The Hostages of the Northmen
From the Viking Age to the Middle Ages

Stefan Olsson

Published by
Stockholm University Press
Stockholm University
SE-106 91 Stockholm, Sweden
www.stockholmuniversitypress.se

Text © Stefan Olsson 2019
License CC-BY

First published 2019
Cover designed by Karl Edqvist, Stockholm University Press
Cover illustration: Gerhard Munthe, Norges Kongesagaer, Heimskringla I, 1914, p. 435.

Cover license: CC BY 4.0

Stockholm Studies in Comparative Religion (Online) ISSN: 2002-4606

ISBN (Paperback): 978-91-7635-107-9
ISBN (PDF): 978-91-7635-104-8
ISBN (EPUB): 978-91-7635-105-5
ISBN (Mobi): 978-91-7635-106-2

DOI: https://doi.org/10.16993/bba

This work is licensed under the Creative Commons Attribution 4.0 Unported License. To view a copy of this license, visit creativecommons.org/licenses/by/4.0/ or send a letter to Creative Commons, 444 Castro Street, Suite 900, Mountain View, California, 94041, USA. This license allows for copying any part of the work for personal and commercial use, providing author attribution is clearly stated.

Suggested citation:
Olsson, S. 2019. *The Hostages of the Northmen: From the Viking Age to the Middle Ages*. Stockholm: Stockholm University Press. DOI: https://doi.org/10.16993/bba. License: CC-BY.

To read the free, open access version of this book online, visit https://doi.org/10.16993/bba or scan this QR code with your mobile device.

Stockholm Studies in Comparative Religion

Stockholm Studies in Comparative Religion (SSCR) (ISSN 2002-4606) is a peer-reviewed series initiated by Åke Hultkrantz in 1961. While its earlier emphasis lay in ethnographic-comparative approaches to religion, the series now covers a broader spectrum of the history of religions, including the philological study of discrete traditions, large-scale comparisons between different traditions as well as theoretical and methodological concerns in the study of cross-cultural religious categories such as ritual and myth.

SSCR strives to sustain and disseminate high-quality and innovative research in the form of monographs and edited volumes, preferably in English, but in exceptional cases also in the French, German-, and Scandinavian languages.

SSCR was previously included in the series Acta Universitatis Stockholmiensis (ISSN 0562-1070). A full list of publications can be found here: http://www.erg.su.se/publikationer/skriftserier/stockholm-studies-in-comparative-religion-1.38944. Volumes still in stock can be obtained through the editors.

Editorial Board

All members of the Editorial board have positions at the Department of Ethnology, History of Religions and Gender Studies at Stockholm University.
Chief editor: Susanne Olsson, Professor
Egil Asprem, Associate Professor
Emmanouela Grypeou, Senior Lecturer
Philip Halldén, Senior Lecturer
Peter Jackson Rova, Professor
Marja-Liisa Keinänen, Associate Professor
Ferdinando Sardella, Senior Lecturer
Olof Sundqvist, Professor

Titles in the series

36. Jackson, P. (ed.) 2016. Horizons of Shamanism. *A Triangular Approach to the History and Anthropology of Ecstatcic Techniques*. Stockholm: Stockholm University Press. DOI: https://doi.org/10.16993/bag
37. Rydving, H. & Olsson, S. 2016. *Krig och fred i vendel- och vikingatida traditioner*. Stockholm: Stockholm University Press. DOI: https://doi.org/10.16993/bah
38. Christoyannopoulos, A. & Adams M. S. (eds.) 2017. *Essays in Anarchism & Religion: Volume I*. Stockholm: Stockholm University Press. DOI: https://doi.org/10.16993/bak
39. Christoyannopoulos, A. & Adams M. S. (eds.) 2018. *Essays in Anarchism & Religion: Volume II*. Stockholm: Stockholm University Press. DOI: https://doi.org/10.16993/bas
40. Wikström af Edholm, K., Jackson Rova, P., Nordberg, A., Sundqvist, O., & Zachrisson, T. (eds.) 2019. *Myth, Materiality, and lived Religion. In Merovingian and Viking Scandinavia*. Stockholm: Stockholm University Press. DOI: https://doi.org/10.16993/bay
41. Olsson, S. 2019. *The Hostages of the Northmen: From the Viking Age to the Middle Ages*. Stockholm: Stockholm University Press. DOI: https://doi.org/10.16993/bba

Peer Review Policies

Stockholm University Press ensures that all book publications are peer-reviewed. Each book proposal submitted to the Press will be sent to a dedicated Editorial Board of experts in the subject area. The full manuscript will be reviewed by chapter or as a whole by two external and independent experts.

A full description of Stockholm University Press' peer-review policies can be found on the website: http://www.stockholmuniversitypress.se/site/peer-review-policies/

Recognition for reviewers

The Editorial Board of Stockholm Studies in Comparative Religion applies single-blind review during proposal and manuscript assessment. We would like to thank all reviewers involved in this process.

Special thanks to the reviewers who have been doing the peer review of the manuscript of this book, one anonymously, and:

Thomas Lindkvist, Professor emeritus at the Department of Historical Studies, University of Gothenburg

He him aðas swor and gislas salde.
He swore oaths to them and gave them hostages.
(*Anglo-Saxon Chronicle*)

Contents

List of Figures   xi
Preface   xiii
Preface to the English Edition   xv

Part I: Introduction   1

Part II: The Æsir–Vanir War (or Peace)   55

Part III: Ritual Actions in Different Areas of Confrontation   81

Part IV: Legal Rights   125

Part V: Place Names   225

Part VI: Hostages in the Areas of Confrontation Between the Swedes and the Geats   251

Part VII: Summary and Conclusions   321

Abbreviations   331
References   333
Index   371

List of Figures

I.1. A schematic description of conflicts and conflict solutions in the Viking Age and the early Middle Ages. 26

I.2. Causes of conflict reported in the *Íslendingabók* and the *Landnámabók*. 34

III.1. Map of the realms of Wessex and Guthrum. 85

III.2. The possible relation between an original, now-lost saga of St. Olaf and later versions. 107

IV.1. Picture stone from Lärbo (Gotland), Tängelgårda IV, which may depict a libation. 165

IV.2. Picture stone from the church of Smiss, Gotland, dated to to the eighth century. The motif could be a woman who performs a sacrificial act with a worm. 166

IV.3. Derivations and compositions with *grið*- in Skaldic and Eddic poetry. 186

IV.4. A manuscript of the introduction to the church section in the *Smålandslagen*, from the Skokloster Castle collection. 191

IV.5. B manuscript of the church section in the *Smålandslagen* in the Arnamagnæan Manuscript Collection in Copenhagen. 192

V.1. Map of Finland including the medieval cities of Viborg and Nöteborg. 230

V.2. Sources to the prescence of Scandinavians in the *sȳslur*. 232

V.3. Comparsion between different text sources regarding rituals. 242

VI.1. The legal districts (Sw. *lagsagor*) of the provincial laws. 257

VI.2. Lands of the Geats (blue) and the Swedes (yellow). 262

VI.3. The hypothetical path of the *Eriksgatan* according to Dick Harrison. 268

VI.4. Provincial laws with or without stipulations about the election of the king and the Eriksgata. 269

VI.5. The distribution of the *husabyar*, and some of the *Uppsala öd*, in Sweden. 274

VI.6. The changing power conditions of the kingship, bishops, lawmen, and country people, according to *The Elder Westrogotic Law* and the Country Law of Magnus Eriksson 280

VI.7. The Junebäck monument in Jönköping. 284

Preface

This study addresses hostages in the Viking Age and medieval Scandinavia. During the work with the study, several researchers have reviewed, read through, and commented on my text or in other ways assisted me. Without their help, this study would have been much more complicated and might not have been made at all.

I would therefore particularly like to thank my principal supervisor, Professor Håkan Rydving, who was at my side from day one of my research studies at the University of Bergen, and who throughout the work – always and tirelessly – gave relevant, stringent comments and generously shared with his vast knowledge. My assistant supervisor, Associate Professor Richard Natvig, has also supported me and contributed to the guidance with a sensitive ear. I would also like to thank, in particular, Professor Olof Sundqvist at Stockholm University, Department of Ethnology, History of Religions and Gender Studies, who introduced me to the field of Old Scandinavian religion. Sundqvist has served as additional assistant supervisor. Others who have been helpful to me are Professor Emeritus Thomas Lindkvist and Professor Emerita Lena Peterson, who read and commented on my manuscript. Senior lecturer Torsten Blomkvist at Dalarna University has responded with overall comments. Docent Torun Zachrisson at Stockholm University has guided me through archaeological sites and helped me avoid some of its pitfalls.

I am also in gratitude to the Department of Archeology, History, Culture and Religion at the University of Bergen, which granted me a scholarship and thus gave me the opportunity for postgraduate education and the opportunity to write the thesis. As a part of my postgraduate research, I organised and participated in two seminars, 'War and Peace in the traditions of the Vendel Period and the Viking Age' and 'Religion, Law, and Justice', which took place in spring 2013 and autumn 2014. The participants in these seminars have directly or indirectly contributed with comments on the texts I presented on these occasions.

Finally, I would like to thank my parents, Lennart and Birgitta Olsson, as well as my brother, Anders Leijon, and his wife, Cecilia; without their support and help, the dream of writing a thesis would never have been fulfilled.

Bergen in February 2016
Stefan Olsson

Preface to the English Edition

This book is a revised version of my thesis, *Gísl: givande och tagande av gisslan som rituell handling i fredsprocesser under vikingatid och tidig medeltid* ('Gísl: Giving and taking of hostages as a ritual act in peace processes during the Viking Age and early Middle Ages').

This new revised edition has been read through and commented on by Professor Håkan Rydving, who also stood beside me from the very beginning of this project. A special thanks goes to Professor Emeritus Thomas Lindkvist, who kindly allowed me to use his English translation of the Elder Westrogothic Law (Swe. *Äldre västgötalagen*). I am in gratitude to PhD candidate Konsta Ilari Kaikkonen for inviting me to the seminar 'Religions around the Arctic' at the University of Bergen, where I presented the paper 'Gyslamarchia and Kihlakunta: Places of hostage' (see Part V). I am also in gratitude to the Editorial Board of Stockholm Studies in Comparative Religion for accepting the manuscrtipt and to the Managing Editor of Stockholm University Press, Christina Lenz, for administrating the making of the manuscript into a book.

This book could be printed due to grants from Lennart J. Hägglunds stiftelse. I hereby acknowledge their support.

Umeå in June 2019
Stefan Olsson

Part I: Introduction

In modern times, the taking of hostage has usually been seen as an act of negative significance. According to the definition of the *Chambers Dictionary*, a hostage is: 'a person kept prisoner by an enemy as security'.[1] In other cases, the taking of hostage is perceived as a purely criminal act, the purpose of which is to extort money from people or the society, as described in the *Oxford Advanced Learner's Dictionary of Current English*: 'a person who is captured and held prisoner by a person or group, and who may be injured or killed if people do not do what the person or group is asking'.[2] In ancient times, this was not the purpose of a hostage. Quite to the contrary, it was a tool for reaching and securing peace. The use of hostages was thus formalised in a way that was different from what it is today, and in the formalisation a ritualization was embedded.

In previous studies, research on hostages has primarily dealt with studies of the culture of ancient Rome and what can be characterized as the medieval study of Ancient Rome, of Continental Germanic history, and of Anglo-Saxon history. Recently, historians have been interested in the concept of the hostage in its socio-political contexts (see further below). Even in these cases, the studies have, for the most part, dealt with Continental Germanic and Anglo-Saxon traditions and conflicts, for example, in the Carolingian Empire; these studies have often concerned themes of Christian values and morality. Few studies have focused on hostages in the Scandinavian countries. These studies have often been based on the idea of a legal development that pertained to the 'private', civil, aspect of hostages – in German, *Borgensgeisel* – in

---

How to cite this book chapter:
Olsson, S. 2019. Introduction. In: Olsson, S. *The Hostages of Northmen: From the Viking Age to the Middle Ages*. Pp. 1–54. Stockholm: Stockholm University Press. DOI: https://doi.org/10.16993/bba.a License: CC-BY.

which a person functioned as assurance that a commitment would be fulfilled. No extensive, systematic study has so far been carried out by the second aspect, about hostages in times of war and peace, which will be my point of departure in this study.

Cornerstones

The main purpose of the study is to investigate the giving and taking of hostages in peace processes during the Viking Age and into the late Middle Ages (16th century) in Scandinavia with neighbouring areas. I understand the exchange of hostages as a ritual act in peace agreements, as an opportunity for both parties – the victors as well as the defeated – to influence their respective negotiating position, and as a way of exercising dominance over further relationships within and between communities.

During the Viking Age and the Early Middle Ages, ceremonies and ritual acts were conducted during peace and negotiation processes that also included the giving and taking of hostages. The surrender of a hostage appears to have been partly formalised and loosely associated with ritual acts. The concept of the hostage also appears as a theme in myths and other stories.

Another purpose is to understand how and why Christian and non-Christian traditions in laws were related to each other in the peace processes, as well as the norms and attitudes formed by these processes towards hostages and people in similar situations. Therefore, in the study of hostages in peace processes, it is possible to establish politico-legal perspectives in addition to the perspectives of the history of religions. I will also take into account the power structures that existed between the hostage takers and the hostages. In some cases, the hostage was killed or severely punished; in other cases the hostage was treated well. I will discuss the structural similarities and differences between hostages and phenomena such as the institutions of foster children and marriages.

These purposes can be summarised in the following questions:

(1) How and why can the giving and taking of hostages be understood as a ritual act in peace processes during the

Viking era through the late Middle Ages (16th century) in Scandinavia? How did the hostages function as objectives of negotiations?
(2) Were there similarities and differences between hostage traditions in different parts of Scandinavia and continuities from the Iron Age into medieval Scandinavian societies?
(3) What were the relationships, or social bonds, between hostages and hostage takers?
(4) What methodological concerns does one encounter if one examines the phenomenon of the hostage? How can the hostage be understood theoretically against the background of peace processes in communities where Scandinavians acted?
(5) What were the similarities and differences between Christian and non-Christian traditions and values in peace and negotiation processes that involved hostages? What were the attitudes to the agreements that were established?

These questions will be answered through an analysis of different source categories with information about hostages, mainly texts, but also other sources such as personal names, place names and archaeological material. As the study will specifically describe phenomena during the Viking Age and the early Middle Ages, a period of religious change that also involved major politico-legal changes, it has been important to choose methodological and theoretical strategies with particular care. These points of departure will be described and discussed below.

Outline of the book

Part I of the book deals with previous research on the giving and taking of hostages in the Viking Age and early medieval traditions, and I provide a summary of earlier research on hostages in Roman, Continental Germanic, and Anglo-Saxon traditions. Research on hostages in Old Scandinavian traditions has not been extensive and is basically non-existent in the history of religions.

A methodological discussion is also conducted. In order to get a perspective on hostages in relation to war and peace, the phenomena is put in relation to a theoretical model of peace processes, as well as different perspectives of ritual theory, where I, among other things, define my use of the concept of ritual action (or rather 'acts').

In Part II, the myth of the Æsir–Vanir War (or Peace) is analysed, and in Part III, the theoretical perspectives I presented in Part I are applied to various cases of hostages in the Scandinavian societies as well as societies outside Scandinavia, including the Danelaw in England and in the meetings between Scandinavians and Franks in the Merovingian kingdom and the later Carolingian Empire (800–888).

Part IV focuses on who became hostages, their legal rights and social value. Here, the relationship between law and tradition is discussed by referring to examples from different parts of Scandinavia and adjacent areas. When analysing the examples taken from different contexts, it is relevant to understand the writers' intentions when they are reporting about various conflicts. This applies not least to the question of ancillary relationships, such as questions about who was the subordinate in a conflict – something that was not always obvious. Furthermore, the role of female hostages is discussed. Medieval Scandinavian contexts with regulations against violence towards hostages are analysed. Finally, two major case studies involving massacres of hostages and their ethical and moral consequences are presented.

In Part V, I further develop an idea of an available hostage: the disposable hostage. This phenomenon can be found in place names that suggest organisational forms around hostages. Also, the Swedish place name *Gyslamarchia*, mentioned in *Gesta Danorum* is discussed. This place name is then compared to other place names with a similar meanings in Finland, Estonia, and Ireland.

In Part VI, everything in the book is put together by an analysis of the *Older Westrogothic Law* in relation to previous analyses. The focus is on two hostage cases in connection with the traditional journey of the Swedish king to the provinces before his coronation: the so-called Eriksgata. This part is concluded with an analysis of Christian II's Eriksgata in the early 16th century. This part brings the observations of the book together and answers to the objectives mentioned in Part I.

Earlier research on hostages

The concept of the hostage has been dealt with in several monographs and articles, mainly in disciplines with a focus on the cultures of Antiquity, and of the Anglo-Saxon and Continental Germanic areas, but a more comprehensive, general study of the phenomenon is still lacking for Scandinavia.[3]

The works that deal with Antiquity, Anglo-Saxon, and Continental Germanic cultures are mainly written from the perspective of legal history or from historical viewpoints. They therefore emphasize the social relations, power ideology, and international law. At the same time some of the authors of these works consistently point out religious aspects when describing hostages.[4] In the Roman Empire, society was touched at all levels of religious practice, which was not bound only to sacred places or festivals. The religions of the Empire included many socio-political activities, such as hostage taking. Nevertheless, studies on hostages in the Roman Republic and the Roman Empire do not explicitly deal with the history of religion. As the Romans came into contact with other cultures during their expansion, hostages were used to regulate or control other peoples, and it is therefore inevitable to take up the meeting between Romans and Germans. The legal historian Stephan Elbern has investigated hostages based on medieval Christian law (*jus gentium*).[5] Elbern also pays attention to some social and religious factors, and his investigation is one of few studies on hostages in which legal and religious elements are not seen as separate from each other.

Some studies have been devoted to hostages in the Old Irish society. The historian Robin Chapman Stacey has shown how hostage taking was a part of the legal practice of the Irish Iron Age Society.[6] The Old Irish material is mainly outside the scope of this study, but I will address some cases as comparisons.

The studies on hostages mentioned in this book are primarily based on legal historical perspectives. Recently, however, some historians have applied social and ideological viewpoints from the perspectives of social history and the history of ideas on hostages. The historian Ryan Lavelle has investigated hostages in Anglo-Saxon societies. He perceives the hostage as a kind of symbolic 'security' during peace processes. Even more important, he shows how the hostage could function as a symbolic representation of power.[7] He also addresses legal contexts and agreements that included hostages and the consequences if these agreements were broken.[8]

The historian Adam J. Kosto has written about Continental Germanic traditions and, in particular, the Carolingian Empire. The taking of hostages was a way to secure the peace between the Christian Franks and the heathen Saxons. Kosto describe ritual actions in connection with the use of hostages and points out the need to understand its mechanics.[9] He has also thoroughly discussed definitions of the term 'hostage', which is something that will be addressed later in this book.

The interest in hostages within Old Scandinavian studies has so far been limited. There are mainly a few historians that dealt with hostages in Scandinavia. Gabriele von Olberg has related to Scandinavian examples in an article about hostages in *Reallexikon der Germanischen Altertumskunde*, but she mainly focuses on Continental Germanic cultures and legal issues.

Another researcher who devoted some attention to Scandinavian material was the legal historian Karl von Amira. His *Nordgermanisches Obligationenrecht 1: Altschwedisches Obligationenrecht* (1882) and *Nordgermanisches Obligationenrecht 2: Westnordisches Obligatierecht* (1895) also included medieval, Scandinavian legal history. He devoted a chapter in each volume to the study of hostage, which he primarily related to Scandinavian civil law: the hostage became a kind of pledge which remained with the debtor until the debt was paid (i.e. *Borgensgeisel*).[10] He did not focus on the contexts of martial law.

A civil law perspective was also applied by the legal historian Ascan Lutteroth (1922). Lutteroth made a general examination of the 'hostage settlement' in the context of martial law, including examples from Scandinavia. According to Lutteroth, it is obvious that the martial tradition occurred in parallel with the civil law that he exemplified with cases from Antiquity to World War I.[11] However, the differences between war and peace may not always have been so clear that such a distinction can be made. Nevertheless, Lutteroth's listing is important because he made a distinction between hostages as an instrument of power relations between individuals (rulers, warlords) and collectives (groupings).

A desire to contextualize hostages in the different Scandinavian communities and to characterize the geographical and cultural conditions in which hostage occurred does not appear to be explicit in any study so far, although the historian Sveinbjörn Rafnsson has a brief note about the hostage taking at Olaf Tryggvason's *hirð* (retinue).[12]

In investigations, hostage taking is seen as a single phenomenon apart from myths and rituals. For example, the historian of religions Andreas Nordberg mentions hostages in connection with the mythical Æsir–Vanir War in his thesis, *Krigarna i Odins sal* ('The Warriors in Othin's hall'), but it is only mentioned in a brief passage where Nordberg concludes that it was common use to exchange hostages in ancient societies.[13]

Hostages have been seen as part of – or a prerequisite for – 'friendship' during the Viking Age or the early Middle Ages.[14] This latter theme has been the subject of intense discussion and research. Studies by the historians Jón Viðar Sigurðsson and Lars Hermanson have been significant.[15] Jón Viðar Sigurðsson has shown that social bonds – as a part of 'friendship' – were as important as family ties for loyalty during the Saga Age (c. 870–1056) and the Sturlunga Era (c. 1180–1264) in Iceland. He also shows how friendships were part of traditional Scandinavian mentality and related to the religious sphere.[16] The historian Ian Miller has investigated the blood feud and the peace makings during the Saga Age. He also addresses traditions regarding fostering and foster children, which may have been an institution of a similar nature to the hostage.[17]

It is evident that the hostage has been described in many different studies, mainly by researchers investigating Roman culture and Continental Germanic cultures. These studies are essentially done from historical or legal historical perspectives, although the perspectives of social history can also be seen in recent studies. The hostage has been seen as something related to religion in only a few studies. There is a need for a study that addresses examples from the Viking Age and early Middle Ages in Scandinavia, Iceland, and the colonies of the Scandinavians that (A) relates hostages to peace processes, (B) puts this in relation to myths, rituals, and ethics, and (C) analyses several source categories: personal names, place names, and archaeological material in addition to texts.

Definitions of hostages

The most comprehensive survey of hostages in medieval Europe between about 400 and 1400 has been conducted by Kosto. He takes his starting point in the Carolingian and Post-Carolingian Empires.

In addition, his ambition has been to review each hostage situation during the period 500–1000 AD (a total of 325 cases), in 'Regions from Russia to Central Asia in the east to the Celtic and Scandinavian borderlands in the west and the north'.[18] Kosto is careful about pointing out the variety of forms of hostages.[19] During the 11th century, different forms of hostages appeared, and women were appointed as hostages.[20] The hostages became more important from this period as representatives of larger groups rather than individuals. Kosto explains several variants of the situations in which hostage exchanges could occur.[21]

Kosto believes that, in addition to variations over time, other factors may have influenced how the hostage was used. This may have included, for example, the view of religion, law, and justice. Kosto sees European Christianity as a unit of common values, which can be problematic, not least in terms of perception of law and morality. He does not go in depth to justify this point of view. How should the researcher, for example, regard Viking rulers such as Eric Bloodaxe (ON *Eiríkr blóðøx*) or Haakon the Good (OI *Hákon góði*), who had their feet in both heathen and Christian traditions?[22]

According to Kosto, the hostage in the Middle Ages could be seen in relation to changing power structures.[23] However, he does not always notice the varying social contexts. To get further clues to the understanding of hostages, it is crucial to analyse and create a comprehensive picture of the political situation where the phenomenon occurred and functioned.

A point of departure for this book is the historian Paul Kershaw's point of view that hostage exchanges, together with oaths, represented the most central moments of peace processes. In addition, the specificities of Scandinavian power relations in the context of peace processes is pointed out in this survey.[24]

Kosto points out the lack of sources to Scandinavian conditions. He mostly leans towards continental chronicles, but also uses some Scandinavian material, such as legal texts, Danish and Norwegian royal annals, and some of the kings' sagas.[25] He seems to regard these sources as valid only for describing medieval conditions, thus eliminating other sources such as Ancient sagas, Icelandic sagas, and even other kings' sagas. Certainly, the Old Norse source material has shortcomings in terms of details compared to the continental sources of the 12th and 13th centuries, but the lack of information can be turned into an advantage. By subdividing Old Norse texts into smaller parts, isolating key concepts, and correlating these with other sources, such as runic stones, skaldic and eddic poetry, place names, iconography, and other types of archaeological material, the texts can provide important information. I relate to the two main forms of hostages Kosto refers to – the bilateral and unilateral – and also to his more specific categories of hostages (outlined below). I do not deny that the power aspect is important, nor that the balance of power between different parties has been uneven, but my intention is also to analyse the situations where a hostage could be an opportunity for the weaker party. In this book, therefore, a main focus is that the hostage was an opportunity for influences under conditions where peace and war presupposed one another in the balance of power between groupings and individuals.

In Part I will rely on Kosto's definition of hostages. This definition – which concerns Continental Germanic and medieval communities – differs to a large extent from our modern perception. Kosto tones down the violence and instead emphasises a contractual role for the hostage: it was essentially a security by temporarily depriving a person of his or her liberty by another person to guarantee a third party's undertaking. The hostage thus has the following characteristics: both one person (the hostage), who was not a prisoner but who was detained for deprivation, and another person for whom the hostage was the security and who was not deprived of his or her liberty.[26] There are also some further characteristics:

(1) A hostage was a person who served as a guarantee for a number of people, and is thus to be distinguished from a prisoner of war or a common prisoner.
(2) The hostage was not the subject of a ransom, but its function was to guarantee that, for example, prisoners were released.
(3) The hostage was a third party – not one of the individuals whose security was guaranteed by the person or the persons who were being hostage.
(4) The hostage was in fact subject to the loss of physical freedom and thus different from other forms of guarantor obligations.
(5) The hostage was given rather than taken. A person might be given as a hostage, but without acknowledgment from both sides (hostage-giver and hostage-taker), the hostage could not be a guarantee that (peace) terms or agreements were being fulfilled.

As a condition, it differs significantly from being a prisoner. Prisoners were taken, but hostages were given.[27] The hostages could, however, be prisoners: the Kurdish ruler Saladin's hostage, for example, became prisoners after the massacre of Ayyadieh in 1192.[28] The hostage could also be exchanged for prisoners. This happened to, for example, the Swedish nobleman – later king – Gustav Vasa and the other hostages in connection with the negotiations between Sten Sture the Younger and Christian II of Denmark in 1518.[29]

Kosto makes a division of different types of hostages that could be considered to be a security:[30]

(A) A conditional hostage, which is transferred as security after violence had been committed in violation of an agreement.[31]

(B) A judicial or procedural hostage, which involves a legal aspect.[32]
(C) True hostages, which are given from both sides as a security: when a (peace) agreement is signed.[33]
(D) A custodial hostage, when a prisoner could chose a hostage as a security prior to his or her release.[34]

In my opinion, a fifth type of hostage could be distinguished: (E) the 'available hostage' or the 'disposable hostage', which we will return to later.

According to Kosto, the above-mentioned types of hostages (aside from the last one) may probably be linked to the 11th century. He is also careful to point out that the characteristics of these forms are not entirely clear but vary in both time and space:

> [W]e cannot be certain, as we can in some cases, that the sureties in question conform to the definition of hostage used in this study; on the other hand, we cannot be certain, as we can in some cases, that they do not conform to that definition. Given the geographical and chronological range as well as the generic variety of the sources examined in this study, there is no fixed rule to follow when attempting to move from the words used in the sources to an understanding of historical practice.[35]

When Latin verbs like *dare*, 'give', *accipere*, 'accept, receive', or *recipere*, 'receive', are used about hostages in Carolingian sources, this could indicate the unilateral hostage form. Kosto believes that hostages were given in different power situations rather than by force.[36]

Basically, there were two types of hostage agreements: unilateral and bilateral. In the former case, one side gave a hostage, in the latter the two sides exchanged hostages.[37] Unilateral contractual forms arose mainly when someone was defeated and the hostage guaranteed that no violent acts should be directed against the victor.[38] The bilateral forms of hostage appear to have been far more common. In that type of agreement, it is much easier to identify an implicit purpose. In these contexts a treaty about a time-limited ceasefire was usually found. Afterwards, the hostage was returned. In this way, a formal ceasefire could be maintained between armies,[39] and – I would add – land areas. Another way in which both bilateral and unilateral hostages could work was by guaranteeing free passage. It could take place in order to protect individuals who were envoys in negotiations.[40]

There were also other types of hostages, both in unilateral and bilateral forms, in different negotiation situations where they were given in exchange for prisoners or on bail.[41] But these forms can be difficult to distinguish in my material. With regard to the unilateral form of hostages, the examples appear to be mainly from the Middle Ages, and in this variant it was often about the settlement of debts, which could happen, for example, between kings and knights, and they belonged rather to 'private' companies,[42] even though that distinction is not entirely clear.

In the present material, I focus mainly on hostages as a part (an element) in peace processes. I discuss the opportunities for influence between competitive parties during conflicts and focus on those who became hostages, from a perspective of the history of religions.

Sources

Old West Norse

My main sources are texts. Of the texts in Old West Norse (Old Icelandic, Old Norwegian, Old Faroese, and Greenlandic Norse), the most important are the skaldic poems.[43] These are the oldest texts that can be dated to the Viking era. Although they only mention hostages sporadically, the skaldic poems are important because they can confirm later depictions of wars and peaces, to the extent that they mention triumphal events such as victories and the taking of hostages as well as prisoners of war. Some of the skaldic poems are tendentious. This may have been the case with the poems composed at the court of the heathen Earls of Lade (ON *Hlaðir*) in Trøndelag and was possibly a reaction to the Christian kings of Vestfold, and this served as a propaganda instrument for the Earls.[44] Some skalds, however, participated in different field campaigns and raids, and their poems, though composed as honours to various rulers, are direct sources of old Scandinavian traditions of pre-Christian customs and warfare.[45]

Another important text source – regarding war and peace – is the Eddic poetry, predominantly preserved in Icelandic manuscripts from the Middle Ages, such as the main manuscript of the Poetic Edda, *Codex Regius*, but also fragmentary in manuscripts containing *Snorra Edda* and *Hauksbók*.[46] These texts are more detailed than the skaldic poetry. But the Eddic poetry is questioned as a historical source to pre-Christian traditions. The author of the latest handbook in Old Scandiavian religion, the professor of English Christopher Abram, considers them to be overrated as sources of old traditions and dates the *Poetic Edda* to about 1270 (the date of *Codex Regius*).[47] On the other hand, some scholars argue that there is palaeographic evidence that the *Poetic Edda* has had a predecessor; Snorri, for example, quotes Eddic poems in his Edda dated to about 1225.[48]

Others claim that there was an oral tradition before the fixation in writing of the Eddic Poems.[49] The historian of religions Jens Peter Schjødt points out that it is hardly possible to determine the age of the Eddic poems based on objective criteria; there are just too few of them.[50] Schjødt also considers it less important for the researcher whether the poems were fixed in writing in the 12th or 13th centuries.[51] However, the difference between these centuries is important for understanding the relationship with other literary works that are central to the understanding of Old Scandinavian myths, such as *Snorra Edda*. It can also be important for analysing different versions of Eddic poems.

Schjødt poses an interesting question in his discussion of the Eddic poems: why would Christian skalds be interested in composing poems about heathen gods? He concludes:

> We may talk as much as we like about a 'Renaissance' in the twelfth century, but it is one thing to collect old material together, something different to compose new poems, and in the twelfth and, for that matter, also in the thirteenth century, paganism was still relatively close, probably so close that it would have been difficult to compose whole poems about pagan gods.[52]

Schjødt's point of view can be compared with that of the philologist Preben Meulengracht Sørensen, who has claimed that in individual Eddic poems we can find remains that survived from an oral tradition into their preserved forms.⁵³ For the researcher, in an analysis of the Eddic poems, the Christian and contemporary material has to be peeled away in order to reach the remnants of the old traditions.

This procedure is something that, for example, the historian of religions Anders Hultgård has recently shown is possible in an analysis of the Eddic poem *Vǫluspá* through a comparative analysis.⁵⁴ Thus, there appears to be a certain consensus about the Eddic poems so far that they convey a message with pre-Christian content but with possible later Christian additions. The Eddic poetry cannot serve as direct historical sources of war and peace, because it does not describe direct historical events like the skaldic poetry does. Instead, the Eddic poems focus on myths about different beings and cosmological events or various hero poems that mostly are set in prehistoric times. However, in the myths of the Eddic poetry there are actions that can be prototypical to the human being and related to various ritual acts. To get information about historical events, the researcher must turn to other Old West Norse texts. Of these, the Icelandic family sagas (OI *Íslendingasǫgur*) are of course most well-known. They mention hostages very rarely, even though they refer to many conflicts at the micro level.⁵⁵ However, they are my main sources of the Old Icelandic Society from the settlement of Iceland (c. 874–930) to the Sturlung Era and the dissolution of the Free State (c. 1188–1264). Many times, interpreters of the sagas have emphasized the discrepancy between the fixation in writing (mainly in the 12th–13th centuries) and the time the texts describe. Likewise, the relationship between oral tradition and the influence of Christian learned traditions has been pointed out. In addition, it has been emphasized that the Icelandic writers strive to describe their ancestors as 'good Christians' or in a glorious light.⁵⁶

In this investigation, I mainly use the *Landnámabók* as the source of the older periods in Iceland, about 870–930. It is considered, along with *Íslendingabók*, written by Ari Þorgilsson (OI *Ari Þorgilsson*) about 1130, to be the oldest of the Icelandic family sagas.⁵⁷ The *Landnámabók* appears in surviving copies of the original manuscripts from the 13th century. A possible original of the *Landnámabók* may have been written down in the first half of the 12th century.⁵⁸ It can be seen as a matrix for the Icelandic family sagas, even though it is not always credible when it comes to non-Christian traditions. Its value lies in describing traditions that can be confirmed by both Icelandic and Norwegian early medieval laws.⁵⁹ Social norms such as attitudes towards prisoners, gender relations, and the bonds between chieftains and their retinues are also important information.

The *Sturlunga* saga contains, like the *Íslendingabók*, several books (or parts); it is a source of medieval conditions in Iceland. *Sturlunga* saga describes conflicts on the micro-level that are limited in time and space, thus providing information on conflicts and solutions to these conflicts in a realistic way.⁶⁰

The kings' sagas (OI *konungasǫgur*) contain very valuable information as they mention campaigns that involved both the taking and the giving of hostages.⁶¹ This is unique material in relation to skaldic and Eddic poetry, as well as Icelandic sagas, since the stories are written by both Icelandic and Norwegian writers. The oldest of these sagas is from the beginning of the 12th century. Some of the stories can be based on older written and oral sources. This is, for example, noted in *Heimskringla* (c. 1230), traditionally attributed to the Icelandic chieftain and skald Snorri Sturlasson (OI *Snorri Sturluson*). Snorri worked like a historian, albeit not in a modern sense, and was able to use skaldic and Eddic poetry as well as other kings' sagas. He also used sources that are unknown or have been lost, for example, the skaldic poem *Hryggjarstykki*.⁶² What may be problematic with much of the Old West Norse literature is that it can be highly biased in favour of the Norwegian kings in the descriptions of war, peace, and other socio-political events. It can make it difficult to fully understand the purpose, background, and results of different conflict lines between the kings and their opponents.

Legendary sagas (*fornaldar sǫgur*) are stories about ancient times, created in Iceland in the 14th and early 15th centuries; the manuscripts were collected in Denmark in the 17th century. These are stories with fictional themes that are set in semi-mythical landscapes of the Older Iron Age (about 500 BC–550 AD), sometimes later, and influenced by continental, romantic and heroic legends.⁶³ Traditionally within research, the uncertainties of the Legendary sagas have caused them to be attributed to a low source value.⁶⁴ Some interpreters of the Legendary sagas have recently wanted to revise them as sources. It has been pointed out, among other things, that the authors did not necessarily have to disregard pre-Christian traditions in the same way as the authors of the family sagas, as they are set in a distant, ancient age.⁶⁵ Other interpreters have attempted to apply comparative methods or isolate pre-Christian elements transmitted in a literary context.⁶⁶

It is given that the details of battles and peace processes are greatly exaggerated in romanticising stories of the distant past. The excesses and, above all, the time discrepancy give the Legendary sagas a low source value, and they cannot stand alone as sources of the Viking Age, but must be seen in relation to other sources. They can primarily provide information about details that are not mentioned in the other text sources. For example, the story of King Vikar (OI *Vikarr*) in *Gautreks* saga gives details about fosterage and hostages, details that can be confirmed by the skaldic poem Víkarbalkr (OI *Víkarsbalkr*), which is quoted in the saga.

Old East Norse literature

In Old East Norse languages – Runic Swedish, Old Swedish, Runic Danish and Old Danish – there is actually no purely literary work of saga character. However, there are some Danish chronicles in Latin such as *Brevis Historia Regum Dacie* (c. 1186), covering the history of Denmark from the early centuries AD up to the 1100s and *Chronicon Roskildense* (c. 1140). The most important feature of these works is that they legitimise medieval Danish royal dynasties.

The source that interpreters of Old Scandinavian religion usually relate to is Saxo Grammaticus *Gesta Danorum*, 'The Deeds of the Danes', by Saxo Grammaticus, from about 1200. Like Snorri, Saxo worked as a collector of material (both oral and written), which he then structured and reinterpreted according to his learned principles. He moralises, however, more than Snorri, and idealises the Danish kingdoms. In addition, he interpreted myths differently than in the Old West Norse literature: the gods are described as human kings and heroes. He may also have known other versions of the myths.⁶⁷ The Danish sources are interesting to compare to the Old West Norse literature in terms of politics, war, and peace.

Names

Place names are particularly important for the interpreter of Old Scandinavian religion because they can confirm institutionalised traditions and social activities. During the first half of the 20th century, the theophoric place names were used as a historical source of religion. But with articles in 1924 and as late as 1950, the place-name researcher Jöran Sahlgren strongly questioned the methods used by former place-name research, implying that the sacred place names could be discarded on a linguistic basis as sources for pre-Christian traditions.⁶⁸

Sahlgren's criticism of the interpretation of certain place names as sacred lasted until 1986 when the place-name researcher Lars Hellberg published an article where he could show that there is sustainable evidence for the interpretation of several place names as being related to a heathen cult. With this article, place names made a comeback in the study of Old Scandinavian religion. A new orientation has been taken by place-name researchers such as Thorsten Andersson, Lennart Elmevik, Stefan Brink, and Per Vikstrand.⁶⁹ When I use place names, I basically focus on the analyses of these place-name researchers. There is, however, little evidence of the giving and taking of hostages in the place-name material. In Scandinavia, one can only make certain assumptions about the insecure place name Gyslamarchia (Da. *Gislemark*).

Another important source are the old personal names that are primarily found in runic inscriptions. The philologist Lena Peterson's *Nordiskt runnamnslexikon* ('Dictionary of proper names in [Scandinavian Viking Age] runic inscriptions') has been central to me as a source of knowledge. The basic meaning of different personal names can provide information about structures lost to the name holders in their lifetime.

The main part of the Futhark runic inscriptions with 16 characters occurs on the runic stones in the Swedish Mälaren Valley and the province of Uppland. These stones have been created in a society that was in transition to Christianity, but still there was the will to maintain the older names. Futhark runic inscriptions with 24 characters are from periods before the 7th century AD. These inscriptions can be hard to interpret but can still provide very valuable information about 'hostage' as a word.

Medieval laws

Medieval laws are important mainly as a source of early medieval Scandinavia and Iceland. Interpreters of Old Scandinavian religion have pointed out that the prohibition of heathen cults in the medieval laws can be interpreted indirectly as a source of customs of ancient times.[70] The latter could be seen in the *Elder Westrogothic law* (Swe. *Äldre västgötalagen*, 12th century) – for this study one of the most important sources – describing the hostage giving between the Swedes (OWN *Svíar*) and the Geats (OWN *Gautar*), which should have been performed during the king's ritual journey, the Eriksgata, in connection with his coronation.[71] The Eriksgata is also mentioned in other provincial laws, such as *Magnus Erikssons landslag* (ca. 1350). For me, the Swedish provincial laws[72] are mainly a source of early medieval traditions.

Norwegian medieval laws can also provide information about both hostages and assembly places. These are traditions created in the transition to an early medieval state society, either retaining or distancing from older, pre-Christian traditions.

The *Gulaþing law* (OI *Gulaþingslǫg*) is the oldest of Norway's provincial laws and probably originates from the 10th century. The law mentions hostages but also different traditions of the organisation of the thing,[73] which may be a legacy of older times.

The later *Frostatings law* (ON *Frostaþingslǫg*) from the Norwegian province of Trøndelag was fixed in writing around 1260, but some of the materials are older than that. The law is most interesting when it comes to medieval conditions because it mentions hostages as a part of the regulations between the king, his followers, and other rulers, such as dukes and earls.

The Icelandic *Grágás*, written around 1117, can provide information about the organization around the Icelandic parliament, the Althing (OI *Alþingi*), and is important especially in terms of legal terminology that may have survived from before Christianity. *Grágás* was the legislation created at the foundation of the Althing in 930.

Continental chronicles and annals

Continental Germanic and Old English chronicles, royal annals, and bishop chronicles are important sources for the study of Old Scandinavian religion and culture. It has been pointed out that these types of texts fulfil a time criterion; they were written in the time period they describe. Examples of such chronicles are Adam of Bremen's historical overview of the archbishops in the Archdiocese of Hamburg-Bremen, *Gesta Hammaburgensis ecclesiae pontificum* ('Deeds of the Bishops of Hamburg' (ca. 1070), and Rimbert of Hamburg's description of the mission of the monk Ansgar in Scandinavia, *Vita Ansgarii* (ca. 875). However, these texts can politically be unreliable when it comes to the criterion of proximity. This may be missing because the chroniclers had to rely on secondary information.

Continental bishop chronicles, such as *Gesta Hammaburgensis ecclesiae pontificum*, are, along with place names and archaeological findings, my main source of conflicts involving hostages in the East Scandinavian areas. Among other things, they disclose conflicts between the Danes and Vends as well as between Swedes and people from the Baltic region.

Other important sources are Anglo-Saxon chronicles of the 10th century. These are not native texts, but some of them are still recorded in Old English, others in Latin. Through the Anglo-Saxon texts, it is possible in various descriptions involving hostages to isolate a terminology that is linguistically closely related to Old Norse. *The Anglo-Saxon Chronicle* consists of annals from about year 1 to the mid-1100s, but the Chronicle was created in the late ninth century.

The Old English *Beowulf* poem depicts conflicts between people called Danes (OE *Dene*), Geats (OE *Ġēatas*), and Sweons (OE *Swēon*). It is a matter of debate whether these conflicts took place between these peoples in the Scandinavian Peninsula or in

Denmark, but for my analysis it is important that this literary work describes the interaction between groupings and individuals in an Iron Age society that commuted between war and peace. It is disputed whether *Beowulf* was created in the 8th century or in the 11th century.[74]

There are also chronicles that depict conflicts between the Carolingian Empire and Vikings (mostly from present Denmark). Here, among other things, the Frankish Royal annals are important (*Annales regni Francorum*) because they depict the strife between Frankish, Saxon, and Danish rulers covering the years 741–829. Most important is the monk Einhart's biography of the life of Charlemagne (*Vita Karoli Magni*). It is considered to have a high source value because Einhart was close to Charlemagne.

Classical sources

Classical sources such as Tacitus's *Germania* (98 AD) and Caesar's Commentaries on the Gallic Wars (*Commentarii De Bello Gallico*, 58–49 BC) are imperative because they mention hostages as words without ambiguities. In these sources, sometimes misunderstandings of situations about how the hostage would be perceived might occur. There is also a time discrepancy of hundreds of years between the pre-Roman Age (about 500 BC–1 AD), the Roman Iron Age (1–400 AD) and the Viking Age (about 750–1100 AD). In spite of these reservations, it is possible to compare the traditions of the Romans with later traditions.

Archaeological material

Archaeological material cannot by itself provide the interpreter with information about hostages. However, it can provide evidence of the existence of social and religious activities at things, burial grounds, cultic places, and other locations by the findings of artefacts and by the mapping of the terrain.

A very significant source is iconographic material, especially Gotlandic picture stones. The motifs on these stones can confirm that myths and legends of the Old West Norse texts also appeared in Eastern Scandinavia. The stones also depict events that are probably unique to Gotland. One problem with Gotlandic picture stones is that they can be misinterpreted. They can reproduce a message that was alive during the time they were created, but that we are shielded from today. Another problem is that the picture stones are eroding, especially those that are outdoors. Picture stones were often restored and painted in the first half of the 20th century. Recently, the Scandinavianist Sigmund Oehrl has shown how a new photographic method – Digital Reflectance Transformation Imaging (RTI) – can illuminate completely different figures and formations on the picture stones than those previously restored.[75]

The above review is intended as a summary of the source material and its characteristics. Some text sources and other sources have been omitted, but we shall return to these sources later. I do not claim to cover all the material regarding hostages. I will now present some methodological considerations.

Methodological considerations

In this investigation, I relate the text material primarily to the time and place the different sources describe. I do not regard these descriptions of traditions as relevant for all the Scandinavian societies.[76] There is, for example, a geographical and cultural division which becomes evident in the Icelandic family sagas that occur in the Icelandic society of the Viking Age or the Middle Ages, compared to the *Anglo-Saxon Chronicle* and the Royal Frankish Annals' descriptions of confrontations between the Carolingian Empire, the Saxons, and the Danes. At the same time, the sources sometimes have cross-cultural references: they describe places, situations, and times the writers have been less familiar with. It is therefore important to pay attention to the writers' attitudes towards the foreign geographic and cultural conditions that they describe, especially in a study that claims to investigate contacts and interactions at the micro level.

Because different sources have different characteristics, several different methods must be used. Preferably, a statement in a source should be supported by at least two other sources, texts, or other types of material (archaeology, etc.). Sometimes it is not possible to confirm the information in an Old Norse source. Then, the information can be compared to analogies in Continental Germanic sources. This method can be fruitful when it primarily concerns comparing medieval societies based on canon law, which had much in common through Christianity. However, the earlier domestic religions across the area of present-day Europe may have differed in many ways, and such a method must be used with caution and can primarily point out what are possible and probable assumptions.

Another method used by some interpreters of Old Scandinavian myths, such as Georges Dumézil,[77] is to try to trace a common Indo-European cultural 'heritage' based on comparative language studies. It has also been attempted to trace a 'Pan-Germanic' legacy in various old legal texts. I do not want to take a stand for or against these methodological approaches. I primarily use analogies to communities that are closest in time, space, and culture to the societies I investigate.[78] Such societies are the early medieval English societies, where the authorities used hostages as security against other people, as in the case of Wales. In 1063, for example, Englishmen came to Wales (OE *Brytland*), took many people as hostages, and killed their King Griffin.[79]

The communities with similar traditions can be exemplified by the Carolingian Empire in its confrontations with the Saxons during the Saxon mission. These societies were contemporary with the Viking Age in Scandinavia. Secondly, I use analogies to societies such as the Old Irish, the Old Finnish, and the Baltic cultures. These cultures did not have the same language as the Scandinavians but were still contemporary, or almost contemporary. Thirdly, I use analogies to societies such as the Roman Empire that differed in terms of time, language, and geographical scope, but which may also have had some cultural impact on Germanic societies.

In some cases, it is necessary to go deeper into individual texts. It may be a word that differs in different text editions. Sometimes the word hostage is not mentioned, for various reasons, in the texts or appears implicit; then I 'observe within the sources'. This way of approaching a text is partly inspired by the historian of mentalities Carlo Ginzburg. I thereby analyse certain specific details that can be understood as what Ginzburg refers to as 'clues' in a specific text. It may, for example, concern information that appears to be untrue to the writer and recorded without reflection. Several such clues can be combined into a pattern that can be combined into a larger structure.[80] The investigation of the underlying details can be summarized in the following points:

(A) Unnoticed details that were not important to the writers and chronicles. Some events during the taking and giving of hostages were never recorded. It may have been about a kind of behaviour and obligations that were not pronounced and perhaps misunderstood by both sides. An example of such an event is the misconception of the hostage exchange that took place between Romans and Gauls during the Gallic War in the first century BC.[81]
(B) Writers may hint at some details without registering them. Some procedures might be considered so obvious that they were not written down. An example may be seen in the appendix of the Elder Westrogothic Law by the scholar Lars Djäkn ('The priest of Vidhem') who mentions that King Ragnvald Knaphövde of Sweden rode into the province of Västergötland without giving a hostage before crossing the border.[82]
(C) Power structures that underlie the textual tradition. Who is assigned the greatest benefits in the text? This may not be obvious because the writers usually sympathized with the Christian side. Other issues may be: How was the violence motivated by both sides? Are there exaggerations or understatements?
(D) Criticism against certain types of behaviour in the texts, a critique that can be implicit as well as explicit. For example, medieval laws can provide us with information about mentalities in relation to taboos as well as the breaking of oaths. This can, in turn, give us some clues regarding the attitudes towards ethics and morals.

Another method that is used was developed by the philologist and historian of religions Preben Meulengracht Sørensen. It gives the interpreter an opportunity to analyse both Christian influences and remnants of myths and ritual actions in the saga literature. According to Meulengracht Sørensen, survivals of the old traditions exist in the saga literature, but they have not been transmitted in an unaffected form. When the writers refer to pre-Christian cult rituals, they mention, in addition to social institutions, things like 'heritage', 'weddings', and 'relationships regarding property', institutions that did not lose their functions after the Christianisation.[83]

I will also use etymologies, especially of personal names and place names. But etymologies, 'derivations of words', have a small source value for, for example, the 10th-century society. Etymologies are created by syntheses of words and sound changes that underlie the origin of a word, not the specific meaning of the 10th century. Sometimes the changes have taken place very quickly, sometimes they have been slower. These changes can be so fundamental that it might not be possible to understand the original meaning of a word. The word, as well as name elements, may have been situational, developed in contexts that cannot be traced through available sources. Nevertheless, there is an opportunity to interpret the 'hostageship' using different elements in personal names and place names, which may give some indications of what contexts – including cultic and martial – they originated in.

The methods I use for text interpretation can be summarized:

1. Collection of all empirical data from the examined texts.
2. Contextualization of collected data.
3. Comparsions with other sources.

This also includes analysis of other types of sources such as place names and archaeological findings. We will now turn to the theoretical framework.

A model of peace processes: Territorial boundaries, consensus, and communicative acts[84]

A conflict may occur either (a) across borders or (b) within a society. In this investigation my concern is with the former, even if the distinction between the two may be difficult to discern. I define these boundaries as areas of confrontation.

If a border, or territorial boundary, was the subject of low-level warfare and temporary peace agreements, it must, contrary to the stable *Limes Germanicus* in the Roman Age, have been maintained by certain instrumental means. The historian Eva Österberg describes such means in an article about householders (or farmers) and central powers in border societies (Småland) in early modern Sweden.[85] Although Österberg describes conflicts within border societies in the 16th and 17th centuries controlled by a feudal state, she emphasises the mutual agreements in certain communicative spaces. She is influenced by the Marxist consensus concept, but she uses it at the microlevel. The concept of consensus is understood as a solution of mutual agreements through a willingness to negotiate and communicate, where the level of interaction is important. Österberg's understanding of conflicts in border societies is crucial for my own understanding of peace processes across areas of conflict. Borders and boundaries are understood as areas that must be upheld communicatively in the areas of confrontation.[86] These existed both within and outside a society. An example of an area of confrontation is the present-day Southern Göteborg Archipelago, which was the venue for various meetings involving trade, but also peace conferences, during the Viking Age and early Middle Ages.[87] The ideas of Österberg might therefore be used to analyse the conflict and consensus of border societies during the Viking Age.[88] In my opinion, her principle of agreements can also be used in analysing Viking Age society.

Certain communicative spaces existed in the areas of confrontation. Österberg mentions the assembly places in Småland, still referred to in the 16th century as the (Swe.) *tingsplatser*, 'things', as such communicative spaces. It seems likely that ritual places, things, and other kinds of gathering places also had this communicative function in the areas of confrontation during the Viking Age. In recent years it has been suggested, for example by the Scandinavist Stefan Brink, that both cult places and things were multifunctional, but this idea has been disputed.[89] I will not discuss this here, but would like to add another aspect: the mobile features of both cult places and things. The mobile cult place might be compared to the traditional practices of nomadic peoples such as the Sami, but also to lifestances and religions such as Islam.[90] A mobile feature of a cult place is mentioned in the *Landnámabók*, when stocks from high seats or coffins were brought from the homelands and discarded off the Icelandic coast.[91] This might be compared to Sundqvist, who claims that the cultic object *seiðhjallr* was used only in times of need and not permanently.[92] The mobile feature could also be a characteristic of things. Torsten Blomkvist touches on the mobile feature of the thing in stressing the distinction between gatherings and places which were fixed in the landscape.[93] The *Hirdskraa* (*Hirdloven* ca. 1273) describes how the spoils of war were divided: they tied a *vébǫnd* and shared the spoils within that area.[94] *Saxo Grammaticus* (Book 8) also mentions this custom. I will not further outline the mobility theme here. It seems, however, that times such as during war, plague, or drought have had some impact on the nature of ceremonies and rituals, which may also have influenced where people met and how they interacted.

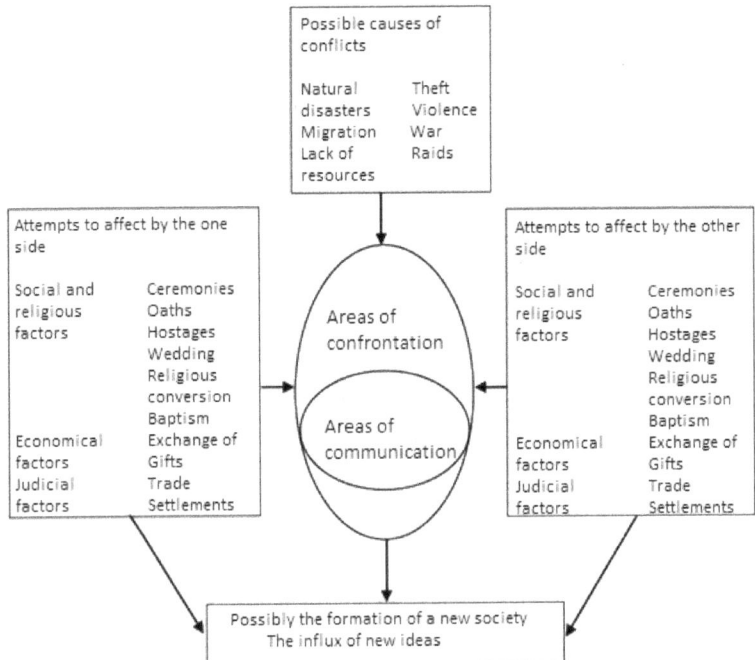

Figure I.1. A schematic description of conflicts and conflict solutions in the late Viking Age and the early Middle Ages.

I will describe the functions of those communicative spaces and in areas of confrontation later in this book. First, it is necessary to describe the society in which the communicative spaces and areas of confrontation occurred.

Development of society, spacial and temporal variation

Some historians have pointed out the importance of temporal variations and societal changes during the Viking Age and the early Middle Ages. Sverre Bagge and Nils Blomkvist, for example, have described a process of change for early medieval Norway and Gotland, respectively.[95] Bagge portrays the pre-state society as decentralised, dominated by a ruler and competitive 'great men' (Swe. *stormän*; OI *mikill maðr*), and a societal web that relied upon personal bondage. The state society was dominated by a king with a dependent aristocracy, ground rents, and a fixed societal hierarchy.[96] The means to achieve this fundamental societal change can be seen in the directed mission in late Iron Age societies such as Saxony (ninth century) and Norway (late 10th century). Archaeologists such as Alexandra Sanmark have also drawn attention to this change.[97]

By 'society' I mean a society in the early stages of state formation. It was characterised by periods of peace and violence. In this period there was also a horizontal division of what Brink,[98] in a study of aspects of space and territoriality in Early Scandinavia, calls the administrative divisions of the Old Swedish *rike*, *land*, and *hundrade*. It is my purpose to distinguish the personal bonds occurring among groups and individuals in and between such administrative divisions.

I will present a model as a tool for understanding the relationships between society, areas of confrontation, and communicative spaces. Its purpose is to describe the dynamic processes before, during, and after a conflict. It is almost a truism among political scientists that a society reshapes after pandemics, war, natural disasters, or other crises. Historians such as Thomas Lindkvist have pointed out that the main reason for war or raids during the Viking Age was plunder.[99] But crises such as drought or plague seem also to have caused migrations and, therefore, engagements (Figure I.1).

Interest – mutual or unilateral – in creating peace may arise during conflicts. In the Viking Age and early Middle Ages such interest was located in communicative spaces at various levels. There were at least three steps in these peace processes.

1. The first step was establishing social relations through ceremonies involving rituals including oaths, gift-giving, banquets, and perhaps a decision to exchange hostages and tributes (ON *geld*) and to intermarry. These ritual performances often (but not always) occurred in communicative spaces such as things and halls. The symbolic expressions of these ritualistic performances varied and depended on the situation in which they occurred.
2. The next step was stabilising economic relations, such as trade or cooperation between crafts and access to resources. This might mean admission to fertile lands, pastures, woods, and coastal areas with harbours and fishing rights, and so on. These trade cooperations or land sharings between opposing sides might be implemented through ritual.
3. Finally, the peace agreement needed to gain legal force. It might be written, but in most cases it was oral. The agreement had then to be accepted by both sides.

These steps were not necessarily communicated at assembly places; they might also be communicated at market or other societal spaces, which were sometimes temporary. These spaces were flexible in their function but existed within the areas of confrontation. An important aspect was the societal consequences of the peace processes. Conflicts may have brought an influx of new ideas that might be seen within the society at the judicial, societal, and economic levels, and these were reflected in the sources that described the events.

The model may help us in our analysis of the opposing sides, their symbolic actions in peace agreements, and their adaption to the society after the conflict. Clearly, as a model it is merely a simplification of reality. It is also important to stress that peace processes during the Viking Age and early Middle Ages were never straightforward. If, for example, one side was stronger, the weaker had to submit. To underline these differing conditions and to exemplify how the model can be used, two case studies are briefly presented. The first deals with the peace processes between Alfred the Great (OE *Ælfrēd*) and the Viking ruler Guthrum (OE *Guðrum*) in late ninth-century England. The second addresses the various conflicts and solutions described in the Icelandic *Íslendingabók* and *Landnámabók*. These include conflicts at both the macro and micro levels.

The peace processes between Alfred and Guthrum

In the second half of the ninth century, Wessex (OE *Westseaxna rīce*) and East Anglia (*Ēast Engla Rīce*) were societies in the midst of dynamic changes that were sometimes at war but also enjoyed periods of peace. After Alfred the Great, the Christian ruler of Wessex, had defeated Guthrum, the heathen ruler of East Anglia, at the Battle of Edington (OE *Eðandune*) in Wiltshire between 6 and 12 May 878,[100] Christianity gradually gained a foothold in the Danelaw.[101] According to Alfred's biographer, Asser (d. 909), the Danes fled to a fortification after the battle. The Danes were besieged for two weeks, enduring much hardship, until they surrendered to Alfred. The peace treaty was much to Alfred's advantage. The written treaties cannot be trusted as neutral documents because they are written from the Anglo-Saxon perspective. However, from the perspective of power balance it is important to note that Guthrum was not completely subjugated: he kept his lands and thus the ability to raise more troops.

Ritual performances

The rituals performed during the peace conferences between Alfred and Guthrum exemplify the activities in areas of confrontation that can be analysed with the help of the model. When the first peace conference was held after the Battle of Edington, the Danes sent hostages to the Anglo-Saxons to guarantee the peace. This is an example of the establishment of communication, as envoys were probably also sent.

Asser claims that the 'heathen' swore to leave Alfred's realm, which implies that oaths were taken within a ritualistic framework.[102]

From other Old English sources we know that these could be ring oaths for the heathens, and an example of what I refer to as the mobile feature of the ritual place, i.e. ritual objects, were moved to a place in the area of confrontation that became a communicative space where the oaths were sworn.[103] Guthrum, however, vowed to let himself be baptised.

Seven weeks later, Guthrum arrived with a retinue of thirty men for a second peace conference at the royal estate of Wedmore. Guthrum was baptised and Alfred became Guthrum's godfather.[104]

There is only a brief explanation of the rituals performed when Alfred and Guthrum negotiated and agreed on peace terms. These ceremonies and rituals are similar to those of Continental Germanic peoples.[105] An understanding of something of its contextual character might be obtained from the theoretical perspective of performance suggested by the historian of religions Catherine Bell.[106] Performance models suggest active rather than passive roles for ritual participants, who reinterpret symbols as they communicate them. Cultural life has come to be seen as the dynamic generation and modification of symbolic systems, as something constantly being created by the community. In performances, actions are important. The exchange of hostages was a performance in the sense that it aimed to reach something beyond itself.

As a description the treaty cannot be considered a neutral text recorded by only one side. Furthermore, it was perhaps written some decades after the peace building. The notion of an Alfred who took pity and chose a limited number of hostages may be a Christian interpolation. Despite this, the treaty must be considered contemporary in its original setting. As the peace processes were very much on the terms of the Anglo-Saxons, one can assume that the symbolism in the account, as well as in reality, expressed the symbolism of the victor. However, the heathen Danes and the Christian Anglo-Saxons seem to have understood the rituals in a similar way, which indicates that the Danes shared similar knowledge of, and presumptions about, peace processes with the Anglo-Saxons. If we accept the accuracy of the gesture of limiting the number of hostages, it may have been a signal of goodwill in an early form of chivalry.

Oath-taking was involved in the peace processes, combined with the giving and taking of hostages; it constituted the essential element of rituals.[107] Formally, the oaths taken by both heathens and Christians were considered equal. This may confirm some of my assumptions of a temporary communicative space, or spaces, if the rituals were performed not only in one location but also on separate occasions. The Danes may have brought sacred objects such as rings and sworn on them.

This ritual probably gave the impression that Guthrum (OE *Guðrum*) had formally submitted to Alfred, and it might be understood as consonant with the ideology of a Christian ruler who had no rival but relied on his own *auctoritas*, 'authority'. However, Alfred also had to give up something to secure this agreement. According to Asser, Alfred gave 'many fine houses', probably estates, to Guthrum.[108]

Guthrum may have seen Alfred as an ally. East Anglia was hardly a unified realm, but was rather several separate territories under earls and chieftains, and successive wars weakened Guthrum. The history of the Danelaw has neglected the importance of ecclesiastical power, but alongside royal power it might also have proved useful to Guthrum as a source of alignment for the control and defence of his territory (cf. Figure I.1) against internal enemies. What is important, however, is that these rituals were performed in communicative spaces, even if the Anglo-Saxons and Danes may have differed in their interpretation of the rituals' significance. The rituals' performances illustrate the first part of the model: the establishment of social relations.

Economic and judicial matters

When Alfred and Guthrum signed a treaty at Wedmore, the border between Wessex and the Danelaw was constituted. Several years later, between 886 and 890, Alfred and Guthrum signed a new treaty, the *Treaty of Alfred and Guthrum*, which is preserved in two manuscripts in a body of legislation from the late 11th century.[109] This agreement included the division of the Thames but also some judicial matters and trade relations, which were to some extent ritualised.[110]

The treaty constituted: (1) the land boundaries asserted through waterflows up the Thames and some tributaries (the Lea, to Bedford, up the Ouse, to Watling Street); (2) the assertion that if a man were killed, whether English or Danish, there should be a fine of eight half marks; and (3) the assertion that if one of the king's thanes was accused of murdering, he should take an oath in the presence of twelve of the thanes, and a man of lower degree in the presence of eleven men, but if he refused he should pay threefold.[111] The swearing of oaths probably occurred in some sort of communicative space, for example, a thing.

The treaty covered some trade issues, including also some rituals. According to the treaty: (4) a guarantor well-known (to both sides) should guarantee the acquisition of slaves, horses, and oxen; and (5) in the oathswearing, it was ordained that neither slaves nor freemen should go to the other side for commerce with cattle and goods without hostages given to show goodwill.[112] These are examples of how rituals or ritual actions connected with commercial interests functioned as an access to effect or regulate the area of confrontation. Hostages were a vital strategy in this regulation to avoid conflict and could be used as a tool by both sides and were not necessarily themselves subordinated. It is also important to note both the degree of subordination in cases like these but also the ability to affect the peaceful relations.

The *Treaty of Wedmore* suggests violence occurred in the area of confrontation. If this were not the case, the regulations would have been unnecessary. It therefore exemplifies the third step in the peace process, in which the agreement became lawful and was accepted by both sides. On this occasion, it appears to have been the end of a lengthy process. Almost a decade elapsed between *The Treaty of Wedmore* and *The Treaty of Alfred and Guthrum*. The latter was probably the result of the experience gained during this interim period.

In this section, examples have been given from larger areas, realms, which might be analysed with the help of this model. Next, we will turn to how the model can be used as an analytical tool for understanding feuds and personal disagreements, with examples from the Icelandic *Íslendingabók* and *Landnámabók*.

Conflicts and conflict solutions in *Íslendingabók* and *Landnámabók*

The *Íslendingabók* and the *Landnámabók* are problematic sources, because there is a time discrepancy of between 130 and 300 years from when they were written to the period they describe, the colonisation and Christianisation of Iceland. I will not address here the extensive debate about their source value. It is enough to note that the conflicts probably originated in the struggle for resources during the Landnám era, during which Iceland was settled.[113]

In early Icelandic society, conflicts often occurred at the levels of kin-based groupings and individuals. There were no rulers with the rank of the Earls of Lade (ON *Hlaðir*) in Trøndelag in Norway, for example. The Icelandic *goðar* had political and judicial as well as religious functions, but their influence was probably limited and their dominance largely depended on their lands in attractive coastal regions with fertile soils, woods, and access to fishing grounds, harbours, and driftwood. Land disputes were the main cause of the 126 conflicts that I have noted in the *Íslendingabók* and the *Landnámabók* (Figure I.2). The blood feud was a special mechanism of violence. In Figure I.2 I have noted the blood feuds that immediately escalated into conflicts where revenge was the single motive. An insult beneath the surface may have caused these feuds.

Other causes of conflict were accusations of witchcraft, heritage disputes, theft, molestation, and murder. The periods of agreement between the conflicts, for which there was some kind of consent, are important here. Naturally the reason for the consent varied. But I would like to emphasise this consent as an attempt at consensus. These are examples of conflict and solutions relieving each other within areas of confrontation.

In the longer perspective the main result of the conflicts during the Landnám era (the time of settlement) was the creation of the Althing, the general assembly, in 930 and the later organisation of legislative districts, *fjórðungar*, which resulted in territorial strengthening. This is not new information; I merely wish to point out that the experiences drawn from the areas of confrontation strengthened the communicative spaces.

Land disputes	35
Blood feud	18
Murder	17
Insult	11
Witchcraft	9
Duel	5
Lawsuit	5
Heritage disputes	5
Theft	4
Molestation	4
Riot of thralls	2
Suicide	1

Figure I.2. Causes of conflict reported in the *Íslendingabók* and the *Landnámabók*.

Areas of confrontation and communicative spaces

A lack of information makes it difficult to define areas of confrontation. Naturally, this is true of the conflicts in the *Íslendingabók* and the *Landnámabók*, where descriptions are cryptic. The locations of the disputes limited the significance of the areas of confrontation: the texts describe how clashes took place on high ground, in valleys, or in the backwoods between farmsteads. These became boundaries when periods of collaboration followed conflict.

In these contexts there are examples of how communicative spaces such as things and farms could be transformed into areas of confrontation. The *Íslendingabók* (Ch. 5) tells of the chieftains Hænsna-Þórir (OI *Hænsa-Þórir*) and Tungu-Odd (OI *Tungu-Oddr*), who fought the lawman Thord Gellir (OI *Þórðr gellir*) several times at the Althing (OI *Alþingi*).

Another narrative in the *Landnámabók* tells how Erik the Red (OI *Eiríkr Þorvaldsson hinn rauði*) broke into the house of Thorgest (OI *Þorgestr*) at Breidabolstead (OI *Breiðabólstaðr*) to retake his high-seat pillars, which he had entrusted to Thorgest. It is not clear if Breidabolstead functioned as a *hof*, a cultic building, but perhaps there were some ritual restrictions linked to this place. The break-in was a crime in any case, and Erik was summoned to the thing. This escalated into a blood feud between Erik and Thorgest.

The feud between Erik and Thorgest is an example of cooperation involving trust from its outset, and it can be compared to the examples given concerning the swearing of oaths. In this case, however, each side may have blamed the other and differed about the nature of Erik's offence. This is another example of regulation in areas of confrontation, because they were both able to affect the result of the feud. Erik and Thorgest met several times at the Thorsness Assembly (OI *Þórsnesþingi*), a communicative space.

The model makes possible an analysis of the details of narratives such as the one about Erik and Thorgest, which assists in understanding the confrontations and communicative spaces, with a focus on various concessions, demands, and compromises. From a broader perspective, mediation between different areas such as hostages, intermarriage, and fostering might then be explained in a wider setting. These were tools to regulate borders or boundaries at different levels and in different contexts in different parts of Scandinavia as well as in the Viking diaspora. The actions could also be seen within a framework in which economy, laws, and social issues belong together and depend on one another.

The story of the issue of Thorsness illustrates the need for balancing structures like the thing and the presence of negotiators.

Ritual definitions

According to the cultural anthropologist Melford E. Spiro and the historian of religions Håkan Rydving, the concept of 'rite' can be used for the smallest meaningful unit in a ritual complex.[114] Several rites forms a unit called 'a ceremony', while a 'ceremonial' are all the ceremonies performed on one occasion.

The rituals could then be categorized according to the subdivision by the folklorist Lauri Honko, Spiro, and Rydving, into (1) calendrical rituals, (2) crisis rituals, and (3) transition rituals.

According to Honko, the first category is group oriented, the second individual oriented, and the last category is both individual and group oriented.[115] Spiro's system is based on a distinction between recurring and non-recurring rituals.

As for the crisis rituals, Honko saw them as recurring, which Spiro did not. Honko claimed that disasters and the like are unique events and the rituals occur in accordance with them.[116]

Rydving points out that the characteristics must apply to all the ritual types, and crisis rituals should be regarded as recurrent: the same ritual pattern can be carried out every time one meets with a certain type of crisis. The same ritual pattern is performed as usual, even if the disaster is a unique event.[117]

It can be difficult to determine the character of different ritual acts if the point of departure is the distinction between the events to which they relate and not to ritual acts themselves. For example, initiations may concern a group as well as an individual. In connection with calendrical rituals, individual-centred elements may occur.[118] This may have consequences for an analysis of peace processes where, for example, recurring cyclical rituals occurred during festivities with the giving of gifts, which had the function of preventing further disputes. Wars are events similar to disasters, and if one categorises the following truce as part of a larger peace process, these rituals can be both individually and collectively oriented.

A leader can be integrated, for example, through honours, marriages, and gifts, and not least by the spontaneous actions of a cult leader – which we will return to in a section below. Settlements between opponents can ritually have consequences for a larger population through collaborations between people, and these may be manifested in trade (e.g. with festivities), as festivals, or in other recurring, common events of ritual character. These are just a few comments about the division and character of rituals.

In this book, I basically refer to Honko's, Spiro's, and Rydving's definitions of rituals as analytical categories. However, there is reason to discuss how the ritual could express itself in space and the division between the sacred and the profane.

Rituals and space

Traditionally, in the research on religious history, one has been interested in where rituals take place. The research usually focus on places with special characteristics and where ritual practices are performed, practices which distinguish them from other places. Such places are therefore often referred to with a special word. Such a special place for ritual acts can be exemplified by the Old Norse *vi* (OI *vé*), 'holy place'. It is the term that is usually associated with cultures in Viking Age Scandinavia and Iceland. At the *vi* place, 'ritual taboos' and 'ritual restrictions' existed.[119]

The word *vi* can be derived from an Old Germanic adjective: **wīhaz*, 'holy'. Other terms for 'holiness' were also used for cult places, such as Old Norse *heilagr* and *helgi*, 'holy'. Words like these were later used by the church in Scandinavia as translations of *sacer* and *sanctus*.[120] The term *heilgar* has thus had the meaning of 'sacred' in the pre-Christian context, although Sundqvist argues that it merely refers to an 'aspect' of sacredness.[121]

However, the discussion of the concept of sacredness linked to certain places can be developed further. Recently, the concept of sacredness has made a sort of comeback within the research on religious history. For example, it can be seen in the historian of religions Veikko Anttonen's study on the concept of sacred. He discusses the boundaries of the sacred by using a domestic term, the Finnish word *pyhä*, as an analytical category. The word *pyhä* can be defined as something authoritative that the cult performers do not question. Anttonen points out why the sacred (*pyhä*) and its ritual performativity has a 'sacred' character:

> [...] it is important to conceptualize the sacred as a category-boundary which becomes actual only in social situations when the inviolability of such categories as person, gender, marriage, nation, or justice, liberty, purity, propriety, are threatened and are in danger of losing their legitimating authority as moral foundations of society and social life.[122]

In order for something to be perceived as sacred, it must be filled with content. This content usually occurs in the meeting of people who relate to each other, i.e., through interaction, rather than – as in a theological perspective – being a question about something separated from the social organization.[123] Instead, sacredness becomes a social construction that depends on the culture it occurs in. The sacredness is constantly undergoing (paradigmatic) changes and is the subject of exchanges and negotiations about what should be included. Anttonen shows how the sacred can be perceived in relation to *pyhä*, which has had a double meaning:

> Terms denoting the 'sacred' in various languages can be viewed as linguistic indices, the semantic scope of which has varied in time according to the systems of meanings whereby distinctions between persons, animals, things, objects, phenomena, topographical points in the landscape, events, experiences and so forth are made. In the Finnish language, the term *pyhä* (denoting the 'sacred') was originally used to designate both territorial borders and the intersections of waterways, allowing groups of settlers to separate themselves from one another and to mark the boundary between the shared inner domain of the territory claimed by them and the outer domain. In place names, *pyhä* signified the outer border of the inhabited area [...].[124]

Anttonen's perception of the sacred in space is essential for my analysis. Rather than interpret *heilagr* as 'holy, sacred' in a modern understanding, I suggest that the term should be used as a unit of meaning within categories such as 'ritual taboos' and 'ritual restrictions', that is 'a sanctioned protection'. I relate *heilagr* to these categories when I discuss the characteristics of the *vi*-place (or other places).[125] The indigenous concepts of *vé*, 'sanctuary', *heilagr*, 'holy, sacred' and *helgi* 'holiness, sanctity', can be used as analytical categories for 'sanctioned protection' at places of communication. But there is also reason to think that this protection (A) can be extended outside the 'sacred places' and (B) can be related to places that were temporarily established in times of war and crises.

In some cultures cult objects, or everyday objects, can be transported during movements. These cult objects can be used on special occasions – sometimes temporarily and in other cases permanently. On these occasions the objects may have cultic functions. The objects can then mark a place where specific restrictions (or a sanctioned protection) exist. This is evident among nomadic peoples like the Sami where the tent (or hut), *goahti*, is multifunctional and traditionally had a cosmological function. In Islam, the prayer rug (Arab. *sajjāda*) marks a cult place when a Muslim puts it down before a prayer. We could define these cult places as 'mobile'. The mobility of a cult place in the Old Scandinavian society can be seen from three different perspectives:

(1) The Icelandic sagas mention how images of deities were brought along and thrown overboard. Where the images landed, a farm was built and – in some cases – the cult buildings called *hof*s. This relates to the establishment of a permanent cult place.
(2) The Icelandic *Landnámabók* describes how the mould from a *hof* in Norway was brought to Iceland, and spread over a land area, which then was sanctified.[126] Thus, something material (the mould) could – when it was moved – be used to create a sanctioned area in a new land.
(3) Cult objects were used to mark a temporarily established cult place, for example, by swearing an oath on a ring that was brought to a certain place; in this case the same sanctioned protection applied as in the case of a fixed cult place.

I would like to add some other features of mobile cult places that could be used in connection with peace processes:

(1) The terms *vé*, *heilagr*, and *helgi* can be related to the place's sanctioned protection. This meant that a person who sought sanctuary could do so in a *vi* place or in a church (during the Middle Ages). Peace meetings in hall buildings such as the *hof* may also have had this type of sanctioned protection.
(2) An area of communications could be temporarily established between conflicting parties. These places were often chosen in the area of confrontations between the opposing sides. Such places may have been both temporary and fixed. Around some of the places, bands, so-called *vébǫnd*s, were tied to mark a meeting place.
(3) Peace meetings were often held in places referred to as 'thing places' in the written sources. The link between the thing place and the *vi* place is, however, not obvious.

However, in *Egils saga Skalla-Grímssonar*, there is a *lausavísa* (a single stanza) that implies this connection since the thing place is referred to as a *vé* (or *vi*).[127] Anyhow, ritual acts were carried out at thing places, too.[128]

(4) A cult object could be brought to a place that was not characterized as *vé*, *heilagr*, and *helgi*. This may have happened in connection with crisis rituals such as when the warriors met for negotiations after a war. Oaths were taken and the performers put their hands on an oath ring. Even crosses that were transported with the armies have had a similar function in the Viking Age as well as later in the Middle Ages.

(5) It could be a matter of a ritual journey,[129] for example the journey of a cult leader such as the Uppsala ruler who moved between different places and received a form of flexible protection. This issue concerned recurring cyclical rites.

(6) Also in the context of rites of passage such as weddings, the purpose may have been to strengthen peace agreements in the Scandinavian society, and in these cases there was a flexible protection. It is mentioned in *Hauksbók*'s and *Sturlubók*'s versions of the *Landnámbók* about Össur the White (*Ozzur hinn hviti*), that he killed someone when he was in a bridal train in the *Oppland*s (*Upplondum*) with the ruler of Hadafylki Sigurd hrisi (*Sigurðr hrisi*).[130] The wording *va víg i veum*, 'killed at the *vi*', suggests that there was the same sanctioned protection in the bridal train as at a fixed *vi* place, where violence was forbidden.

(7) The division of war booty was important as a vertically directed ritual to maintain the social bonds within a war retinue. The division took place at temporary (thing) places, which is described in the Norwegian medieval *Hirdskraa*, where it is stated that the war booty could be divided within an area surrounded by a *vébǫnd*.[131]

To sum up: Indigenous denotations such as *vé*, *heilagr* and *helgi* may have been used to indicate sanctioned protection, taboo, etc. The sanctioned protection was applicable not only to permanent places but also to temporary places and sometimes outside of these areas.

The performativity of rituals

In recent years, the research on rituals has focused on the dynamic and changeable aspects of rituals.[132] One way to approach the contextual character of ritual was suggested by the historian of religions Catherine Bell. Bell emphasized that performing ritual models point to active rather than passive roles for the participants in rituals.[133] She also meant that actions could be more or less ritualized. In order to further understand the ritualized action, Bell specified three different characteristics for how it should be analysed, something that could be related to how the individual acts and moves in a ritual context:[134]

(1) The ritualized action must be understood within its context. Only then can one fully understand why the action is different from other actions.
(2) The central feature of the ritual action is the primacy of the body. The body moves within a specifically designed space while at the same time the body both experiences and defines the norms that orders the surroundings. Participants do not understand how they themselves have contributed to the creation of the surroundings, which are perceived as being controlled by forces beyond the immediate situation.
(3) The result is a situation where the ritualization tends to strengthen the authority of forces considered to be from the outside.

Ritualization therefore involves a number of practices that are 'flexible sets of schemes and strategies acquired and deployed by an agent who has embodied them'.[135] Through this kind of analysis, it is possible to determine the varying degrees of ritualization, the difference between different cultural systems, and what kind of ritualization it is about. Thus, the writing analyst can answer questions about what distinguishes the ritual action, why it is performed, and its results compared to non-ritual actions. Bell's way of defining ritualization means that it is possible to interpret spontaneous expressions as ritualized actions and that different – more or less ritualized actions – can be analysed.

The ritual action has also been discussed by Caroline Humphrey and James Laidlaw. Similar to Bell, they use the term 'ritualization', and like Bell, they mean that there is a basic connection between everyday activity, the ritual practitioner's intentions and the identity of the ritual actions that is performed.[136] Humphrey and Laidlaw argue that the ritual commitments of the ritual practitioner are not intentional, but stipulated through established rules, different archetypes, and that they constitute different named entities with their own history. Since the ritual action is perceived as external, it is understandable to the practitioner. Thus they determine a characteristic that is crucial to the way ritualization is to be considered.[137] Therefore, in Humphrey and Laidlaw's analysis, one can see the same intent as with Bell: the concept of ritual is regarded as elastic.

The key to my analysis is that the use of the concept of ritualization is a help in a flexible analysis that tests the boundaries of what is considered to be a ritual action, focusing on the performativity of ritual actions. According to Bell's definition, it means that the ritual action is an attempt to create an understanding of society since the ritual action constructs the perceptions and values of society. At the same time, the ritual act in society, which is constantly changing, becomes a way to get past the opposition between tradition and change.[138] Therefore, I choose to refer to 'ritual act' and not 'ritual'.

Sundqvist has pointed out that performativity in Old Scandinavian religion could also contain violent elements. For example, might have been to harm the one who had power over the place where the ritual action was carried out. Sundqvist therefore points out that the performativity of rituals had the 'capacity of change' and that the practitioners could focus on the outcome of the actions and the attention was also turned to the intent of action, its utterance, and how it affected them as individuals.[139]

By means of two examples from Old Norse sources, I will show how the performativity could occur in ritual situations where both conflicts and consensus occur in ritual acts.

An example of performativity in an Old Icelandic context can be seen in the *Kristni saga* when the *gyðja* Friðgerðr speaks when she is sacrificing in the *hof*, probably at (or on) a *stalli*. Meanwhile the bishop Friðrekr is preaching at the nearby thing of Hvammur. They can both hear each other. This event is reproduced in a *lausavísa* by Þórvaldr Koðránsson – who was present during these events according to the saga – from the 10th century:

Fork með dóm enn dýra;	I preached the precious faith;
drengr hlýddi mér engi;	no man;
gǫtum háð at hreyti,	we got scorn from the sprinkler
hlautteins goða sveni,	– priest's son – of blood-dripped branch.
en við enga svinnu	And without any sense,
aldin rýgr við skaldi	old troll-wife against poet
(þá kreppi goð gyðju)	– may God crush the priestess –
gall of heiðnum stalla.[140]	shrilled at the heathen altar.
	(Transl. Siân Grønlie)[141]

Sundqvist believes that the Christian Þórvaldr and the bishop upset the *gyðja* so much that she 'screamed' (or 'shrilled') to them from the sacrificial altar.[142] Friðgerðr was also sacrificing in the *hof* when the bishop made his visitation. This act can be interpreted as a protest or demonstration conducted by the *gyðja* towards the Christians in a place and in a time when there was room for doing such performances. In this way she wanted to claim her influence over the cult place threatened to be destroyed by external forces.[143]

There are also examples of ritual acts that demonstrated consensus during peace negotiations. In *Orkneyinga saga*, written around 1230 by an unknown Icelandic writer, a peace meeting between two great men of the Orkney Islands is mentioned. Earl (or *jarl*) Rögnvald Kali Kolsson (ON *Rǫgnvaldr Kali Kolsson*) meets Sweyn Asleifsson (OI *Sveinn Ásleifarson*) at 'Rognvald's Island' (ON *Rǫgnvaldsey*, Eng. South Ronaldsay) in an initially aggressive way, but then a truce shield (ON *friðskjǫldr*) is set to signify peace, and they meet on the island to discuss peace.[144] Then they see Sweyn's enemy, Harald Earl Maddadsson (*Haraldr jarl Maddaðarson*), approaching, and Rögnvald advises Sweyn to seek shelter at the island of Struma (ON *Straumey*).[145] There lives a man named Amundi Hnevason (*Ámundi Hnefason*), who is a relative of Sweyn and a friend of Harald. He settles the feud between Harald and Sweyn and claims that the settlement that was agreed upon last year should apply. Then Amundi puts them both in the same bed. After this settlement (*sætt*) on the peace, Harald and Sweyn return to their homes.[146]

The story contains much of what I mentioned earlier: in the area of confrontation between Harald and Sweyn an area of communication is established in Amundi's house, where the parties can meet and interact on peaceful terms. We cannot know if there were any particular form of peace in the house, but Amundi seems to act as a mediator between the parties, and some kind of mutual respect for the location must have existed. When Amundi puts Harald and Sweyn in the same bed, it can be perceived as a ritual act as it conveys a symbolic message of consensus. It was a good idea to do this act during this occasion because there was a storm and it was crowded in the house.

The fact that they were brought together was thus a ritual act with a demonstrative function regarding the position of the bodies – a performativity that was a result of external circumstances such as the storm and the hostility – as compared to Bell's discussion. But my main point is that the action can be related to the above discussion of what can be counted as a ritual act. The example can be compared with the theory of Humphrey and Laidlaw, pointing out that it is not a (performative) act, like bowing, which makes this ritualized action effective, it is the context:

> If you bow during a state ritual you are by that very act constituting yourself as a subject, not just symbolizing a relation which 'really exists' elsewhere. However this observation does not tell us anything general about ritualized action, since a bow is a bow in ritual or outside it. It would be ethnocentric to assume that bowing is a necessarily 'a ritual' just because you yourself do it only in rituals.[147]

The results and expectations of what can be a ritual act in a particular cultural context are thus important aspects to pay attention to when a researcher analyses his or her material. The above discussed analyses of ritual acts are important in cases that include the hostages, since the giving and taking of hostages could appear in connection with – or as a result of – critical moments (like during wartime conditions) where the performativity could be a part of a power demonstration, as well as a part of a power strategy and where it was a question about displaying the intentions of the practitioners.

Concluding remarks

In this part it is presented how hostages in ancient cultures have been viewed in various research disciplines. Legal historians and historians have focused on the Roman Empire, Continental Germanic, and Old English cultures. In some cases, Scandinavia has also been touched upon, mainly with a focus on legal history issues.

Studies have been made within social-historical perspectives on hostages, for example by Adam J. Kosto and Ryan Lavelle, mainly with interests in the Carolingian Empire and the Anglo-Saxon societies. It has been argued that peace negotiations with hostages also involved ritual actions (not least in the Roman Empire); however, the connection between hostages and ritual acts has been discussed to a limited extent. In these studies, sources that are not texts, such as place names and archaeological material, are seldom used. Thus, there are several approaches and source categories that have not been used on the study of hostages in Scandinavia during the Viking Age and the early Middle Ages.

The starting point for the book is the assumption that there were two types of hostages: as a guarantor of business transaction or as a hostage given in war. The latter form is the focus in this survey. It is important to stress that the hostages were given in these contexts, which can be related to unilateral and bilateral contractual forms. The latter form is interesting because it concerned certain areas during negotiations between adversaries. The unilateral form is of interest in this case because it was about receiving people as hostages.

Because the use of hostages occurred during both war and peacetime activities, which at the same time could associated with religious aspects, a number of methodological considerations must be discussed. Each case that is referred to in this book should be studied based on its geographical and temporal conditions.

Understanding hostages in relation to peace processes is also relevant to the study. By 'process' is meant the times of war and peace and the time in between. There is also a native terminology with words for hostages and peace.

In accordance with scholars of medieval studies, the concept of 'bounds of friendship' is used, in this context with a focus on the horizontal rather the vertical longitude. The focus is on both the victorious and losing side of conflicts, that is, the recipients and givers of the hostage.

The conflicts were located in what I refer to as areas of confrontation and in areas communication. The negotiations were conducted at different levels, legally (peace agreements), religious (ring oaths), socially (festivities), and financially (trade agreements). The experiences of previous peace processes or the ongoing conflict could form the basis of a peace ending during the Viking Age and later in the Middle Ages. A theoretical model for these events is presented. The model describes how conflicts could be managed in border areas, at both macro and micro levels, that is, between larger land areas, such as the kingdoms as well as between landowners at the local level. The model is, of course, a simplification of reality, but as an analytical tool it is relevant to this book.

By two case studies, of the peace between Alfred the Great and Guthrum (ON *Guðrum*), ruler of Northumbria in the late ninth century, and of conflicts in the *Landnámabók* (Sturlubók) and *Íslendingabók*, I exemplify how the model can be applied. The conflict between Alfred and Guthrum occurred in a society that was about to unite under a government, while the conflicts in Iceland preceded a society that was decentralized and without ruling power. Thus, the conditions were different in these two cases.

In this part, the concepts of 'ritual' and 'holy place' are applied. Scholars such as Lauri Honko, Melford Spiro, and Håkan Rydving have defined different types of rituals with the division into calendrical rituals, transitional rituals, and rites of passages that are regarded as basic analytical categories. In order to characterize the places where ritual acts were carried out, one can use indigenous terms as the Old Norse *heilagr* or *helgi*.

Although these concepts did not have had the same meaning, they could be related to the devoted, 'sacred place', where special restrictions and taboos were established. This raises a discussion about the nature of the 'sacredness' of the 'holy places', which could be compared to Veikko Anttonen who discusses the concept of *pyhä*. Instead of talking about 'sacredness' domestic concepts such as *vé, heilagr,* and *helgi* can be used as analytical categories to denote 'sanctioned protection' at places.

The discussion of 'sacred places' can also be related to a discussion about the performativity of the ritual, that is, its elasticity and change. Ritual theorists such as Catherine Bell, and Caroline Humphrey and James Laidlaw, who pointed out what distinguished the ritual act from other acts. They meant that there is a connection between everyday activity, the intentions of the ritual practitioner, and the ritual actions performed. Performativity, according to Bell, expresses that ritual acts, among other things, contribute to creating hierarchies. The performativity could also contain violence, for example, when protecting a sacred place. Such performativity can be seen in the *Kristni saga* which describes how the *gyðja* Friðgerðr protects her *vé*-place against a missionary bishop in Iceland by shouting and thus 'protesting'. In the *Orkneyinga saga*, from the later half of the 12th century, it is described how the house of Amundi Nevason transforms into an area of communication where two enemies shared the same bed signifying a symbolic unification.

These case studies are important because they exemplify how performativity in ritual acts could include demonstrations of power including the use of hostages during peace processes.

Notes to Part I

1. CD 1998: 776.

2. *Oxford Advanced Learner's Dictionary of Current English* 2010: 753.

3. Cf. Aymard 1961; Matthews 1989: 38.

4. See Phillipson 1911: 42, 399 ff.

5. Elbern 1990.

6. Chapman, Stacey 2007.

7. Lavelle 2006: 270 ff., 295.
8. Lavelle 2006: 290–296.
9. Kosto 2002: 142.
10. von Amira 1882: 691 ff.
11. Lutteroth 1922: 212.
12. Sveinbjörn Rafnsson 2001: 138 f.
13. Nordberg 2003: 118.
14. See Andrén 2014: 99.
15. Jón Viðar Sigurðsson 1999; 2010; Hermanson 2000; 2009.
16. Jón Viðar Sigurðsson 2010: 12.
17. Miller 1990: 122 ff; 171 ff.
18. Kosto 2012: 20.
19. Kosto 2012: 92.
20. Kosto 2012: 21.
21. Kosto 2012: 24 ff.
22. See Hultgård 2011.
23. Kosto 2012: 8.
24. Kosto 2012: 132 ff.
25. Kosto 2012: 22.
26. Kosto 2012: 9 ff.
27. Kosto 2012: 13.
28. Kosto 2012: 104.
29. See Part VI.
30. Kosto 2012: 15 ff.
31. Kosto 2012: 15, 30.
32. Kosto 2012: 15 f.
33. Kosto 2012: 15.

34. Kosto 2012: 16 f.
35. Kosto 2012: 18.
36. Kosto 2012: 13.
37. Kosto 2012: 24.
38. Kosto 2012: 25.
39. Kosto 2012: 28.
40. Kosto 2012: 29.
41. Kosto 2012: 29 f.
42. See Kosto 2012: 30.
43. Simek 1993: 287.
44. See, for example, Schier 1981.
45. Simek 1993: 287.
46. *Edda* a–c (ed. Anthony Faulkes); *Landnámabók* II, Hauksbók ([ed.] Finnur Jónsson).
47. Abram 2011: 16 ff., 20.
48. See Steinsland 2005: 47 and Schjødt 2008: 89.
49. Meulengracht Sørensen 1993: 12. It is open to debate whether the Eddic poems originate from Iceland or Norway. However, the environmental descriptions may show Norway rather than Iceland. During the excavations of Bryggen, in the present city of Bergen, runic inscriptions from 1200 to 1400 were found with a similar content (Liestøl 1964: 25, 30 ff., 50 f.; Hultgård 1996: 27).
50. Schjødt 2008: 89.
51. Schjødt 2008: 89.
52. Schjødt 2008: 91.
53. Meulengracht Sørensen 1991.
54. Hultgård 2016.
55. *Egils saga Skalla-Grímssonar* ([ed.] Sigurður Nordal); *Eyrbyggja saga, Brands þáttr örva, Eiríks saga rauða, Grænlendinga saga,*

Grœnlendinga þáttr ([ed.] Einar Ól. Sveinsson & Matthías Þórðarson); *Orkneyinga saga* ([ed.] Finnbogi Guðmundsson).

56. See Abram 2011: 21.

57. *Landnámabók* I–III ([ed.] Finnur Jónsson).

58. Jakob Benediktsson 1969: 276 f., 282 f.; Sundqvist 2007: 26.

59. Sveinbjörn Rafnsson 2005: 613.

60. *Sturlunga Saga* ([ed.] Gudbrand Vigfusson).

61. For example in *Saga Ólafs hins helga*, *Heimskringla* 2 ([ed.] Bjarni Aðalbjarnarson).

62. Kristinn Jóhannessons preface in *Nordiska kungasagor* I ([ed.] Johansson): 14.

63. For example *Heidreks saga*, *Hervarar saga ok Heidreks konungs* ([ed.] Jón Helgason); *Hrólfs saga kraka og Bjarkarímur* ([ed.] Finnur Jónsson).

64. See, for example, Hultgård 1993; Abram 2011: 24.

65. Clunies Ross 2010: 10.

66. Schjødt 1999: 35; Røthe 2010: 21 ff.

67. Steinsland 2005: 59.

68. Sahlgren 1924; See Hellberg 1986: 42 ff.

69. Andersson T. 1992a; 1992b; 1992c; 1993; Brink 1997; 1999; Elmevik 1999; 2003; 2013; Vikstrand 2001.

70. See Sundqvist 2002: 55.

71. Rättlösabalken, *Äldre västgötalagen* II ([ed.] Wiktorsson): 84 p. (text), 85 f. (transl.) (pages 21r–21v).

72. I mainly use Åke Holmbäck and Elias Wessén's translations, *Svenska landskapslagar* ('Swedish provincial laws'), published in the 1930s and 1940s. I also rely on Per-Axel Wiktorsson's new translation of the *Elder Westrogothic law*. To access the original Swedish text, I rely on Carl Johan Schlyter's editions of the original texts (1827–1877). Currently a project with new translations is being conducted by the Centre for Scandinavian Studies, Aberdeen. I am aware

that this project may change the view on the interpretations of the Swedish provincial laws.

73. In this book I use the word thing (ON *þing*) for the assembly.

74. For an overview see Kiernan 1981.

75. Oehrl 2017: 87–122.

76. I use the word 'Old Scandinavian' to characterize religion as well as society. This can be derived from the historian of religions Anders Hultgård's (1991: 161 f.) term 'Old Scandinavian religion', which refers to the groups in the Nordic countries who spoke the Old Norse languages, but not those who spoke the Sami languages or Old Finnish.

77. Dumézil 1966.

78. See Rydving 1990: 172 p.

79. *The Anglo-Saxon Chronicle* 7 MS E (ed. Irvine): 86 (year 1063).

80. Ginzburg 1989: 96–125.

81. See Part IV, n. 131.

82. See Part VI, p. 252 ff.

83. Meulengracht Sørensen 1992.

84. Preliminary versions of the following sections has been published in Olsson 2017: 266–275 and 2018: 159–170.

85. Österberg 1989: 73 ff.

86. According to the OED 'conflict' means 'strike together', 'clash', 'contend' (OED 1989: 713). It may further be related to 'collision', 'to clash', 'to be at variance', 'to be incompatible' (OED 1989: 713). I will instead rely on the OED definition of 'confrontation' as 'the bringing of persons face to face; esp. for examination of the truth' (OED 1989: 719). It may also be related to 'the coming of countries, parties, etc., face to face: used to a state of political tension with or without actual conflict' (OED 1989: 719).

87. Several sources describe Brännö (*Brenneyja*) as an island where kings met every third year for festivities.

88. Österberg 1989: 74 ff.

89. Brink 1997: 403 ff. See also Sundqvist 2002: 101 ff. In a recent article the archaeologists Sarah Semple and Alexandra Sanmark (2008: 245–259) cast some doubt on the multifunctional thing. Andreas Nordberg (2011: 21) is cautious concerning the division between funeral place and cult place.

90. The *goahti* of the Sami could be multifunctional even if the construction differed depending on location. In Islam the prayer mat becomes a cultplace.

91. This custom can be intermingled with Christian imaginations, since Christians in the *Landámabók* practise the same custom.

92. Sundqvist 2012.

93. T. Blomkvist 2002: 104 ff.

94. *Hirdloven* Ch. 33: Um Þat skipti et guð getær sigr [oc] hærfong.

95. Bagge 1986: 158 ff.; T. Blomkvist 2005: 265.

96. Bagge 1986: 81 ff., 92 f., 97 f.

97. Sanmark 2004: 43–53, 91–106.

98. Brink 1997: 403 f.

99. Lindkvist 1988: 32 f.; cf. Stylegar 1999: 116 f., 122 ff.

100. *The Anglo-Saxon Chronicle* MS F, 71 f.

101. The term 'Danelaw' (OE *Dena lagunema*) appears for the first time in the *Doom Book* (*Code of Alfred*) of 1008. The term was used more frequently in the 11th and 12th centuries, when the term denoted Yorkshire, Derbyshire, Leicestershire, Northamptonshire, and Buckinghamshire (Hadley 2000, 2 ff.).

102. *The Medieval Life of King Alfred the Great*, 33; *The Anglo-Saxon Chronicle* MS F, 71 f.

103. See Olsson 2012: 69.

104. *The Anglo-Saxon Chronicle* MS F, 72.

105. See Lundgreen 1995: 603–612; see also Olsson 2012. This could be compared to the reception and baptism of King Harald (Klak) at the court of Louis the Pious, recorded by Ermoldus Nigellus, which is taken up in Part III of the book.

106. Bell 1997: 159–162.

107. See Kershaw 2011: 17.

108. *The Medieval Life of King Alfred the Great*, Ch. 35; *The Anglo-Saxon Chronicle* MS F, 72.

109. The manuscripts (MS 383) are preserved at Corpus Christi College, Cambridge (Kershaw 2000: 44, 48). The treaty should not be confused with the 11th-century agreement *Laws of Edward and Guthrum*, written by Archbishop Wulfstan II.

110. *Die Gesetze der Angelsachsen* 1, 126 f.

111. *Die Gesetze der Angelsachsen* 1, 126 f.

112. *Die Gesetze der Angelsachsen* 1, 126 f.

113. Orri Vésteinsson 1998: 8–9; Hayeur Smith 2004: 16–17; Jón Viðar Sigurðsson 2008: 51.

114. Spiro 1982: 199 ff.; cf. Rydving 1993: 93 ff.

115. Honko 1975: 75; Rydving 1993: 94.

116. Honko 1979: 378; Rydving 1993: 95.

117. Rydving 1993: 95.

118. It can be seen during annual festivals such as the award of the Nobel Prizes in Sweden and Norway. In addition, the Nobel Peace Prize can be given to both groups (organizations) and individuals.

119. Sundqvist 2007: 182.

120. Sundqvist 2016.

121. Sundqvist 2016.

122. Anttonen 2000: 276 f.

123. Anttonen 2000: 277.

124. Anttonen 2000: 280.

125. Cf. Sundqvist 2015, where he argues that the 'sacredness' was designed and applied in the context of power relations.

126. Enligt *Landnámabók*, Hauksbók ([ed.] Finnur Jónsson): 94 (Ch. 258).

127. *Egils saga Skalla-Grímssonar* ([ed.] Sigurður Nordal): 163 (Ch. 56, stanza 28); see Sundqvist 2007: 189, n. 98.

128. Steinsland 2005: 371 f.

129. See Hultgård 2001: 438 f.

130. *Landnámbók*, Hauksbók ([ed.] Finnur Jónsson): 116 (Ch. 331); *Landnámbók*, Sturlubók ([ed.] Finnur Jónsson): 225 (ch. 376).

131. *Hirdloven* ([transl.] Steinar Imsen): (Ch. 33); see Olsson 2016.

132. See *Ritual, Performatives, and Political Order in Northern Europe, c. 650–1350*, [ed.] W. Jezierski *et al.*, for examples from the Old Scandinavian societies.

133. Bell 1997: 72 ff.

134. Bell 1997: 81 f.

135. Bell 1997: 82.

136. Humphrey & Laidlaw 1994: 260.

137. Humphrey & Laidlaw 1994: 263.

138. Bell 1997: 74 ff.

139. Sundqvist 2016.

140. *Den norsk-islandske skjaldediktning* A 1 ([ed.] Finnur Jónsson): 105.

141. *Íslendingabók – Kristni Saga*, Grønlie ([ed.] Faulkes & Finlay): 36 (Ch. 1).

142. Sundqvist 2007: 65.

143. *Kristnisaga* ([ed.] Kahle): 9 (Ch. 2, 11).

144. *Orkneyinga saga* ([ed.] Finnbogi Guðmundsson): 267 (Ch. 96).

145. *Orkneyinga saga* ([ed.] Finnbogi Guðmundsson): 267 (Ch. 97).

146. *Orkneyinga saga* ([ed.] Finnbogi Guðmundsson): 268 (Ch. 97).

147. Humphrey & Laidlaw 1994: 263.

Part II: The Æsir–Vanir War (or Peace)

In a myth, the tribes of deities – the Æsir and the Vanir – fight each other. In the Æsir–Vanir War, both sides experience both success and adversity. Finally, they decide to make peace. As a part of the peace agreement, hostages are exchanged. From the Vanir come Njǫrðr, Freyr, Freyja and (in one version) Kvasir to the Æsir, and the Æsir sends Hœnir and Mímir to the Vanir.

Because the giving and taking of hostages are mentioned in this myth, it could be said to have a function on the cosmological level. However, the myth is reproduced in various medieval redactions and it appears in two different versions that may not be compatible. The hostages are only mentioned as a central part of the peace agreement in one version.

Below, an interpretation of the versions of the myth in the various medieval redactions of the *Poetic Edda*, the *Snorra Edda* and the *Heimskringla* is made. The details here are important as well as answering the question: what is the central message of each version? Ultimately the myth of the Æsir–Vanir War has been altered and reworked in relation to the time when it was first fixed in writing.

Vǫluspá

The oldest known source for the myth of the war is the skaldic poem *Vǫluspá* in the *Poetic Edda*, stanzas 21–24. In the Old Norse literature, the Eddic poems about the deities constitute a special genre.[1] But the *Vǫluspá* could contain some unique characteristics for the North Germanic regions.

How to cite this book chapter:
Olsson, S. 2019. The Æsir–Vanir War (or Peace). In: Olsson, S. *The Hostages of Northmen: From the Viking Age to the Middle Ages.* Pp. 55–80. Stockholm: Stockholm University Press. DOI: https://doi.org/10.16993/bba.b License: CC-BY.

The *Vǫluspá* is found in the *Poetic Edda*, which is preserved in the manuscript *Codex Regius*, written around 1275, in the *Hauksbók* (Book of Haukr), written in Iceland and Norway at the beginning of the 14th century, and in the Icelandic *Flateyjarbók* (late 14th century). Another important manuscript is AM 748 I 4 to, dated to the beginning of the 14th century.

In the *Vǫluspá*, the history of the world is narrated by a seeress, a *vǫlva*, through images. The images refer to different myths, of which some are known from other sources, some of them are unknown to us. The traditions may therefore have originated during different periods of time, something which is common with traditions that are orally transmitted.

There is a theory that it is primarily the Icelandic writers – the medieval editors – who created this story. But that theory does not currently have so many followers.[2] Recently, the *Vǫluspá* has been dated to the first half of the 11th century by the Scandinavianist John McKinnell.[3] The Germanist Kurt Schier – who builds on an idea by Helmut de Boor – argues that the poem was composed in Norway as early as in the ninth century as a tribute to the heathen earls of Lade and as 'anti propaganda' against the Christian rulers in Vestfold.[4]

The overall content of the *Vǫluspá* visualizes a mythical and cosmic space. The *vǫlva* depicts the creation and the fall of the world and the time in between. The end of the world is called Ragnarök (OI *ragnarǫkr*), the 'fate of the gods'. The myth can therefore be related to eschatological and apocalyptic ideas.[5] It is also a cosmological myth and explains how the world order is maintained. During her divination, the *vǫlva* reveals events from primeval times, but also from the future. The plot has a causal perspective: one event or activity causes another.

The *vǫlva* describes the existence of the gods during the early days as 'happy', but in the end the bliss of the gods is shadowed by the arrival of the feminine being Gullveig, which leads to the war between the Æsir and the Vanir. The events can be summarized as follows, partly after Folke Ström:[6]

> (1) (Stanza 21) The prelude to the war. Gullveig, which could mean 'golden thirst' or 'gold wish', arrives to the Æsir. She seems, according to the poem, to be sent from the Vanir.

The Æsir try to kill Gullveig. She is burned three times, but is reborn every time.

(2) (Stanza 22) Gullveig returns under the name Heid (*Heiðr*) and brings evil *seiðr*, 'sorcery'. The greed is awakened among the gods.

(3) (Stanzas 23–24) The Æsir hold a meeting to discuss whether they should pay fines for the killing of Gullveig. However, the first war in the world begins. Odin throws his spear over the head of the Vanir as a sign of this.

(4) (Stanza 24) The Vanir are victorious, possibly because of their sorcery skills. They shatter the shield wall of the Æsir or manage to come inside their defensive wall.[7]

Then the *Vǫluspá*s version of the myth of the Æsir–Vanir War is ended. We are not further informed about the peace agreement and the hostage exchange between the Æsir and the Vanir as described in other sources.

Several interpreters of the *Vǫluspá* agree that the events described in connection with the war between the Æsir and the Vanir constitute a turning point: it leads forward towards Ragnarök.[8] The war is described as the world's first battle between peoples (*þat var enn fólcvíg fyrst í heimi*). There are also events that indicate that the war is prototypical: when Odin throws his spear over the Vanir it is a ritual action. The myth can thus be related to a cosmological period. In the beginning of the Æsir–Vanir War, greed is awakened and a sudden murder occurs. One can compare with the end of *Vǫluspá* (45), which tells how moral decay escalates and that there is 'violence in the world' (*hart er í heimi*), 'adultery' (*hórdómr*), 'axe time' (*sceggǫld*), and shields that are broken.[9] But the *Vǫluspá* does not mention the peace conditions between the Æsir and the Vanir. In order to understand that part of the events, we are dependent on other sources, most of which are of a later date or have been under the influence of the medieval period when they were written down. Different versions of the peace process are described in these texts.

Snorra Edda

In the version of the myth of the Æsir–Vanir War in the *Snorra Edda*, it is a part of the story of the creation of the skaldic mead (or the 'Mead of Poetry'). Researchers like the philologist and historian of religions Georges Dumézil and the historian of religions Folke Ström regarded this version of the myth as central to the understanding of the peace process.[10] In this chapter it is argued that the connection to the peace in this version of the myth is weak and that it should be interpreted as a myth of the origin of the skaldic mead.

In his *Edda*, Snorri Sturluson has systematized and explained the world of the Old Norse deities. He does so by referring to and clarifying older skaldic and eddic poems, as well as other text sources. For example, he cites a version of the *Poetic Edda* that partly differs from the version of the manuscript *Codex Regius* (ca. 1270), which contains most of the eddic poems. In addition, he may have built on oral tradition, but it also possible that Snorri brought in literary material that was popular in the scholarly circles of the continent.[11] Snorri also created his own coherent prose versions of the old traditions. As a possible consequence, the myth of the war can be depicted with entirely different motives than in the *Poetic Edda*. The *Snorra Edda* has this prelude to the myth of the creation of the skaldic mead:[12]

> And Ægir went on: 'How did this craft that you call poetry originate?'
> Bragi replied: 'The origin of it was that the gods had a dispute with the people called Vanir, and they appointed a peace-conference and made a truce by this procedure, that both sides went up to a vat and spat their spittle into it. But when they dispersed, the gods kept this symbol of truce and decided not to let it be wasted, and out of it made a man. His name was Kvasir, he was so wise that no one could ask him any question to which he did not know the answer. He travelled widely through the world teaching people knowledge, and when he arrived as a guest to some dwarfs, Fialar and Galar, they called him to a private discussion with them and killed him. They poured his blood into two vats and a pot, and the latter was called Odrerir, but the vats were called Son and Bodn. They mixed honey with the blood and it turned into the mead whoever drinks from which becomes a poet or scholar. The dwarfs told the Æsir that Kvasir had suffocated in intelligence because there was no one there educated enough to be able to ask him questions. [...]']'[13]

(Transl. Anthony Faulkes)

Later Galar and Fjalar invite the giant Gilling and his wife. For reasons that are not mentioned they kill both the giants. Suttungr, son of Gilling, avenges his parents by putting the dwarves on a rock in the sea. To redeem themselves, the dwarves offer Suttungr the skaldic mead. Suttungr brings the mead to a mountain and his daughter Gunnlöð stands as guard. But Odin slips into the mountain in the shape of a snake. He persuades Gunnlöð to give him three sips but empties all the vats. He shifts shape into an eagle and fly away. Suttungr chases him, but Odin manages to escape to Asgard; however, he spits out the mead during his flight, thus giving it to the skalds.

The introduction of the paragraph can be described as a study section. The book, *Skáldskaparmál*, 'the language of poetry', in the *Snorra Edda* is primarily intended as a textbook for skalds. Therefore, this introduction in the *Skáldskaparmál* is presented as a dialogue between the deities Ægir (or Hlér) and Bragi. Since the aim of the *Snorra Edda* was to educate skalds, the depictions of the myths can have been subordinated to this purpose. It was the skaldic poetry itself that was important, citing sources in a correct way. Snorri himself may have embroidered the text and added elements from his contemporary scholarly circles. This may apply to all parts of the *Snorra Edda*. However, much indicates that some of the prose stories in the *Skáldskaparmál* are based on older traditions, because Snorri refers to the circumlocutions called 'kennings' in the poems. These are alliterative compounds of old age that survived in the poems. He also mentions the names of the skalds in some cases.

Some interpreters argue that the story about the skaldic mead goes back to ancient Indo-European traditions.[14] This idea can be based on the description of the manufacturing process: honey mixed with yeast turns into mead. The saliva was used in an ancient brewing method. The saliva contains the enzyme alpha-amylase, which is a starch. By chewing berries and then spitting them out, yeast was added to the brew.[15] The fact that alcoholic drinks had a ritual significance in Indo-European cultures can be traced through name etymologies. According to the Germanist and historian of religions Jan de Vries, there is a possible, though dubious, etymology of the name Kvasir: Icl. *kvasa* (verb) 'to exhaust, to make powerless' < Old Icelandic *kvasu*, 'kvass'; cf. Danish *kvas(s)e*, 'squeeze juice', Middle Low German *quetschen*, 'squeeze', < Proto-Germanic **Kvasāiaz*.[16]

So far there is a possible connection to Indo-European cultures with the brewing of the mead. But how could a ritual that actually seems to describe the creation of an alcoholic drink be linked to the peace process? Ström suggested that the saliva 'of different peoples came into use in acts of friendship. As a symbolic act, the blend of the spit of both parties has the character of a social bound.'[17] Ström does not give any further explanation to whom he refers to as 'peoples'. As a source, he relies on an article by the historian of religions Rudolf Stübe about Kvasir and 'the magical use of spit'. Stübe reports many different uses of saliva, although he does not explain the difference between the spitting as a ritual action and the use of spit as a medical cure. Actually according to Stübe, the alcohol itself binds people together into peace agreements, not the spitting as a ritual action.[18]

Alcohol is also the factor that Dumézil considered to be crucial to peace. He believed that the Hindu myth of the being Mada, the personified alcoholic drink, which was created in the war between the Nasatyas (or the Ashvins) and Indra (*Mahābhārata* III), has parallels in the myth of the creation of Kvasir.[19] It is noteworthy that Mada was originally produced as a weapon before being finally transformed into alcoholic beverages under peaceful conditions, something that has nothing to do with the spitting.[20] Dumézil's interpretation postulates a division of the functions of the deities, something which cannot be read in the prose story of *Skáldskaparmál*. A given circumstance in the comparative model of Dumézil is that the versions of the medieval editors correlate with each other. The Scandinavianist François-Xavier Dillmann has in contrast argued that the different versions of the Æsir–Vanir War are 'incompatible'.[21]

Spitting has several functions in many cultures, not only Indo-European and it could be crucial to distinguish between the spitting as action and the saliva as ritual component.[22] Spitting and saliva can be included in many aspects of religions: in creation acts as well as in healing rituals or curses.[23]

Previously, it was common practice for researchers to look for parallels in other cultures. That is also the case with some interpretations of the myth of the skaldic mead. For example, the Egyptologist and philologist E.A. Wallis Budge referred to a study of the Luwo (or Jur) people in present South Sudan by the botanist and ethnologist Georg August Schweinfurth. Schweinfurth described how spitting was a sign of belonging, faithfulness, and friendship.[24] This is, however, a completely different culture than the Old Scandinavian without any kind of relationship between them. As a single component, the spitting does not necessarily have anything to do with the settlement of battles between groupings as in the Æsir–Vanir War.[25]

According to the above-mentioned interpretations, it is as transformed alcoholic drink that the role of Kvasir is to be understood in the context of the peace between the Æsir and the Vanir. Ritual drinking and toasts was, by all means, an important element in peace processes. But the step from the spitting to the transformed skaldic mead goes through several steps before it is finished. Fjalar and Galar have a not insignificant part in the creation when they add the so important honey to the mead.

When the skaldic mead finally reaches the Æsir through Odin, there is no longer any peace to settle. One can compare this with an idea from the historian of religions Ulf Drobin that Odin can be seen as the god who exemplarily takes part of the mead in various myths.[26]

Thus the version Snorri reproduces should be understood as a myth of origin of the brewing of an alcoholic drink that transforms into the skaldic mead. When the gods spit, a yeast component is delivered to the brew. Actually, the process is repeated in this version when Odin spits out the skaldic mead, which is confirmed by the kenning *arnar kjapta órð*, 'the seed of the eagle nib'.[27] The action has a parallel in the legendary saga *Hálfs saga ok Hálfsrekka*. In this story, Freyja and Odin aid two women who are competing about who can brew the best beer. Odin spits in the brew of one of the women and it swells up.[28]

As a peace pledge, the spitting is weakly linked to the traditions of peace and war. Snorri could also be said to make an interpretation of the material he compiles. The word he uses for the pledge of peace (i.e. the spitting), *griðamark* (n.), does not occur in any runic text in skaldic or eddic poetry, only in the *Skáldskaparmál*. There are no poetical compounds at all alluding to the conclusion of peace between the Æsir and the Vanir.

In this section, it is argued that spitting and saliva as a cultural phenomenon had many different meanings in different cultures and as an individual component cannot be linked to the peace between the Æsir and the Vanir. The giving and taking of hostages, on the other hand, is more specifically linked to peace processes, where the purpose is to regulate another grouping. The hostage is of more central importance in the peace process than in the version of the *Ynglinga saga*.

Ynglinga saga

The first book in the *Heimskringla*, the *Ynglinga saga*, is a historical survey of the grouping called the Ynglings (or the *Ynglingar*) in Uppsala and their origins.[29] In the *Ynglinga saga*, Snorri presents another version of the myth of the Æsir–Vanir War that is much more informative about the peace than the version in the *Snorra Edda*:[30]

> Óðinn went with an army against the Vanir, but they put up a good fight and defended their land, and victory went alternately to both sides. They each raided the other's land and did damage. But when both sides grew weary of this, they arranged a meeting of reconciliation between them and made peace and gave each other hostages. The Vanir put forward their noblest men, Njǫrðr the Wealthy and his son Freyr, and the Æsir in return the one called Hœnir, and they claimed that he was very suitable to be a ruler. He was a large and most handsome man. With him the Æsir sent the one called Mímir, a very clever man, and in return the Vanir put forward the wisest in their company. He was called Kvasir. [13] But when Hœnir came to Vanaheimr he was at once made a lord. Mímir always told him what to do. But when Hœnir was present at councils or meetings where Mímir was not nearby, and any problem came before him, he always answered the same way: 'Let others decide.' Then the Vanir suspected that the Æsir must have cheated them in the exchange of men. Then they took Mímir

and beheaded him and sent his head to the Æsir. Óðinn took the head and smeared it with herbs that prevented it from decaying, and recited spells over it and imbued it with magic power so that it spoke to him and told him many secret things. Njǫrðr and Freyr Óðinn appointed as sacrificial priests, and they were gods among the Æsir. Njǫrðr's daughter was Freyja. She was a sacrificial priestess. She was the first to teach the Æsir black magic, which was customary among the Vanir. When Njǫrðr was among the Vanir he had been married to his sister, for that was the law there. Their children were Freyr and Freyja. But it was forbidden among the Æsir to cohabit with such close kin.[31]

(Transl. Alison Finlay & Anthony Faulkes)

In this account there are literary influences that can be derived from literature of antiquity and the Middle Ages, a fact that must considered before an interpretation of the *Ynglinga saga* can be made.[32] Because of these continental literary influences, the historian of religions Gabriel Turville-Petre suggested that the version of *Skáldskaparmál*, with its references to skaldic poetry, would be closer to an original myth than the version in the *Ynglinga saga*.[33] For some historian of religions, this does not have to be a major problem. Schjødt reports for example, that Snorri probably did not reflect on the consequences of the discrepancies between the two versions of the myth as his goal was to preserve the basic structure of both versions.[34] Snorri's sources and the different versions of the myth should then be reviewed and compared with contemporary sources as far as possible. Snorri has compiled several different traditions and he has known several different versions of the myth. He may also have had some sources at his disposal that are unknown to us.

The purpose of the *Heimskringla*, including the *Ynglinga saga*, is to create a story about the medieval Norwegian ruling dynasty beginning with Ynglings in Uppsala. Snorri's main source is the skaldic poem *Ynglingatal,* which is attributed to the skald Þjóðolfr of Hvinir. The dating is much debated, but recently, the Scandinavianist Edith Marold has convincingly argued for a dating to the ninth century.[35]

The introduction of the *Ynglinga saga* is historically and geographically speculative. It depicts how the Æsir emigrate from

Asia and the battle between the Æsir and the Vanir is set in an area called Vanaland or Vanaheimr, more specifically at the river of Tanakvisl (Don), or Vanakvisl, floating into the Black Sea (*Ynglinga saga*, ch. 1–2). Snorri is here inspired by continental literary influences, which can be seen in alliterations such as Æsir and Asia, Vanir and Vanakvisl, places Snorri probably had little knowledge about, but which were used as reference points in contemporary historical descriptions.[36]

Other literary elements can be seen in the euhemeristic perspective that Snorri uses when depicting the Æsir with a human origin. The Æsir are described as mortal rulers with cultic functions. When Odin, the leaders of the Æsir, sends his men to battle or as messengers, he blesses them.[37] His men call upon him and think he can aid them in battle. Thus Snorri describes Odin as a mortal man who is worshiped as a god, thereby distancing himself from 'heathenism'.

In an earlier research tradition, the emigration of the Æsir was interpreted to be historical. The myth of the Æsir–Vanir War has been conceived as a war between an older megalithic culture (in Scandinavia: the Funnelbeaker culture, c. 4300 BC–2800 BC) and an immigrant Battle Axe culture (c. 3000 BC–1000 BC).[38] However, later structuralist research was more restrained in terms of the historical perspective. Under the influence of Dumézil, the war between the Æsir and the Vanir has been interpreted as reflecting a mythical division into a warlike social grouping (the Æsir) and a more peaceful farming and business fraction (the Vanir). Later researchers have dissociated themselves from Dumézil's theory, although it still has its followers.[39]

The historian of literature Margaret Clunies Ross (1994) has a structuralist approach: she claims that ancient Scandinavian myths reflect conflict lines between classes during the Age of the Sturlungs (c. 1180–1264) in medieval Iceland. Her point of departure regarding the myth of the war in the version of the *Heimskringla* is that it is based on a medieval map (*mappa mundi*) where the Old Asgard (Troy) is near the center of the world (*nær miðri verǫldunni*), that is, Jerusalem. Through this placement, and that the Vanir become the first people to be defeated, the superiority of the Æsir is proven. This reflects, according to Clunies Ross, the superiority of some dominating Icelandic groupings.[40]

The text of the *Ynglinga saga* does not support the idea that the Æsir defeats the Vanir. As it is stated in Chapter 4: "Óðinn went with an army against the Vanir, but they put up a good fight and defended their land, and both sides were victorious." Rather, Snorri describes a subsequent peacemeeting between equal parties.

The structuralist interpretations made by Dumézil and his followers are crucial for my own understanding. I also understand Chapter 4 as a reflection of an older myth. Snorri had a model for his text that was originally orally transmitted by skalds. But it is not necessary to compare with Vedic or ancient myths to understand the role of the hostages, with some examples of such parallels, even if the comparative perspective can be useful in some cases.

The myth version in the *Ynglinga saga* can primarily be related to Snorri's own sources as well as other Old Norse texts; it can also be compared to ritual traditions that still existed at the time of Snorri. Below, I will present this source material and how it can be understood in relation to the different elements in Chapter 4. First, I list the events in the chapter in sequences:

(1) The outbreak of the war: Odin marches against the Vanir with an army. The war is a struggle between equal opponents, both sides experience victories and losses. Finally, the two sides are settled at a meeting. They decide to exchange hostages. The Vanir send the wealthy Njörðr, his son Freyr, and his daughter Freyja. The Æsir, in return, give the handsome Hœnir, whom they call 'very suitable to be a ruler'.

(2) The Æsir provide another hostage, the wise Mímir, while they in return receive the wisest of the Vanir, Kvasir. Hœnir is made chieftain of the Vanir. Mímir becomes Hœnir's adviser, but when he is not present at the assembly, Hœnir says that others should advise. The Vanir suspect that the Æsir try to fool them. The Vanir cut off the head of Mímir and send it to the Æsir.

(3) Odin takes Mímir's head and awakes it by embalming it with herbs and the singing of charms. The head can then reveal hidden things to Odin.

(4) Njörðr and Freyr are appointed to *blotgoðis*, 'sacrificial priests',[41] and they are *diar*, 'gods', together with the other deities. Freyja teaches the Æsir the practice of *sejðr*.

(5) Earlier, when Njörðr lived among the Vanir, his sister was his wife, and with her he had the children Freyr and Freyja. But marriages between siblings are forbidden among the Æsir.

Sequence 1 can be related to the cause of the war and the depiction of the war in the *Vǫluspá*, one of Snorri's sources.[42] Snorri had access to the Eddic poem *Vafþrúðnismál*,[43] which is considered to be one of the older of the Eddic poems. In the stanzas 38–39 of the *Vafþrúðnismál*, we are informed that Njörðr was given as hostage to the gods (*seldo at gíslingo goðom*), i.e. the Æsir:

Óðinn qvað	Othin said:
38 'Segðu þat iþ tíunda, allz þú tíva rǫc ǫll, Vafþrúðnír, vitir, hvaðan Niǫrðr um kom með ása sonom; hofom oc hǫrgom hann raeðr hunnmǫrgom, oc varðað hann ásom alinn.'	'Say as the tenth, since the sacred gods' fates thou, Vafthrúðnír, dost wot: whence came wise Njorth among holy gods– [temples and fanes full many hath he–] yet was not begot among gods?'
Vafþrúðnir qvað:	Vafthrúðnír said:
39 'Í Vanaheimi scópo hann vís regin oc seldo at gíslingo goðom; í aldar rǫc hann mun aptr koma heim með vísom vǫnom.'[44]	'In Vanaheim Vanir begat him, and gave him as hostage to gods; at the world's last weird he will wend again home to the wise Vanir.' (Transl. Lee M. Hollander)[45]

In the *Vafþrúðnismál*, the war between the Æsir and the Vanir is not mentioned, nor do the Vanir receive any hostage in exchange. Instead, stanza 39 describes a giving of one individual as hostage only. The verb *selja*, 'send', and the preposition *at*, 'to', indicate that a hostage was sent and received by the gods as a collective (*ása synir*). The hostage is sent by *vís regin*, 'the wise powers'. *Regin* is a diffuse expression for 'powers', but it is specified by the compound *vísir Vanir*, 'the wise Vanir'. The plural forms indicate that there are groups involved and it is consistent with the ancient hostage form between collectives. It is very important (stanza 39) that Njörðr returns to Vanaheimr after Ragnarök. This is the only information that connects the theme with the hostage to the larger eschatological and apocalyptic themes of the *Vǫluspá*.

An interesting analysis of stanza 39 has been made by the folklorists Frog and Jonathan Roper. According to them the stanza could certainly be interpreted that Njörðr was given as hostage to the gods and that he will return to Vanaheimr with the wise Vanir. However, following an idea by Lotte Motz and, later, Rudolf Simek,[46] that the function of the word Vanir is synonymus with 'gods and elves' in general, and not as a single group of deities, Frog and Roper mean that Njörðr: 'will die along with most other gods (and elves?) during the ethnic apocalypse – *ragna rǫc* ["doom of the *regin*"] – and together they (the vanir) will return "home" to Vanaheimr'.[47] But this latter interpretation does not consider the function of the hostageship of Njörðr. A hostage must be given and it is the result of an agreement between opposing sides. If the Vanir did not give Njörðr as hostage, then who did? The hostage giving actually suggests that there was a division of groups of deities rather than the opposite. Nontheless, the words of Vanir and Vanaheimr could be disambiguous in the skaldic and eddic poetry and may have been misinterpreted by Snorri.

Another source that Snorri probably had access to, the Eddic poem *Lokasénna* (stanzas 34–35), indicates that Njörðr was sent to the Æsir as hostage: *vart austr heðan gíls um sendr at goðom*, 'was sent eastward to the gods as a hostage given'.[48] Here neither the Æsir–Vanir War is mentioned, nor does Njörðr return to Vanaheimr after Ragnarök. In the *Gylfaginning* – the first book in the *Snorra Edda* – however, it is mentioned that Njörðr was given in exchange for Hœnir in order to secure the peace between the Æsir and the Vanir. This may indicate that Snorri had sources in addition to what has been preserved in the *Codex Regius*.

Sequence 2 is difficult to understand compared to other sources. Hœnir's role is so complex that we shall return to this in a later article. The information about the Vanir's dissatisfaction with Hœnir and violent action against Mímir is not reproduced elsewhere. That Kvasir comes from the Vanir to the Æsir is only reported in the *Ynglinga saga*. Probably, as I mentioned earlier, Kvasir belongs to another myth. It may be that *Snorri* simply used this character to embroider the text.[49]

In sequence 3, the information about Mímir's talking head can be derived to the *Vǫluspá* (Stanza 46).[50] However, the episode when Odin awakens Mímir's head is unknown in other Old Norse sources. Recently, the philologist Annette Lassen has explained the presence of Mímir's talking head as a *topos* and suggested that Snorri were inspired by speaking bronze heads which was a topic in medieval literature.[51] At the same time, it can be argued that Snorri describes the necromantic act (the awakening) with domestic terminology. The verb *magna* (of the noun *magn*, 'force, strength'), 'to grow, strengthen' occurs (in the *galdr* or other songs of sorcery), during the awakening (or summoning) of *draugr*, 'ghosts'.[52] Mímir's head is not included in this text in the same apocalyptic scenery as in the *Vǫluspá* (stanza 46), which refers to the demise of the gods. Nor in the *Snorra Edda* is that picture given. In such cases, the myth may originally have depicted the situation in times of peace, and therefore be prototypical, since the theme in Chapter 4 is an ideal peace.

Sequence 4 may be based on older information that can be traced through etymologies. The Old Icelandic word *díar* (pl.) is considered to be derived from the Old Irish word *día* < Proto-Celtic *dīyo-*.[53] Perhaps the word *guþ*, 'god', was too sensitive to Snorri in his euhemeristic perspective and he replaced it with an older poetic word for 'gods'. Snorri consistently uses the word *díar* (or *hofgoðar*) to describe the Æsir in his historiographical, narrative style: the style where they are portrayed as humans. When he mentions the Æsir as 'gods', he emphasizes that they were worshiped as gods and not that they were gods.

In the *Vafþrúðnísmál* (stanza 38), it is said that Njörðr was the custodian of many *hof*s (cultic buildings) and *hǫrgr*s (stone altars, cult places, or stone settings).[54] This is in line with the traditional tasks of the *goði*s in Old Scandinavian society. The information that Freyja teaches the gods the art of *seiðr* is similar to the fact that Gullveig/Heid brings 'evil sorcery' to the gods in the *Vǫluspá*. It is therefore believed that Freyja and Gullveig are identical.[55]

In sequence 5, Njörðr's incestual relation with his sister can be confirmed by the Eddic poem *Lokasenna* (stanza 35). But in the place name material there is also support for this information. Several historians of religions, and some place name researchers, argue that Njörðr and the goddess *Njärd (> Lat. *Nerthus*) belong together, which can be seen in theophoric place names, e.g. Nälsta, Spånga parish, in the province of Uppland, and Mjärdevi, Slaka parish in the province of Uppland.[56]

To summarize: some parts of Chapter 4 of the *Ynglinga saga* are not only based on other sources with continuity back in time but: they also reflect traditions from times of peace and war in Snorri's own age, such as the giving and taking of hostage. Nevertheless, this is a compilation made by Snorri and, at best, a reflection of an older myth. Some pieces of information comply with the version of the *Snorra Edda*, or can be confirmed by other sources such as Eddic poetry. An example of this may occur in the stanzas 34–35 in *Lokasenna*, where it is implied that Njörðr was sent 'eastwards' as hostage.[57] These stanzas, however, are difficult to interpret.

When someone, as a stranger, came to a new collective, one had to try to be accepted through active actions, as reflected in the (beneficial) functions supplied to the Æsir through the addition of deities like Njörðr, Freyr and Freyja. At a cosmological level, it may be possible to explain different roles of beings, which were defined (possibly redefined) when they entered into a new collective of deities (or were added to a new pantheon). This is a phenomenon which also occurs in other archaic religions. I will below give examples of how this may also occur with other beings who are hostages through an analysis of Chapter 4 of the *Ynglinga saga* on both the literary and the mythical levels.

Comparative perspectives

As Snorri presents the end of the war in the *Ynglinga saga*, both parties are assumed to have opportunities for good peace conditions. In this context, the handling of the hostages appears to be institutionalized, even if no details are given about what happened after the actual exchange.

In Snorri's version of the myth, the apocalyptic depiction of the *Vǫluspá* is missing. Perhaps Snorri's version may be based on oral material, and the original purpose of which was to describe a prototypical peace. The result of the hostage exchange can be seen as ideal. Both sides are assumed to benefit from the exchange; the implied amoral act of the Æsir can also be seen in other narratives, especially when Odin acts in a fraudulent manner (for example, in the myth about the skaldic mead).

When the Vanir execute Mímir – perhaps a separate addition by Snorri – the limitations of the rights of the hostages are described. Behind this, there may be a moral: one side uses cunning to get the most out of the peace agreement without losing on the settlement. In this confrontation, it appears that the knowledge that accompanies the hostages is an important factor.

The structuralist interpretations of this version often focused on the functions of the deities and their positions in an ordered pantheon. Gabriel Turville-Petre's interpretation – inspired by Dumézil – was that the story is a creation myth that explains why the Vanir and the Æsir could live in peace and friendship. It would also explain why and how people with different interests and aspirations can live in harmony.[58] The historian of religions Torbjörg Östvold thought that the myth reflects an assimilation where a god is transferred from an old functional sphere to a new one.[59] According to Schjødt, the hostage exchange allows for the exchange of 'knowing objects' (like the head of Mímir) that both sides have access to; it is an example of successful integration where the different functions of the gods are arranged.[60]

The concept of function, however, suggests fixed positions for the deities, something that has been debated within research.[61] Instead, I would like to describe it as a transfer of knowledge made possible by the hostage exchange.

The fact that foreign deities are brought into another pantheon is not an unusual phenomenon in myths and there are parallels in nearby cultural areas (to Scandinavia).[62] Gabriel Turville-Petre compared, for example, the Æsir–Vanir War with the Old Irish legend of the battle of Mag Tured (Old Irish *Magh Tuireadh*). In the second battle of Mag Tured, the gods, the *Túatha Dé Danann*, defeat another tribe of gods, *Fomhoire*. Bres ('the beautiful') Mac Elatha, who according to this tradition originates from Fomhoire, is elected ruler of the *Túatha Dé Danann*.[63]

Under the rule of Bres, Ireland falls into decay, which leads to insurgency. Bres joins the hostile tribe, the *Fomhoire*. But the *Túatha Dé Danann* finally succeeds, in alliance with Lugh, whose attributes are similar to those of Odin, defeating the *Fomhoire*, and Bres is captured. Bres tries to buy his life with the offer that if he is set free the cows of Ireland will never run out of milk and the harvest will grow every quarter of the year. The offer is rejected, but in exchange for advice on plowing, sowing, and harvest, Bres will keep his life.[64]

Comparisons between the Æsir–Vanir War and the second battle of Mag Tuiread can be misleading because in the latter case it is not a peace between equally strong opponents. The *Fomhoire* and the *Túatha Dé Danann* do not live in harmony. However, the principle that new knowledge is added to the community is an interesting parallel.

The importance of the hostage to glorify a ruler tradition could also be found in another Irish legend. The Irish High King (Old Irish *ard rí*) Niall Noígíallach was probably a real person (fourth century),[65] but the stories around him could also be said to be mythical.

According to the legend he was named Noígíallach, 'the nine hostages', because he had taken hostages from the surrounding Irish tribes. Níall's hostage takings cannot be related to an equal peace, but reflects the practice of allowing certain areas to provide hostages.[66] The role of hostages in the legendary stories of Níall was to represent submission. For the medieval writer, there may also have been an effort to demonstrate the geographical extent of the Irish realm.

Níall also captured people from the disintegrating Roman Empire, including Saint Patrick (or *Succat*) who later was responsible for the Christianization of Ireland. St. Patrick's knowledge of Christianity did not reach Ireland until later, but the information reveals the importance of associating an important symbol of Ireland with one of its most famous kings.[67]

The legend provides the kingship with a symbolic capital in the form of significant persons. The medieval editors who compiled these stories may have wanted to create a prerequisite for the rulers. A number of important features and skills are provided to them in the story. This may have served as an ideological basis in the regulation of their own society (as an instrument of propaganda). A similar agenda can be found in the works of Snorri. When he constructs the meeting of the Æsir and the Vanir as a hostage exchange, it is to explain the long history of the Ynglings and their connections to antiquity. Thus, the names of the Norwegian kings can be added to the Æsir, like Odin, and to Njörðr and Frey. In this way he can rely on other Icelandic and Norwegian literary traditions that claim genealogical origins back to Odin and Freyr. On the other hand, as a mythical reflection, it is possible to understand the purpose of a hostage on a cosmological level in the form of the transfer of knowledge between different gods.

Concluding remarks

The myth of the Æsir–Vanir War depicts a war between the Æsir and the Vanir habits that ends with a peace where hostages are exchanged. Nevertheless, the myth of the war exists in two different versions that are partly incompatible.

In the version of the eddic poem *Vǫluspá*, the war – and the causes of the war – are mentioned, but not the accompanying peace. The war in the poem is introduced into a clearly eschatological and apocalyptic setting and can be understood at a cosmological level.

In *Snorra Edda*'s version, it is described how the gods jointly spit into a vat, which has been interpreted as a ritual and part of a prototypical peace process. It is here argued that this is a misinterpretation and instead should be understood as a myth of origin: the creation of the mead of poetry. In Chapter 4 of the *Ynglinga saga* is the actual description of the hostage exchange between the Æsir and the Vanir. This myth version is heavily influenced by literary phenomena such as euhemerism, but this myth version was also built on different traditions, some of them very old. The purpose of the hostage exchange – as it is described in Chapter 4 – is to add the names of Vanir deities to the pantheon of the Æsir, which may be a stroke of the pen by Snorri as well as an old tradition. The actual giving of hostages, however, cannot simply be dismissed as a literary phenomenon, because it is mentioned in skaldic poetry, and these sources need to be considered in their own contexts.

Notes to Part II

1. Cf. Mundal 2013.
2. See Gísli Sigurðsson 2007: 533.
3. McKinnell 2008: 9.
4. Schier 1981: 415 ff.; cf. Steinsland 1999: 37 f.
5. The eschatological and apocalyptic ideas in the *Vǫluspá* have led to a discussion about the degree of Christian influence. For example, diffusion theories have been presented. The folklorist Axel Olrik (1902) claimed influence from Germanic, Latin, and Celtic cultures as well as from Christianity, while the philologist Richard Reitzenstein (1924) vowed for Gothic and Iranian influence from Manichaeism. Other researchers, such as the philologist and historian of religions Georges Dumézil (1966), explained them as a more direct influence from Indo-European cultures. See also Steinsland 1999: 31 ff. Modern interpreters have attempted to single out Christian motifs and influences (e.g. John McKinnell 2013, Petúr Petúrson 2013). Christopher Abram (2011: 86), on the other hand, indicates that the poet was heathen but with the purpose of describing the end of the world, i.e. 'the downfall of paganism' and thus the limitation of the old religion. According to Anders Hultgård, an influence of Christian tradition is not likely because there are major differences and that similarities with Iranian eschatology can hardly 'have arisen through an Iranian influence'. Instead, he states that it is about 'two independent eschatological traditions, the Scandinavian and the Iranian' (Hultgård 2016: 235).
6. Ström 1997: 102.

7. *Edda* ([ed.] Neckel & Kuhn): 5 f. (stanzas 21–22); 6 (stanzas 23–24).
8. *Edda* ([ed.] Neckel & Kuhn): 10 (45); see Gísli Sigurðsson 2007: 533.
9. For a comparison between *Vǫluspá* 45 and the medieval Book of Revelation, see McKinnell 2008: 23.
10. Dumézil 1966: 32; Ström 1997: 104; cf. Schjødt 1991; 2008: 108–172.
11. There are also different manuscript traditions where the authors themselves may have added information.
12. Ok enn mælir Ægir: 'Hvaðan af hefir hafizk sú íþrótt er þér kallið skáldskap?'
Bragi svarar: 'Þat váru upphǫf til þess at guðin hǫfðu ósætt við þat fólk er vanir heita. En þeir lǫgðu með sér friðstefnu ok settu grið á þá lund at þeir gengu hvárirtveggiu til ein kers ok spýttu í hráka *sínum. En at skilnaði þá toku goðin ok vildu eigi láta týnask þat griðamark ok skǫpuðu þar ór mann. Sá heitir Kvasir; han er svá vitr at engi spyrr hann þeira hluta er eigi kann hann órlausn. Hann fór víða um heim at kenna mǫnnum frœði, ok þá er hann kom at heimboði til dverga nǫkkvorra, Fialars ok Galars, þá kǫlluðu þeir hann með sér á einmæli ok drápu hann, létu renna blóð hans í tvau ker ok einn ketil, ok heitir sá Óðreyrir, en kerin *heita Són ok Boðn. Þeir blendi hunangi við blóðit, ok varð þar af mjǫðr sá er hverr er af drekkr verðr skáld eða frœðamaðr. Dvergarnir sǫgðu ásum at Kvasir hefði kafnat í maviti firir því at engi var þar svá fróðr at spyrja kynni hann fróðleiks [...].'
Edda (b) ([ed.] Faulkes): 3 (ch. 57).
In the *Uppsala Edda* there is neither the introductory section or the prose story about the Mead of Suttungr, except as a brief introductory commentary in the *Skáldskaparmál (Uppsala Edda* [(ed.) Heimir Pálsson]: 224 ff. [ch. 37]) on theories describing the poetry and a reference in a quote of the scale Stentor (*Steinþór*).
13. *Edda* ([ed. and transl.] Faulkes): 61 f.
14. Dumézil 1966; Ström 1997: 104; Simek 1993: 184 f.
15. Ström 1997.

16. de Vries 1961: 336; cf. Bezlaj 1982: 116.

17. Ström 1997: 104.

18. Stübe 1924: 500 f.

19. Dumézil 1966: 33.

20. Dumézil (1966: 33 ff.) is aware of this difference but refers to the fact that different traditions arose after the Indo-European split.

21. Dillmann 2001: 41.

22. Rudolf Stübe (1924: 503 ff.) points out parallels in Finnish, African, and American rituals.

23. In ancient Egyptian mythology, it was the god Ten whose saliva gave rise to the gods Shu and Tefnut (Budge 1973: 204). In Islam, descendants of the Prophet Muhammad are perceived to cure people by spit (Budge 1973: 204). In Hindu traditions, animal saliva is believed to have a special effect in healing rituals (Abott 1984: 36). For Hindus, spitting can also be of significance to curses when someone is to emphasize another's misfortune (Abott 1984: 35). In Swedish traditions, the tradition is found to spit three times if a black cat runs across the road. See Bengt af Klintberg *Svenska trollformler* 1988 (1965): 65ff., 77.

24. In Budge 1973: 204.

25. For example, spitting appears as an apotropic (protective) action against jinns in Cairo, which is described by the anthropologist Barbara Drieskens (2008: 15 f.). In Islam, spitting also occurs during exorcism and as a medication against evilness or obsession (Dols 1992: 253, 257, 269).

26. Drobin 1991: 131.

27. Näsström 2001: 131.

28. *Hálfs saga ok Hálfsrekka* ([ed.] Andrews): 70 f. (ch. 1, stanzas 3–6).

29. *Íslendingabók, Ættartala* ([(ed.) Jakob Benediktsson]: 27), which is attributed to Ari Þorgilsson 'the wise'. Ari presents a list of kings where he links his own family to the Ynglings. He begins his list with

Yngvi Tyrkjakonungr, number 2 is *Njǫrðr Svíakonungr*, and number 3 Freyr. The Ynglings are also mentioned by other Icelandic writers.

30. IV. KAPÍTULI
Óðinn fór með hér á hendur Vǫnum, en þeir urðu vel við ok vǫrðu land sitt, ok hǫfðu ýmsir sigr. Herjuðu hvárir land annarra ok gerðu skaða. En er þat leiddisk hvárum tveggjum, lǫgðu þeri milli sín sættarstefnu ok gerðu frið ok seldusk gíslar. Fengu Vanir sína ina ágæztu menn, Njǫrð inn auðga ok son hans, Frey, en Æsir þar í mótt þann, er Hœnir hét, ok kǫlluðu hann allvel til hǫfðingja fallinn. Hann var mikill maðr ok inn vænsti. Með honum sendu Æsir þann, er Mímir hét, inn vitrasti maðr, en Vanir fengu þar í mót þann, er spakastr var í þeira flokki. Sá hét Kvasir. En er Hœnir kom í Vanaheim, þá var hann þegar hǫfðingi gǫrr. Mímir kenndi honum ráð ǫll. En er Hœnir var staddr á þingum eða stefnum, svá at Mímir var eigi nær, ok kœmi nǫkkur vandamál fyrir hann, þá svaraði hann æ inu sama – „ráði aðrir," kvað hann. Þá grunaði Vani at Æsir myndi hafa falsat þá í mannaskiptinu. Þá tóku þeir Mími ok hálshjoggu ok sendu hǫfuðit Ásum. Óðinn tók hǫfuðit ok smurði urtum þeim, er eigi mátti fúna, ok kvað þar yfir galdra ok magnaði svá, at þat mælti við hann ok sagði honum marga leynda hluti. Njǫrð ok Frey setti Óðinn blótgoða ok váru þeir díar með Ásum. Dóttir Njarðar var Freyja. Hon var blótgyðja. Hon kenndi fyrst með Ásum seið, sem Vǫnum var títt. Þá er Njǫrðr var með Vǫnum, þá hafði hann átta systur sína, því at þat váru þar lǫg. Váru þeira bǫrn Freyr ok Freyja. En þat var bannat með Ásum at byggva svá náit at frændsemi.
Ynglinga saga, *Heimskringla* I ([ed.] Bjarni Aðalbjarnarson): 12 f. (ch. 4).

31. Alison Finlay & Anthony Faulkes 3–4 (ch. 4).

32. Because the introduction of the *Heimskringla* differs from *Snorra Edda*, researchers believe that Snorri did not write both of them. In the various manuscript versions, additions could have been made by the medieval editors. See *Saxo og Snorre* 2010 for this discussion.

33. Turville-Petre 1964: 157.

34. Schjødt 2008: 158; cf. Dillmann 2001: 41.

35. Marold 2012: 5 f.

36. For example, Geoffrey of Monmouth claims King Arthur's descent from Troy in the *Historia Regum Britanniae* (see Mortensen 2010: 126).

37. *Ynglinga saga, Heimskringla* I ([ed.] Bjarni Aðalbjarnsson): 11 (ch. 2).

38. Salin 1903: 139; Höckert 1926: 295, 299 ff.; Lindqvist 1936: 260–281.

39. E.g. de Vries (1957) 1970: 213; Östvold 1969: 202; N.Å. Nielsen 1976: 315); DuBois 1999: 56; Schjødt 2008: 383.

40. Clunies Ross 1994: 55, 58, 116 f.

41. Regarding the concept of 'priest', see Sundqvist 2007: 22 ff. From the perspectives of a historian of religions it is problematic to use the term 'priest' because it designates a religious specialist within a codified hierarchical institution. No such characteristic is visible in the text material regarding the *goði*s. Sundqvist suggests the more neutral concept 'cult functionary' (Sundqvist 2007: 22 ff.).

42. Parts of the *Vǫluspá* are quoted in the *Snorra Edda* (a) ([ed.] Faulkes): 9 (ch. 4), 12 (ch. 8), 14 f. (ch. 13–14), 17 (ch. 15), 20 (ch. 18), 35 (ch. 42), 49 (ch. 50), 51 (ch. 51).

43. Snorri quotes two stanzas of the *Vafþrúðnismál* (30–31) in *Snorra Edda* (a) ([ed.] Faulkes): 10 (ch. 5).

44. *Edda* ([ed.] Neckel & Kuhn): 52.

45. *The Poetic Edda* ([ed. and transl.] Hollander): 49.

46. See Simek 2010.

47. Frog & Roper 2011: 33.

48. *Edda* ([ed.] Neckel & Kuhn): 103.

49. In the *Gylfaginning*, Edda (a) ([ed.] Faulkes): 48 (ch. 50), Snorri mentions Kvasir in the myth of Baldr, although he should actually be deceased. Kvasir appear as the one who figures out the secret of the charred net (*Heimskringla*), but he should have been transformed into the skaldic mead at this stage. According to Schjødt (2008: 167), either Snorri simply needed a character and he 'forgot' that Kvasir

was already dead or – an explanation which Schjødt thinks is more likely – the myth of the net really does not belong to the story about the death of Baldr but for some reason was placed there.

50. In the *Vǫluspá*, it is mentioned that *Mím(r)*'s speaking head advises Odin. It is a matter of debate whether the nameform *Mím(r)* refers to Mímir. The Germanist and philologist Rudolf Simek (1993: 217) points out that Snorri considered the names to be identical. The compound *Míms höfuð* ('Mím's head') is also found in the Eddic poem *Sigrdrífomál* (*Edda* [(ed.) Neckel & Kuhn]: 192 [stanza 14]).

51. Lassen believes that the episode about Mímir's head may have been influenced by a story by the English 11th-century historian William of Malmesbury. In his *Gesta regum Anglorum*, it is mentioned how Gerbert of Aurillac (the Pope Sylvester II), who lived in the late 10th century, devoted himself to 'occult' actions with a speaking bronze head (*Gesta regum Anglorum* [(ed.) Mynors et al.]: 292 f. [text], 293 f. [transl.] [ch. 172]). The talking bronze head also occurs in Robert Green's *The Honorable History of Friar Bacon and Friar Bungay*, c. 1589 (Lassen 2010: 224 ff.). However, it can be argued that in the text of William (*Gesta regum Anglorum* [(ed.) Mynors et al.]: 294 [text], 295 [transl.] [ch. 172]) is a matter of the talking head of a statue (*statuae caput*) and it is not mentioned whether it would be of bronze. In the case of speaking bronze- and brassheads as literary phenomena, it appears to be common only during the Renaissance (McCorduck 2004: xxiv, 8, 12). It may well be that Snorri knew of William of Malmesbury because the latter was a famous historian and mentions several Norwegian kings. On the other hand, the size of the medieval bookshelf in Scandinavia and Iceland is unclear. Some scholars tend to assume that the Icelandic writers had access to a number of specific learned works, which, for example, can be compared with the Scandinavianist Carl Edlund Anderson's analysis of the *Beowulf* poem where he mentions that a historian (Lars Hemmingsen) assumed that the writers in Denmark in the 1100s and 1200s had access to works by so divergent writers as Adam of Bremen, Henry of Huntingdon, Dudo, William of Jumiéges, Paulus Diaconus, Jordanes, Procopius, and Malchus (C.E. Anderson 1999: 112; cf. Hemmingsen 1989: 57 f.).

52. de Vries 1961: 375; Janson 2008: 199. The denomination is found in the Icelandic sagas and later tales such as the *Þorgeirsbola* (http://www.snerpa.is/net/thjod/thorgeir.htm). The Sparlösa Runestone (Vg 119) provides the noun *makin(i)*, which, according to an interpretation, can be understood as 'sorcery' (Norden 1961: 256 ff.). Odin's connection to the *draugr* can be seen in the name *Draugadróttinn*, 'Lord of the undead'.

53. The word *día* occurs in a skadlic poem by Kormakr Ǫgmundarson from the 10th century (*Den norsk-islandske skjaldedigtning* A 1 ([ed.] Finnur Jónson): 79 (stanza 1).

54. This is also confirmed by the *Grímnismál* (*Edda* [(ed.) Neckel & Kuhn]: 60 [stanza 16]), which mentions that Njörðr is the custodian of the *hargr*.

55. *Edda* ([ed.] Neckel & Kuhn): 4 (stanza 22); Turville Petre 1964: 159; Näsström 1995: 63; Nordberg 2003: 100.

56. See Näsström 1995: 53 ff. and Vikstrand 2001: 95 ff., 101 f. Vikstrand reports that the place names as individual sources cannot confirm that the *Njärd*-names refer to a female god. Cf. Elmevik (2013), who claims that no Scandinavian, feminine, theophoric place names can be confirmed in the place-name material.

57. *Edda* ([ed.] Neckel & Kuhn): 103 (stanzas 34–35).

58. Dumézil 1966: 31 ff.; 1970: 70 ff.; Turville-Petre 1964: 161 f.

59. Östvold 1969: 200.

60. Schjødt 2008: 384 ff., 394.

61. Cf. E. I. Haugen 1967: 858 ff.

62. Saxo Grammaticus (*Gesta Danorum* [(ed.) Friis-Jensen]: ch. 1.7.2) reports of the stranger Mithothyn who takes Odin's place as leader of the gods when he is gone. The phenomenon may also have occurred in a myth tradition from Estonia. Tharapita – a god associated with the island of Saaremaa – migrated from the province of Virumaa in northeastern Estonia (see Part V).

63. Turville-Petre 1964: 161; *Keltiske myter* ([ed.] Rekdal): 1–44.

64. Berresford 1999: 23 f., 27 ff.
65. *Medieval Ireland* ([ed.] Duffy): 353.
66. See Part V.
67. Patrick and Níall may not even have been contemporary. However, Patrick is supposed to have baptised Eochaid, the son of Níall (MacKillop 1998: 10, 305 f).

Part III: Ritual Actions in Different Areas of Confrontation

Hostages in peace processes

The purpose of this part of the book is to elucidate how the giving and taking of hostages can be understood within a ceremony (or several ceremonies). The analysis must in part be carried out as a reconstruction because the medieval writers sometimes saw the giving and taking of hostage as irrelevant during negotiations: there were more important events to describe, such as the conversion of heathens. At the same time it is important to understand the use of a hostage as a major or essential part of a wider context: the peace process. The central parts of ceremonies are also analysed in this part, the treatment of the hostages, and how they were valued as persons. These ceremonial patterns may have taken altering expressions – regulations, and procedures – in different areas of confrontation and must therefore be understood by identifying their contextual factors. Initially Anglo-Saxon areas of confrontation are described and analysed, as well as some other contexts. In particular, it is emphasized that there were specific conditions for each individual conflict, with a subsequent peace, where personal interests may have been decisive for the outcome as well as other social mechanisms related to competitive groupings. Additional examples will also be taken from other confrontational areas involving Scandinavians: the Carolingian Empire, Denmark, and Norway.

How to cite this book chapter:
Olsson, S. 2019. Ritual Actions in Different Areas of Confrontation. In: Olsson, S. *The Hostages of Northmen: From the Viking Age to the Middle Ages.* Pp. 81–123. Stockholm: Stockholm University Press. DOI: https://doi.org/10.16993/bba.c License: CC-BY.

Confrontations, peaces and hostages in the Anglo-Saxon confrontation areas

The chronicler Asser (Ch. 47) reports how King Ceolwulf II of Mercia gave hostages to Vikings in 874.[1] According to the *Anglo-Saxon Chronicle* (874), The Great Heathen Army (OE *mycel heathen here*) had come from the kingdom of Lindsey to Repton in Mercia for winter quarters. They drove away Burgred, the king of Mercia, and all lands were subdued. That same year they granted Ceolwulf – a thegn (OE *þegn*) of the king – the rulership. Ceolwulf took an oath and gave hostages who would be at the Northmen's disposal any day they would need them. According to the *Anglo-Saxon Chronicle*, Ceolwulf would also be available for military service.

Obviously, the hostage appeared in this context in connection with the swearing of oaths. But in order to understand the ritual features of the hostage in this context, a historical survey is required. I have divided this overview in sequences year by year. I have deliberately limited the time span between the period 865 and 879, and only dwelt on conflicts – and events that involved hostages – between kingdoms in the Heptarchy (the kingdoms of East Anglia, Essex, Kent, Northumberland, Mercia, and Wessex) and what is referred to in the chronicles as the 'Great Heathen Army'. Naturally, a discussion of the conflicts 787–896 could also be subject to a broader discussion of the different opportunities for the conflicting sides to influence the outcome of the peace processes and the formation of societies (or state formation). In this context I refer to these limited time periods because they involve events with hostages.

> 865. The Great Heathen Army stops at Thanet in Kent, South East England. They make peace with the residents of Kent, who promise them money (debt) in exchange for peace. Despite the agreement, the Danes carry out raids in East Kent. In the same year, the Great Heathen Army goes into winter quarters in East Anglia. They are provided with horses by the residents and make peace with them.

> 866. This year, the Great Heathen Army goes into Northumbria and plunders York. There is an inner split among the Northumbrians who

dispose their king and replace him with Ælla. The Northumbrians assemble an army that is beaten at York. The surviving Northumbrians make peace with the Danes.

867. The Great Heathen Army goes into winter quarters in Mercia in the current English Midlands. Mercia allies with Wessex.

869. The Great Heathen Army returns to York and stays there for a year.

870. The Great Heathen Army goes through Mercia to East Anglia. The ruler Edmund of East Anglia falls in battle with the Danes. The Danes raids the monastery of Petersborough. They go to winter quarters in Thetford.

871. The Great Heathen Army enters Wessex and fights four battles against king Æthelred and his brother Alfred. The Great Heathen Army is divided into two parties. One party is led by the kings Bagsecg and Halfdan, the other by some earls. Both parties are beaten at Ashdown. Two weeks later, the Great Heathen Army defeats Alfred at Basing. Two months later, the Army triumphs over both Æthelred and Alfred at Merton. The same year comes a 'great summer fleet'. Æthelred passes away. Alfred takes over the throne and fights ten battles against the Army. An agreement is made.

872. The Great Heathen Army goes from Reading to London and sets winter quarters there. The Mercians make peace with the raiding army.

873. The Great Heathen Army enters Northumbria and sets winter quarters in Torksey at Lindsey. The Mercians re-launches the peace treaty with the Army.

874. The Great Heathen Army ranges from Lindsey to Repton. King Burhred is driven away. The Danes, instead, allow the deployment of one of Burhred's thegns as king. The new king must give oaths and a hostage, which is on stand-by for the Danes whenever they wish. The king, with his retinue, shall be ready for military service for The Great Heathen Army.

875. The Great Heathen Army ranges from Repton to Northumbria. Halfdan takes a part of the Army and ranges along the Tyne. The

kings Guthrum, Oscytel, and Anund arrive in Cambridge with another part of the Army. Alfred wins a naval battle.

876. The Great Heathen Army retreats to Wareham, Dorset. King Alfred makes an agreement with the enemy fraction at Wareham. They swear before him on their holy ring that they will never return. They leave a hostage to Alfred.[2] With the temporary peace treaty as protection, the Great Heathen Army descends towards Exeter in Devon during the night. That same year, Halfdan share lands in Northumbria and start working the soil.

877. A part of the Great Heathen Army retreats to Exeter, sets sails to the sea, and loses 120 ships outside Swanage, Dorset, scattered in a mist. The second, mounted, part of the Army takes shelter from the pursuing Alfred in a fort. Then they give hostages to Alfred, as many as he wants, and swear 'grand' oaths. They maintain peace. Another part of the Army enters into Mercia, divides the country and gives a part of it to Ceolwulf.

878. During the Christmas month, a part of the Great Heathen Army enters Chippenham and invades Wessex. Alfred manages to flee. He builds a fortress (*burh*) in Athelney and musters an army. There is a battle at Edington where the Great Heathen Army is utterly destroyed. The rest of the army escapes to the fortress in Wareham. After two weeks, the Great Heathen Army surrenders. They give Alfred a prominent hostage; they give oaths, promise to leave Wessex, and their king (Guthrum) vows to take the baptism. Three weeks later, Guthrum comes to Aller, near Athelney, where Alfred receives him for baptism. At Wedmore his bound is removed.[3] He stays twelve days at Altheney, and Alfred gives him many gifts.[4]

This division of events is not without contradictions because it is a matter of real events. Some years also overlap each other in different manuscript versions. The layout is primarily intended as an overview of the course of events and to clarify the actions that are essential for my reasoning. The division follows a timeline that largely corresponds to not only the scriptures of the *Anglo-Saxon Chronicle* but also with Asser's biography of Alfred. The political stages depicted in the division are crucial for understanding different ritual aspects of hostage exchanges, which we will turn to below.

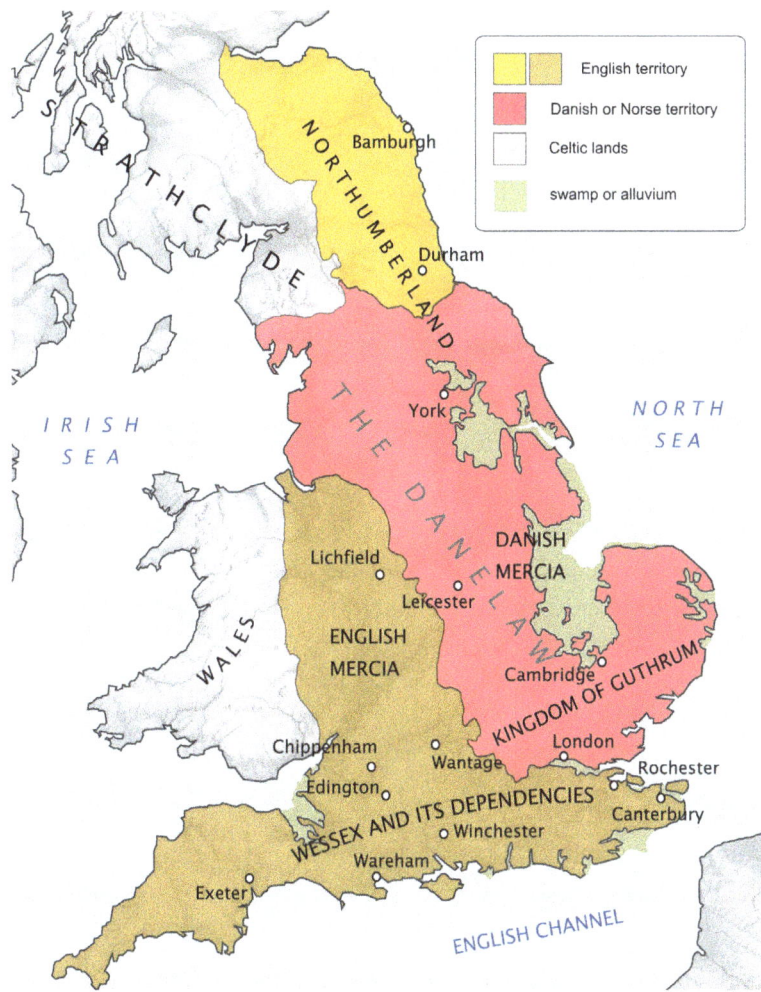

Figure III.1. Map of the realms of Wessex and Guthrum. Source: Wikipedia, Attribution-ShareAlike 3.0 Unported (CC BY-SA 3.0) https://sv.wikipedia.org/wiki/Danelagen#/media/Fil:England_878.svg (2019-06-20).

Legal, religious, social and economic aspects of hostages and other ritual acts

As pointed out in the Part I, the side with the strongest military force is usually the one who dictates the terms. In the introduction, it was also mentioned that this was not always evident for the real situation of the Danelaw, which was ruled by several great men and different fractions of the Great Heathen Army, as is evidenced by the above sequences.[5] The so-called Great Heathen Army was divided and led by several leaders. The fact that they were ascribed with titles such as 'king' and 'earl' did not necessarily meant that they corresponded to the titles of the Anglo-Saxon nobility. This division of the Army made it inevitable that there were several bases of support for different Scandinavian great men, something that is important to remember when different types of negotiations occurred even if it was not wartime. Thus, the concept of the Great Heathen Army could be misleading since it was not a unit in practice but consisted of groupings led by various great men with different interests.

According to the above timeline, different impact attempts were made by both sides (the Danes and the Anglo-Saxons) to regulate their counterparty. This can be compared to Figure I.1 in Part I, where some of the means used to affect the outcome of a peace or to regulate a threatening violence are listed: ceremonies, oaths, guest attendance, hostages, weddings, exchanges of gifts, trade, and peace agreements. Such an attempt took place in 865 in Thanet, Kent, when the residents were allowed to pay tribute in return for peace, but the debt did not provide enough protection for the eastern part of Kent. The tribute can be seen as a gift (see below), but it was not a matter of economic cooperation in accordance with step two of the model in the introduction. This event took place before tributes were put into system.[6] A similar attempt was made when the residents of East Anglia gave horses to the Danes and thus made an agreement. An alliance was also a way of influencing or strengthening a position vis-à-vis counterparties. Both Anglo-Saxons and Danes tried to build separate alliances. In 867, Mercia allied itself with Wessex. The part of the Great Heathen Army that entered Mercia in 873 drove away king Burhred and installed Ceolwulf as ruler in 874. In exchange, Ceolwulf had to support the Great Heathen Army with auxiliary troops, which may be understood as if Ceolwulf was involved in an alliance, although built on a subordinate relationship.

In 877, when the Great Heathen Army suffered some defeat, they divided the lands in Mercia and gave a share to Ceolwulf, that is, the Army wanted to make a bond with him, thus strengthening the alliance when they were under pressure from other parts of the Heptarchy such as Wessex (see Figure III.1).[7]

The hostage, who in any case was unilateral according to Kosto's definition,[8] appears in the case of Ceolwulf to have been a way to get free passage for the Army. They could then continue their plundering in other parts of the Heptarchy. However, the purpose of the hostage was also probably to regulate Ceolwulf; as a third party, the hostages guaranteed that Ceolwulf would not unite with anyone else or turn against the Danes.[9] These were the same tactics that were used by Continental Germanic rulers. The Danes appear to have been familiar with these manoeuvres.[10] A particular aspect of the hostage in this case was that it was available for the Great Heathen Army not once but on request. The procedure can be compared with Kosto's point of view that the hostage was distinguished from other forms of personal security, like prisoners of war, since they were not routinely distributed.[11] Moreover, if the giving of hostages can be understood as ritual acts, it means that the procedure was repeated. This hostage form in which hostages stood in constant preparedness through a peace settlement has been overlooked by Kosto in his study on various forms of hostage exchanges. However, the giving of hostages occurs in different contexts as in the aforementioned agreement between Guthrum and Alfred and the hostages mentioned in the *Elder Westrogothic law* when the ruler Ragnvald Knaphövde rode into the province of Västergötland in the 1130s.[12] Some place names could indicate a similar function of hostages. One could therefore categorize this form of hostage as a disposable hostage. At the same time, it should be noted that the purpose of this kind of hostage could differ, although free passage may have been a common purpose.[13] This could be compared to how the historian David Hill describes the border between Mercia and Wales as dynamic, during an occasionally violent period, between 704 and 1066 where both sides tried to adjust the border, which also involved the English (Wessex) attempt to control Wales. In these contexts, hostages were also used: 'the mechanism for the control may be seen through the hostages mentioned in the "Ordinance concerning the Dunsæte", and there clearly is some recognized person who will meet *bona fide* travellers at the frontiers'.[14]

With the defeats of 876 and 877 against Alfred, the situation was the reversed for the Great Heathen Army. Suddenly they were the weaker party during the negotiations. During the following peace summit, the Army had to provide hostages and they participated in ritual acts as the giving of oaths with the promise to leave Wessex. The writer of the *Anglo-Saxon Chronicle* noted that Alfred took as many hostages as he could (*swa fela swa he habban*).[15] In this case, the number of hostages may have been exaggerated. Lavelle thinks that this was the case because it was uncertain whether Alfred had the upper hand in 877.[16] In 878, however, the victory was real.[17]

The hostage giving of 876 may still be interpreted as linked to the promise of the Army to leave Wessex. Such a promise was probably something of a literary cliché in both Anglo-Saxon and Continental-Germanic literature.[18] Nevertheless, in the *Anglo-Saxon Chronicle*, at least outwardly, the purpose of the hostage is stated: keeping the Danes outside of Wessex. In the other cases, in 877 and 878, the hostages were rather a symbolic expression of submission.[19] In 878, the subordination is clear because it was a prominent hostage that was given with people belonging to the political elite of the society. The hostage taking also has a ritual aspect in this case. The giving of the hostage is described with the Old English formula *gislas salde*, 'gave hostages',[20] which can be compared with Marcel Mauss's theory of the gift: it must have a value that surpasses the (earlier) gift of the recipient. One can also note the financial counterperformance of Alfred; he gave extensive gifts, including estates, to Guthrum and members of his retinue.[21] The comparison with Mauss's theory of gifts demands a more comprehensive analysis and we shall return to this matter later in Part IV.

In 876, the Danes swore an oath on the holy ring (*helgan beage*) during the peace conference. This ring was an indigenous cultural object of the Danes and could have been rejected as 'pagan' by the Anglo-Saxon. It is interesting that the *Anglo-Saxon Chronicle* depicts how the Danes and the Anglo-Saxons participated in a common ceremony that appears to have been formally respected by both sides. Perhaps it can be described as an acculturative moment. The fact that the cultural object was brought to the place of meeting could be an example of a place that served as a mobile, cultic place.[22] In this case the place was respected by both sides by the giving of hostages as a sign of good will. And the agreement that was settled seems to have been regarded as legally binding, as in the case of the oath.[23]

Asser has another version of the swearing of oaths by the Danes in 876. According to him, the Danes gave as many hostages as Alfred demanded and the oath was sworn on all the relics the king regarded as 'the highest after God'. They swore not to return to the kingdom of Alfred (as raiders). Asser also adds that the Danes had not sworn such an oath to any other people before.[24] It is difficult to evaluate these two contradicting sources. Nonetheless, it is interesting that the Welsh monk Asser considers the relics to be crucial and implicitly the powers they turned to, which is a recurring theme in chronicles describing conflicts between Christians and heathens.[25] At the same time, the giving of hostages and the giving of oaths are not actions that the *Anglo-Saxon Chronicle* or Asser deny.[26] A similar pattern regarding the giving and taking of hostages and oaths can be found in descriptions in other contexts and under different political conditions (see below). The Scandinavian holy ring in the one case and the Christian relics in the other exemplify the use of cultural objects in ritual acts in both Scandinavian heathen and Anglo-Saxon Christian contexts. Interestingly the Christian Anglo-Saxons accepted the oath by the heathen Danes. It is likewise interesting that the 'heathens' accepted oaths that were Christian in content. When Guthrum swore his faithfulness to Alfred in 878, it is perceived by Lavelle as either a subordination, or a submission, where Guthrum became 'Alfred's man'.[27]

In my view, it is in the light of the symbolism of these submissions that the giving and taking of hostages and the swearing of oaths should be understood in this case. Which deity the Danes turned to was probably not so important – probably more important to the Anglo-Saxons – because the Christian god was perceived as a god among others for the polytheistic Scandinavians.

But even in a warlike situation, pragmatic reasons may have played a significant role. The Scandinavians faced a situation in which parts of the Great Heathen Army began to use the land in the conquered areas (e.g. 876 and 877), and this may have contributed to a standstill and a period of peace. That is not to state that this was a straightforward development, or that the will for peace would have been entirely intentional; on the contrary, the plundering continued for a while.[28] But what I refer to as a 'regulation' – the ability to utilize the resources offered to achieve as favourable results as possible within the area of confrontation – emerged. Here the actual performativeness of the ritual acts can be considered; both sides were given the opportunity to demonstrate their dependence on (or association with) their own traditions while establishing their adaptation to the new political situation.

During the ceremony – or ceremonies – in connection with the giving and taking of hostages between the Anglo-Saxons and the Danes, several ritual acts were performed:

(1) The giving and taking of hostages.
(2) Swearing of oaths at sacred objects.
(3) Baptism.
(4) The giving of gifts.

Probably – although this is not mentioned in the sources – joint festivities were held. During these celebrations, most likely toasts were made, a tradition that the Scandinavians could recognize from Scandinavia. In addition, a hunt could have occurred during these events. Lavelle has analysed various royal estates in Wessex in his doctoral dissertation.[29] Some rulers in Wessex seem to have had several hunting cottages. At the same time, Lavelle points out that the evidence of royal hunting is less evident in the time before the conquest (in 1066).[30]

There were several advantages with a hunt. According to Lavelle it had a symbolic, as well as psychosocial, function in which the hunt could be a form of 'controlled aggression' that broke the boredom of negotiations.[31] As a power manifestation, the hunt may also have impressed the subjects and made the ruler appear vigorous before the comprehensive retinue and the dignitaries.

Asser (Ch. 22), for example, praises the hunting skills of Alfred: 'he strives [...] in every branch of hunting [...] for no one else could approach him in skill and success in that activity, just as in all other gifts of God'. According to a local tradition, King Alfred's hunting lodge was in the market town of Chippenham, Wiltshire.[32] In such cases, it is possible that it was used in some of the negotiations between the Danes and the Anglo-Saxons, although this is something we only can speculate about.

The confirmation of Olaf Tryggvason

The depiction of the giving of hostages in Southampton in 994 is one of the most interesting in the early medieval sources, as it describes how a Scandinavian ruler could participate in ceremonies where power strategies were displayed. The *Anglo-Saxon Chronicle*, which can be regarded as a primary source, describes several ritual acts in connection with a hostage giving. The description involves the kings Sweyn Forkbeard (ON *Sveinn Tjúguskegg*, OE *Swegen*) from Denmark and Olaf Tryggvason (OE *Anelaf*) from Norway. When the giving of hostages at Southampton was completed, the political situation was different compared to seven years earlier when both Sweyn and Olaf conducted small-scale raids. Both rulers had ambitions of their own: Olaf aspired to become ruler over Norway, and Sweyn wished to appear as a ruler of the same character as the Christian Anglo-Saxon kings. Initially, the purpose was to collect tributes, the so-called Danegeld.[33] But with larger armies, Sweyn conquered England, while Olaf achieved his goal of becoming king of Norway – but only for a while. He fell at the battle of Svolder in the year 1000.

In 994, Sweyn and Olaf attacked London. According to the *Anglo-Saxon Chronicle,* the Londoners offered hard resistance. Then the Scandinavians raided the rural areas of Essex, Kent, Sussex, and Hampshire instead. A tribute was offered to the staggering sum of 16,000 pounds by the Anglo-Saxons.[34]

Olaf and Sweyn went to winter quarters in Southampton and the tribute of London was sent to them. Then Æthelred II, king of Wessex, sent bishop Ælfeach and the ealdorman Æthelweard to retrieve Olaf. The Anglo-Saxons also sent hostages to the ships of the Scandinavians. The bishop and the ealdorman brought Olaf to Andover, where he was received and led to the king who bestowed him with royal gifts. Olaf made the promise to never return as an enemy of the English people, a promise he held according to the chronicle.[35]

The ceremony at Andover was a confirmation (*ad confirmandum*),[36] because Olaf was already baptized, although this is not explicitly mentioned in the text. As a part of the ceremony, the bishop first led Olaf to Andover under great honours (*hi þa læddan Anlaf mid mycclum wurðscipe to þam cynge to Andeferan*) and handed him ritually to King Ethelred, who received him from the bishop's hands (*se cyng Æðelred his anfeng æt biscopes handa*).[37] The leading was a ritual act that was conducted during coronations in the Early Middle Ages in Scandinavia. The leading could take a variety of forms. The *Magnússona saga* reports how the Norwegian king Sigurd I Magnusson (OI *Sigurðr Jórsalafari*) visited a duke in Sicily.[38] During a banquet, Sigurd led the Duke to the high seat and confirmed his royal title. In the Norwegian *Hirdskraa*, it is mentioned that the king shall take the hand of an earl and lead him to the high seat (*þa skal konongr taka i honð hanum oc sætia han i hasæte*).[39]

The king had the function of godparent (or godfather; OE *fæder*) during the confirmation and exercised spiritual guardianship over Olaf, whereas Olaf could symbolically show that he could humble himself. The Christian tradition of a spiritual father might have originated in the mysteries of Isis, where a cult officiant had the function of *meum iam*, 'my father'. In Eastern Christianity, particularly, there was a conviction that a person was guided and instructed by a 'spiritual father', usually the bishop in a smaller congregation. Later, in early Europe, the importance of the spiritual father was reduced and should not be confused with a godfather.[40]

The ritual acts and the giving of hostages appear – as in the previous examples – as each other's prerequisites. The purpose of the confirmation ceremony might have been to display King Æthelred as the one with the highest rank. He had to avoid losing face.[41] And the siege of London had been a tactical victory for him if one is to believe the version of the *Anglo-Saxon Chronicle*, even if the siege as an incident does not need to be doubted. On the other hand, the payment of the Danish tribute was a significant loss for Æthelred, and the military and political situation was precarious. According to Joseph H. Lynch, Æthelred's intention was to complete the ceremony, a splitting up the Danes by binding Olaf to himself.[42] In any case, it may have been a symbolic prestige for Æthelred that Olaf outwardly submitted to the confirmation ceremony and then disappeared from his kingdom.

Why did Olaf submit to this ritual act of confirmation? One answer may be that he considered himself equal to the Christian Anglo-Saxon kings. On the other hand, they did not consider the Scandinavian rulers as equal. It was not until Canute the Great (ON *Knútr inn ríki*) became ruler of England that a king of Scandinavian birth was counted as an equal of English kings.[43] If the case of Guthrum and Alfred was an example of submission, then this case was a situation that Olaf could use to his advantage, which had to do with the real political situation; there were different interests of the various participants in the ceremony. However, on a symbolical level the ritual acts were something people from the Scandinavian countries recognized, the oaths none the least.[44] At the same time, there was another symbolism in the ceremony that could be related to the warrior elite, for example gift giving in the pre-Christian context. There is no direct correspondence to the confirmation ceremony, but according to Lynch, similar ritual acts, which marked paternity, may have existed in Continental Germanic areas. It may have been about cutting a young man's hair or beard or to give him his first weapon.[45] It is obvious that it created a close bond similar to that of kinship. This method of using a symbolic relationship had a horizontal effect in this case because Olaf had (or was obliged) to leave Æthelred's territories in England.

In Part IV I will further show how relationships, including in a father-and-son–like relationship, as a social bonding mechanism, could have an impact on people who became hostages.

The hostages provided by Æthelred had the function of guaranteeing Olaf's personal security. There are no hints about what persons constituted the hostages. The hostage procedure can be compared with Lavelle's view that the hostage, as it appears in the writer's perspective of the *Anglo-Saxon Chronicle*, had only a practical role in guaranteeing Olaf's person.[46] In my view, however, hostages, as described in the *Anglo-Saxon Chronicle*, may have had the function of honouring Olaf Trygvason. He was the one who had to come to Æthelred and not the opposite. In such cases, it is comparable to Lavelle's idea that the hostage should reflect the status of the hostage taker.[47] Olaf was brought 'under honours' to Andover, which could indicate that the moment was perceived as a part of the same ceremony and thus a ritual act.

It is interesting that the hostages had to wait aboard the ships. The reason was probably pragmatic; it was the easiest way to control the hostages. But there was also a certain symbolism displayed. The ship was undeniable Scandinavian 'territory', and having the hostages there reinforced the impression that it was at the disposal of the Scandinavians and that they were dominant.[48]

As a result of these ritual acts, Olaf symbolically strengthened his social position. The symbolism was not about England, where he had no further political interests.[49] The motivation would also have been strengthened by the part of the tribute that was given to Olaf. Consequently, the fulfilment of this holy promise could be seen as a performative act. And the performative actions became a reflection of the negotiations between the participants in the ceremonies (Olaf and Æthelred).

Thus, in this case the following ritual elements appear:

(1) The leading of Olaf to Andover under honours.
(2) The taking of hostages that would be related to Olaf's pride.
(3) The reception at Andover where Olaf was ceremonially attended by Æthelred.
(4) The actual confirmation.
(5) The giving of gifts.
(6) Olaf's pledge to never return to Æthelred's lands.

Everything is not evident from the description in the *Anglo-Saxon Chronicle*, but some ritual acts are merely implied or implicit in the text. All the ritual acts can be related to the negotiations that Bell considered being an important part of performativity. For both sides in the area of communication, in this case, it was important to demonstrate both power and humbleness. Such an order of power must, however, be understood on the basis of its political context, which can be seen through examples from the Carolingian Empire.

Negotiations in the areas of confrontation in the Carolingian Empire

Between the 8th and 10th centuries, there were numerous negotiations dealing with disputed land areas, plundering, and alliance-buildings between Danish rulers and the Carolingian royal power. These negotiations are reported in the *Royal Frankish Annals* (*Annales regni Francorum*). The following conflicts and peace processes involved the Danes:[50]

> 777. The Saxon Widukind does not appear before the court of Charlemagne in Paderborn. He is looking for a refuge with the Danish ruler Sigfred (or Sigurd Hring).
>
> 782. The emperor Charlemagne holds a meeting outside Cologne with the Saxons. Even the envoys of Sigfred attend.
>
> 804. The Danish ruler Godfred (or Gudfred) comes with a fleet to Sliesthorp (later Hedeby), at the border between Godfred's lands and the Saxons, to negotiate with Charlemagne. Emissaries are sent.
>
> 808. Godfred enters the land of the Obotrites with an army. Godfred returns and establishes the trading emporium Reric. He decides to fortify the boundary of his realm.
>
> 809. The Emperor is angry over Godfred's campaign. Godfred decides to reconcile and sends his men for a meeting with the Emperor's envoys (from the nobility) in a place north of Elbe so that both sides can express their views on the conflict. The negotiation ends in locked positions. At the request of Godfred, the Sorbian ruler Thrasco gives his son (Ceadragus) as hostage to the Danes. Godfred then summons troops, with auxiliary troops from the Saxons, and ravages the territory of the Veleti (or Wiltzes).[51] Thrasco is later murdered by Godfred's men at Reric.

810. Godfred's troops arrive to Friesland. All islands on the coast are invaded, and the Danes defeat the Frisians in three battles. The Frisisans have to pay 100 pounds of silver in tributes. Charlemagne marches with an army to the mouth of the river Weser. Godfred withdraws but is murdered by one of his men. Hemming, Godfred's brother, takes over the throne and concludes a peace with the emperor.

811. A peace meeting is held at the river Eider with men from both the Carolingian Empire and the Danish realm.

812. Hemming dies. There is a war between Hemming's relatives Sigfred and Anulo. These two throne pretenders fight a battle where they are both killed. Anulo's party is victorious from the feud, and his brothers, Harald Klak and Reginfred, become kings. They ask the emperor for peace through messengers and make a request that their brother Hemming (a hostage?) is to be handed over.

813. A meeting occurs between Frankish, Saxon, and Danish noblemen above the river Elbe. The peace is confirmed and Hemming is handed over. Harald and Reginfred make a campaign in Britain. When they return, the son of King Godfred, together with some Danish great men who lives in exile in Sweden, starts a war against Harald and Reginfred. The kings are driven away.

814. Harald and Reginfred gather forces once again. New battles between Harald and Reginfred and the sons of Godfred. Reginfred is killed. Harald seeks support from the King of the Franks, Louis the Pious. Louis asks him to wait in Saxony for the right time.

815. Louis raises forces with Saxons and Obotrites in support of Harald. They march over the river Eider into Sinlendi (Schleswig) and camp. Godfred's sons settle on an island 30 kilometres off the mainland. The forces of Louis and Harald fortify the coast and force the locals to give hostages to Louis. The sons of Godfred do not intervene.

817. Godfred's sons beg Louis for peace, but this is considered hypocrisy. Sclaomir (or Slavomir), ruler of the Obotrites, is in dispute with Ceadragus on shared royal power. Sclaomir breaks off from Louis and allies with the sons of Godfred. With the support

of Danish troops, he falls into Nordalbingen and makes a siege on the border fortress Esesfelth. Finally, Sclaomir breaks the siege.

819. Sclaomir is sent to Louis in Aachen and is declared an outlaw. Ceadragus becomes ruler. Harald sails on the order of Louis to Denmark to take the power. Two of the sons of Godfred join him. Two other sons are driven out of the country.

821. Harald and the sons of Godfred share the rule over the Danish realm.

822. Messengers are sent from both Harald and the sons of Godfred (who were driven away) to Louis.

824. Harald arrives at Compiègne and asks Louis for aid against the sons of Godfred, who threaten to throw him out of the country. Louis sends a delegation to negotiate with the sons.

825. Godfred's sons send a messenger to Louis, who decides that the peace they ask for will be settled with a meeting in their border regions.

826. Harald comes to Mainz and is baptized in the St. Alban's Abbey.

Over the Danish-Frankish (and Saxon) areas of confrontation, which consisted of border areas, several alliances and counter-alliances were formed between the Danes, the Franks, the Obotrites, and the Saxons. The Carolingian Empire's kings and emperors and the rulers of the Danes appear to have occasionally acted as reasonably balanced parties in negotiations.

The areas of communication consisted of temporary campsites that were prepared by the counterparties before the peace meetings.[52] These places were often situated at watercourses, the rivers that formed natural boundaries. Characteristic to these areas was also the infrastructural effort by both the emperors and kings as well as the Danish rulers to consolidate their positions of power by fortifying their borders.

Boundaries can be considered as areas of communication within or in the immediate vicinity of the area of confrontation. Others were far from the areas of confrontation such as the emperor's base in Compiègne. The strengthening of the fortification line called *Danevirke* and the commercial site Reric – known archaelogical sites – can thus be characterized as attempts to regulate the areas of the confrontation.[53]

The construction of the trading place can be understood as the beginning of collaborative forms in accordance with step two of the model, although it may not have given immediate results. Short periods of calm, however, appear to have occurred, if one is to believe the *Royal Frankish Annals*.

For the counterparty, those who were plundered, there were regulatory means such as tributes to cope with the robbery. Hostages also filled the function of regulating areas of confrontation and could provide an opportunity as it could both be given by one party and used by the other to prevent further attacks. The actions of Thrasco, the ruler of the Obotrites, as described in the the *Royal Frankish Annals* is interesting in this case. After his son became a hostage of the Danes, he instead focused his interest on the Veleti. By uniting himself with the Saxons, he was able to plunder the lands of the Veleti. By the spoil he took and his new alliance, he could strengthen his failing position with his people. These acts are likely to have had a symbolic significance as well as pragmatic.

The above is intended as a characteristic of the area of confrontation and different communicative aspects. It also serves as the following analysis of why and under what conditions Harald Klak approached the king (or emperor) Louis the Pious at his court in Mainz.

The alliance between Harald Klak and Louis the Pious

Harald Klak's alliance with the king, later emperor, Louis the Pious, is depicted in a poem by Ermold the Black (Lat. *Ermoldus Niegellus*), called *In honorem Hludovici emperatoris*, 'In honour of Emperor Louis'. In 826, Harald (Lat. *Herioldus*) came with his family to Louis's court in Mainz (or Ingelheim). Then Harald and his family agreed to be baptized.[54]

The Emperor Louis the Pious (Fr. *Louis le Pieux*) personally dressed Harald during the baptism in the same way that he dressed recently converted men at the baptismal font. According to Lynch, this ritual act was specific to the Franks.[55] Louis gave gifts in accordance with Harald's position, and afterwards they held a banquet.[56] Interestingly, Lynch points out that one of the gifts consisted of French clothing with metals and precious stones that 'suited their taste'.[57] What the Scandinavians thought of this symbolism we do not know. Probably it was a way for them to get acceptance, symbolically appearing equal, and above all to gain an alliance. This impression may have been reinforced at the baptism ceremony when the queen (or the empress) Judith stood as the godmother of Harald's wife, and Lothar, the emperor's son, was a sponsor of Harald's son. This can be compared with a remark by the historians Birgit and Peter Sawyer: the Franks perceived Denmark as a unit and not a land area ruled by two or several brothers.[58] There was not any hereditary title; the choice fell upon the person who could obtain support from the most dominant within the king's immediate circle, often after violent settlements. Thus, Louis may have thought he was dealing with a person with higher social capital than he might have, a person who, with this act, became subordinate in the vertical sense. For Harald there was nothing to lose. A few days after the banquet, Harald and Louis completed their alliance-building ceremony. Louis and Harald, now regarded as a 'godson', had then strengthened a friendship that they had begun already in 814.[59] These ritual acts can be perceived pragmatic and what later has been referred to as *Realpolitik*. The degree of submission by Harald Klak can be judged by relating to the conditions constituting a prerequisite for the area of confrontations with these constant alliances and counter-alliances. Compared to the conditions of Olaf Tryggvason's confirmation, the conditions for Harald were harsh: he had lost his position. Therefore, the role of the emperor as a sponsor can be emphasized to a higher extent than in the case of Olaf and Æthelred, in which it was about restricting Olaf from taking future tributes. Harald was given an expensive costume and the county of Rüstringen in Friesland. But Harald's position as a ruler of Rüstringen was unclear because it says in the annals that he could seek his refuge there with his household 'if necessary'.[60] Nor were the families of Harald and the emperor intermarried.

Most importantly, of course, was the assurance of a wider alliance and retaliation of Harald's power position in Denmark. Still, Harald became a weak ruler who only managed to retain power for a year. Then he retired to Rüstringen.[61] Although the giving of hostages was not a necessary measure in this particular case, some of the actions of Louis can be compared to step two in the model: During antiquity, the Romans 'invested' in the offspring of foreign rulers. This method was primarily applied to hostages from the eastern provinces and was ritually displayed in ceremonies.[62] Similar methods and traditions might have continued into the Early Middle Ages. Louis's actions could likewise be understood so that he tried to show himself as a mediator of Christianity, as can be seen by the presence of the monk Ansgar – one of the earliest missionaries in Denmark and Svetjud – who travelled with Harald. It is worth noting the observation of Rimbert in *Vita Ansgarii*. Through a common belief in God, it would be possible with a more intimate friendship between the emperor and the Danish king. A Christian people could also aid Louis and his followers in their struggles.[63]

Between Harald and Louis, ritual acts took place, similar to those in England during the confrontations between the English and Scandinavian rulers. In this case, it was:

(1) Acceptance of baptism.
(2) Baptism (including sponsorship).
(3) Ritual dressing.
(4) The giving of gifts.
(5) Banquet.
(6) Symbolic confirmation of alliance.

Events also probably occurred, including rituals, that the sources do not mention, such as the oaths in connection with promises of alliance.

In order to further deepen the understanding of the above-mentioned ritual acts, one can compare this with Bell's commentary on how important symbolic acts are for those who compete for power, as ritual acts construct political submission and dominance.[64] All this can be seen in the above case, as in the previous examples from confrontations between Anglo-Saxons and Danes. The one who possessed the most power was the one who could best determine the order and thus the direction of the display of power.

Everything indicates that the above cases exemplify a vertical subordination between a Scandinavian and a Carolingian ruler where the power relations were uneven. There are also examples of peace negotiations from other places, times, and power relationships in Scandinavia where rival rulers met on a more horizontal, equal level, and there were ritual acts with hostage of the same kind as in the Anglo-Danish and the Carolingian-Danish areas of confrontation.

The peace negotiations between Harald Hardrada and Sweyn Estridsson

In 1064, the Norwegian king Harald Hardrada (ON *Haraldr harðráði*) and the Danish king Sweyn II Estridsson (Da. *Svend Estridsen*, ON *Sveinn Ástríðarson*) met for a peace meeting at the river Göta älv. Two years earlier, Harald had defeated Sweyn in the battle of the river Nissan (in present Sweden) as described by the skald Þjóðólfr Arnórsson in the poem *Sexstefja*, which was a *lausavísa* composed in 1065, a set of stanzas not connected to a grand narrative, which is now almost completely lost.

The later peace negotiations are depicted in a poem simply called *flokkr* (from ca. 1064) by the skald Halli stírði (or *stríði*, 'the stern'), reproduced by Snorri in the *Saga of Harald Hardrada* (OI *Haralds [harðráða] saga Sigurðarsonar*) in the *Heimskringla*. In the following analysis, I will rely on this skaldic poem to scrutinise the negotiations which were conducted over the area of confrontation between the two sides and how ritual actions and hostages were used by both sides in the area of communication, at the river of Göta älv.

In the poem, the second stanza describes how King Harald is a man to be trusted to keep his oath (*eiðfastr Haraldr*):

Gerðir opt fyr jǫrðu Oath-fast Harald! Thou oft
eiðfastr Haraldr skeiðum. Didst gird the land with ships.

Sveinn skerr ok till annars	Swein, too, through the sounds
eysund konungs fundar	Didst sail to meet the king.
Út hefra lið lítit	The high-praised raven-feeder
lofsnjallr Dana allra,	Who locked up every inlet with stems
hinn es hvern vág sunnan,	Had out a mighty host
hrafngrennir, lykr stǫfnum.[65]	Of all the Danes from the South.[66]

(Transl. Erling Monsen & Albert Hugh Smith)

The mentioning of the oath can be linked to the meeting between the two counterparties. The stanza also describes how Harald forms a blockade around his country and how the kings are about to face each other.

The poem's epithet for Harald as 'trustworthy' (*eiðfastr*) implies that the present peace meeting had a ritual meaning. As a prerequisite for the meeting, oaths had to be taken to preserve the peace. In the *Saga of Harald Hardrada*, it is mentioned that the peace meeting had been preceded by the sending of envoys between the two parties.[67] Both sides respected the messengers. If the prose version of the *Heimskringla* is credible, it is implicit in the text that the messengers acted as witnesses of the assurances of the kings. And both kings agreed to meet at Älven (the river Göta älv), that is, at the border between the realms.

According to the third stanza of the poem, both sides approach the border (*landamæri*) and agree to hold the meeting (*mæltrar stefnu*).[68] There is no further information about the meeting place either in the prose text or in the poem. The meeting could have taken place on an island or on the mainland. If it was a meeting place that was organized *ad hoc*, it could be compared to my hypothesis about the mobile cult places that I presented in the introduction.

By relying on the theories on liminality by the anthropologists Arnold van Genneps and Victor Turner, it is possible to generally designate certain areas at borders as 'liminal'.[69] In this case, such liminality could also characterize the meeting place where the political situation allowed the present householders (or farmers) from both sides to raise their voices. This arrangement can be related to Turner's hypothesis on 'Betwixt and Between', a kind of intermediate mode during ceremonies where opposition towards the authorities is possible. This kind of order might be seen in stanza 4 describing the meeting:

Telja hǫtt, es hittask,	The brisk bonders said
hvartveggja mjǫk, seggir,	Such words loudly
orð, þaus angra fyrða	Even such as, when men meet,
allmjǫk, búendr snjallir.	Most anger the others.
Láta þeir, es þraeta,	Men who quarrelled about everything
þegnar, allt í gegnum,	Did not want
svellr ofrhugi jǫfrum.	To seek an early peace.
eigi brátt við sǫttum.[70]	The wrath of the princes grew.[71]

(Transl. Erling Monsen & Albert Hugh Smith)

Great men were present during the meeting. The noun *þegnar* (pl.) is ambiguous as a poetic expression for 'men' or as a title.[72] It seems as if there was opposition among the present great men towards the kings. According to the prose text, it was due to all the damage by the plundering people suffered during the war.[73] The skald describes the wrath of the kings as 'dangerous' (*Ofreiði verðr jófra allhæt*). The anger of the kings threatened to break the ongoing negotiation.

Some actors – other than the kings – had a significant impact on the outcome of the negotiations. In stanza 5, it is mentioned that some managed to communicate between the different sides:

Ofreiði verðr jǫfra	The wrath of the princes would be
allhæt, ef skal sættask.	perilous
Menn þeirs miðla kunnu,	If peace was in sight.
mǫl ǫll vega í skǫlum.	Had to weigh all in the scales.
Dugir siklingum segja	It suited the kings to say
slíkt allt, es her líkar.	All such as the armies like.
Veldr, ef verr skulu hǫlðar,	Ill would result if the bonders
vili grindar því, skiljask.[74]	Were left in a worse position.[75]

(Transl. Erling Monsen & Albert Hugh Smith)

It is noteworthy that these mediators were celebrated in this context. Obviously, they filled an important function in communicating the message between the king, the great men, and their men. The lines 5 and 6 of stanza 5 are key lines in this context, because it is said that 'It is honourable to say what the army considers' (*Dugir siklingum segja slíkt allt, es her líkar*), which is to be understood that the men were weary of the war and wanted to see an end of it. At the very least, the poem gives the impression that the kings appear as equal parties.

They also decided to give hostages to each other to secure the peace:

Hitt hefk heyrt, at setti	I have heard that gladly
Haraldr ok Sveinn við meinum,	Did both Harald and Swein
guð sýslir þat, gísla	Give hostages one to the other;
glaðr hvárrtveggi ǫðrum.	God brought it about.
Þeir haldi svá sœrum,	May they keep their oaths
sǫtt lauksk þar með vǫttum,	And fully hold their peace.
ok ǫllum frið fullum,	Nobody can break the treaty;
ferð at hvǫrgi skerði.[76]	It was sealed by witnesses.[77]

(Transl. Erling Monsen & Albert Hugh Smith)

The giving of hostages was a result of the negotiations and – in this area of confrontation – gained the function of regulating both sides so that further violence could be prevented. It is likely that the hostages were left indefinitely. This case, however, is comparable to the Anglo-Saxon examples in which the giving of hostages was used to regulate future cooperation between different peoples in the Heptarchy and the Dane law.

A bilateral situation arose that can be compared to step three of the model (see Part I): after a long conflict, the two sides reached consensus under a certain pressure of other groupings such as the householders. Attempted mediation had been carried out and finally an agreement was accepted as legal by all the involved.

There are no hints of gift giving during these negotiations. But the skaldic poem of Halli stirði can be seen as a kind of gift that had been performed as a compliment during later hall ceremonies. In the poem, both rulers are attributed with similar characteristics of warriors and rulers as their heathen ancestors. These are the kennings and *heiti*s for Harald and Sweyn.

Harald: *eiðfastr* 'oath-fast', *jǫfurr* 'prince, wild boar'
Sweyn: *ljósnallr* 'the honorable King', *jǫfurr* 'prince, wild boar', hrafngrennir 'raven-feeder'

These are examples of how traditions of old age survived into the time when Christianity was accepted in Denmark and Norway. There are also examples of meetings between heathens and Christians in Norway where there was a consensus about the ritual acts that were linked to the actual peace negotiations, while the confrontation between 'belief systems' appears to have been more loaded with subjective judgements.

The hostages of Dale-Gudbrand

In the *Heimskringla* (Ch. 111–113), in the saga of Olaf Haraldsson, it is reported that the Norwegian king Olaf II Haraldsson (later St. Olaf) – with his said ambition to Christianize and to conquer the whole of Norway – raids the county of Oppland. Olaf relies on bases in places like the regions of Dovre and Lesja. He forces the inhabitants of the Oppland to accept Christianity and give their sons as hostages.

In the Gudbrand Valley (No. *Gudbrandsdalen*), lives the heathen chieftain (ON *hersi*) Dale-Gudbrand (ON *Dala-Guðbrandr*) at a farm called Hundtorp around 1021. He sends his son with a retinue of householders against Olaf and his men. But the householders fly after a few spearthrows from Olaf's men and Gudbrand's son is caught. Olaf gives the son mercy and he is sent back to his father with the announcement that the king shall soon come to the thing at Hundtorp.

The son tells his father of Olaf's skills as warrior and advises Dale-Gudbrand to submit. Dale-Gudbrand refuses. During the night Dale-Gudbrand has a horrible dream of a terrible shape that mentions that he and all his men will die if they do not submit to King Olaf. The next day Tord Bigmaw (OI *Þórðr istrumagi*), who is a cult functionary called *hófgóði*, tells Dale-Gudrand that he had the same dream.[78]

[—] In the morning they had a thing called and said that it seemed advisable to them to hold a thing with this man who came from the north with new words of bidding and get to know with what truth he fared. Then Gudbrand said to his son: 'Thou shalt now go to the king who gave the peace, and twelve men with thee'; and so it was done. And they came to the king and told him their errand that the bonders would hold a thing with him and make peace between the king and the bonders. The king said it seemed a good thing to him, and they now bound it with terms between themselves for as long as the meeting should last. After they went back and told Gudbrand and Tord that peace was made. The king then went to the place which was called Lidstader and was there five nights. Thereupon the king went to meet the bonders, and held a thing with them, but there was much rain that day. When the thing was set the king stood up and said that the folk in Lesjar and in Loar and in Vaga had taken Christianity and broken down their temples of blood offerings, 'and now they believe in the true God who shaped heaven and earth and knows all things'. After that the king sat down and Gudbrand answered: 'We know not of whom thou talkest. Thou callest by the name of God Him whon neither thou nor anyone hast seen. But we have a god whom we can see every day; he is not out to-day, because the weather is wet. He will seem awe-inspiring and mighty to thee and I think fear will come upon thee when he comes to the thing. But since thou sayest that thy God can do som much, let Him now do so that the weather to-morrow be cloudly without rain, and let us than meet here'. The king then went home to his room, and Gudbrand's son went with him as hostage, but the king gave them another man in return. In the evening they asked Gudbrand's son how their god was made. He answered that 'he is marked like Thor and he has a hammer in his hand, is big of build and is hollow inside, and there is a stand on which he rests when he is outside. There is no shortage of gold and silver on him, four loaves of bread are brought to him, and meat withal'. After that they went to bed, but the king awoke in the night and was at his prayers. But when it was day the king went to Mass and then food and so to the thing; the weather was now such as Gudbrand had wished for.[79]

(Transl. Erling Monsen & Albert Hugh Smith)

One day later at the thing, the sun rises and King Olaf refers to it as his god before the heathen householders. One of Olaf's men, Kolbeinn, breaks down the idol of Thor. When the idol breaks apart, mice, lizards, and snakes crawl out. The householders[80] are frightened and convinced of the incapability of their god. They accept the king's friendship and Christianity. The bishop of Olaf baptizes Gudbrand, his son, and all other inhabitants of the valley. A church is later built in the Gudbrand Valley.[81] The legendary saga of St. Olaf was probably written around 1210. Snorri Sturluson possibly had this version as the model of his version in the *Heimskringla* (cf. Figure III.2). Even though it is disputed, there may have been an older, now lost, version of the saga of St. Olaf, probably written around 1190, which Snorri may have relied on.

Previous research has often referred to the episode of Dale-Gudbrand's confrontation with King Olaf, but the episode has not been subject to an extensive analysis, except for the one made by the historian of religions Gro Steinsland. She has thoroughly analysed the episode in the *Heimskringla* called 'the drama of Hundtorp' and pointed out the lack of interest among researchers.[82] Previous research has focused on the source value of the story, which is now generally considered to be low.[83]

For researchers in the early 1900s, such as the historian and politician Edvard Bull, the story was important as a part of the confirmation of an early state formation. For him it was important that it was a Norwegian history. Bull stated that Snorri used a local legend and that archaeological evidence such as burial mounds and stone settings indicated a central place. Additional

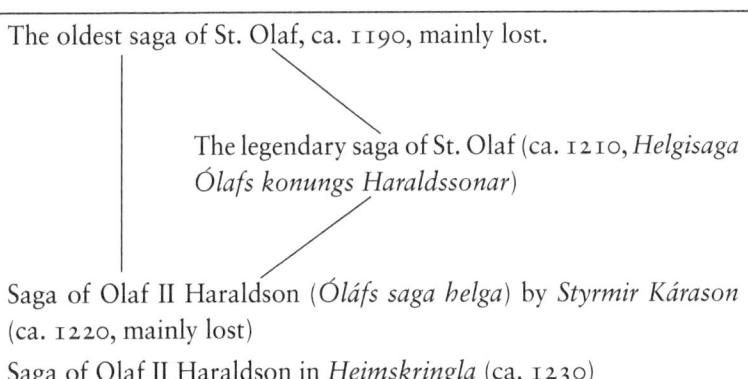

Figure III.2. The possible relation between an original, now lost, saga of St. Olaf and later versions.

evidence was found in place names, skaldic poetry, and medieval diplomas.[84]

More recent researchers are more concerned about whether it is really a Norwegian story. The philologist Theodore Andersson argues that the oldest story of St. Olaf was not the original source. Instead, it may have been built on the presumed *Kristni þáttr*, which might have been written around 1210.[85] The story is therefore Icelandic and not Norwegian. Perhaps the Icelandic chronicler Ari Þorgilsson may have written this part, which was later used by both Snorri and the author of the legendary saga of St. Olaf. Andersson tries to show how some specific Christian ideas might have inspired Snorri in the miracle-like events of the *Heimskringla* version.

Steinsland refers to the philologist Anne Asplin, who analysed the manuscript of the episode with Olaf Haraldsson and Dale-Gudbrand. According to Steinsland, Asplin succeeds in distinguishing some Norwegian linguistic features.[86] The depiction of the landscape could indicate the Norwegian origin of the story. Steinsland therefore assumes that the story may be built on a local tradition.[87] She interprets the episode with Olaf and Dale-Gudbrand as a way of reproducing an ideal picture of how a Christian Germanic king would appear.[88] According to Steinsland, following the theologian James C. Russell, Christianity brought new means to kings of Norway, including the stave churches and a general ritualization of the traditions of the saints. This kind of Christianity was characterized by a salvation ideal in which apocalyptic ideas were central. In the 'Germanic communities', the old tradition (*forn siðr*) touched upon the cultural identity and solidarity of the groupings.[89] The new tradition (*inn nýi siðr*), i.e. Christianity, had to be adapted to the old identity and solidarity. Through the new Christian ideal, Christ was interpreted as a conquering warlord; on early Scandinavian crucifixes he is depicted as a king with a golden crown. It was also important to show Christ as a victor who defeats the dark powers, often regarded as being embodied in the old, indigenous deities.[90]

I agree with Steinsland that one cannot completely deny the possibility that Snorri built on sources that may have been unknown to us, but the story itself must be seen in the light of the ambition to make Olaf Haraldsson a saint and cannot be taken for a realistic account. Writers like Snorri tend to focus on religious matters such as the worship of heathen gods, which is set in opposition to the Christian doctrine of a 'true god'. For me, however, it is not the Christian conversion but the interaction between the actors that is interesting. Certain aspects of the story may be authentic regarding the use of hostages and references to older legal traditions. Because the versions in the *Heimskringla* and the legendary saga cannot be regarded as realistic accounts of all the events, there is the possibility that the medieval writers did not see any threat to parts in the story that was no direct challenge to the conversion and the adoption of the new tradition.

Below, I outline the traditions in the stories that can be related to hostages and the traditions of assemblies like the things and how these can be understood against Christian literary traditions. To clarify, a division of the events in the story can be made into sequences:

(1) The summoning to the thing. Dale-Gudbrand sends his son with twelve men to invite King Olaf to the thing.
(2) King Olaf accepts the invitation.
(3) The son returns to Dale-Gudbrand and confirms that there is a truce (*grið*).
(4) The king travels to the farm Listad (*Liðsstaðir*) and remains there for five days.
(5) The first day of the thing.[91] The kings speak and proclaim his new faith. Dale-Gudbrand gives his answer. Both the king and Dale-Gudbrand give hostages. Dale-Gudbrand sends his son with the king to Listad.
(6) The second day of the thing. At dawn the king visits the mass, eats his morning meal, and walks to the thing.
(7) The third day of the thing. The king demonstrates that his faith is the strongest. When the sun rises, the idol of Thor bursts and mice, lizards, and snakes crawl out.

The sequences can be interpreted in the following way:

Sequence 1. That there were just twelve men may have had Christian connotations; Jesus had twelve disciples. According to

Theodore Andersson, these manœuvres with military movements are just a way to dramatize the end of the story.[92]

Sequences 2–4. Even if the story does not refer to real events, this (ritual) act itself does not need to be 'dramatized' but may be consistent with previous examples of peace processes in the Anglo-Danish areas of confrontation.

Sequence 5. It seems that Snorri, in other chapters about Olaf's life, reports how he paid his respect to old laws and traditions during various assemblies even if the king's word was final, even this information must be taken with a grain of salt. At the same time, Steinsland points out that the king also opposed the householders on occasions by violating their old traditions (*brióta lǫg vár*).[93]

Sequence 7. As the sun rises and the idol of God breaks, it is – according to Gro Steinsland – a sign of the power of the *majestas*, 'the divine monarch'.[94] It is not a question about salvation or condemnation but rather relates to early Christianity in which the ruler identified himself with Christ. When the saints break down idols, the devil can materialise in the form of a dragon or worm.

It is possible that the king is presented in the text according to a *Rex Justus* ideal, i.e. the 'righteous king', whose power stems from his piety.[95] On the other hand, it is not certain that just the giving of hostages and other ritual acts upon the summoning to the thing are inaccurately described, even if the story itself is fictitious. Before Snorri, these kinds of traditions were not an immediate threat to the new tradition. On the contrary, the above example, with hostages, illustrates that it occurs in situations where both parties respect the hostages for different reasons. It is rather how the fight is made between the counterparts that are important to the writer and that the Christian faith appears as the strongest when heathen gods are positioned against the Christian god. The traditions that are not a threat to the king as *Rex Justus* is of less importance in Snorri's account. The procedure with the hostages certainly follows this line. Dale-Gudbrand dare sends his son, which was a sign of respect and trust. The noun *einkamál* can be interpreted as a 'pledge' or 'promise'.[96] Thus, the actual negotiations and the actions associated with the conflict are overlooked. This does not mean that the description would generally be free from idealization or influence from literary traditions and Christian values, a topic that we will return to.

Some characteristics

The similarities between *Heimskringla*'s version (Hkr) of the *Saga of Olaf II Haraldson*, The *Anglo-Saxon Chronicle* (ASC), Halli's *Flokkr* (F), Asser's (A) *Biography of Alfred* and the *Royal Frankish Annals* (Fk) can be structured as a series of events of ritual acts involving hostages and other ceremonies that took place in the context of negotiations of peace:

(1) Messengers and envoys are sent.   [Hkr, ASC, A, F, Fk]
(2) An agreement of where to meet. The   [Hkr, ASC, F]
   promise not to break the peace at the
   meeting place.
(3) The giving and taking of hostages
   performed at an area characterised by
   liminality, which could be:
     (a) a river (b) an area of communication   [Hkr, ASC, F, A, Fk]
       such as the thing. The hostage giving
       took place:
     (α) before (β) during or (γ) after the
     meeting.
(4) Negotiations at: [ASC, A]
     (a) assemblies such as the thing or   [Hkr, F]
     (b) in the hall (or the royal court)   [Fk]
(5) Ritual actions, including:
     (a) the giving of gifts   [ASC, Fk]
     (b) oaths/promises   [ASC, Hkr, A]
     (c) the performances of skaldic poetry or   [F]
       other celebrations
     (d) baptism   [ASC, A, Fk]
     (e) the casting of lots   [Hkr]
     (f) other types of demonstrations   [Hkr, Fk]
(6) Festivities.   [ASC]
(7) Hunt.   [A]

Some of the above-mentioned ritual acts have not been touched upon. This applies to the casting of lots, alternatively dice games, and the possible hunt (see above). The casting of lots, however, is mentioned in the *Heimskringla* and some other sources. For example: Olof Skötkonung and Olaf Haraldsson play dice as to whether the island of Hisingen should belong to Norway or Sweden.[97]

What is refered to as 'peace process' in this survey could extend over several years, as the examples from the Anglo-Danish and Frankish-Danish areas of confrontation show. Therefore, it may not always be right to describe the ritual acts as one ceremony, rather there were acts that occurred with many years apart. The ritual actions can be related to the three steps of the model:

(1) The establishment of social relations through ritual actions.
(2) The stabilization and establishment of (new) trade relations and other types of economic cooperation.
(3) The peace treaty is ratified by both parts.

The middle step is visible to a lesser extent in the examples I have discussed. The peace agreement between Guthrum and Alfred, as well as the statistics of the *Íslendingabók* and the *Landnámabók*, provide empirical evidence that economic cooperation really occurred between opposing sides. The relationship between steps one and three is marked by the time that occurred between the establishment of the contact and the meeting. The first contact was ritually conditioned by the promise of no further hostilities and to keep the peace at the meeting place. Step one could also include all of the above-mentioned ritual actions. Step one may also have resulted in a temporary truce. Sometimes it took a long time, with interruptions for fighting, before the peace agreement could be completed, that is, step three. Then other interests from various groupings, as in the case of Harald Sigurdsson and Svend Estridsen, could have had an effect on the outcome.

Through the ritual acts, there was room for different power demonstrations that were symbolically important and were performed in ritual acts. Some of these ritual actions may not fit into a normal pattern for what is commonly referred to as 'ritual' but can still be compared to what Bell refers to as 'ritual-like'. On the other hand, many researchers are willing to see gift-giving as a ritual act in ancient Scandinavian traditions.[98] Mauss, for his part, was willing to see the gift in Germanic societies as something that also included acts like hostages and marriages. He described the 'Germans' as loosely organized tribal communities that 'communicated' through gifts. The alliances were based on pledges and hostages, as well as celebrations and gifts that were as generous as possible.[99] Even though Mauss did not relate these actions to peace processes, as I do, he still attributed to them a symbolic value within social systems. The symbolic value was contextual; the giving of gifts, which could include enormous sums (i.e. the Danegeld), must at that time be submitted in such a way that it marked generosity in return for promise (not to return, not to plunder, etc.). Even ritual acts such as baptism and confirmation became means that a Christian ruler could use to symbolically demonstrate his supremacy before the great men/nobility, the ecclesiastical power, or the assembled commonality.

The source material suggests that a heathen ruler could understand the demonstrations. Such a demonstration can be seen in the peace meeting in 911 between Rollo, identified as the Norwegian Gaange Rolf (ON *Gengu-Hrólfr*), and the French King Charles the Simple (Fr. *Charles le Simple*) at the agreed site of St Clair, Normandy.[100] The armies stood on each side of the river Epte. According to the historian and dean Dudo of Saint-Quentin (d. 1043), Rollo sent an archbishop with the message of the lands he wanted. After several bids, the king finally promised that Rollo would get Brittany beyond the land area he already had. The king passed this information to Rollo by sending Duke Robert and Bishop Franco as envoys. Rollo then followed them to Charles, a hostage was given for his safety, and oaths for safe conduct were sworn. At the request of the Franks, Rollo put his hands on Charles's knee, something Rollo did not do for anyone else earlier, including his father, according to Dudo. The king gave his daughter Gisla as wife to Rollo and the land from Epte to the sea as agreed upon. But Rollo did not accept another humiliating act: to kneel down and kiss the king's foot. In Rollo's place, one of his men went forward and took the king's foot to his mouth, leaving Charles fallen on his back to the amusement of the surroundings. This is a dubious story because Dudo lived several decades after these events and had to rely on second-hand information. William of Jumièges (Fr. *Guillaume de Jumièges*, d. 1070), a follower of Dudo, does not mention the episode with the foot.[101]

Because the cases mentioned in this part mainly occurred between Christians, or between Christian and heathen rulers, it is tempting to understand the cases as what we refer to as 'religious' in a Christian sense. Still, the perception of what was symbolically valuable may have differed from case to case; the 'heathens' interpreted the situation in a different way than the Christian writers did. Obviously, there were room for spontaneous, demonstrative expressions of power or other expressions that might be perceived as more important to the actors. The historian Gerd Althoff points out that the 'non-verbal' actions were part of such demonstrations and they also meant to demonstrate peaceful intentions.[102] Additionally, the actions followed so closely that the dividing line between the sacred and the profane became fluid; it is therefore possible to describe them generally as ritual acts.

The ritual acts were thus a part of the situation of realpolitik, something that can be seen in the cases listed above. To speak with Bell, the ritual acts became something that both sides constructed from their perspective.[103] The conflicting parties went stronger from the ceremony but could use it differently to later gain political benefits. In this way not only were societies changed through the ritual acts, but the future relationships between individuals and societies were also affected. The way the hostage was treated may also be associated with important symbolic mechanisms. These issues will be addressed later in this book.

Concluding remarks

In this part various examples of confrontations involving hostages are given. The areas of confrontation that is described occurred in present England, France, and Denmark. The examples are compared to the model presented in Part I.

The Dane law was ruled by factions of leaders and competitive groupings with different interests. The giving of gifts, trade, peace treaties, and the use of hostages were all used to affect the out come of peace processes and thus the building of alliances. A special function of the use of hostages, in this case, was its availability as a personal security on request. Ceolwulf was given the rule of Mercia. In exchange he made sure that a hostage was always available to the Danes. According to the agreement he was also ready to support the Danes with forces on request.

The use of hostages could also be symbolical. The kings Sweyn Forkbeard from Denmark and Olaf Tryggvason from Norway were to receive the Danegeld from the king of Wessex in 994. Hostages were exchanged and other rituals were perfomed when Olaf arrived to Andover. Olaf was ritually led to the king by the bishop and was confirmed. Thus, rituals, or ceremonies, like these – that occurred in the Anglo-Danish area of confrontations – contained ritual acts like the use of hostages, oath-takings, baptism, and gift-givings. Both Olaf and the English ruler could symbolically benefit from these rituals. There are similarties in the alliance between Harald Klak and Louis the Pious in the Frankish-Danish area of confrontations. As a part of the ceremonies, Louis personally dressed Harald during his baptism. This was a ritual act that was specifically important to the Franks. Rituals like those could be perceived as part of a realpolitik in which Scandinavian rulers searched for support from continental rulers without caring so much about the old traditions of their home lands. It was more attractive to have the continental rulers as models.

In 1064, the Norwegian king Harald Hardrada and the Danish king Sweyn II Estridsson met for peace negotiations at the river Göta älv. In a poem by Halli stírði, the negotiations are reported: It was decided about the hostages and how the boundaries would be drawn. In this case the use of hostages was linked to the establishment of the borders. During the negotiations, the householders were able to speak their minds about the outcome of the negotiations, and they were able to restrain the rulers from further hostilities. This was an important part of the negotiations: the representatives of the peoples had the ability to affect the outcome of the peace. As a comparsion, this is not evident from the story about the negotiations between Olaf Haraldsson and the heathen chieftain Dale-Gudbrand as reported by Snorri in *Heimskringla*. Because the story is about Saint Olaf, it focus on themes such as the *Rex Justus*-ideal and the conversion of the heathens rather than rituals that surround the negotiaitons. In the story, Dale-Gudbrand dares to send his son as a hostage during the negotiations, which could be interpreted as a token of trust and thus something that is subordinated to the main theme, the conversion of the heathens, but nonetheless important in the reality.

It is thus in these contexts that the giving and taking of hostages must be understood as a ritual act about symbolic demonstrations of power. However, the purpose of a hostage as a symbolic show (or demonstration) may have varied. The role of the hostage did not end with the peace negotiations themselves. On the contrary, it may have played a symbolic role in embellishing the triumph of the victor, who was exposed many times in different ways, not least in the hall where the status of the ruler was constantly confirmed by skalds and various festivals that included many ritual acts.

Notes to Part III

1. *The Medieval Life of King Alfred the Great* (ed. Smyth): 22 (Ch. 47).

2. This giving of hostages is not mentioned in the MS A (see *The Anglo-Saxon Chronicle* MS A [(ed.) Bately]: 50 [year 876]).

3. A white bandage – or a hair tie – was knot around the head of the one who was going to be baptized. Before that, he or she was greased with oil. The bandage was removed a week later.

4. *The Anglo-Saxon Chronicle* MS E ([ed.] Irvine): 48 ff. (year 865–878); *The Anglo-Saxon Chronicle* MS F ([ed.] Baker): 66 ff. (year 865–878).

5. As, for example, the division of the Great Heathen Army in 871.

6. The Danegeld was raised in 991. In France, however, the tradition occurred even earlier (the ninth century). The Danegeld may be similar to a tax system, which means that there was also some kind of

counterperformance service in return, for example military protection (Larsson 2008: 71).

7. Cf. the years 867–877 in the timeline.

8. See the introduction.

9. The Welsh monk Asser (see Asser, *The Medieval Life of King Alfred the Great* [(ed.)] Smyth]: 22 [Ch. 46]) have another explanation of the hostage taking by the Danes:

After he had been expelled, the Pagans subjected the whole kingdom of the Mercians to their rule. But they entrusted not it to the agreed custody of a certain foolish thegn, whose name was Ceolwulf, on the deplorable condition that if they wished to have it again at any time, he should give it peaceably to them. He gave hostages to them under this provision and he swore that in no way would he go against their will but that he would be obedient to them in all things.

(Transl. Alfred P. Smyth)

10. Cf. Kosto 2012.

11. See Part I.

12. See Part VI.

13. See Part I.

14. Hill 2001: 173 ff., 182.

15. Lavelle 2006: 280.

16. Lavelle 2006: 280.

17. Lavelle 2006: 280.

18. See Part IV. The promise is repeated in several chronicles.

19. Cf. Lavelle 2006: 280 f.

20. See Parts I, IV.

21. See Part I. Cf. step two of the model.

22. It is quite possible that the meeting took place in some hall or fortification in Wareham, but we can only speculate about the location. However, it is impossible to imagine that the Danes would have

performed at something similar to the cultic building of a *hof* in Wareham, where the ring would have been kept and oaths would have been sworn as described in the *Eyrbyggja saga*. See Sundqvist 2007: 175 ff. and Olsson 2012: 68 ff. for evidence and a discussion about rings and oaths.

23. Regarding morality and ethics associated with hostages, see Part IV

24. Asser, *The Medieval Life of King Alfred the Great* ([ed.] Smyth): 23 (Ch. 49).

25. See Parts I, III, IV in this volume.

26. Cf. Ginzburg's (1989) remarks.

27. Lavelle 2006: 280.

28. See Part I.

29. Lavelle 2007: 75.

30. Lavelle 2007: 73.

31. Lavelle 2007: 73.

32. According to David Hill (2001: 181), the hunting lodges of the kings of Wessex also occupied the border areas between Wessex, Wales, and Cornwall. One reason may have been that these areas were not settled due to raids and plundering. The wastelands were therefore suitable as hunting areas. Cf. the theoretical discussion in Part I.

33. Haywood 1995: 111 f.

34. See Part IV where I discuss the sum 16,000.

35. *Anglo-Saxon Chronicle* MS F ([ed.] Baker): 89 (year 994).

36. *Anglo-Saxon Chronicle* MS F ([ed.] Baker): 89 (year 994).

37. *Anglo-Saxon Chronicle* 7 MS E ([ed.] Irvine): 61 f. (year 994).

38. *Heimskringla* III ([ed.] Bjarni Aðalbjarnarson): 247 (Ch. 28).

39. *Hirdskraa* ([ed.] Imsen): 82 (text), 83 (transl.) (Ch. 11).

40. Lynch 1986: 165, 168.

41. Cf. Lavelle 2006: 285.

42. Lynch 1998: 225.

43. Haywood 1995: 113.

44. See Sundqvist (2002: 324) on the continuity of oaths into Christian times in Scandinavia.

45. Lynch 1986: 180.

46. Lavelle 2006: 289.

47. Lavelle 2006: 295.

48. Cf. Parts I, IV.

49. Cf. Larsson M. G. 2008: 55.

50. Den frankiske Rigsannaler, *Vikingerne i Franken* ([ed. and transl.] Albrechtsen): 11–24 (years 777–826).

51. The tribal federation of the Veleti had its settlements east of the Obotrites and was from the late ninth century named as the Lutici. They were divided into different tribes: the Kessinians of Lower Warnow, the Zirzipanians (alt. Circipanians) between the Recknitz, Trebel, and Peene rivers, the Tollensians to the east and south of Peene, and the Tollense and the Redarians to the south and east of Tollensee and Upper Havel (*Die Slawen in Deutschland* [(ed.) Herrmann]: 8).

52. Compare the discussion about mobile cult places in the introduction.

53. Through the construction of a trading venue there, it was possible to impose duties and other means of taxing goods. The control of land areas based on the fortifications meant that there was an opportunity to demand land interest rates, or similar taxation systems or similar forms of taxation, although such systems were characteristic of the late Viking era and the early Middle Ages. However, some form of primitive taxation system was used (see Part IV on taxation systems).

54. Ermoldus Nigellus, In Honor of Louis, *Charlemagne and Louis the Pious* ([ed.] Noble): 176 ff. (Book 4).

55. Lynch 1986: 175 f.

56. Ermoldus Nigellus, In Honor of Louis, *Charlemagne and Louis the Pious* ([ed.] Noble): 178 ff. (Book 4). This ceremony is reported by

Rimbert too in *Vita Ansgarii*. (*Boken om Ansgar* [(ed.) Hallencreutz]: 22 [Ch. 6]).

57. Lynch 1986: 176.

58. B. & P. Sawyer 1993: 52.

59. Lynch 1986: 176.

60. Den frankiske Rigsannaler, *Vikingerne i Franken* ([ed.] Albrechtsen): 24 (year 826).

61. Den frankiske Rigsannaler, *Vikingerne i Franken* ([ed.] Albrechtsen): 25 (year 828).

62. See Parts I, IV.

63. Boken om Ansgar ([ed.] Hallencreutz): 22 (Ch. 6).

64. Bell 1997: 133 ff.

65. Haralds saga Sigurðarsonar, *Heimskringla* III ([ed.] Bjarni Aðalbjarnarson): 159 (text) (Ch. 71).

66. The History of Harald Hardrade, *Heimskringla, Or the Lives of The Norse Kings* ([ed.] Monsen & Smith): 550 (transl.) (Ch. 71).

67. Haralds saga Sigurðarsonar, *Heimskringla* III ([ed.] Bjarni Aðalbjarnarson): 159 (Ch. 71).

68. Haralds saga Sigurðarsonar, *Heimskringla* III ([ed.] Bjarni Aðalbjarnarson): 160 (text) (Ch. 71).

69. van Gennep 1977: 10 ff.; Turner 1969: 94–130.

70. Haralds saga Sigurðarsonar, *Heimskringla* III ([ed.] Bjarni Aðalbjarnarson): 160 f. (text) (Ch. 71).

71. The History of Harald Hardrade, *Heimskringla, Or the Lives of The Norse Kings* (ed. Monsen & Smith): 551 (transl.) (Ch. 71).

72. There is another example of opposition from great men and the assembly present at the thing. At the thing of Uppsala, Torgny lawmen spoke against king Olof Skötkonung and even threatened him (*Óláfs saga helga, Heimskringla* II [(ed.) Bjarni Aðlarbjarnarson]: 114 ff. [Ch. 80]). Even though there were different political conditions in the Swedish, Danish, and Norwegian realms, this type of

opposition still seems to have been a prerequisite for the function of the things, otherwise they would not have been needed.

73. Haralds saga Sigurðarsonar, *Heimskringla* III ([ed.] Bjarni Aðalbjarnarson): 160 (text) (Ch. 71).

74. Haralds saga Sigurðarsonar, *Heimskringla* III ([ed.] Bjarni Aðalbjarnarson): 161 (text) (Ch. 71).

75. The History of Harald Hardrade, *Heimskringla, Or the Lives of The Norse Kings* ([ed.] Monsen & Smith): 551 (transl.) (Ch. 71).

76. Haralds saga Sigurðarsonar, *Heimskringla* III ([ed.] Bjarni Aðalbjarnarson): 161 f. (text) (Ch. 71).

77. The History of Harald Hardrade, *Heimskringla, Or the Lives of The Norse Kings* ([ed.] Monsen & Smith): 551 (transl.) (Ch. 71).

78. Kap. 112

[—] Ok um morguninn létu þeir blása til þings ok sǫgðu þeim þótti þat ráð, at eiga þing við þann mann, er norðan fór með ný boðorð, ok vita með hverjum sannendum hann ferr. Síðan mælti Guðbrandr við son sinn: "Þú skalt nú fara á fund konungs þess, er þér gaf grið, ok xii. menn með þer" –ok svá var gǫrt. Ok þeir kómu á fund konungs ok segja honum sitt Ørendi, at boendr vildu hafa þing við hann ok setja grið í mílli konungs ok bónda. Konungr lét sér þat vel þokkask, ok bundu þat við hann einkamálum sín í milli, meðan sú stefna væri; ok fóru þeir aptr við svá búit ok segja Guðbrandi ok Þórði, at grið varu sett. Konungr fór þá til boejar þess, er Liðsstaðir heita, ok var þar v. nætr. þá fór konungr á fund búanda ok atti þing við þá; en væta var á mikil um daginn. Síðan er þingit var sett, þá stóð konungr up ok segir at Læsir ok á Lóm, á Vága haft tekit við kristni ok brotit niðr blóthús sín –"ok trúa nú á sannan guð, er skóp himin ok jǫrð ok alla hluti veit". Síðan sezk konungr niðr, en Guðbrandr svarar: "eigi vitum vér, um hvern þú roeðir; kallar þú þann guð, er hvern má sjá, ok er þú sér eigi ok engi annara, er vér eigum þann guð, er hvern dag má sjá, ok er því eigi úti í dag, at veðr er vátt; ok mun yðr hann ógurligr sýnask ok mikill fyrir sér, vænti ek, at yðr skjóti skelk í bringu, ef hann kømr á þingit. En með því at þú segir, at guð yðarr má svá mikit, þá láttu hann nú svá gera, at veðr sé skýjat í morgin, en regn ekki, ok finnumk hér þá". Síðan fór konungr heim til herbergis, ok fór með honum sonr Guðbrandz í gísling, en konungr fekk þeim annan mann í móti. Um kveldit þá spyrr konungr son Guðbrandz, hvernug goð þeira væri gǫrt. Hann segir han var merkðr eptir Þór – "ok hefir han hamar í hendi, ok mikill vexti ok holr innan, ok gǫrr undir honum sem hjallr sé, ok stendr han þar á ofan, er hann er úti; eigi skortir hann gull ok silfr á sér; iiii. hleifarbrauðs eru honum foerðir hvern dag ok þar víð slátr". Síðan fóru þeir í rekkjur, en konungr vakði þá nótt ok var á boenum sínum. En er dagr var, fór konungr til messu ok síðan til matar ok þá til þings; en veðrinu var svá farit, sem Guðbrandr hafði fyrir mælt. Óláfs saga Helga, *Heimskringla* II ([ed.] Bjarni Aðalbjarnson): 186 f. (Ch. 112).

79. The History of St. Olav, *Heimskringla, Or the Lives of The Norse Kings* ([ed.] Monsen & Smith): 331 (transl.) (Ch. 112).

80. By 'householder' I here refer to the OSw *bondi*, ON *bóndi*, which also could be interpreted as 'farmer'. The ON *bóndi* is from the present participle of *búa* ('to reside').

81. *Olav den heliges saga, Nordiska kungasagor* II ([ed.] Johansson): 156 f. (Ch. 112).

82. Steinsland 2000: 119.

83. See Steinsland 2000: 119.

84. Bull 1917: 158 ff.; Engen 2010: 31.

85. T. M. Andersson 1988: 265.

86. Steinsland 2000: 118.

87. Steinsland 2000: 119.

88. Steinsland 2000: 121, 123, 127 ff.

89. Steinsland 2000: 90.

90. Steinsland 2000: 90 f.

91. According to the local historian Arnfinn Engen (2010: 31), the thing place was probably situated nearby the farm of Hundtorp. After the Christianization, the thing was moved to the mountainside above Hundtorp.

92. T. M. Andersson 1988: 83.

93. Steinsland 2000: 126.
94. Steinsland 2000: 123.
95. See the discussion in Steinsland 2000: 104.
96. *Íslensk orðabók* 1992: 167.
97. *Óláfs saga helga, Heimskringla* II ([ed.] Bjarni Aðalbjarnason): 157 (Ch. 94).
98. See Sundqvist 2002: 204 ff.
99. Mauss 2002: 77.
100. *Normandiets historie under de første Hertuger* ([ed.] Albrechtsen): 62 ff. (Ch. 28–29).
101. *De normanniske hertugers bedrifter, To normanniske krøniker* ([ed.] Albrechtsen): 35 f. (Ch. 11).
102. Althoff 2004: 136 f.
103. See Part 1.

Part IV: Legal Rights

It has previously been mentioned how hostages as rituals during peace processes – which in the sources may be described with an ambivalence, or ambiguity – and how people could be used as social capital in different conflicts. It is therefore important to understand how the persons who became hostages were vauled and how their new collective – the new household – responded to its new members and what was crucial for his or her status and participation in the new setting. All this may be related to the legal rights and special privileges, such as the right to wear coat of arms, weapons, or other status symbols. Personal rights could be regulated by agreements: oral, written, or even implied. Rights could also be related to the nature of the agreement itself, what kind of peace process the hostage occurred in and the type of hostage. But being a hostage also meant that a person was subjected to restrictions on freedom and mobility. What did such situations meant for the hostage-taking party? What were their privileges and obligations? To answer these questions, a point of departure will be Kosto's definition of hostages in continental and Mediterranean cultures around during the period 400–1400, when hostages were a form of security for the behaviour of other people.

Hostages and law

The hostage had its special role in legal contexts that could be related to the discussion in the introduction of the relationship between religion and law. The views on this subject are divided

---

How to cite this book chapter:
Olsson, S. 2019. Legal Rights. In: Olsson, S. *The Hostages of Northmen: From the Viking Age to the Middle Ages*. Pp. 125–224. Stockholm: Stockholm University Press. DOI: https://doi.org/10.16993/bba.d License: CC-BY.

among scholars. Sundqvist shows in an article on morality how the concept of *siðr*, 'custom', 'tradition', 'morality', or 'religion', could characterize traditional legislation. On the other hand, the Germanist Klaus von See argued that religion and justice were as different entities in the Old Scandinavian society.[1] As evidence, von See referred to a few procedural texts in which the concepts *lǫg* (law) and *siðr* appear distinctly separated from each other, as in the *Íslendingabók*: *hǫfum allir ein lǫg ok einn sið* ('one is to keep one law and one religion/ritual/custom'). According to Sundqvist, there are texts that contradict this, such as the Norweigian Frostathing law (I, 3): *Enn um siðsemi á Frostoþingi* ('and through a custom at the Frostating'). In *Egil's saga*, 'law' and *siðr* appear as equivalent concepts during a negotiation at the Gulating (ON *Gulaþing*).[2]

Hostages could also be linked to laws and thus indirectly to *siðr*. The link between hostages and laws can be relevant for the understanding of the hostage as a ritual tradition. Written agreements are – although they are not laws – legally binding and can therefore function as an instrument of power.

The only preserved written agreement from the Viking Age that includes Scandinavians and an agrement on hostages is the settlement between Guthrum and Æthelred. However, oral agreements would have been binding because several peace negotiations between Scandinavians and Anglo-Saxons involved hostages according to the *Anglo-Saxon Chronicle*, as previously mentioned. Even if these 'oral agreements' do not mention the exact role of the hostage, we can assume that they implicitly stipulated that the hostage should be respected.

In Norwegian and Swedish medieval legislation, hostages are mentioned in different contexts. These texts are remnants of old traditions, which we can refer to as *siðr*. The hostage cannot be directly linked to this concept in the texts, but words of hostage appear in formal expressions and in ceremonial contexts, that is, in traditional contexts.

Selection of hostages

In peace processes, a particular selection of hostages occurred. After a conflict, both sides tried to manoeuvre from an advantageous position when it came to determining who would be hostages in both unilateral and bilateral peace agreements. The selection was due to what degree one side was subjected to the other, but at the same time it could be a game in which the opposing party tried to get as good hostage as possible, preferably a person with special qualities. Different variants of hostage givings may have given room for some maneuvering regarding the selection. This game is imprinted in myths and stories as well as in a cultic behaviour. Who then were the hostages and why were they selected? In order for a hostage to act as security for both party and it must have had a definite social value. The person who would be hostage must have been in some kind of close relationship with the person, or persons, whom he or she was a guarantee of. Generally in Continental Germanic societies, children (mainly sons), parents and relatives were the ones preferred. Persons who were not relatives but who appeared within the framework of 'friendship' could also be hostages.[3] In the continental forms of hostages, Kosto explains: to serve as hostage was 'almost a standard element in the curriculum vitae of a medieval prince'.[4]

There are many similarities with being a hostage and a foster child, but there are also some differences. Basically, to be a hostage meant that you were given as a security for other persons during, before, or after negotiations, as has been discussed earlier in this book. The fosterage, on the other hand, was not the result of a conflict but a formal agreement between families or groupings, i.e. a social bond. In the Icelandic law *Grágás*, the rights of the foster child is described: The fosterage period was between the ages of eight and sixteen. The fosterfather received a so called *fóstrlaun*, a compensation, for the costs of fostering the child. It was the right of the father to bring a child back home if the child was being mistreated, and then the provision would return the child. This was also the case if the child was sent home by the foster parents. But if the father took away the child without cause, then the provision would remain at the foster home. The heirs of the foster parents had the right to take over the tutelage and the compensation.[5] This was the difference between being a hostage and a fosterchild: In the former case the time of the hostageship could last could last for a lifetime, while a period as foster child lasted for eight years. The return of the hostage was a decision by the hostage giver, which was also due to altering political conditions such as the outcome of a war. A hostage could not be released for money unless they became prisoners of war. The biological father of a foster child still had the opportunity to retribute his children when he wished to do so.

The fostering will be further discussed in this part of the book. We will now turn to the role of the female hostages.

Women hostages

Could women become hostages during the Viking Age? In the time of Ancient Rome, Germanic peoples took female hostages according to Tacitus (see further below). Kosto considers that information uncertain. He points out: that are only 'a handful of' sources from antiquity, their source value can be questioned, and there are even fewer from the 8th to the 10th century, but from about 1200, female hostages became routine. They were, however, disconnected from their families. Instead, Kosto claims that they were handed out as wives.[6]

The procedure with women given as wives is precisely described in the *Annales Alamannici*: Conrad I of Germany and Erchanger, Duke of Swabia, established peace. In 913 Conrad was married to Erchanger's sister, Cunigunde, who is described in the annals as a 'peace hostage' (*tamquam obsidem pacis*).[7]

Tacitus depicts, in Histories (*Historiae*), negotiations between the Romans and romanized Ubians in the colony of Agrippina (Cologne) and the Romans during the Batavian rebellion (69–70 AD). The revolution leaders Civilis and Classicus had given some of their relatives as hostages of the the Agrippinenses in the colony including Civilis's wife and a daughter of Classicus.[8] The wife of Civilis was hardly a possible potential wife for the hostage takers or their nearest circle, though she had an important symbolic function as a wife of Civilis. By contrast, Classicus's daughter could have been used in a marriage arrangement. However, in order for a marriage to be concluded, one must first reach a standstill. The example may possibly indicate different motives for taking a woman as hostage.

Another case may be the bishop of Lyon, Eucherius (d. 449), who depicted the siege of the Visigoths on the Gallo-Roman city of Bazas (or Civitas Vasatica) in Aquitaine in 414. The Roman poet Paulinus of Pella became hostage of the ruler of the Visigoths, Athaulf. In return, the Romans recieved an Alanian 'queen' and a 'prince'.⁹ Here, as in the case of the wife of Civilis, it was a question of a married woman because she is called 'queen'. Thus, these cases represent two exceptions to the general rule that there were unmarried women who acted as hostages. There may also be examples of forced labor in connection with war and robbery. In the epic poem *Beowulf*, the modifier *Weolh-*, in Weolhþeow's name, could mean 'celtic', 'foreign', or 'slave' and the head *-þeos* could have the meaning of 'slave', 'servant', or possibly 'prisoner'.¹⁰

According to the chronicle *Annales Vedastini* from the Abbey of St. Vaast in Arras, a 'Norman king', Godefrid (*Godefridus*), attacked Emperor Charles the Fat in 882. Charles would have given Friesland to Godefrid and married him to Gisela (or Gisla), King Lothar's daughter, for the promise that the Normans would leave the kingdom. Gisela's function was like a hostage because the marriage was a guarantee that Godefrid would not attack again.¹¹

The question is then how to interpret the sparse evidence that describes women as hostages between 500 and 1000. Kosto points out that from the 11th century, 'women, and most often daughters, regularly served as hostages per se'; before that, daughters were given as wives rather than hostages.¹² Kershaw, on the other hand, mentions that 'with few exceptions [the women] were all adults, aristocratic but left to the dominant party'.¹³ Kosto claims to have found only seven cases of female hostages during the period 400–900 AD.¹⁴

Rather than going into the details of Kosto's and Kershaw's arguments, I should like to problematize the image of the woman's position before the new collective. For example, how should one interpret this statement in the *Þiðreks saga*: 'She was often put as hostage' (*Hon war tit sat till gisl*)?¹⁵ Does it suggest that the person in question was used as a hostage, also when married, and still had a certain social value? The *Þiðreks saga* can be rejected as unreliable as it is a late source (fixed in writing in the 13th century), but such data on sources are generally often uncertain. With this example I simply want to emphasize that women may have had changing status and, depending on culturual values, could have been valued differently in connection with marriage alliances.

The fact that women could be politically important during 'The Dark Ages' (The Migration Period of c. 400 to 800 AD) can be illustrated by an example involving Theodoric the Great. After a feud with the Kingdom of Thuringia, Theodoric married his niece Amalaberga to the ruler Hermanfrid (532). Amalaberga brought a letter of introduction to her husband-to-be, which described her skills; she was assumed to have skills that were important in her future marriage.[16]

In general in the Old Scandinavian society, women were regarded as representatives of the household (cf. *husfrú*). Although it is uncertain whether they participated in war actions, they may have had certain roles in the context of peace and warfare. These functions made them – based on Kosto's statement that they were given as wives – interesting as actors regarding in peace processes. At the same time, the sources – both continental and Old Norse – leave no room for any far-reaching conclusions as to whether women became hostages. We will return to the cultural and social roles of women in war and peace later.

The game of hostages

In a few ancient and medieval stories, the value of the hostage is indicated by the will to maintain it. Perhaps, therefore, a tactical game was displayed to keep important persons. This can be seen in the story of the birth of the Roman festival *Nonae Caprotinae* (7 July). According to *Bíoi Parállēloi*, 'parallel biographies', by Plutarch, the Romans were threatened by the Latin under the command of Livius Postumius.[17]

The commander Livius deployed his troops not far from Rome, sending a hero with the message that the Latins wanted to renew their friendship with the Romans through marriage alliances. The Romans were invited to send many maidens, or widows, in exchange for friendship and peace as they had done before with the Sabins. The Romans hesitated regarding what to do: either handing over their women – which they thought were the same as sending them to captivity – or go to war. A maid (*ancilla*) called Tutula, or Philotis, advised them to use a stratagem. She and other maids dressed up to resemble the free-born Roman women and were sent to the Latins. At night they would light a signal fire for the Romans, who would sneak into the camp. This was done; a fig tree was ignited, and the Romans could surprise their enemies. In memory of this event, the festival *Capratine* ('Figs') was celebrated, during which maidens went into Rome in a procession, while joking with people, performed a ritual battle, and feasted in the shadow of figs. Plutarch, however, is careful to point out that this is a legend and that the festival could also have been celebrated in memory of Romulus's passing.[18]

According to the myth about the war between the Æsir and the Vanir, the Æsir obviously used a stratagem to fool the Vanir in the exchange of hostage, which may have involved to ursurp the powers of the goddess Freyja. Implicitly in this myth, there was the will to keep deities with a special symbolic capital.

The game about the selection of hostages – where it was important for the hostage giver to keep and for the taker to get a person of as high a value as possible – can be compared with a gift-giving institutional custom described by the anthropologist Annette Weiner, who was inspired by Mauss. Weiner formulated through the paradox 'Keeping-While-Giving' the idea that some items were too valuable to be transferred to others.[19] At the same time, it is important to point out differences between cultures. Lavelle claims that it was voluntary to enter as a hostage in the Anglo-Saxon society, even if the other side could influence or dictate the peace agreement.[20] There are indications of similar approaches to agreements and peace processes in areas of confrontation involving Scandinavians. For example, at the siege of Apuolė in Courland 854 (see further below), there was a willingness among some citizens to volunteer as hostages to the Swedes even though the degree of 'volunteering' can be discussed.

As the hostage owner did not have full control of the identity of the hostage, the knowledge of who was appointed must have been essential. This reasoning will further be developed below and in the next parts.

Hostages in different peace processes must have had a certain social value, a social capital. Otherwise they would not have been used. Perhaps the value of hostages may have been reflected in what we today refer to as their 'legal capacity' if they were attending the negotiations. The legal historian Gabriele von Olberg claims that the hostage itself had a 'legal capacity' because it could serve as witness. As a source, she uses a paragraph from the Lombard law, *Edictus Rothari*: *gisil id est testis*, 'hostage, that is the witness'.[21] An example from another time period may confirm this. In 414, during the siege of Bazas (or Civitas Vasatica) in Aquitania, the Roman poet Paulinus of Pella went as a negotiator to the ruler Athaulf of the Visigoths and ended as a hostage.[22] In the Old Irish *The Airgíalla Charter Poem* (written in the seventh century), it is described without ambiguity that persons who would be hostages witnessed and swore oaths during a peace treaty (see the *The Airgíalla Charter Poem*, part V). Naturally this was due to the conditions in Gaelic Ireland. Implicitly, one can assume that the hostage generally witnessed peace treaties. However, I have not found any evidence in peace talks that included Scandinavians and where the hostage was actively able to influence the negotiations except for 16th century Sweden (see the final part).

Kosto believes that the status of the Continental Germanic hostage was reflected in how the hostage was treated – or could be expected to be treated – because they came from well-off homes:

> Because of the nature of the sources, particularly for earlier periods, most of the hostages we know about were either noble or wealthy enough to merit (or negotiate) good treatment. Furthermore, many hostages of lower status were handed over pursuant to agreements negotiated by powerful people and thus the conditions of their confinement reflected their patron's influence. When hostages are treated well, in other words, it is as likely to be because of who they were as because of their status as hostages.[23]

In addition, it may be added that the persons who decided who would be hostages – and handed them over – could play a decisive role as much as the ones who received them. Whoever gave hostages may have relied on the nature of the agreement, the degree of dependence to the victorious side, and how the bonds of 'friendship' were expressed. The giver and the recipient of the hostage were responsible for the delivery according to the 'regulations', and they must have been percieved to have 'legal capacity' and to be authorized to take part in the negotiation and drafting of the peace agreement.

Naturally, the decision could lie with the one who exercised the greatest influence over the peace process, the winning side. This is given in the case of the Roman Empire, which could affect hostages through various agreements. But such a power-making ruling may have been less evident in other and later cultures, such as the Continental Germanic, at least if there were settlements between fairly equal parties. Even in the Roman Empire it was complicated to decide on peace and hostages because these judgments were partly ritualistic in their character. The Romans used different types of war treaties. The treaty *foedus deditio* meant that a defeated country submitted to the Romans without reservation. The war treaty, *foedus aequum*, was used when Rome negotiated with a country whose sovereignty they could, or would, not restrict, i.e., fairly equal nations such as Carthage before the final defeat or Parthia. The *foedus iniquum* meant that the new partner was obliged to respect Rome's sovereignty. Hostages were used as security in all treaties.[24] During the negotiations a group of cult specialists were present: the fetials (*fetiales*).[25] The fetials accompanied the hostages when they were delivered. These specialists appear to have had influence over both the declaration of war and the taking of hostages. Before peace processes, Roman commanders were obliged to relate to activities and decisions of the fetials, especially during the times of the Kingdom and the Republic. During the Empire, their influence seems to have diminished. Such cult specialists are found neither in Continental Germanic nor in pre-Scandinavian traditions.

In Old English sources it is mentioned how ealdormen and bishops are mentioned regarding the surrender of hostages.[26] These officers were members of the king's counsel and could influence the election of the king. Similar functions can be attributed to the lawmen and bishops mentioned in the *Elder Westrogothic Law*. These were also able to influence the outcome of the royal election.

In the Swedish realm, a lawman appointed the hostage to be taken to the border between Östergötland and Västergötland during the king's journey in the 13th century, the Eriksgata (see the final part).[27]

These latter cases with clergys and lawmen refer to Old English and medieval Scandinavian contexts, but, as with the Roman cult specialists, they routinely discussed peace processes and thus how to use the hostage.[28] Another common factor during the early Middle Ages was that the ecclesiastical power was able to express its views on peaces. Hence, various rulers had to relate to people with both worldly and spiritual office when they made decisions.

Generally, in the context of peace processes, other persons or groupings, for example in a parliamentary assembly, as in the case of the peace meeting between Harald Hardrada and Sweyn Estridsson at at Göta älv (River of the Geats), could influence the outcome (see further below). All these groupings – great men or nobility, men belonging to the worldly or the ecclesiastical spheres – could directly or indirectly influence decisions including the appointment of hostages.

According to *Annales Bertianni*, some 'pirates' attacked parts of Friesland in 839 and caused major damages to the border areas, including the Danish parts of Friesland. The Danish ruler Horic then sent an embassy to the Frankish emperor Louis the Pious.[29] He also sent his nephew (*nepos*) and gifts. One of the messengers was a man whose advice Horic seem to have paid attention to more than anyone else. With this embassy, Horic would consolidate the peace and the alliance, which was maintained between his lands and the Frankish empire.[30] The episode in *Annales Bertianni* contains no explicit information regarding whether Horic's nephew would be a hostage to secure peace, even if this was the case. The role assigned to Horic's adviser is more relevant. The messenger seems to have been the one authorised to negotiate and was responsible for the delivery of the gifts. Hypothetically, he could also have been the one who surrendered the hostage.

The sources are often written from clear perspectives. The medieval writers chose – possibly based on their own interests – sometimes to focus on rulers, sometimes on others. Next, such a hostage case will be discussed.

The peace between Magnus the Good and Harthacnut

A peace agreement between the Norwegian king Magnus the Good (*Magnús góði*) and the Danish ruler Canute III Hathacnut (ON Harðacnut or Hǫrða-Knútr) in about 1036 is mentioned in *Ágrip*:[31]

> However, in Denmark Sveinn had died and so had his father Knútr in England, and Denmark was then ruled by Sveinn's brother, who was called Hǫrða-Knútr, and he led an army against Magnús and they met at Brenneyjar. Wise men acted as intermediaries and an agreement was proposed and made in such a way that since Hǫrða-Knútr thought he had rightful claim to Norway because his father had won it and his brother had ruled it – and Magnús thought too that his father had suffered great wrong at the hands of Knútr, betrayal, exile, death – this agreement was reached: the one who lived the longer was to rule both countries, but each would rule his own kingdom while both lived. Then hostages were exchanged. Knútr died first, and Magnús then took Denmark without opposition, because the sons of the most important men were held hostage.[32]
>
> (Transl. Matthew J. Driscoll)

The background was that Magnus – who was the son of Olaf II Haraldsson and born out of marriage – had been raised in Novgorod. With the help of Swedish and Norwegian great men, he managed to expel the King of Norway, Svein Knutsson (ON *Sveinn Knútsson*), son of Canute the Great. Magnus had been coronated King of Norway in 1035. Harthacnut of Denmark, Svein's brother, then tried to take the Norwegian throne, something he considered himself entitled to since his father was King of England, Denmark, and Norway. War and negotiations followed.[33]

As mentioned, the two kings meet at the islands called Brenneyjar, in the archipelago of presentday Gothenburg, for negotiations. They concluded a treaty with the agreement that if one outlived the other, he should take over his kingdom. The treaty is referred to in both Norwegian and Danish texts, but historians consider them to have a low historical source value. The historian Claus Krag comments on this in Aschehoug's *History of Norway*:

Both the later sagas and Danish chronicles explain what happened when Magnus and Harthacnut had already entered into an agreement in 1036 that the one who lived the longest would inherit the other. But there are no hints about any such agreement in the contemporary sources, and most historians in recent times have therefore assumed that the agreement has never existed.[34]

Despite the low source value, it may be of interest to look more closely at how the various writers and chroniclers reproduce the event. The chronicles, kings' sagas and annals describing the episode use a terminology that differ between different works and therefore can give different perspectives on the story. Of these sources, *Ágrip*'s version is most relevant because it exemplifies the role that the hostage could have in conflict. It also has a darker view of the actions of the kings than other versions.

I will also tend to the other sources to compare differences and similarities. In that way, it is possible to discern the different views of the different writers. For example, in *Ágrip*'s version, 'wise men' (*vitrir menn*) have an influence over the peace process. In other versions (see below), it is claimed that it was Magnus's and Harthacnut's low age that was the reason why other men who ruled their kingdoms had to deal with the negotiations and arranged settlement and peace, but that is not evident in *Ágrip*. The kings appear as fully capabale players who could lead armies against each other. No willingness to establish peace is noted. Instead, the mediators utilize a stratagem by arranging it so that both kings can retreat without losing face through the deal.

In the quoted paragraph there is no word for peace, for example, *friðr*. Instead there is a word for peaceful settlement, *sætt*. The word *friðr* is ambiguous, and in the Icelandic skaldic language it could mean: (1) 'love', (2) 'friendship', (3) 'peace, peaceful relationship', (4) 'peaceful living', and (5) 'heavenly peace, bliss'. ON *friðr* can also have the double meaning of 'peace' in general or 'peace' in the Christian sense, but it may also refer to 'settlement, truce'. Peace can sometimes be described in texts with the less ambiguous ON *grið*, 'safety for life and limbs, armistice, truce'.[35]

The word *sætt*, 'settlement, agreement', is thus used in the above paragraph to describe the peace. The term indicates that this kind of agreement was so fragile that it had to be secured with hostages. It is not evident from the text what influence the great men had on the actual arrangement with the hostages, because the kings are depicted as competitive warlords, but it is quite possible that it was a part of their scheme.

After the death of Harthacnut, Magnus was able to secure his position as ruler in Denmark, since he possessed the hostages. Reading this paragraph gives room for several interpretations where different wills are set against each other. Obviously, the 'wise men' are a part of this. Men like these were surely made up of bishops and lawmen, because they had knowledge of what could be called 'state affairs', but there were probably other great men, perhaps war chieftains, who served as intermediaries. These events correspond to some of the processes that I described in my model. The rulers were not entirely self-determined when it came to how peace would end. The area of confrontation was here, as well as in some other conflicts between Norwegian and Danish rulers in the 11th century, the outflow of Göta älv where the Brenneyjar formed the area of communication. However, *Ágrip* reproduces events that are 150–200 years back in time and other sources partly contradict this version.

Norweigian and Icelandic sources

In other sources, the tone is softer in terms of the actions of the kings. Indeed, in *Fagrskinna*s version, the encounter is described in almost mythical words: one meets at the river (the river Göta älv) and the aim is to achieve a 'world peace' (*veraldarfrið*), which should last as long as the 'world is in existence' and 'for ever' (*allan aldr*). The agreement also in this version arranged by the 'foremost men' (*enir beztu menn*) from the retinue – the *hird* – of each king. Twelve of the richest men from each kingdom swear to keep the peace as long as they live. This version does not mention any threats from either of the two kings. The treaty between Magnus and Harthacnut is described as brotherly: 'Then King Magnus will have the whole kingdom, and to be heir shall be his right, as his [Harthacnut] born brother' (*þá skal Magnús konungr eiga allt ríki ok vera arftǫkumaðr hans réttr, sem borinn bróðir* *hans*).³⁶ In this version the great men have lesser ability to maneuver in relations to the kings. In this case there is a reference to the (peace) meeting (*stefna*) at the river where the kings had previously made peace (*friðr*). This can be an indication that it was a matter of routines and hence tradition. Here too, the word *sætt* is used to describe the agreement.

In *Heimskringla*'s version of the *Saga of Magnus Góði* (*Uphaf Magnús konungs goða*), decisions seem to be taken by the officials rather than by the kings. Magnus and Harthacnut travel with their fleets (*ledung*s) up to the river (*Elfr*) for a battle. However, learned men (*lender menn*) in each army send messages to their relatives and friends that they will make peace between the kings. Since the kings are too young, their realms are run by great men (*ríkismenn*) who were elected in each country. A conciliation meeting is agreed in the name of both kings. They meet and talk about conciliation (*sáttmál*). It ends with the kings becoming brothers (*brœðralag*); they make a peace agreement and decide about the succession.³⁷

In this version, the kings are united in brotherly love, which could be a topos or literary feature, as well as the fact that both countries are represented as each other's reflection: the great men call upon each other and the succession is established equally. At the same time, other men are credited with the success of the peace work; the two kings are too young to influence the outcome.³⁸ Even according to this version, 12 of the finest (*ágætastir*) men of each kigdom swear to keep the peace.

Morkinskinna's version does not differ essentially from the ones in *Fagrskinna* or *Heimskringla* except for the beginning of the story where householders (or farmers) exercise a significant influence over the peace:³⁹

> When the warfare between the kings had gone on for a time, each succeeded in wreaking much damage on the other. This was a burden on the farmers, and they were eager to improve relations between the kings. The farmers from both realms assembled and consulted wisely and propitiously on behalf of the kings, who were both young men, amenable and willing to be guided by their followers. They arranged a meeting at the River Elfr (Götaälv).⁴⁰
>
> (Transl. Theodore M. Andersson and Kari E. Gade)

Otherwise, *Morkinskinna* follows the other chronicle and saga traditions. Nevertheless, the householders hold their own meeting, which does not appear in the other texts in which 'envoys' are mentioned.

In the Icelandic *Knytlinga saga,* it is only mentioned that Harthacnut takes control of England and Denmark and that Magnus, the son of St. Olaf, controls Norway and is 'brother of oath' with Harthacnut.[41] The author, who may have been the Icelandic skald Ólafr Þórðarson hvítaskáld (d. 1259),[42] refers only to other Norwegian kings' sagas in this case.

The Norwegian chronicle of the kings, *Chronicon Regum Norvegiæ*, written in Latin, is laconic, but contains all the basic elements found in the other versions. Here too, the low age of the kings is mentioned, how nobility worked on both sides to achieve a settlement with peace, and and an agreement on the succession, which was confirmed with an oath endorsed by a grouping of nobility.[43]

To conclude: The details of the peace meeting with related terminology regarding the meeting place and the hostage exchange seem to have been of less interest for the writers than details about the intentions and actions of the kings and the great men. It is probably due to the purpose of the writers to legitimise the kings' power.

The fact that, in some cases, the writers used a terminology that, in earlier times, was associated with peace processes may indicate that the episode in *Morkinskinna* could have had an older story as a frame. The islands of Brenneyjar as well as Göta Älv were meeting and trading places during the Viking Age and the Middle Ages.

Danish sources

Danish sources – mainly chronicles and annals – are generally more laconic. In the 'Annals of Ryd' (*Annales Ryenses*) from 1288, it is mentioned that when Harthacnut learned that Magnus had become king of Norway, he sailed with Danish and English ships to Norway. It is also mentioned that the friends of Harthacnut and Magnus made a standstill (*saanæ*) between them and that they agreed that the one who lived the longest would have both realms.[44]

21, 2 While this happening, Cnut, as deeply upset by the report of Norway's treachery as he was by that of his father's death, began to be worried, for if he turned his efforts to with his neighbours, in the delay caused by his absence he might find himself deprived of England; he therefore judged it more prudent to tolerate the revolt of the lesser country than give an opportunity to the larger one for a similar attempt; he considered that the fear alone of a graver event outweighed a smaller distress. For this reason he concealed his displeasure at the insult and approached the rebel with certain terms, stipulating on oath that whichever of them died first should yield his kingdom to the survivor, this would avoid a situation where a new division of the realms tore apart the old acknowledged authority and divided the supreme power, which had formerly had the advantages of unity. So he strove to keep Denmark and Norway under a single command, his preference being to subordinate one to the other instead of letting each exercise rule individually; he would rather foreigners held sway over his country than that his country should exclude foreigners from those it governed. Surely that agreement, inasmuch as it was more subject to chance, came all the nearer to foolishness, in that it would produce for one or the other realm either a glorious sovereignty or mean servitude. Each party took an oath agreeing to abide by the convenant.[45]

(Transl. Peter Fisher)

According to this version, it is of loyalty to Denmark that Harthacnut entered into the agreement with Magnus. There is no mentioning of a mediation by great men from both sides. Instead, it is entirely Harthacnut's own initiative that saved Denmark from fragmentation.

The Danish chronicle traditions differ from the Norwegian by merely implying that the meeting took place at the river of Göta älv. Perhaps the Danish chronicle tradition are independent of the Norwegian, but here too is the problem of time discrepancy and – especially in *Gesta Danorum* – the tendency to legitimize the Danish royal power. The texts give different explanations of how and why the meeting would have taken place, with dissimilar descriptions of the characteristics of the two kingdoms. The accounts of the kings' decision to meet differ between the sources as well as the depiction of the men who – in some versions – independently made decisions.

Obviously the mentionening of hostage in *Ágrip* appears to be a remission. Whether the version of *Ágrip* – the oldest of these texts – really can build on actual information cannot be determined with certainty. What can be noted is that the same terminology was used during peace processes in both the Viking Age and the early Middle Ages. Whether the contexts say anything about a real situation is uncertain, though.

In the next chapter the question is brought up whether hostages – as described in different chronicles and in saga literature – could have been perceived as a symbolic subordination or not.

Subordination and triumph: Different opinions

In the Roman Empire, the arrival of the hostage was a triumphal ritual act. The historian of ideas Joel Allen describes how such a procession with the hostage would appear. The case concerns the Roman politician and general Titus Quinctius Flaminius who returned to Rome in 194 BC and was awarded a triumph after several victories, not least against Philip V of Macedonia, who gave his support to Hannibal during the Second Punic War:

> As Livy [34: 52] tells it, the festivities lasted for three days, with a parade of unusual riches and spectacles of a Roman triumph […]. Works of art, weapons caches, and wagons loaded with ingots of precious metals and mounds of coins were carted through the streets. Brightly colored placards and tableaux would have depicted events in the war, as well as conquered territories, city walls breeched by the Romans […]. A horde of prisoners of war would have chocked the streets, hundreds of them destined for slavery. Such an array of conquest must have been deeply impressive to the audience […]. [—] The climax of the third day, when dozens of Greek boys trudged along in front of Flaminius, who as the *triumphator*, would have appeared as a near-god decked in purple and with his face painted in red as he rode in a four-horse chariot up to join Jupiter on the Capitoline Hill. The Greek youths before him were about twenty-five in number […]. [—] Viewed together, they formed a memorable entourage: as children of the nobility, all of them would have been well dressed; as adolescents, many of them would have been gangly and uncomfortable, both

in Rome and their own skins. [...], failing to understand the Latin cries all around them, making their way before Flaminius's chariot, which bore down on them from behind, [...], the hostages must have seemed utterly pathetic and powerless. That appears to have been the point: here at zenith of the triumph, the man responsible for it all came shepherding a final and peculiar asset for Rome's future, a next generation.[46]

Allen describes what was central in the use of hostages in ancient Rome. It was first and foremost a symbolic expression of the victory of Rome and utilized in the triumphs that were granted to certain generals. The hostage was placed in front of the triumph wagon, a place that was also reserved for the most valuable spoils of war after a campaign.[47] But hostages also represented an 'investment' in the future, as the Macedonian boys could become future leaders in their home country. They also provided valuable capital of knowledge because they were educated in the Greek intellectual traditions, which had a strong impact on the Romans. The boys thus had valuable functions in addition to be a security for the behaviour of their parents.

In the Old Scandinavian and Continental Germanic communities, similar beliefs about hostages may have occurred even if one must be aware of the different societal conditions for of these cultures. The taking and display (in public) of hostages may, in some cases, reflect a symbolic submission, but in some cases it may not be that obvious.

Lavelle discusses whether the hostage was a triumph for the hostage taker or a subordination for the donor in the Anglo-Saxon society. Neither the legal functionality of hostage, nor its practical and symbolic values was the only dominant factor for the 'hostageship'.[48] But for writers and chroniclers, it could be a way of demonstrating a ruler's triumph over Viking leaders:

> [T]he taking of Viking hostages by West Saxon kings (both Alfred and Edward the Elder) remained one convenient shorthand way for writers to demonstrate power, even where the kings' actions may have been motivated more by practical necessity and where tangible authority may have been less apparent. Therefore, it may be concluded that the importance of hostages lay in the mixture of

the practical threat with political status. The rituals inherent in the making of peace presumably remained important, but the different circumstances under which hostages were used (peacemaking with external enemies, the assertion of the submission of external enemies, the assertion of lordship within the Anglo-Saxon kingdom and the use of local legal guarantees) show a flexible application of hostageship – or at least multi-layered meanings of hostage-holding which are not always immediately perceptible in the sources. The flexible use of and abuse of hostages show that both Anglo-Saxon rulers and their opponents could be far more imaginative in their dealings than we sometimes give them credit for.[49]

Lavelle points out something central: for the chroniclers, the moment of submission was important just as to portray 'strangers' and 'pagans' like those who broke the hostage agreement. Lavelle's examples, however, are limited to Anglo-Saxon England about 800–1000. A comparison between different chronicle traditions would reveal how complex the reality was, as Lavelle suggests. Even what Lavelle regards as less important – the legal and symbolic value of the institution surrounding the hostage – could be emphasized. It is necessary to turn to both Old Norse and Continental Germanic sources to discuss the hostage in a broader perspective. In this part, it is discussed how men from the groupings around great men were treated as hostages. The intention is to investigate the different political and religious contexts they encountered. The role of women is also discerned. In addition, both the major forms of hostages that Kosto defines as bilateral and unilateral, as well as the breaking of oaths and cases of violence against hostages *en masse,* are scrutinezed.

Submissions

Total submission involving hostages seems rarely to have occurred, possibly except for in ancient Rome, especially during the imperial era. An example from the antique world with a similar category – a prisoner – could illustrate a symbolic exposure of a total submission: Caesar mentions in his comments on the Gallic War (*Commentarii de Bello Gallico*) how Vercingetorix, the ruler of the Gauls, was handed over to the Romans after the battle of Alesia in 52 BC and threw his arms to Caesar's feet; despite this, he was later executed by Caesar.[50]

A more recent symbolic exposure of submission – which involved hostages – can be seen in the story of Niall Noígíallach, whose legendary epithet can be interpreted: 'he who has nine hostages'. The name Noígíallach is probably fictitious, but it may have been used to embellish the ruler and thus legitimize the king's power in a later period. A stanza by Sigvatr skald (*Sigvatr Þórðarson*) (Sigvatr Thórðarson) in the memorial poem of St. Olaf (*Erfidrápa Óláfs helga*) can be linked to a similar context:

(2) Upplönd fekk til enda
óss neista ok þar reisti
kristnihald þats heldu
hvers veitir, sverðs beitar.
Àðr stýrðu þeim eyðar
ellifu fyrr hella
mildings máls enn guldu
menn vísliga gísla.[51]

The giver of gold (i.e., the king) conquered the Highlands to each end (i.e., from border to border), and established Christianity there, which the sword-wielders (men) kept. Eleven kings (lit., wasters of the cave-lord's interest) ruled them (i.e., the Highlands), but the men wisely gave up hostages.[52]

(Transl. Jón Skaptason)

In these cases, it was the prerogative of the victor to receive the hostage and dictate the terms of his or her time as hostage. At the same time, there may be a difference between text and reality. This can be seen in another example of a possible total submission involving hostages, in the Carolingian *Annales Bertiniani*. It depicts how the Saxons fought the *colodici*, a Sorbic tribe, at a place called Kesigesburg (location unknown) in 839, a fight that ended with the death of the Sorbian ruler (*regeque ipsum*) Cimusclus (or Czimislav). The Saxons – then Christians – managed to defeat the Sorbs 'with divine aid' (*celestibus auxiliis fulti*). A new 'king' (*rex*) was elected by the Sorbians, and the Saxons took an oath of loyalty from him. He gave hostages and some of the lands of the *colodici* were confiscated.[53]

The chronicle reveals what may be a cliché of continental chronicles: the idea that it was divine intervention that made the Christian Saxons triumphant. The information about a Saxon victory does not necessarily have to be wrong, but it may have taken a long period before peace had been achieved. Why was the hostage needed if a tributary king was deployed and the Sorbs swore oaths? Was not the Christian victory total? The text does not mention if the Sorbs in this case were Christianised. In this case, the hostage implicitly functioned as assuring the obedience of the Sorbian ruler, but in the text it is mentioned as part of a submission in addition to the taking of oaths and the conquest of land areas. This is comparable to how the hostage was often given by the Saxons during the confrontations with the Carolingian Empire, but they often broke the peace despite hostages. How subjected the Sorbs really were by the Saxons can thus be open to discussion. Annals can provide incorrect information about the role of hostages. They have been recorded by monks who – although they were active in the ninth century – were far from the area that is described. The Carolingian Emperor, the victory of the Christian side, and theological questions about miracles were the themes that were most central to them, while themes of realpolitik became less important.

There are several examples of how the victory over heathen enemies is described in a triumphal way by chroniclers. The hostages in their texts are mentioned as an important part of the victory as well as the baptism of the defeated enemies. The specialist in Old English Peter S. Baker points out that peace negotiations were often followed by forced repentance,[54] and Lynch gives the baptism of Guthrum as an example of such submission.[55] However, the comments of Lynch and Baker may be taken with a pinch of salt. In Part I, I discussed the possible actual situation based on strength and geographical relations between the realms of Alfred and Guthrum. The willingness of the 'heathens' to accept baptism may have been of political nature and represented a syncretistic or acculturative attitude where the Christian deity was not necessarily understood in the same way as within Christianity.[56] Thus, there may have been many ways the hostage was perceived when heathens and Christians met for negotiations. Kosto points out how the sources are often written from a subjective perspective:

> [...] the sources, most written from the perspective of the stronger party in these encounters, understandably report events in a way that favours their subjects; what appears to have been a submission may in fact be closer to a negotiated settlement, and the grant of hostages for safe passage communicates that this was the case.[57]

Kosto exemplifies this with the episode of the *Anglo Saxon Chronicle*, where Olaf Tryggvason was convinced by the English king Æthelred II to meet him at Andover. Olaf received gifts and was baptised, a ceremony secured by a hostage. The hostage may in this case have been perceived as a symbolic sign of submission, as well as the baptism and the gifts. Instead of giving the 16,000 pounds in silver that Olaf demanded, this ceremony could be carried out. According to the text, Olaf also promised not to return to England. The hostage was in fact a guarantor of a safe passage, according to Kosto, in many different cases on the continent where the symbolism surrounding hostages was important.[58] In this case it is not quite clear what is a description of the course of events and what is a rhetorical device. The number '16,000' is also interesting because it is close to another number that occurs in the *Vita Ansgari*, and could indicate 'an (indefinite) but very large amount' in the same way as other large numbers (see below).

There are examples of those who were forced to give hostages also mentioned in positive terms even if they were subjected to submission. In the *Vita Ansgari*, Rimbert reports about the siege of Apulia (Apuolė, in present Lithuania) in Courland in 854. A Swedish king, Olof I of Sweden, carried out raids into Courland and burned Seeburg (Liepāja) before he turned to Apulia. Rimbert claims that 15,000 'fighting men' defended the city for eight days and that there were heavy losses on both sides. On the ninth day, the Swedes were so exhausted and scared that they considered making a retreat. In their fear they could only find one resort: to cast lots to find out if their gods would help them win or if they had to retreat. After the casting, they could not understand the will of the gods.⁵⁹ The courage left them, but among them there were merchants who reminded them of the bishops' teachings (from the mission in Sweden [Svetjud]) and advised that they should cast lots to understand the will of Christ. The lots showed that Christ was willing to help them. The Swedes were filled with fighting will and when the citydwellers saw it, they asked for negotiations for peace, something Olof granted them. The Curonians promised to give the Swedes the war booty (gold and armor) they took last year from the Danes and a pound of silver for every man in the city. They would pay the same tribute they had previously given and give hostages to show their submission and the obedience that had previously existed. Therefore, the Swedes could take a massive tribute and 30 people as hostages.⁶⁰ When peace had been established between the two parties, according to Rimbert, the Swedes accepted Christ and embraced Christian traditions.

The description contains several interesting details, but in this case I will focus on some possible misconceptions, literary insertions, and learned clichés that can be found in the text. *Vita Ansgari* was written about 857 and meets the critical source criterion of being contemporaneous with the course of events that are described (the contemporarity criterion). However, it does not live up to the criterion of having been written in the area that is described (the proximity criterion). There may be a rhetorical maneuver in the depiction of the heathens. Two examples can illustrate this. Firstly, the casting of lots is portrayed as ineffective when it was directed towards the Swedes' own deities, and this is presented as having resulted in uncertainty and fear. However, the self-esteem was strengthened as soon as the Swedes turned to the Christian god, a *topos* that is common in conversion stories.⁶¹ Secondly, some of the numbers mentioned in the chronicle can be related to numbers in both the Old Testament and the New Testament: the 30 people who would bring the tribute and the siege that was broken on the ninth day.⁶² When some people from the fortress volunteered as hostages it may be associated with martyrdom, in which some people sacrifice themselves for the majority, but this is only a hypothesis. It can also be a symbolic Christian fraternization, because the Swedes later declared their willingness to celebrate Easter when they were converted.

The willingness to give hostages is emphasized rather than the subordination.

There are also some other things that can be deduced from learned insertions. The luxurious riches of gold are most likely based on ancient literary genres; insignificant, immense human masses like the 15,000 fighting men belong to this genre as well as the presence of a 'king of the Swedes'. Such learned embroideries make it ambiguous whether the text can be used as a source of actual circumstances. But it can also reflect a syncretistic situation in which Christ is regarded as a god among others.

It should be noted that the siege of Apulia is not supported by other written sources, but an archaeological survey outside of Apuolė, conducted in the 1930s. The archaeologists found the remnants of a fortification; additionally there were findings of iron arrows (at least 150). This type of arrow has also been found in the cemeteries of the town of Birka in Lake Mälaren, Sweden. They were common in Scandinavia but unusual in the eastern Baltic countries. Many of the arrows were found at the fortified wall, and some of them were broken. All the arrows were found in the same earth layer and can be dated to the ninth century. This could confirm that attacks on the fortification took place in that time.[63]

The above are thus examples of how the chroniclers and writers could portray the hostage in positive terms. There are also literary examples that describe how main characters have been the hostage of an enemy and how it could be turned into a triumphal flight, such as Walther in *Waltharius*, or revenge, as with Vikar and Starkad (*Götreks saga* [*Gautreks Saga*]; *Víkarsbalkr*).[64]

As literature, a story from the king's saga *Ágrip* can also be mentioned. It does not mention a hostage, but it uses the related category 'captivity'. The story is about how the three-year-old Olaf Tryggvason fled from the Orkney Islands over Sweden to Novgorod (ON *Hólmgarðr*). In the Baltic Sea, he is captured near the island of Saaremaa and his foster father Þórólfr is killed. But since Olaf is divinely chosen, there is a solution. An envoyee from Novgorod is at Saaremaa to collect taxes. He pays the ransom for Olaf who has been thrall for nine years. Olaf can later avenge his foster father.[65]

These examples show how the hostage situation may have been perceived as subordination because the protagonists had to cope with or master the situation they were put in after the defeat of their parents. The main characters are taken or given to the enemies as hostages when they are children or youths. These examples are found in literary genres such as skaldic poetry, legendary sagas (*fornaldarsögur*), and Medieval Latin poetry. As a literary theme, the state of hostage in these texts appears as something negative. However, from continental chronicle traditions there are examples of an opposite attitude towards hostages. Theoderic, who would later become 'the Great', son of Theodemir, was sent to the emperor of Constantinople as a part of a peace process when he was seven or eight years old. In the version of this event related in *Getica* by Jordanes, it is not quite clear who had the upper hand. Between the Ostrogoths and the Eastern Roman Empire, wars alternated with periods of peace in an area of confrontation.[66]

According to *Getica*, the Ostrogothian ruler annually sent gifts to the Emperor Marcian (d. 457) to secure a peace treaty. Valamir – belonging to the family-based grouping called the Amali – discovered that another grouping was in friendship bonds with the Romans, which also meant that they received annual gifts. The Amali, on the other hand, did not receive any gifts. Therefore, the Amali plundered in Illyria, whereupon the emperor softened and promised to continue the giving of gifts. As a pledge of peace, the Amali decided to send Theoderic as a hostage.[67] Theoderic returned to the Amali at the age of eighteen.

Valamir's choice to send Theoderic away does not indicate submission. Rather, the transmission may had the same meaning as a symbolic, valuable gift, and can be seen in relation to Tacitus's statement that the Germans were always prefering nephews as hostages; they would have been particularly valuable.[68] If the Germans perceived Theoderic as a person of great value that exceeded the gifts of the emperor, the hostage, in this case, could be understood in relation to the value of the gifts. The value of the hostage to exceed that of the gifts of the Romans and the recipient could therefore not 'pay' back, something Mauss thought of as the basic idea of the potlatch economy.[69] In this way, submission was created in an interchange relationship. As seen from the Byzantine side, this follows a tradition that other leaders or prominent persons from areas adjacent to the Roman Empire also had experienced.[70] During the final period of the Western Roman Empire, Romans also appear to have experienced this tradition when the Roman Empire was exposed to increasing pressure from opponents such as the Visigoths and Huns. As a child, the general Flavius Aetius was held as hostage by the king of the Visigoths, Alaric I (around 408), and later the warlord Uldin of the Huns. Flavius Aetius later married a highborn Gothic woman and their son, Carpilio, was sent as hostage to the Huns in 425.[71] However, it must be noted that the well-developed Roman traditions of hostages were partly different from those in the Continental Germanic areas. Nevertheless, the Scandinavian foster institution has features that correspond with Theoderic's situation.

Foster children

Procedures with foster children raised at a foreign court, like the Roman and Byzantine Empires, can be seen in the Danish-Continental area of confrontations, where Danish rulers sometimes acted as enemies and sometimes as allies to the Carolingian Empire. In the early ninth century there was some Danish rulers were interested in seeking support from the Caroligians when their own realm was characterized by internal feuds. At the same time, the Danes raided the Carolingian territories or the regions of their allies.

There were in this area of confrontations instances that show that the use of hostages and the institution with foster children could be almost identical. Hemming, son of the Danish king, also called Hemming, was found at the court in Aachen in 812, according to the Royal Frankish Annals (*Annales Regni Francorum*), probably as a foster child (OWN *fóstri*). He could also have been a presumptive hostage, because his brothers Harald and Reginfred asked for peace and that Hemming should be handed out.[72]

A similar case is found around the character of the legendary Ogier the Dane (Da. *Holger Danske*) who – according to some continental chronicle traditions – became a hostage of Charlemagne. It is difficult to determine whether Ogier was a historical person or not. He has been identified as Ogier of Denmark (*Ogier de Danemarche*), or Ogier the Dane (*Ogier le danois*) in the *Song of Roland* (*La Chanson de Roland*), which has survived in ten manuscripts, the oldest being dated to 1100: the Oxford version. According to the Oxford version of the *Song of Roland*, Ogier has a prominent position at the court of Charlemagne. He is responsible for leading the rearguard during the retreat over the Pyrenees (stanza 748–750).[73] The oldest source that is considered to confirm Ogier the Dane as a Danish great man in the Carolingian Empire is a chronicle about Olgerus, who restored the monastery St Martin in Cologne in 778.[74] He is refered to as *dux daniæ*. However, if Ogier was a hostage of Charlemagne, he seems, according to literary traditions, to have received some kind of 'education' as a warrior.

During the late Viking Age and early Middle Ages, when Danish rulers also became kings of England, at least one case of extradition of sons appears as something between the giving of foster sons (OI *fóstri*) and the use of hostages. According to the *Anglo-Saxon Chronicle*, Canute the Great and earl Thorkel the Tall (OI *Þorkell inn hávi*, OE *Þurkyll*) exchanged their respective sons in 1023; Canute took Thorkel's son to England, and Thorkel kept Canute's son in Denmark. Lavelle believes that it was primarily about fostering as an institution rather than a matter of hostages.[75] Here the political context should be considered. Thorkel then served Æthelred II and defended England against the invasions of Sweyn Forkbeard and Canute in 1013.[76] After the death of Sweyn, Canute withdrew from England. Thorkel also fled from the reprisals of Æthelred against the Danes. He allied himself with Canute and accompanied him to England, and after the conquest he became earl of East Anglia. But a new conflict arose between them in 1021. Canute outlawed Thorkel, who had to return to Denmark. Thorkel's tendency to take a stand against the king may well have played a role for the status of his son, but that is a hypothesis; we have no further information in this case.[77]

Another demanding settlement involving a foster person – who practically functioned as a hostage – can be seen in *Heimskringla*'s version of the Saga of St. Olaf (*Óláfs saga helga*), which generally runs parallel to the probably older *Orkneyinga saga*, dating back to about 1190. The saga describes how Olaf Haraldsson had a few confrontations with the earls of the Orkney Islands and the Shetland Islands.[78] The confrontations consisted mostly of negotiations, alternating with threats by the king, whereupon some of the earls restored the settlement with the king as much as possible.[79] They had previously reached an agreement with the King of the Scots and have contended among themselves. Olaf could claim the Orkney Islands with reference to the fact that Norwegian kings had previously landed there, and therefore he regarded them as his inheritance.[80] Some of the earls chose to unite with Olaf, but especially the earl Thorfinn Sigurdsson (ON *Þorfinnr Sigurðsson*) resisted. Earl Brusi Sigurdsson (ON *Brusi Sigurðsson*), brother of Thorfinn, chose to ally with Olaf. Thorfinn had supported his grandfather, the Scottish king, but his territory was only one third of the islands, while Brusi had two thirds and Thorfinn wanted half of the islands.[81]

The two earls participated in things and other meetings as their friends tried to reconcile them. Then Brusi, who was the weaker, paid a visit to King Olaf with his ten-year-old son Rögnvald (ON *Rǫgnvald Brusason*). Brusi offered the king his friendship. The king set the condition that Brusi would be his henchman, but at the same time he gave him the isles as bestowment. Unless Brusi agreed to this agreement, the king required the properties on the islands that his ancestors and predecesors previously possessed. The earl agreed to the settlement after having consulted with his friends.[82]

The earl became the king's henchman (*handgenginn*) and the agreement was confirmed with oaths. Later, the king made the deal that Brusi was to have two thirds of the Orkney Islands, but to bound him as his henchman, he took Rögnvald as hostage. Rögnvald was attributed with positive qualities in the *Orkneyinga saga*:

> Hann var allra manna fríðastr, hárit mikit ok gult sem silki. Hann var snimma mikill ok sterkr. Manna var hann gørviligastr bæði fyrir vits sakir ok kurteisi. Hann var lengi síðan með Óláfi konungi.[83]

Rognvald [sic] was one of the handsomest of men, with a fine head of golden hair, smooth as silk. At an early age he grew to be

tall and strong, earning a great reputation for his shrewdness and courtesy, and he stayed on with king Olaf for a long time.[84]
(Transl. Hermann Pálsson & Paul Edwards)

Naturally, he received these positive qualities when he lived with the holiest of all the kings of Norway.

It could be difficult to understand Olaf's actions – whether these took place in reality – filtered through Snorri's elucidation. Snorri points out that Olaf understood how Brusi was somewhat unhappy with his actions: '*at Brusi gekk tregliga at ǫllu sáttmálli, en mælti þat eina um, er hann ætlaði sér at halda* (that Brusi went slowly to all the negotiations, but never gave promises that he would keep)', but the text is similar in the *Orkneyinga saga*.[85] Thorfinn willingly makes an agreement with Olaf, who, on the other hand, suspects Thorfinn of making changes to the deal. Thorfinn has the stronger military on the islands through his grandfather's support.[86] Perhaps Olaf wanted to take Rögnvald as hostage to assure the full support of Brusi so that he would not become a turncoat. The hostage does not appear in this case as a word but with a euphemism: '[...] *ek vil festa trúnað með því, at ek vil hér sé eptir með Rǫgnvaldr, sonr þinn* (I will bind your faithfulness to me by looking after Rögnvald, your son)'.[87] The text does not mention whether Rögnvald is a foster son, but implicity it seems to be the case. The hostage was a tool that hade been used in the areas of confrontation between the Orkney Islands and the Norwegian Kingdom ever earlier, e.g. when Hunde became a hostage of Olaf Tryggvasson (see below).

It is also interesting that Olaf, according to the texts, always refers to the actions of his ancestors regarding his power ambitions on the islands. By such means of power legitimation, the traditions of hostage were formed in this context. But in this case, we are dependent on the versions of *Heimskringla* and the *Orkneyinga saga*; no skaldic poems mention anything about the hostage. Nevertheless, it is mentioned by Sigvat the Skald (*Sigvatr Þórðarson*) in his drapa of the death of Olaf that Olaf used hostage as an instrument of power to control chieftains in Norway. In another drapa, by the skald Óttarr the Black (*Óttarr svarti*), it is mentioned that he landed on the Shetland Islands (*Hjaltland*) and the Western islands (*eyjum vestan*).[88]

Foster children in Iceland

In Iceland, there seems to have been a type of institution with foster children that concerned families and their friendship instead of the regulation of major areas such as kingdoms (see the introduction). The historian Ian Miller has described the foster institution as it is reproduced in the Icelandic genealogies. He points out that children could be a burden: they were costly, and it took time and effort to raise them, something that could have been an underlying factor in why foster parents sometimes undertook their care.[89] He divides foster parents into three groups based on their rank:

(1) If the recipients were of a lower grade, they could be forced to commit themselves by fostering a child.
(2) If the recipients were of an equal rank as the donors, the receipt of the foster child was a way of bridging conflicts.
(3) There may have been an obligation to receive someone within a family-based grouping that may have brought an advantage through the fact that the foster children grew up in a wealthier household. This meant that the children were taken care of by a servant or the equivalent from the great man's own estate.[90]

In some cases, those who gave away their children as foster children were superior to the recipients, while in other cases they seemed to have been the opposite. According to Miller, there were several binding mechanisms within the foster institution that could take place at one and the same time, involving several exchanges between relatives. Sometimes sons were sent only to preserve the peace of a household, a way to get rid of 'messy children' or to protect young women from men's interests.[91]

Another variant was that children could have a foster parent from their own home that was responsible for their education.[92] Thus, there was a complex social fabric with many different varieties of fostering in the Old Icelandic society. On the other hand, foster children were never intended to be hostages as Miller puts it:

> In each of these instances the offer was an act of kindness, of reconciliation; but at another level, the child also looked a little like hostage to secure the maintenance of a nervous peace. [...] In fact no evidence in the sagas indicates that such children were perceived as hostages. There are no examples of a foster-parent threatening to harm the child, nor any instances of natural parents acting out of fear of what a foster-parent might do to the child. The [foster] children, it seems, were treated no differently than any other child would have been.[93]

I agree in part with Miller. As previously mentioned, it is not possible, based on the analysis I made of conflicts mentioned in the *Íslendingabók* and the *Landnámabók*, to claim that hostage was used as an instrument of power in conflicts and peace processes between individuals and groupings in the Old Icelandic society. But it occurred in at least a few cases between the Icelanders and the Norwegian royal power. One case was when Kjartan Olafsson (ON *Kjartan Ólafsson*) and a few Icelanders became hostages at the court of Olaf Tryggvason in 999, which is described in *Laxdæla saga*.[94] Another case was when the great man Jón Snorrason was held hostage by the king Håkon IV Håkonsson (ON *Hákon Hákonarson*) in 1221, when Iceland was subdued by the royal power.[95]

Miller's motivation for his claim that a hostage did not appear as a foster child is vague because he relies only on Old Icelandic texts. It may be that hostages in other contexts are not mentioned with words, and there may have been variants where it is not possible to distinguish a pattern with sharp dividing lines between hostages and foster children. It can be noted that Miller does not completely reject the possibility that the foster institution held up a fragile peace as a binding mechanism. With Miller's reasoning, the foster institution could thus have acted as a stabilizing factor for peace in its own right, and the foster child could have been more than just "a little like a hostage"[96]

The historian Auður Magnúsdóttir has a different view of the foster institution in the medieval Icelandic society than Miller. Auður argues that foster children could only be part of a subordination because they were given and thus represented a vertically oriented action. According to Auður, the foster institution was therefore a stronger binding mechanism than relying on biological family bonds, because through this confidence, subordinate householders could maintain their loyalty to their superior great men.[97]

Auður's reasoning could, in part, explain the absence of hostages – despite the similarity with the foster institution – in Iceland during the Viking Age and the Middle Ages. The foster institution became vertical with the establishment of the great families, or groupings, during the Middle Ages.[98] This means that during previous periods the foster institution could have been horizontally oriented, used between householders that were more equal. Perhaps later, a vertically directed foster institution became sufficient to control underlying territories in the immediate vicinity of these dominating groupings.

The hostage, on the other hand, was, generally both horizontally and vertically oriented. That the use of hostages did not occur in the Old Icelandic society during these periods when war and peace shifted may have been due to the size of the individual households. In other cases, in Scandinavia, there was competitiveness between great men and rulers with the ambition to control a kingdom or a region. The longer the distances and larger the areas, the more likely that the 'real' hostage could be used as a regulating factor. This can partly confirm my hypothesis that hostages in peace processes in Iceland only began to be used once the territorial division became clearer. It can also be compared to Jón Viðar Sigurðsson's hypothesis about the island communities of northmen as more 'peaceful' and collaborative.[99]

The above example shows that there are cases where the giving of hostages is not only associated with a symbolic submission, although several examples indicate this. Thus, the hostage was not only part of arrangements of superiors and subordinates, but also it was done in a complex manner, with geographical and temporal variations. To this could be added the different views of writers and chronologists on the degree of submission.

There is no unambiguous picture of hostages as subordinate in the Old Icelandic litterature. As an institution within the

Scandinavian countries, it was corrected by varying legal, religious, political, and social circumstances. One could summarize the conditions as follows:

(A) There was some confusion about who was to be counted as hostage, by continental chroniclers and Nordic writers.
(B) Geographical distances contributed to the confusion.
(C) It is difficult to see hostage merely as 'pure submission', even if that type occurred.
(D) Gift-giving conditions could occur between equal parties.
(E) Political considerations in it was important to keep in with one's opponents which could be some of the reasons for taking and giving hostages.
(F) 'Investments' for future alliances was another reason for hostage exchanges.
(G) The difference between foster children and hostages was in some cases difficult to discern in Scandinavia.

In the case of A, C, and D, it is almost exclusively about a foster institution. A and D were not necessarily about warlike conditions but could apply to steps two and three according to my model, where one gradually tries to ease the tensions at the same time as unrest could threaten to erupt again.

Conduct and loyalty

The conduct of the hostage had consequences in much larger contexts than that of the 'guest' of the nobility who could seek exile and protection of his or her own choice. A person who was a hostage was in a more vulnerable position – where others made the decisions – but it could also be a matter for the hostage to show loyalty toward the hostage taker, and the taker must have been bestowed with certain responsibilities.

Cases with 'trust'

I have previously pointed out how the social bonds must be actively maintained through actions associated with the foster institution.

It is comparable to Lavelle's idea that hostages in some cases had to prove their loyalty symbolically.[100] He gives examples of how a hostage of the Anglo-Saxons shot an arrow against the Viking army during the Battle of Maeldun, in Essex in 991. It was Æscfrith, son of Ecglaf, who showed his loyalty to Earl Byrhtnoth and the Anglo-Saxons in this way.

Kosto mentions a similar example from the *Anglo-Saxon Chronicle*. It concerns an Anglo-Saxon (Welsh) hostage who was the only survivor after an attack by Cyneheard on King Cynewulf of Wessex.[101] Obviously, the Welsh hostage fought on Cynewulf's side because he was severely injured. In both cases, it is not a standpoint against its own side. However, the symbolic significance of the action should not be underestimated.

In Continental Germanic traditions, hostages fighting for their recipients are a recurring theme, but they are literary works that can possibly build on oral traditions. In the *Waltharius* poem (first half of the 11th century), for example, three Frankish and Germanic kings were forced to hand over hostages and some treasures to Attila to avoid invasion.[102] As a result, Walther (*Waltharius*), a son of a Frankish king, grows up at the court of Attila, battles on his side, and eventually becomes almost an honored son. He flees together with the princess Hiltgund, a Burgundian hostage, and takes some treasures with him. The story can be interpreted as Walther restoring some of his lost glory in the form of the stolen treasure and the rescue of Hiltgund.

There are some possible parallels to this behaviour, even in Old Norse literature, for example in *Gautreks saga* in which King Vikar (OI *Vikarr*) and other sons of great men become hostage to King Herthjóf (OI *Herþjofr*) of Hordaland, Norway.[103] Vikar was raised at Herthjóf's household and seemed to be treated well. For example, he got the confidence to guard a beacon. But because Herthjóf killed Vikar's father, he must avenge this, and he did, together with his foster brother, Starkad (ON *Starkaðr*), who was raised parallel at the island of Fenhring (present Askøy outside city of Bergen) by Hrosshársgrani (a name of Odin).

These texts also testify to ambivalence because they depict rebellion against the hostage taker. Walther, like Vikar, broke up with their hostage takers. There might be a moral issue in these stories;

the confidence can suddenly be broken in the case of former enemies, even if it is implicit in these texts. Nevertheless, trusts were important for both symbolic and pragmatic reasons. Hypothetically, the reason for such confidence could be that it involved functions primarily in the household, including different constellations of companionship. Loyalty attached to the close sphere became at least initially easier to control than outside that sphere.

From the point of view of the hostage taker, the presence of the hostage may indicate his status. The tradition is best known from Old Irish contexts: 'he is not king who has hostages in fetters'.[104] Whether or not this symbolic approach was expressed in Old English, Continental Germanic, or Old Norse traditions, we do not know. However, as both Lavelle and Kosto emphasize, the hostage also deals with reciprocity, i.e. the hostage was in several cases given, not only taken.[105] In such a constellation, it may have been important not only to symbolically manifest the subordination but also the loyalty: the guarantor's obligations towards the hostage.

In Old Western Norse sources, perhaps the clearest expression of a possible symbolic, subordinate relationship is in Sigvat the Skald's drapa of St. Olaf. In the poem it is said that it is 'wise' to provide hostage to Olaf Haraldsson. In this case, there are subversive 'kings' in the conquered county; it is a political situation that is in line with the first step in my model with the establishment of social relations, but perhaps, in this case, does not reflect a reality. To provide hostages in this context can nevertheless also be interpreted as an opportunity to secure peaceful relationships. A situation like this might have been a reason for good behaviour: the hostage would secure its position by proving its loyalty and thus securing future good relationships and alliances, regardless of the deprivation of the recipient side. Some unambiguous explanation for the trust hostage received in exchange for loyalty and good conduct is not possible to give; these situations were probably due to both the political situation as well as purely individual.

Female hostages

As previously mentioned, researchers like Kosto have claimed that women who were handed out would primarily become wives. If it were common in Continental Germanic contexts that future brides were given to a possible enemy, it is likely that this custom occurred in Scandinavia too, although, as far as I know, there are no texts that explicitly use the word 'hostage' for a bride (or potential bride). Therefore it is interesting to compare the functions of married and unmarried women before a regular wedding. For example, was a bride price given, or a dowry, in these contexts as a part of peace processes? In my view, however, it is a reductionist approach to assume that women would only have functions related to marriage. Perhaps such functions must primarily be derived from Old English or Continental Germanic, contexts. In Scandinavian contexts, there were several functions for women. For example, according to the historian Michael Enright, the queen Weolþeow had a 'warden role' connected to the peace in the mead-hall Heorot, which prevented the fighting between men.[106]

If women possessed certain functions before marriage, captivity, or hostageship, these functions could be transferred to the new household. In such cases, these functions can be related to the traditions of the non-Christian Scandinavian societies that did not necessarily fit into the values of Christian writers and chroniclers. Some of these traditions can be related to war and peace. They can therefore be compared to how the functions of women could be linked to a symbolic capital in a similar manner to the men who became hostages.

In Scandinavia and Iceland, some women – including wealthy widows – had a special social value. We know that some widows had specific functions that could be related to, among other things, the functions of the goðar on Iceland, which is an additional aspect of women's social value for peaceful solutions of war and other conflicts. Aud the Deep-Minded (ON *Auðr djúpúðga*) in the *Laxdœla saga* held ceremonial banquets and ruled over both her own farm and other subordinate units.[107] These honorable women could themselves have affected the outcome of conflicts with more indirect instruments than men.

A woman who was married into a new household may have contributed with new knowledge and other social capital in the environment of the foreign hall and in other areas of communication that she now took part in. For example, Hildeburh in the *Beowulf* epic organized the pyre of her son, her brother Hnæf, and her husband Finn, which could be compared to the role of Weolþeow in the mead-hall.[108] The ritual act can be interpreted as an attempt to create new bonds during the peace that followed; it became a way to reconcile symbolically.

Continental Germanic literature mentions other types of functions. Hiltgund becomes treasurer and is tasked with managing Attila's treasury.[109] It could be a literary, stylistic feature freely based on old traditions; still, one could compare this with the married woman's situation in the Old Scandinavian society: she brought the dowry to her new home and took custody of it.

The above examples can be compared with Kershaw's hypothesis about the situation of the male hostage arriving to the new home:

> The contrast with male hostage is noteworthy: men in foreign households were acculturated, women in foreign households were agents of culture. For royal women seeking to foster peace under their own initiative and free from a male-dominated framework a further strategy was available: prayer, either their own or the formal commissioning of prayers for peace from religious communities, an approach favoured by both Radegund and Balthild in the later seventh century according to their biographers.[110]

Kershaw's examples primarily concern women in Continental Germanic and Anglo-Saxon socities. The married woman in the Old Scandinavian society had primarily cultural functions attached to the home and the cult buildings. In Old Western Norse sources there are some hints that women also had other cultural functions, including some that could be related to war and peace.

Women and the thing

In some research, Scandinavian women have been considered excluded from the thing, an area of communication where decisions about war and peace were made. Recently, the archaeologist Alexandra Sanmark has problematised the image of women's role in relation to the assemblies. Contextual differences appear to have existed between the Norwegian and Icelandic things.

Sanmark, who relies on the Icelandic law *Grágás* and Norwegian medieval laws, describes five different 'scenarios' that existed in Norway and by which women could approach the thing:[111]

(1) Women inherited after the death of other family members (husband, child).
(2) *Baugrýgr*, 'ring woman', an unmarried woman who inherited both land and esatates and had no close male relatives.
(3) In the event of a conflict between women, only women could claim compensation for the matter at the thing.
(4) Warden of a household.
(5) Female witnesses at the thing.

It appears that women, according to these scenarios, were entitled to conduct negotiations at the thing. In Norway, the ring women could inherit (additional) manors and receive fines. The fourth group could act on the thing on behalf of their men if they were unavailable. Sanmark points out with reference to Else Mundal that female witnesses could testify in almost all kinds of cases, not only in special circumstances such as murder cases.[112] The same rights for women are not found in the Icelandic laws, even though the degree of their freedom there was higher than has been assumed.[113]

Sanmark's hypothesis about women's ability to influence political outcomes at the things can be compared to my own model: there were different ways to mediate messages of reconciliation in the areas of confrontation. If women had these opportunities, they could certainly have influenced the outcome of peace processes in other arenas than in the above-discussed hall environment.

I have mentioned that women who were in hostage-like situations could (a) have been that directly after a peace process or a war campaign, or (b) have been given as a wife (implictly as hostage). They may also (c) have become wives after a period as *fóstra*, 'foster daughter' (see later section). Did these women have the same rights as in 'normal' marriages? There is nothing that contradicts certain restrictions due to the conditions regarding the marriage. This can be seen, for example, with women with some form of restricted degrees of freedom such as the thrall Melkorka in *Laxdæla saga*, who is originally captured in Ireland. She became mistress (ON. *frilla*) of the chieftain Hoskuld (OI *Hǫskuldr Dala-Kollsson*) and was then driven away from his household by his wife. As expressed in the *Laxdœla saga*, Melkorka had privileges that imply a free position. She received a new estate as a gift from Hoskuld: Melkorkastead (OI *Melkórkustaðir*). Later she married Thorbjorn Skrjup (OI *Þorbjǫrn skrjúp*).[114]

In *Sturlubók*'s version of *Landnámbók*, king Hjörr of Hordaland (ON *Hörðaland*) raided Bjarmaland and took Ljufvina, daughter of the king of the Bjarmians, as a prisoner of war (*herfenginn*). She gave birth to two sons of Hjörr. They were dark-skinned and were given the names Geirmund (OI *Geirmundr*) and Hamund (OI *Hamundr*). Ljufvina replaced them with the children of a female thrall because they were fair-skinned. Even here, it seems to be descent rather than privileges that matter as in the case of Melkorka, who is described as the daughter of an Irish king, Myrkjartan (OI *Muirchertach*). Nevertheless, the text still suggests that Ljufvina acted as the wife of Hjörr and was called 'Queen'.[115]

Women as cult leaders

According to Sanmark, women were important as cult leaders, and she points out the connection between the cult and the things, something which supports the assumption that women participated in 'assembly rituals'.[116] As cult leaders, they may have presented warlike messages. This suggests that they may also have had other types of functions that made them valuable as hostages. To further understand how women functioned symbolically in connection with war, we must turn to ancient texts.

The relationship between men and women as cult performers could be exemplified by a narrative in the *Commentaries on the Gallic War* by Caesar. The Romans had confrontations, which included both talks and battles, with the ruler of the Suebi, Ariovistus. Caesar claims that the Suebi did not show up in the morning during the decisive battle. He then withdrew his troops to the camp. At noon, Ariovistus attacked the camp and retreated at sunset. Caesar asked the prisoners why the Suebi did not attack at dawn and was told that the married women read whether the battle would go wrong or not through rituals of divination. The women said that it was the will of the gods that the Suebi would not battle until full moon.[117] This story may be due to Ceasar's political ambition and not fully reliable.

Veleda, a seeress of the Germanic tribe Bructeri, was an important political player in the Roman-Germanic conflicts. Veleda seems to have exerted a great political influence on German tribes. Tacitus mentions that she was worshiped as a goddess by some.[118] With her, political and cultural functions coincided. Among other things, she played a crucial role during the Revolt of the Batavi in 69–70 AD. She stood in a tower from where she spoke to the insurgents, answering questions about the outcome of the war. According to the poet Statius, Veleda was captured by the Roman general Callicus.[119] From neither Tacitus nor Statius is it apparent how the Romans treated Veleda during captivity, but it was symbolically important that they held her as a prisoner, or as presumptive hostage, which is evident from Statius's text.

Veleda has been compared with the Old Scandianvian *vǫlur*.[120] Sundqvist and the historian of religions Catharina Raudvere has pointed out that the *seiðr*, 'witchcraft, sorcery', was performed when they ambulated between different places.[121] This is one of the reasons why the texts describe the *vǫlur* as 'strange' or 'exotic'. They are described in the Old Western Norse literature as deviant in terms of age, sex, and geographical location. Their functions can be related to war and crisis, and because they could behave in aristocratic environments, they may have been actors with purposes that are not always harmonised with the will of the great men.[122]

Women of other social belongings than the *vǫlur* also had cultic functions during war- and peace-setting contexts, and it may be of interest to examine some of the sources. Outside the text material, a few motifs on Gothic picture stones can confirm that women had cultic functions related to both war and peace.

The importance of ceremonial toasts has previously been mentioned. The historian Agneta Ney has analysed women in the Iron Age society of Gotland and compared motives on picture stones representing a woman who is giving a drinking horn to a man, sometimes sitting on a horse, with the description of the queen Weolhþeow in the *Beowulf* epic.[123]

Figure IV.1. Picture stone from Lärbo (Gotland), Tängelgårda IV, which may depict a libation. Source and copyriht: Photo: Ola Myrin, The Swedish History Museum. License: CC BY 4.0.

The picture stone from Lärbo (Figure IV.1), Tängelgårda parish in Gotland, shows that the subject with horn that is given is not only found in literary contexts. Furthermore, this ceremony does not appear to have taken place in the hall but also outdoors, as can be seen on this picture stone from Lärbo. At the same time, the picture stones do not necessarily represent women in peaceful contexts. On some stones, women are depicted as in warlike situations,

Figure IV.2. Picture stone from the church of Smiss, Gotland, dated to to the eighth century. The motif could be a woman who performs a sacrificial act with a worm. Photo: Stefan Olsson.

for example on the motif on the stone from the church of Smiss (Figure IV.2). This motif has by several researchers, including the folklorist Aðalheiður Gudmundsdóttir, been linked to the the being called Hild (ON *Hildr*) in the legendary battle *Hjaðingavíg*, where she resurrects fallen warriors. Apart from the parallel from the legend, we can identify some cult objects on the picture stone. The woman holds what seems to be a snake in her hand, an animal that has been associated with Odin and perhaps with war.[124] The woman leans over what appears to be an altar (ON *stallr, stalli*, or possibly a *hörgr*). Swords, ships, helmets, and shields may not be interpreted as individual cult objects but appear in this case to be associated with warlike activities. The men move into what seems to be a procession. Clearly, the picture is depicting a warlike situation with a woman in a leading position.

Aðalheiður believes that the *Hjaðingavíg* in its ancient Scandinavian versions reflects the wish of men to be healed after their death on the battlefield (as in the myth of Valhall and the einherjar). Thus, it could be a symbol of women's reaction to the destructive forces of warlike societies and a desire to restore society.[125] By assuming this type of role, women could take the consequences of men's mistakes.

Other sources implictly suggest that women had functions during political negotiations where a hostage was a resource. *Knytlinge saga* contains a story about Emma, the wife of Canute the Great. Canute was married in 1016 to the widow Queen Emma of Normandy, who had her sons, Edward and Alfred, with Ethelred II of England.[126] According to the much earlier *Encomium Emmæ Reginae* (probably written in 1041), Emma cunningly refused to become the bride of Canute unless he promised to not appoint the son of any other woman as heir to the throne. Canute accepted the terms and took an oath to not appoint any other son than the children of him and Emma. Thus Emma made arrangements for her offspring. The *Encomium* further reports that the marriage of Canute and Emma ended the ongoing war with the English king Edmund Ironside (who passed away the same year).[127] Later Emma gave birth to Harthacnut who became the heir of Canute.

According to the *Knytlinge saga,* the sons of Emma opposed Canute, who made a siege on London, which was held by the sons. Both sides sent emissaries for negotiations, hostages were given, and a truce was signed to more confidently discuss the negotiations.[128] Did Emma have an impact on these negotiations because she had close connections to both sides? The accuracy of this information must be regarded as unclear because the *Knytlinge saga* was written in the mid 13th century. According to the Icelandic philologist Ármann Jakobsson the general tendency of the saga is 'the institution of kingship as such, and with the virtues of kings', some of these kings and good others evil.[129] The conflict with the sons are not mentioned in the *Encomium,* which only reports that the sons of Emma and Canute was jointly sent to France while Harthacnut was kept in England.[130] Was this a way to avoid conflict? Still, the example might illustrate how a woman could have an intermediate position that could be decisive for the outcome of the peace, or war, even if it was directly or indirectly through a council as it is implied by the *Encomium*.

Gunnhild

One of the few named Scandinavian women who can be identified as hostage is Gunnhild who lived in the early 11th century.

She belonged to the Danish royal family because she was sister of Sweyn Forkbeard. She was probably married to the chieftain Pallig Tokesen, who served with Æthelred II in England. On the 13th of November in 1002, she was supposedly executed in the so-called St Brice's Day massakre. Ethelred II had all the Danes he could find executed. According to the historian Ann Williams, the objective was probably to wipe out the Danes who were in the service of Æthelred and not the Anglo-Saxons with Danish ancestry in the shires. The Vikings, who were divided into different groupings, were considered false and prone to betrayal.[131]

The 'St. Brice's Day massakre' is reported in the *Anglo-Saxon Chronicle*, but neither Gunnhild nor Pallig is mentioned. Much suggests that the 'St. Brice's Day massakre' is a late construction because it is only mentioned in medieval chronicles. William of Malmesbury has the most information about Gunnhild (or Gunnhilda). According to him, Gunnhild, together with her husband, voluntarily entered the hostageship as guarantor of an Anglo-Danish peace.[132] The motif – that they would have volunteered as hostages – could be compared with the previously mentioned hypothesis that hostages could be acquired because they were valuable persons. In any case, one cannot assume that Gunnhild alone took this decision.

William of Malmesbury describes Gunnhild as 'beautiful'. When she came to England, she converted to Christianity. When she was killed, she behaved with 'courage' and did not lose her beauty even after she was killed, William writes.[133] This is in line with the cliché image William gives of historical women: primarily as non-violent, beautiful, virtuous, and with good mental qualities, something comparable to female characteristics as they are presented in other types of source material.

Female warriors

Whether female warriors ever existed in Scandinavia is a much-debated issue. Researchers including the archaeologist Neil Price, the historian of religions Britt-Mari Näsström, and the historian Agneta Ney argue that some women acted as warriors.[134] There is, however, weak support for this in text sources such as

Gesta Danorum (Book 9), where it is told that the evil king Frø of Uppsala put women of noble lineage into a brothel. The hero Ragnar Lodbrok (ON *Ragnarr Loðbrók*) attacks Frø and is aided by the female warrior, 'shieldmaiden', Lagertha (ON *Hlaðgerðr*), who fights with 'locks flowing loose over her shoulders'.[135] Näsström points out that an inspiration for Saxo Grammaticus could have been the Catholic virgin martyrs that flourished in the fourth century. In the hagiographical, these martyrs try to keep their virtue sometimes by fighting like Thekla, a follower of Paul, who fought in the Amphitheatres.[136] Other sources, such as the *Gesta Hammaburgensis Ecclesiae Pontificum* by Adam of Bremen, report of 'amazons' in the heathen Scandinavian societies. This kind of information must be regarded as fiction; it was a common theme in literature from the seventh century onward to describe female warriors and huntresses.[137]

Recent archaeological findings and reinterpretation of earlier findings have reignited the debate on female warriors. An investigation of a warrior grave (Bj 581) at the island of Birka, in Lake Mälaren, showed that it contained a presumed male skeleton and the equipment of warrior: a sword, an axe, a spear, armour-piercing arrows, a battle knife, two shields, and two horses. A recent analysis of the genome-wide sequence data showed that it was not a man but a woman that was buried. The woman was probably not of Birka origin. According to Hedenstierna-Jonson *et al.*, this is proof of not only a female warrior but also a female war-leader.[138] In addition, findings from Norway may also be interpreted as burials of female warriors. At the farm Nordre Kjølen in Trøndelag, a mound was excavated in 1900 where grave goods such as a sword, axe, spear, shield, and arrows, and a skeleton of a horse were found together with a skeleton of a woman.

In spite of these findings one must be careful to conclude that it was a question about female warriors. The archaeologist Frans-Arne H. Stylegar points out that the findings were made in the 19th and early 20th centuries and circumstances were not ultimate; for example, in the Norwegian case it could be a double burial, with a man and a woman. The women may not have used the weapons actively in life.[139] The archaeologist Leszek Gardeła examined the funerary material of some burials with possible remnants of female warriors. According to Gardela, there is proof for the existence of female burials with weapons.[140] The most common weapon types for these burials were axes, which is troublesome because these items functioned not only as weapons but also as tools. Gardela concludes that we cannot be sure whether women used the weapons that they were buried with and that the interpretation of the burials must follow the contextual circumstances.[141] Nonetheless, the reinterpretion of these old findings adds fuel to the ongoing discussion.

If there ever were female warriors they would certainly be suitable as hostages.

Although it is not possible to see a unique pattern of the role of women, their qualities and abilities, their social capital, that the texts support, they seem to have had important functions in times of war as well as times of peace. These functions could be compared to the multifaceted functions that male hostage seems to have had. One problem to be aware of is the Christian influence in that kind of context. These sources are also tendentious by describing events in different times and areas. Nevertheless, it can be concluded that women in the cultures described in the sources did not have one but several functions in addition to being a wife in a household. In this way, women became important actors in negotiations, among other things. Thus, the above mentioned examples could illustrate some of the reasons that women became hostages.

The unsuccessful agreement

Although oaths were taken and hostages given in bilateral agreements, sometimes peace agreements failed. For example, such failures can be seen in the *Royal Frankish Annals* for the years 804, 808, 809, and 810.[142] The Danish king Godfred (or Gudfred) arrived at the border area between South Jutland and Friesland in 804 and exchanged messengers with Charlemagne. Godfred made a peace agreement, a personal settlement, with Charlemagne, but in 808 he attacked the Obotrites, according to the Royal Annals. The following year, Charlemagne's emissaries failed to negotiate a peace. In 810 Godfred assaulted the coasts of the Frisians and forced the householders to pay 100 pounds in silver.[143]

In this type of failed peace process, hostages sometimes appear to have had restrictions on personal freedom, something that may have been perceived as extremely offensive to those who came from the upper strata of society. The hostage may also have become a pawn in a political game between the various groupings in which the loyalty of the hostage was not always clear. It could also be the ultimate destiny of the hostage to be executed or die far away from relatives and friends. An example of this is found in a story in the *Orkneyinga saga*. According to the story, Olaf Tryggvason arrives to the Orkney Islands. There he encounters earl Sigurd Hlodvirsson (OI *Sigurðr Hlöðvisson jarl*) and demands that he and his people accept Christianity. Sigurd wishes to obey Olaf, who then takes Sigurd's son Hunde (OI *Hundr*), or Whelp (OI *Hvalpr*), as hostage. Hunde is baptized and Olaf gives him the name Hlaudvir (or *Hlǫdvir*). When Olaf returns to Norway, he brings Hlaudvir, who lived there for only a short while until he died. After the death of Hlaudvir, Sigurd no longer feels bound to his promises to Olaf. In this case, the hostage had played its part. Whether Hunde died a natural death is not apparent from the text, though it is likely.

The above examples lead to questions: Which restrictions were imposed on a hostage? Did violence occur, and in such cases, why? These are themes we shall turn to in the next sections.

Unviolable hostage?

A hostage was never completely without rights, but these must be seen in relation to the current circumstances as well as the political and religious contexts. There were various reasons why hostages were violated. They were due to the degree of the protection that was stipulated. If the hostages were violated, it could have to do with how the relationship was percieved by the taking side. Misconceptions and suspicion may have arisen during the course of events. Another possible reason for the hostage being treated badly – as mentioned earlier in the discussion of the foster institution – may have been that they became a financial burden: a person from the upper strata needed an expensive support.

In the Roman Empire there were apparently hostages who were protected by the written treaty and the hostage takers were obliged to ensure that they were not violated. According to the legal historian Stephan Elbern, the treaty (*foedus*) ensured that hostage (in some cases) even became 'sacrosanct'.[144] Elbern does not explain the concept of 'sacrosanct' but suggests that the hostage had connections with religious traditions.

Elbern's position has been discussed by Walker, who argues that in the Roman Empire it was the design of the agreement that constituted the hostage rather than the hostage itself. The treaty (*fides*) was the verbal expression of an agreement, while the hostage itself was the physical expression of the agreement. Walker points out that Dionysius of Halicarnassus describes how Lucius Tarquinius Superbus, Rome's last king, used violence against the hostage whose bodies were considered sacred (ιερά σώματα).[145] Allen, on the other hand, indicates that the sacrosant status of the hostage is mentioned very few times, such as by Dionysius of Halicarnassus, so that it can not be considered as legio; no other of the hundreds of references to hostages suggests that they had a holy status.[146]

The hostage was the guarantee that the agreement would be held by the donors.[147] There is nothing in these contexts that indicates that hostage was considered as 'holy' and enjoyed sanctioned protection in the same way as holy objects – and sacrosanct persons – and that they would therefore have been inviolable.

Suspicion during negotiations

Since the giving and taking of hostages were part of peace processes, misconceptions about them as persons could arise during the negotiations. Because the hostages were escorted to the areas of communication by the afore-mentioned cult specialists (in the Roman Empire) or by other men with the power to negotiate, they may have been viewed with the same suspicion as the negotiators.

The negotiators received a special protection. Certain rules of conduct appear to have existed for the messengers, who were inviolable, as guests, at least during negotiations between the Romans and Germanic peoples. In 374, the Suebian ruler Gabinius was invited by the Roman army commander Marcellinus under a special sacred, guest right. That kind of protection can be related to the international law – within the Roman legal system – *jus gentium*, a part of the civil law, *jus civile*. The protection concerned, according to Roman perception, messengers, but the Germanic side may have had a different opinion about its 'legality'.[148]

Suspicions could arise before peace meetings. This is a recurring theme in some Continental Germanic and Old Scandinavian myths. An example is found in one of the origin myths of the Saxons that explains the name 'Saxon'. At a peace meeting with the Thuringians, the Saxons are said to have hidden their *seaxes*, knives, under their robes, thereby the name Saxons.[149] The myth of Týr and Fenrir described in Snorri's *Edda* portrays a similar context.[150] These myths could primarily have served as example of what might happen if one did not act cautiously and correctly during negotiations, regardless of different 'sanctioned' protection at places of peace meetings.

Being hostage meant restrictions on personal freedom. But freedom was far greater for people with higher status than for a common prisoner or a slave. At the same time, this could change when the social capital of the hostage disappeared, something that could be seen in the case of Theoderic and Childebert, the sons of Gallo-Roman senators who were used as hostages in the early sixth century to secure a treaty between the sons of king Clovis I. When the peace was broken, the sons lost their value as hostages; they became slaves.[151] The protection was no longer applicable because their fathers no longer held any influential positions. The example suggests that the treatment of a person who was hostage also was dependent on the safety of the hostage taker.

In *Getica*, Jordanes claims that the West Gothic ruler Theoderid (or Theodoric) had a daughter who married Huneric, son of King Gaiseric of the Vandals. In the beginning of the marriage they were content. Eventually Gaiseric suspected that Theoderid's daughter tried to poison him, so he cut off her nose and truncated her ears. Then he sent her back to her father in Gaul. According to Jordanes, the intention was to provoke Theoderid to claim revenge.[152] In this case, apparently, marriage was originally a part of an alliance formation. Perhaps Gaiseric felt the marriage was an arrangement that did not suit him. If the tradition of marrying someone can be related to procedures of gift givings, we can see a vertical friendship here: the delivery of a bride becomes a forced subordination in this case by giving the bride. Gaiseric's suspicion became the triggering factor and, thus, the excuse for breaking the agreement in a position where he felt strong enough to challenge Theoderid.

A unique paragraph is found in the medieval Frisian law code *Lex Frisionum* (XX), which has a ban on executions of hostages.[153] The law is written in Latin around the year 785 and is featured during peace talks between Franks and Frisians. Despite the fact that the law was made due to the Frankish initiative, it contains old Frisian law.

The above Continental Germanic examples may indicate that the cause for an abusive treatment of a high-ranking person who was given as a hostage depended on many things, including the political situation. Nevertheless, I have not found many cases or traces that a hostage as part of an agreement would have been treated poorly during Viking Age Scandinavia. The examples that I have already mentioned are the most extreme cases I could find in peace processes or bilateral agreements. To get further information about violence against hostage in Scandinavia, we must turn to medieval sources.

Medieval contexts

A few details in some medieval texts from Scandinavia – such as the Norweigian law *Magnus lagabøters landslov* – can provide us with information that the hostage has suffered violations and been subjected to violence. These details can be compared to Kosto, who points out late medieval continental examples in which the hostage was treated poorly, e.g. being starved or killed. However, according to Kosto, the hostage was generally treated well during the Middle Ages, although there were exceptions. As pointed out earlier, Kosto believes that the treatment of hostages was determined by how they were socially valued and how they were expected to be treated:[154]

[...] particularly for earlier periods, most of the hostages we know about were either noble or wealthy enough to merit (or negotiate) good treatment. Furthermore, many hostages of lower status were handed over pursuant to agreements negotiated by powerful people and thus the condition of their confinement reflected their patrons' influence. Where hostages are treated well, in other words, it is as likely to be because of who they were as because of their status as hostages.[155]

Similar structures with examples of social differences in the treatment of hostages can be found in the sagas (medieval cases) and in the medieval Scandinavian laws and diplomas.

It was a duty to return a hostage unscathed, as pointed out by the Scandinavianist Dag Gundersen; should it, on the other hand, be forfeited, the hostage could be blinded.[156] One can assume that the hostage was treated well if someone did not violate the agreement, which is stated in the *Magnus lagabøters landslov*. If the King mistrusted the householders to not give him support in a conflict they were expected to give hostages to prove their loyalty. The king was also expected to return the hostage 'not mutilated'.[157] Here, it is explicitly mentioned that it was mutilation that awaited the hostage and not death, which we will return to. It is also suggested in the law, which was an instrument of power, that the hostage was not to be used in direct negotiations. The king would use this tool if the householders refused to perform military service in wartime. The lives of a householder might be less valuable in this context. This is the question of the conditional hostage, i.e. the hostage was used as security because the houeseholders in such cases violated an agreement that existed between them and the royal power.

Another of Gundersen's sources is *Orkneyinga þáttr*, a part of *Flateyjarbók*'s version of *Olafs saga hins helga* (*Saga of St. Olaf*). Thorfinn (*Þorfinnr*), son of the Earl of the Orkney Islands and Caithness, Harald Maddadsson (ON *Haraldr Maddaðarson* [d. 1206]), was held hostage by the Scottish king William the Lion (ON *Vilhjálmr*). William had Thorfinn blinded. In the *Orkneyinga saga* it is briefly mentioned that William previously had Thorfinn whipped.[158]

There are several cases of blindings in the *Orkneyinga saga*.[159] At one occasion Earl Harald arrives to the castle Scrabster (ON

Skarabólstaðr) in Caithness. He then blinds the bishop and cut off his tongue. The bishop was then aided by a woman who brought him to the grave of Saint Triduana (ON *Trollhœna*), where he got his vision and speech back. The case is obviously a miracle story, and then one can interpret the blinding as a topos that is linked to a New Testament model.[160] There are even other cases of blinding in Old Western Norse literature. In *Heimkringla*'s version of Saint Olaf's saga, Olaf Haraldsson surrounds – as was his custom – a building with oposing 'kings'. After capturing them, he had King Hrœrekr blinded because he did not trust him and cut off the tongue of King Gudrøðr. The others had to swear to leave Norway and never return.[161]

Based on only the sagas, it is not possible to conclude that hostages could be blinded in case of breaches of the agreements that were secured with hostages. However, in medieval legislation, it was implicit that violence was actually used against people who were held hostage, at least in the Norwegian medieval realm. In the above stories, the distinction between being a captive and a hostage also emerges: in the former case it is a person that was handed over through the mercy of their capturer. The well-being of the hostage depended on the behaviour of their own side and thus responded to a completely different political situation. Still, there are cases where medieval legislation can provide information about both the protection of hostages and the violence directed against them, which in both cases can be related to negotiations.

In the medieval provincial laws, it can be difficult to distinguish between a 'personal hostage' (Germ. *Borgensgeisel*) and a 'public hostage'. The lawyer and political scientist Poul Meyer believed that the former category is the oldest in the Danish provincial laws.[162] However, in the Swedish provincial laws there is a distinction between the public hostage and the personal hostage. In the *Upplandslagen*, the provincial law of Uppland and the *Östgötalagen*, the procincial law of Östergötland, there is a difference in how to value the hostage. In the *Östgötalagen*, a special crime is stipulated in the section about manslaughter (Sw. *Dråpsbalken*): if a criminal is removed from the captor, he has violated the law of hostage (*gislingabrut*).[163] The same crime is also stipulated in the section about crime that is accidentally committed (OSw *Vådamålsbalken*) and the section about lawsuits (Sw. *Rättegångsbalken*).¹⁶⁴ He who had the main responsibility should forfeit 40 marks. These cases concerned individuals and groups on a private, personal, level.¹⁶⁵

In the paragraph on personal peace (Sw. *Manhelgdsbalken*) in the *Upplandslagen* it is stipulated that if a person who is hostage is beaten or killed, he (or his kin) shall be compencated with the much higher amount of 140 marks:

Nu kan kunnugær gislæ hawæ. wærþer han (wæghin ok slaghin (gildær mæþ hundræþe markum ok firuætighi.¹⁶⁶

§ 8. Now the King may have a hostage; if he is beaten and killed, he shall be fined for with a hundred marks and forty.¹⁶⁷

(My transl.)

This protection applies to the traditions around the Eriksgata, which are listed in several provincial laws, including the *Upplandslagen* (confirmed 1296).¹⁶⁸ The fine in the paragraph on 'personal peace' is equated with other types of crimes that also render 140 marks in fines. These crimes concerned different types of violations within locations where people received some protection:¹⁶⁹

§ 1. In their homes or within the four boundary markers (Sw. *råmärken*) of the common lands of the village.

§ 2. At a church or a graveyard within the distance of sixty fathoms.

§ 3. At a thing place that is 'ancient' and 'lawful'.

§ 4. A father who is killed in the home of a married son, or at his own farm, within the distance of a spearhead and an axe-haft from the farm.

§ 5. In the forge or within the distance of a hammerthrow or a pair of nippers from the forge.

§ 6. If a man has tried to deceive concerning a homicide outside the communities.¹⁷⁰

§ 7. A sick person who has been left on an island.

§ 9. The king's tax collectors and servants are beaten and killed when they are out traveling.

§ 10. If a lawman is beaten and killed when he when he pronounces judgement on the law of the country.

It is possible that some of these paragraphs go back to older provisions such as the measure of how far a hammer can be thrown. According to the lawyer and legal historian Åke Holmbäck and the philologist Elias Wessén, the distance of sixty fathoms has replaced the (older?) measures of hammer and spear throws.[171]

Paragraph three on the protection at a thing place that is 'ancient' and 'right' is even more important, in my view. Holmbäck and Wessén do not comment on this characteristic, but the reference to the age of thing places suggests that if they were used in elder days, they built on an authority that was anchored in the local community. The right to protection may very well go back to older traditions. It is therefore interesting that even the lawspeaker, whose traditional role was to memorise and recite laws, is also mentioned in the paragraph on personal peace (or safety).

Because the protection with personal peace involves both towns and villages as well as the king's hostage during the ritual journey of the Eriksgata, one can compare the latter example with the mobile cult places. The possibility that hostages traveling to thing places had a specific protection could also be the case during peace negotiations. However, it cannot be argued that those persons who had this kind of protection were untouchable in the sense that they had a holy or sanctified protection.

Violence took place in the places listed in the paragraphs, despite the protection, which, in its medieval context, was mainly by the law except for the protection at the churches that was constituted by the Canonic law. One can compare this with Elbern's assertion of hostages in the Roman Empire as 'sacrosanct'. In fact, the paragraph on personal peace suggests that assaults on hostages actually occured. However, it is possible to speak of a 'protection' with its roots in earlier times.

Of the above-mentioned texts there are two main situations where the hostage is used that correspond to the basic premise for bilateral and unilateral hostages:

(A) At an occasion with a more or less voluntarily given or taken hostage on an uneven basis. There was no room for compromises and the behaviour of the side of the hostage largely governed the treatment. This feature had a vertical structure and can be said to have been unilateral as in the case of the law code of Magnus IV of Norway, *Magnus lagabøters landslov*.

(B) Situations in which the hostage had (personal) protection during peace negotiations and the protection was regulated by legal rules for different areas of communications. The protection also concerned the 'hostage' on an even more personal level (see the case of Prince Valdemar, below). In these situations, a horizontal structure is found, which was both bilateral and unilateral. The behaviour of the hostage's own side was crucial for his or her well-being, but to a lesser extent. The social value of the hostage was also of significance.

There is additional information to add to the discussion on the personal protection. This can be done through a review of places and terms for protection in peace talks in Viking and medieval contexts. Before that, the hostage case of Prince Valdemar of Denmark is described.

Prince Valdemar as hostage

In a Danish medieval diploma from the 13th century, it is stated that the hostage should reside in a particular place and not leave it without the consent of the hostage agency. The background was that Count Henry I of Schwerin managed to capture Valdemar II 'the Victorious' (Da. *sejr*) of Denmark and his son Valdemar 'the Young' on the island of Lyø, south of Funen in May 1223. Henry was actually a vassal of the Danish king. However, he negotiated with the Holy Roman emperor Frederick II – who acted as a third party – so that Valdemar and his son were to be extradited to the emperor. In the agreement, Henry demanded that all the lands conqured by Valdemar in the province of Holstein would be handed over to him and Valdemar was obliged to pay 52,000 pieces of silver to the Count and his friends.[172]

The agreement also stipulated that 'the young king of Denmark' should be kept at the castle of Harzburg (in the present Lower Saxony) under the supervision of 'captains' (Da. *høvedsmand*)

and ministerials in the emperor's service.[173] 'The Old King of Denmark' would remain with Henry of Schwerin:

> until Most Reverend Archbishop of Cologne and the above-mentioned Count of Schwerin [Henry] wishes to inform, whether they can engage the kings of Denmark to acquire the mercy of the emperor and of the king, either by payment or by repatriating the lands they have deprived emperor and kingdom, or whatsoever any other means.[174]
>
> (My free translation)

Although the word 'hostage' is not mentioned in this paragraph of the diploma, it is implicit. The hostage guaranteed that the agreement should enter into force. The Danes rejected the requirements, and without Valdemar they suffered a defeat in January 1225. Not until Easter 1226 were Valdemar and his son released upon the payment of 18,000 pieces of silver, and Valdemar's three other sons were admitted as hostage.[175]

This later arrangement could be compared to what Kosto refer to as 'custodial hostage'. The sons stood as a guarantee for a third party while the remaining sum would be collected. The diploma contains no more details about how Valdermar's son, the future king Valdemar, should be treated. It must not be doubted that it was anything but an 'honorable' custody. It was thus the captivity and detention that was the purpose of hostageship and not the external violence. Such a thing occured elsewhere in Scandinavia. Prince Valdemar was thus treated due to his position.

Places and terminology for protection during negotiations

In places with protection during peace negotiations, it was possible to safeguard the hostage during the negotiations and the delivery of the hostage. These places were what I refer to as ares of communication. In order to understand how these places were designed, it is necessary to investigate the terminology that was used. I therefore discuss the words describing peace and a state of restrictions on violence: *friðr* and *grið*.

Friðr

For the temporary hostage used during peace talks, special safeguards might have been applied. The hostage probably had the same protection as the person for whom it was pledged as security. This protection was mainly derived from the negotiations in the areas of confrontation between the Anglo-Saxons and the Danes or other Scandinavians, as described in various chronicles. The hostage form primarily used in direct negotiations was the 'true hostages' (see Part I), but there may also have been other forms of hostages. Thus, protection and regulations for hostages can be mainly related to the places where negotiations took place. But it is also important to clarify the difference between the Old Western Norse concepts of *friðr* and *grið*.

In Old English there are terms for protection during negotiations at certain places. The term *frēoðo-burh* (alt. *frēo-burh*) that can be translated as 'town, stronghold [...] the sacred peace attaching to the king's dwelling in the laws'.[176] The modifier in this designation can be derived from the Old English *frēod*, 'peace' or 'friendship'. There is an analogy in the Old English *friþ* (alt. *frið*), the verb *frēogan*, 'to liberate' or 'to love', and the adjective *frēo*, 'freedom', 'noble', or 'happy'.[177]

The Germanist Heinrich Tiefenbach states in his characteristic of the Germanic and Scandinavian 'peace' (ger. *Friede*) that:

> On the whole, the finding can be interpreted that apart from the function of designating ties within the closest social group ('love, friendship'), the meaning components 'protection, security' were dominant in the Germ[anic] **friþu*. The features 'state without war/conflict', which can be: detected early on, have probably above all received its coining power for the hist[ory] of the meaning of the word under the influence of Christian ideas of p[eace].

According to this definition, the word could have initially been used within a closed community, as in the environments of the halls. The definition can be compared to the historian Johannes Steenstrup's view that peace (*friðr*) eventually came to mean something that was more 'objective' (than *grið*) and existing throughout the society.[178]

Kershaw believes that Old English *friþ*, with cognates in both Scandinavian and in West Germanic languages, may originate from the perceptions of order in the relationships of family and friendship.[179] The Old English word *friþ* seems to characterize the order in different types of places such as the king's hall, a saint's crypt, the sanctuary of the church and the monastery. Sometimes this arrangement could comprise an entire area. It was primarily places with the significance of an ideal order. This applies primarily to the order prevailing in Anglo-Scandinavian areas of communication as described with Old English terminology. As a comparison, it is relevant to see if a similar terminology, which indicates the level of protection during negotiations, can be found in Scandinavian areas of confrontation, using information in skaldic and Eddic poems.

To understand places with protection, it is essential to highlight the contextual differences between the Old Western Norse words *friðr* and *grið*. As far as peace is concerned, it is evident that in late skaldic poems (13th–14th centuries), such as the *Máriuvísur*, it appears in Christian and biblical contexts with the meaning of 'heavenly peace'. The transcripts made by the earliest skalds and directly related to war are more relevant. Among other things, Sigvat wrote the poem in his *erfidrápa* (11th century) on the death of Olaf Haraldsson (c. 1040) 'that there was an end to peace' (*friðbann var þar monnum*) when archers fired their arrows at Stiklestad (1030).[180] The word *Friðbann* could be interpreted as a kind of standstill before the battle. However, the head *-bann* can be related to the verb *banna*, 'to forbid', 'to condemn', or 'to curse'. The word *friðbann* is a kenning that suggests that peace is broken rather than a direct connection with the war.

Several places with names that include the modifier *friðr-* are mentioned in Old Norse sources even if the actual meaning is not always evident. *Friðland* appears as an idyllic land in the skaldic poetry. In the skaldic poem *Háttatal* (stanza 43), *Fróða friðbygg* is mentioned, but it is a metaphorical description of the 'peaceful order' under the mythical ruler Fróði. In addition, a stanza in the skaldic poem *Velleka* (10th century) by Einar Helgason (ON Einarr Helgason) refers to the fact that there was no warrior on earth who arranged such peace (*slíkr friðr*) as Fróði.[181]

There is plenty of proof for the word *friðr* in pre-Christian contexts, but neither in the Eddic poetry nor in the skaldic poetry is it directly linked to negotiations. The combination of *gefa* and *friðr* denotes metaphorical rewritings to break the peace of another person, an enemy or a victim: *gefr hánum engi frið* (*Havamál*), 'gave him no peace', or *at giæfim gridbitum frid litinn*, 'to give the breakers of the truce little peace'.[182]

There is one exception where *friðr* is recorded as a single word, in the phrase *friðar at biðja* ('to ask for peace') in the eddic poem *Hárbarðsljóð* and in the skaldic poem *Haustlǫng* (stanza 8) *varð Þors* [...] *friðar biðja* ('Thor's friend [Loki] [...] asked for peace').[183] The poetic expressions appear ambigious in these cases. It could be interpreted as an appeal for a desired sanctified protection rather than a peace treaty, because it is not evident that the myths alluded to are between groups such as the gods and the jötnar or between the indivdiuals Loki and Thor. Otherwise, the word appears in the metaphorical rewritings for the breaking of peace, or the 'truce', for example, *frið glepsk*, 'the hurting peace'.[184]

There are also places for protection with *friðr-*, 'peace', in the modifier as in the Old English *friðgearð* och *friðsplott*, 'peacekeeping' and 'peace plot'. According to Tiefenbach, these places would be 'heathen', but at the same time have to do with the 'heavenly dwelling' (Germ. *Gefilde*) and Christ.[185] One can compare with the suggestion by Elmevik: Friggeråker (OSw *Frig(g)iæraker*) in the district of Gudhem in Västergötland may be derived from a possible Old Western Gohtic **Friðgærð(ar)aker*.[186]

According to the language researcher, the linguist Johan Fritzner the word *friðgerð* (f.) meant 'peacemaking', 'settlement of peace'. The word is found in the title of the *Friðgerðarsaga*, a story about peace makings in Iceland. In *Stjorn: Gammelnorsk Bibelhistorie*, published in 1862, the word *friðgerðarlǫgmál* appears, which Fritzner interpreted as 'truce' or 'settlement'.[187] Evidently, these sources are vague and belong to medieval contexts. Perhaps *friðgerð*, in its pre-medieval contexts, refered to the 'peace' at the *vi*-place, which was surrounded by a *vebǫnd* as proposed by Elmevik.

No evidence in the skaldic poetry indicates that there was a place with the modifier *friðr-* where negotiations were conducted outdoors. However, there is an Old Western Norse adverb *friðssamligr*, 'peaceable', and an adjective that may suggest that such a word existed before the 12th century. Both of these words are found in the *Flateyjarbók* (II) from the 14th century, and again it is a matter of contexts that indicate a peaceful state.[188]

As a condition, peace may have been important for the 'peace'-like state that existed in the hall, for example during a banquet. The personal name Hallfred may possibly suggest that there was a peace in the hall, e.g. in the Runic Swedish female names *Hallfriðr* (Hall- + *-(f)reðr/-(f)røðr*) and *Hallfríðr* (*Hall-*, 'hall', + *-fríðr*, 'peace').[189]

In the *Eyrbyggja saga*, in the episode about Thorolf Örnólfsson (OI *Þórólfr Ǫrnólfsson Mostrarskegg*), the word *friðstaðr* is used by the writer. The farm Hofsstaðir that Thorolf built on the foreland of Þórsnes by the river Þórsá in the fjord Breiðafjörður was inside declared 'to be in peace' (*friðstaðr*).[190] In this episode, there are some interresting names and descriptions of Thorolf's land ownership around Þórsnes. For example, the township at Þórsnes was a 'holy place' (*helgistaðr*).[191] The sanctification of these places may reflect a will where the hallowing of the land coincided with the ambition to legitimize the land ownership, not only legally but also by religious tradition. The word *friðstaðr* does not appear in any version of the *Landnámabók*'s version of the story about Thorolf, so it is hard to know if the word, in this case, is a part of an authentic tradition or not.

As an example of a possible temporary protection before negotiations, the truce-shield, *frið-skǫldr*, could be mentioned. In connection with the use of the truce-shield, there is an example in which one side wanted to ritually demonstrate their peaceful intentions during peace processes where hostages were used. At the same time, they violated the terms of truce, and the area of communication was therefore deliberately turned into a confrontational area. *The Annals of Fulda* (*Annales Fuldenses*) describe how a Frankish army under Charles the Fat (Fr. *Charles Le Gros*) laid siege to a group of Scandinavians at a fortress called Asselt in Friesland in 882. According to the annals the Scandinavian chief, Godafrid, called *dux*, bribed the 'false' bishop Liutward and his associate count Wigbert to convince the Emperor not to attack the Northmen.[192] Liutward introduced Godafrid to Charles. The Emperor was kind to Godafrid and made peace with him, whereupon the hostage was exchanged. The Northmen took it as a good sign and raised the truce shield to show their good intentions. When some Franks entered the fortification to trade, the Northmen immediately lowered the shield and closed the gates. All Franks inside the fortress were killed or captured for later use in ransom negotiations. The Emperor chose to ignore the incident. Later Godafrid accepted baptism and received some lands in Kennemerland as a gift. Other Northmen returned to their homelands with robbed goods and 200 prisoners, and they waited for the next occasion for plundering.[193] The chronicle is tendentious as it is angled from the perspective of the Franks. The case exemplifies, though, how people were not inviolable during negotiations even though there was formally a 'truce'. The truce shield marked a place where it was supposed to be a temporary peace.

Grið

The word *grið*, as mentioned previously, seems to have a clearer connection with negotiations in the sense that the word indicated that the warriors had temporary protection from further acts of violence. In various medieval legal conflicts, there is a sanctioned protection for individuals, either (a) a homeless woman (*griðkona*) or a man (*griðmaðr*) who is accepted into another's home, or (b) a temporary protection in a place before a trial.[194]

The concept of *grið* occurs in the skaldic language in different contexts about truces (Figure IV.3). Of particular interest are the combination verb + *grið* as in *nefna grið*, 'announce (to) peace'. In *Þórgeirsdrápa*, there is *griða æsta*, 'to pray for truce (or safe conduct)'. Arnórr Þórðarson jarlaskáld's memory drapa dedicated to Harald Hardrada (*Erfidrápa um Harald konung harðráða*) indicates that the Norwegians did not want peace (*vilja grið*) but preferred to fall with the king.[195] In a skaldic stanza in *Ragnars saga*, Ragnar's wife, Kráka, asks if he wishes to keep the peace (*ef vilttu griðum þyrma*).[196] The verb expresses actions such as 'to will', 'to ask', 'to desire', 'to hold', or 'to give' in combinations with *grið*, which in the more unambiguous sense meant that a truce,

186 The Hostages of the Northmen

Word	Meaning	In contexts	Sources
grið (pl.)	'safe conduct, truce, security'	gefa grið	Bjarni Kolbeinsson *Jómsvíkinga drápa* 44 (13th century)
	'truce; life' (the time of safe conduct a killer has before trial)	selja einum grið	*Sólarljóð* 21 'The song of the son' (13th century)
		nefna [...] (?) grið	Sigvat skald *Flokkr about Erlingr Skjalgsson* 4 (1026)
		æsta griða	Þórmóð Bersason Kólbrunarskald *Þórgeirsdrápa* 11 (1030)
		vilja grið	Arnórr Þórðarson jarlaskáld *Erfidrapa of king Haraldr harðráði* 15 (1067)
		halda griðum	Gizurr Þorvaldsson *Drapa of Hakon the Old* (13th century)
		þyrma griðum	Stanza in *Ragnars saga loðbrókar* 3 (13th century)
		koma griðum við[sic.]	Oddr breiðfirðingr *Illugardrapa* 2 (1000)
		iðrask griða	Grettir Ásmundarsson *Lausavísur* 9 (1028)
		ræna griðum	Bjarni Kolbeinsson *Jómsvíkingadrápa* 19 (13th century)
		véla í griðum	Stanza in *Hálfssaga* VI 4

Figure IV.3. Derivations and compositions with *grið-* in Skaldic and Eddic poetry. Source: *Lexicon Poeticum* ([ed.] Finnur Jónsson): 203.

Legal Rights 187

Word	Meaning	In contexts	Sources
	'attempting to break the truce'	hyggja á griðum	Atlamál 33 (Eddic poem)
		grið létusk	Hallr Þórarinsson Háttalykill 14b (1140s)
		grið grennask	Ingjaldr Geirmundarson Atlǫguflokkr 5 (1244)
	'to give gold without conduct'	láta slitna grið gulli	Einar Skúlason Øxarflokkr 6 (?)
	'safe conduct from the einherjar'	Einherja grið	Eyvindr Finnsson Skáldaspillir Hákonarmál 16 (961)
	'someone who bites, the truce, trucebreaker'	griðbítr	Hásteinn Hrómundarson halta Lausavísur4 (955)
		griðbítr	Gunnlaugr Leifsson Merlínusspá I 18
griðfastr (adj.)	'holders of safe conduct'	griðfastir friðmenn	Þórarin lovtunga Tøgdrapa 5
griði	'to give safe conduct'	Grímr griði minn	Vǫlundarkviða 10 (eddic poem)
griðkona	'maid, female servant'		(Þórðr Kolbeinsson) Lausavísur 1
griðmildr (adj.)	'who likes to give (enemies) truce and safe conduct, (about Hakon the Old)'		Sturla Þórðarson Hrafnsmál 6 (1263)
griðningr	'someone who breaks their truce promise, trucebreaker'		Árni Jónsson Guðmundardrápa 42 (14th century)

Figure IV.3. Continued

including negotiations, were to be conducted (Figure V.3). One can thus give and receive *grið* in the event of a war.[197] Other skaldic stanzas, as in *griðningr*, indicate a possible breaking of the truce, the peace, or the safe conduct which suggests that a special 'peace' during the truce could not be broken.

In the case of *grið*, we can see place names with the combination of *grið* + a word for place. These places with *grið-* in the modifier may have been places of negotiations which involved the use of hostage as a security. This is supported by the combination (OSw) *gilzla* and *grutha* in Swedish medieval laws (see further below).

At least one Old English source refers to a building called *griphus* where negotiations were conducted. It could be compared to an English place name, Gribthorpe, Yorkshire, (OE *Grīp's thorp* [1231]), which can be derived from an Old Danish *grip* or an Old Western Norse *grið*.[198] There are no known Old Western Norse or Old Eastern Norse sources mentioning a special building for truces and negotiations. However, in the Old Western Norse sources there are names such as *griðasala* and *griðastaðr*. The latter word can be seen in the prose introduction of the eddic poem *Lokasénna*: *Þar var griðastaðr mikill*, 'it was a great place of peace'.[199]

According to Steenstrup, *grið* was used as the designation of 'peace' or 'protection' in a single place, which, according to Steenstrup, could be the cult building of a hof or a church; it was the place that was protective and not what was protected; it was an asylum right rather than the sanctity of churches.[200]

There is also a specific term for the ritual act through which a place was determined to serve for negotiation: *griðasetning*. Alternatively, it is only about the Old Norse *sætt* or *sett* seen There is also a specific term for the ritual act through which a placewas determined to serve for negotiation: griðasetning, 'treaty' or 'fraternity'. The term *griðasetning* should more accurately reflect how peace should be understood as a place of negotiation and can be related to contexts as in *Eyrbyggja saga*: *at grið varu sett með mǫnnum, þar til att hverr kœmi til síns heima*, 'so that a truce was issued between the men, which lasted until every man came to his home'.[201]

Obviously, there was a sanctioned protection – which was perceived as strong – in connection with *grið*, as suggested by the use of *kenningar* for 'truce-breaker', like *griðbítr*, and *griðníðingr*, such epipithet was not desireable. As a negotiator or participant during negotiations, one had a sanctioned protection through the *grið*. The sanctioned protection can be found in various stories. In the skaldic poem *Hákonarmál*, King Hakon will have safe conduct from the ever-violent *einherjar* as a mark of honor when he arrives at Valhall.[202]

In the same category is the story of the battle of the Alptafjord in *Eyrbyggia saga*, when Snorri Goði and Steinþórr meet to confirm the truce (*gríð*). Steinþór asks Snorri to hold out a hand. When Snorri does, Steinþór strikes with the sword against Snorri's hand; the blade hits the *stallahringr*, the ceremonial ring, which breaks but the hand remains unscathed.[203] The episode can of course be interpreted in several different ways but may possibly be perceived as an intervention from some kind of being who caused the ring to come between the sword and the hand, thereby protecting the *gríð*.

In *Grágás*, a medieval, Icelandic law, *grið* figures prominently in combination with *friðr* in a formal manner, but it clearly shows that the two words had different meanings.[204] In paragraph 122 the law says: *Það er uphaf að þessu máli að eg set grið ok frið á milli þeirra N. og N*, 'As introduction to this case I proclaim truce and peace between N.N. and N.N.'[205]

The same word pairs are found in *Heimskringla*'s version of the Saga of St. Olaf, in the aforementioned peace meeting between the Norweigians and the Swedes at Uppsala in 1018. At the thing the lawspeaker Torgny responded to the king of the Swedes, Olof Skötkonung, and his expansive plans in Norway. There is a dialogue between the king and Rögnvald Earl from Västergötland, during which the king accuses the earl of having made a truce and peace (*hafði gort grið ok frið*) with King Olaf Haraldsson.[206]

In these contexts, *friðr* is the peace you are striving for, while *grið* stands for the temporal truce and is limited in time and space. These concepts appear as an alliterative word pair that reinforces the impression of continuity from older traditions. There is also other medieval Scandinavian legislation with alliterative word pairs with words for peace and hostage.

gilzla *and* grutha *in Swedish medieval laws*

In the Swedish medieval laws, there is a text formula that can be related to both hostage and *grið*. In the laws describing the Eriksgata – the king's ceremonial journey to different provinces before the coronation – there is the formal expression *mæþ gruþum oc gislum*, 'with safe conduct and hostages'.[207] This expression meant that the king was promised safety for his life, with hostages as a security and safe conduct, as he traveled to the thing during his Eriksgata. This will be addressd in Part VI.

Alliterations are common in Old Norse texts, which for example can be seen in a section in the Icelandic law code *Grágás*, known as the *Griðamál*; there are alliterative formulas such as *grið og fullan frið, fégrið* and *griðníðingur er griðum*.[208] However, one law text has been perceived as standing apart of the Eriksgata traditions and can be derived from an independent oral tradition. In the *Smålandslagen* ('the law of the province of Småland', alt. *Tiohärads lag*) the Church section says:

> Gwz frither oc sancte marie. vari meth us. hiit komande. oc haethan farande. The seen alle skylde till gilzla oc grutha. ey æru bilthuga eller banzatte. alle the som boa innæn mioahalt. oc myrtleiks. oc. maellin brutabek oc biureiks.[209]

> God's peace, and holy Mary's, is with us, who have come here and shall depart. They are all obliged to give hostage and safe conduct, [those] who are not outlawed or bannished, all those who live within Mjöhult and Mörtlek and between Bråtabäck and Björkö.[210]
> (My translation)

The Church section is preserved in two manuscripts from the 14th century: the A manuscript from the Skokloster collection at the Swedish National Archives (cf. Figure IV.4) and Schlyter's B manuscript (cf. Figure IV.5), today in the Arnamagnæan Manuscript Collection in Copenhagen.

One phrase in particular in the Church section has been discussed: *The seen skylde till gilzla oc grutha*. A question historians and legal historians have asked has been in what relationship this text passage stands vis-à-vis other provincial laws. The legal historian Carl Johan Schlyter theorized that the passage consists of

Figure IV.4. A manuscript of the introduction to the Church section in the *Smålandslagen*, from the Skokloster Castle collection (today in the National Archives of Sweden, Stockholm). Source: *Samling af Sweriges gamla lagar*, ed. Carl Johan Schlyter; the word *gilzla* is marked. Photo: Stefan Olsson.

material from an elder King's section that was transmitted from some of the manuscripts on the Eriksgata because these texts (*Upplandslagen*, *Magnus Erikssons landslag*) mention that the king had the right to receive hostages and safe conduct before he entered the provinces with his retinue.

He therefore concluded that the Church section was not of old age because the *Tiohärad lagsaga* (an ancient legal district based on the *härad*s, 'hundreds') was not formed until 1296. Only then can it be confirmed by the *Upplandslagen* that the people of the *Tiohärad lagsaga* received the king during the Eriksgata.[211]

Holmbäck and Wessén claimed in their commentaries on the law that this phrase was a part of an earlier King's section (Sw. *kungabalk*) that was added through a transfer from other law traditions and it was older than the fixation in writing of the law of Uppland (*Upplandslagen*).[212] They nevertheless considered the province of Småland to be inclueded by the journey of the Eriksgata and that the concepts of *gilzla* and *grutha* belonged to this tradition. At the same time – according to both the Westrogothic laws – the jurisdictional district of Småland (Sw. *Tiohärads lagsaga*) was not included in the Eriksgata.[213] Those who were to be handed out by the Eastern Geats (Sw. *östgötar*) as hostages only

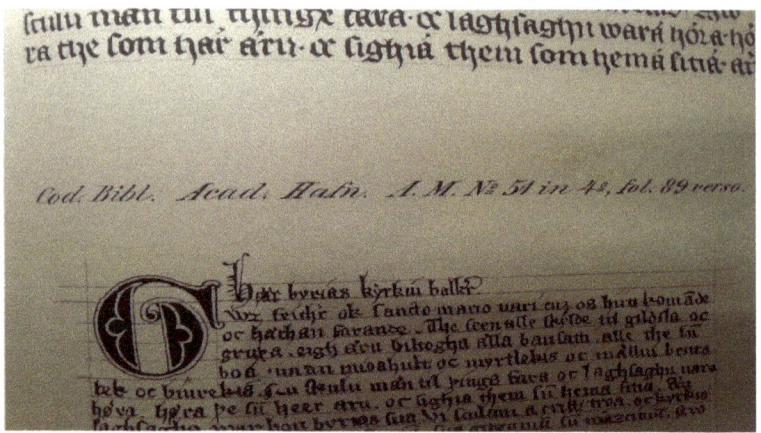

Figure IV.5. B manuscript of the Church section in the *Smålandslagen* in the Arnamagnæan Manuscript Collection in Reykjavík. Source: *Samling af Sweriges gamla lagar*, ed. Carl Johan Schlyter; the word *gildsla* is marked. Photo: Stefan Olsson.

followed the king to Junabäck (at present Jönköping) to meet the Westrogoths (Sw. *västgötar*). On the other hand, in the King's section of the law of Uppland, this had changed: the representatives of Småland would meet the king with the hostages at Holaved in Östergötland and follow him to the river Junebäcken.[214]

The historian Folke Dovring dated the Church section to an earlier time than the 13th century. He assumed that the text could be analysed based on its age-old character. Dovring pointed out that the phrase *gilzla oc grutha* was structured as alliterative word pairs, as was the case with several other phrases in the Church section.[215] The wordpair *gilzla* and *grutha* did not refer to any outlaws because they stood outside the society and did not have reason to attend the celebration of the king. Instead, the word pair refers to the conditions within the jurisdictional district and designated the peace of the assembly. According to Dovring the word *skylde* meant 'guilty' or 'mutually connected'.[216] Dovring thus translated the text: 'They were obliged to give each other "hostage" and "safe-conduct", all who came here (to the thing) and travel away, all that are not outlawed or banished'.[217] Dovring considered it likely that there had originally been a formula – which also existed

in the King's sections of the provincial laws – regarding safe conduct at the things. Thus there was a tradition in the Church section that conserved hostages through the formulistic phrase *gilzla oc grutha*, which stood outside the other traditions of the provincial laws that described the Eriksgata.[218]
Dovring's interpretation was met by hard criticism. The legal historian Gösta Hasselberg pointed out that mistakes have already been made in early interpretations into Latin during the 18th century.[219] A Latin interpretation of the law according to the manuscript from Skokloster was edited by the historian and librarian Magnus von Celse in 1735. It was printed as *Fragmentum Legis Smolandicæ* in *Acta litteraria et scientiarum Sueciæ* in 1738, where the Church section was translated as follows:

> Pax Dei sanctæque Mariæ sit nobiscum, adventibus och discedentibus; omnibus, qui pace publica fruuntur, qui non extorres neque excommunicati sunt; omnibus denique intra Mioaholt & Myrtleiks, atque inter Brutarek, & Biurekis habitantus.[220]

> God's peace, and holy Mary's, be with you, who have travelled here and away; for all those who enjoy the peace of the public, who had not been driven out or is banished, all who live within Mjöhult and Mörtlek, all who live within Bråtabäck and Björkö.
> (My translation)

Hasselberg refered to an interpretation by Johan Ihre, an 18th-century historical linguist. In *Glossarium Suigothicum*, Ihre meant that the word *gilsla* was a distortion in a transcript.[221] In his glossary he pointed out alternative forms: *Gissel*, *Gisle*, *Gisslan*, *Obses*. He translated the phrase from the Church section with:

> Illi omnes jure tutelæ frui debent, qui proscripti non sunt aut excommunicati.[222]

> Those who are not criminals or outlawed shall have legal protection.
> (My translation)

Ihre – like Schlyter – saw *gilzla* as an error in writing for *gizla*.[223] Later interpreters of the text – like Dovring – had, according to Hasselberg, simply used the emendation *gizla* for *gilzla*. The A manuscript has *gilzla* and the B manuscript *gildsla*. In fact, Hasselberg stated, it was a matter of the Old Swedish form *gilzli*, which is found as name element in the word *afgärþabyagilzli*, which denote special usufruct and access rights in villages.[224] This word is found in two medieval diplomas preserved in original (DS 1448, DS 1551), dated to 1304 and 1307. The diplomas concern property rights in Småland.[225] Hasselberg concluded that the noun *gilzli* belonged to the adjective *gilder* in Old Swedish legal writing. The word *gilzli* was derived from the adjective *gill*, 'to be valid', meaning to be 'valid' in a legal sense: when a person had legal security and any violation was to be payed for by fines. Finally Hasselberg translated the word *skylder* with 'just' or 'legitimate' (Sw. *berättigad*) and *gilzli* with 'valid' in the Church section.[226] He did not reject the interpretation of the words *griþ* or *gruþ* as a pledge for peace and safe conduct, but he did not make any comment on Dovring's observation that it was an alliterative word pair.

I have some critical and methodological comments regarding Hasselberg's analysis:

(A) *Gils-* as a rewriting for *gisl-* is not rare in Old Norse sources. This is evident from eddic poem *Vafþruðnismál*, stanzas 34–35 with the Old Icelandic forms *gíls* and *gísl*.[227] The forms *gils-/gisl-* are so common in Old Western and East Norse contexts that they are mentioned in several standard texts.[228]

(B) It is not unusual that words were written in different ways in languages without a standardized orthography; most likely the forms <z> and <ds> were two ways of writing one sound.

(C) In the Saga literature the words *gísl* ('hostage') and *grið* are used as an alliterative word pair, e.g. in *Heimskrigla*, Saga of St. Olaf: *at grið varu sett* [—] *í gísling*.[229] In the *Anglo-Saxon Chronicle* (MS E) there is also an alliterative word pair for 'hostage' and 'peace': *þa gernde he griðes* [*and*] *gisla*.[230]

(D) There could be other explanations of usage of the word *afgärþabyagilzli*: The word occurs only in the two letters, i.e. *afgärþabyagilzli* could be a local form.[231]

(E) To remove the word element from its context and translate with the Swedish *gill* is problematic. It is usually the

Old Swedish *gilder* that is translated with the Swedish *gill*.[232] Hasselberg's claim that the word *gilzla* in the A manuscript meant *gill* has a weak support in the sources because that word was *gilder* (alt. *gylder*).

Hasselberg's argument is therefore not convincing. In recent editions of the *Smålandslagen*, Holmbäck and Wessén did not mention or comment on Hasselberg's claims at all.[233] Given that alliterative phrases occur in Scandinavian medieval laws that reflect older traditions, it might be possible – as Dovring thought – to claim that the Church section of the *Smålandslagen* was outside the King's section, as it was reproduced in other Swedish traditions.

Violence against hostages *en masse*

Sometimes in medieval Scandinavia, conflicting sides used what Kosto refers to as the unilateral hostage form. It was not the question of standing as security for a person, but hostages were used as a means of pressure that aimed at pushing someone for concessions or to undermine a subversive population. The latter form is expressed in the Norwegian law of Magnus the Lawmender (*Magnus Lagabøters landslov*), and it could also be exemplified by the medieval skaldic poem *Runhenda* (1155) by Einar Skulason (ON *Einarr Skúlason*) about the Norwegian king Eystein Haraldsson (*Eysteinn Haraldsson*):

Vikverjom galt	The Mild and generous king
varð þannug hallt,	Made return against
gǫrræði gramr,	The Vik-dwellers' strife;
gjafmildr ok framr.	He had luck in battle.
Flest fólk varð hrætt,	Most folk were afraid
áðr fengi sætt,	Before they sought peace.
en gisla tók	He took hostages
sás gjǫldin jók.	And fines of every man.[234]

(Transl. Erling Monsen & A. H. Smith)

The skaldic poem implies that many people were taken as a hostage after a rebellion of warriors in today's Swedish province of

Bohuslän, and threats were made to use violence against the hostage unless the population stayed calm.

Naturally the purpose of the method of taking many people as hostages was to cause a deterrent effect with an implicit or explicit threat of retaliation against hostages if an agreement was not fulfilled. At the same time, violence against hostages seems to have been unusual and even in cases where it occurred, there may nevertheless have been some restrictions, albeit implicit ones. Massacres are mentioned in chronicles but the same type of violence – that is, mass mutilations – also occurred, which is discussed below.

The story of Thietmar

In 994, hostages taken from Stade in Lower Saxony were massacred. The German bishop and chronicler Thietmar of Merseburg was personally affected by these events because several of his relatives became victims of the massacre. He later described the events in his chronicle on the history of the city of Merseburg, 908–1018.

In June 23, 994 Thietmar's uncles Udo, Heinrich, and Siegfried, met pirates who ravaged their district in a sea battle in the Elbe River. Udo fell in the battle while Heinrich, Siegfried, and Count Adalger had to give up and were taken captive with others. Quickly the news of this misfortune was spread among the Christians. Duke Bernhard, who was staying nearby, immediately sent negotiators who would discuss with the pirates the ransom for the prisoners' release and a peaceful solution.

The pirates demanded an 'enormous sum'. Many contributed to the ransom. Thietmar's mother gave everything she had and could otherwise get hold of. When the pirates had received some of the money, they were given Siegfried, the only son of Heinrich, as hostage, and they also received Gerward and Wolfram in exchange for Adalger, among other people.[235]

The pirates released the prisoners when they received the remaining sum of the money. They only kept Siegfried. As he had no son to stand as security, he asked Thietmar's mother for help. Finally, it was decided that Thietmar himself would depart and enter as hostage.[236] However, during the night Siegfried managed to escape despite his wounds. A priest was blamed for Siegfried's escape. The pirates weighed anchor and lay out in the Elbe River. The next day, Thietmar's cousins and all the other hostages were jettisoned. Before that thay were severly mutilated: noses, ears, and hands were cut off. Then the pirates sailed away. Some of the hostages could be rescued but were marked for life.[237]

It is easy to interpret the massacre through Thietmar's eyes as something unthinkable and horrifying, which may have colored the depiction. In addition, Thietmar, as a clerk, had preconceptions about the inviolability of members of the clergy. But these events were something that happened in his immediate vicinity. Although Thietmar did not witness the massacre himself, his text must be regared as a primary source.

An interesting thing about this description is the complex structures that appear to be found behind the actions of the 'pirates' (most likely Danes or Wends) and the Saxons' perception of what was legal and illegal. For example, the execution of the hostage did not necessarily violate Continental Germanic traditions. As far as I know, there is no Continental Germanic legislation from this period, except the law code *Lex Frisionum*, that explicitly prohibits the execution of hostages. On the contrary, the law code *Lex Salica* (ch. 58, § 6) states that a hostage could be killed if an agreement was not fullfiled.[238] This notion seems to have followed all the way into the early modern era, at least when it comes to *borgensgeisel*.[239] There are also other reports on the mutilation of hostages in Continental Germanic legislation (see The retaliation of Canute the Great below). This does not mean that people adhered to these traditions in practice.

The actual hostage giving seems to have been correct. In this case, hostage was a third-party guarantee until the ransom was paid. In this form of extortion, the procedure resembles the modern hostage phenomenon. However, one should distinguish between prisoners of war and hostages in this case. The former category was made up of the men who were taken as prisoners in the Elbe River and it is therefore not entirely relevant to classify them as hostages. The true hostages were rather the ones that the 'pirates' required as a guarantee to ensure that the debt was paid. It was when a person tried to escape that the 'pirates' believed that the hostages had been forfeited. In Thietmar's story, the killings are described as an unconditional, irrational, action more for the pleasure of perpetrators rather than anything else. But that does not seem to have been the case. Initially, the 'pirates' seem to have followed the rules for the treatment of prominent prisoners of war.

When the mutilation of the hostages was carried out, it might have been an act of revenge. Interestingly, there were noblemen and other important persons among the hostages. The 'pirates' must have considered them as 'expended' and thus dehumanised. But there may also have been a moral that had to do with the killings: these actions could be seen as a preventive.

In the book it has been pointed out how the mutilation of hostages lay explicitly and implicitly within the medieval Scandinavian legislation. Mutilation was actually something that was associated with thralls. Brink believes that the mutilation of slaves grew out of a tradition of the slave system of antiquity. Slaves could be marked by their masters to distinguish them. Their ears could be cut off, they were branded with annealed iron, or the owner's name was tattooed on the slave's body.[240] Brink equates this practice to livestock branding. The practice survived into Continental Germanic times, and then concerned mutilations of one foot, ears, one hand, tongues, or lips as the mark of thralldom. If a slave escaped, a similar punishment also awaited those who helped the slave to escape, according to Brink. Possibly the marking could also have had a preventive effect because the slave was identified by the deformation.[241] At the same time, one could also claim that slaves – not the least during antiquity – represented a value and a (future) resource. Marking them through branding or mutilating them may have jeopardized their health, perhaps with a long-term recovery as a result, and this could be costly. Brink is careful to point out that the mutilation of slaves is not supported by sources describing Iron Age Scandinavia. However, in Danish medieval legislation there are references to the cutting of a nostril as the mark of a thrall and in the Norwegian Gulating law there is a note of the truncation of an ear of a thrall woman as a punishment for theft.[242] Brink argues with these examples that the method of truncation may have occurred during the Viking Age.[243]

There might have been rational reasons behind the mass mutilation at Stade: a marker for what the person was, but also a preventive measure. In the year 991, for example, the Danegeld had been lifted for the first time after the Battle of Mældun in England. As in the case described by Thietmar, it was necessary to ensure that the tribute should be paid and the mutilation was executed as a warning for what was to happen during future expeditions if people disobeyed or acted 'dishonostly'.

Can the size of this conflict have anything to do with the brutality of the actions of the 'pirates'? Was it a small-scale or large-scale conflict and, if the latter case, was there a greater inclination for violent behaviour? Some archeologists make a distinction between ritualized warfare and large-scale war. The archeologist Anders Andrén, for example, argues that such distinction may have occurred in Scandinavia with reference to Guy Halsall's investigations on Anglo-Saxon England (450–1050) and Leslie Alcock's on the Celtic parts of Great Britain and Ireland.[244] The ritualized warfare meant that raids were carried out by 'aristocratic' groupings that could give a prestigious booty through goods such as slaves, cattle, and horses. These raids would not change the balance of power. In this type of warfare there was a clear 'criterion' with which the contenders could choose the battlefield. Parts of the war booty could be returned and instead of fighting, a tribute was given that included exchanges of ties of friendship.[245] The large-scale war, on the other hand, would not have the same 'code of honour' as was found in the ritualized warfare. These wars could instead wipe out communities that were replaced by others:

> The conflicts could change the balance of power, by shifting the boundaries of political units and allowing the rule over an area to be wholly or partly taken over by another king. In the whole Anglo-Saxon area, large-scale wars are mentioned roughly every three years, but for each individual kingdom a large-scale conflict occurred roughly every twenty years […].[246]

From the above it is easy to get the impression that all 'small-scale wars' were 'ritualized' and thus less violent. But it can be difficult to draw a clear line between 'small-scale' and 'large-scale'. According to Lavelle, the Great Heathen Army involved complex structures: on the one hand small-scale raids, on the other great hosts in motion involving thousands of people. But it is difficult to estimate the number on the basis of chronicles and similar source material. As Lavelle points out:

> It is logical to presume that the numbers of belligerents in 'large-scale' warfare gradually increased proportionately with the size of political units and as the resources that could be obtained from them increased. By the eleventh century, more resources were certainly needed for warfare: the historical sources bear out the scale of the 1066 campaingns [...]. It does not necessarily follow that peace agreements could have been easier to reach in small scale-warfare; a feud could continue indefinitely until [...] it was settled, while large armies were difficult to keep together for long. [—]. With a large army, peace could very quickly have become a practical necessity.[247]

Small-scale raids could also be bloody and may not be easily distinguished from major warfare. The distinction between ritualized warfare and large-scale warfare is not clear because ritual actions also occurred in the latter case. As far as hostages are concerned, this study has shown the reverse: hostages were used in conflicts between territories. Seeing the ritual actions as something delimited and distinguishable from other societal activities can be difficult in these contexts.

As suggested with the model, it could be more fruitful to observe a development – between war and peace – where it was a question about taking advantage of the resources to get the best possible negotiating position. It does not mean that the term 'ritual warfare' is wrong, but to argue that warfare is 'ritual', the term must be defined more clearly. The hypothesis of 'ritual warfare' can be compared with Lavelle's claim that the symbolism of war and peace was about nothing more than just violence and non-violence between various chieftains/great men in Anglo-Saxon England.[248] Thus, there was no sharp difference between war on the one hand and 'ritual warfare' on the other in the Anglo-Saxon society. It is not unlikely that a similar pragmatic approach – the symbolism with a message of warning – included the events that took place at Stade in 994, a terror that had devastating consequences for those who were exposed to it.

The retaliation of Canute the Great

In 1014, Canute the Great – according to the *Anglo-Saxon Chronicle* – 'released' his hostage, while he had their hands, ears, and noses cut off. This event has not been paid much attention to within the research. The action is an example illustrating Kosto's point of view that it was far more common to spare hostage than to kill it. Certainly, there was a kind of 'gentlemanship' between nobles, but the reason could also have been pragmatic: killing the hostage meant that it ended as an idea and institution. Did Canute feel so safe that he could 'spend' his hostage or were there other reasons behind the mutilations?

Between Canute, his father Sven, and Anglo-Saxon England, a number of confrontations occurred until 1014. These confrontations can be listed after the *Anglo-Saxon Chronicle*:

994. The siege of London. Olaf Tryggvason and Sweyn Forkbeard recieve Danegeld.[249]

1002. The St. Brice's Day massacre, 13 November. Æthelred II orders the killing of all Danish people in England, because of suspicion of a conspiracy.

1003. The Danes plunder Exeter and enter Wiltshire.

1004. Sweyn arrives to Norwhich with his flett. He burns Norwhich.[250]

1005. The Danish fleet returns to Denmark. There is a great famine in England.[251]

1006. At midsummer the Danes plunder Sandwich. Wessex and Mercia mobilize but cannot defeat the Danes. The Danes go into winterquarter on Isle of Wight.

1007. In the spring of 1007 Æthelred decides to pay Danegeld of 30,000 pounds.[252]

1009. A Danish force comanded by Thorkel the Tall arrives to Sandwich and later to Canterbury. The inhabitants of East Kent make peace with Thorkel and pay him 3,000 pounds. With Isle of Wight as base the Danes ravage Sussex, Hampshire, and Berkshire.

They go to winter quarters in Kent. After Christmas they plunder and burn Oxford. At the rumor of an army that is about to be sent against them they return to Kent.²⁵³

1010. After Easter the Danes arrive in East Anglia and lands at Ipswich. There is a great battle between Danes and Anglo-Saxons during which some of the relatives of Æthelreds fall. Then the Danes control East Anglia and plunder Thetford and Cambridge. The Danes are mounted and can easily move between different parts of England and back to their ships. Consequently there is little time to organise resistance against them. By Christmas they return to their ships.²⁵⁴

1011. Æthelred sends envoys to the Danes with promises of Danegeld and supplies if they cease with their raids. By then the Danes have ravaged large parts of England. At the same time they have tried to achieve truce (*grið*) and peace (*frið*) at the local level, but the plundering continues. Between September 8 and 29, Canterbury is under siege and the Archbishop Ælfeah, together with other men and women belonging to the Ecclesiastical elite, are captured.²⁵⁵

1012. After Easter, the Danes receive an amount of 8,000 pounds. Archbishop Ælfeah refuses to have a ransom payed for him. He is executed on April 19th. Thorkel the Tall comes with 45 ships to Æthelred. He promises to defend the king's land in exchange for supplies and equipment.²⁵⁶

1013. Sweyn comes up along the River Trent to Gainsborough. The Earl of Northumbria, Uhtred, submits as well as the Danish territories of the Five Boroughs in Mercia. Hostages are given from each shire. Sweyn receives supplies and horses. He travels south and leaves the ship and the hostage to his son Canute. Sweyn goes to Oxford and then Winchester. The residents of these cities give him hostages. However, he cannot go to London where Æthelred and Thorkel are staying. Sweyn goes to Wallingford where the Ealdorman Æthelmær gives him hostage. The whole of England acknowledges Sweyn as king. The residents of London then submit to him and give him hostages. Sweyn requires payment and provision. Thorkel located in Greenwich requires the same.²⁵⁷

1014. Sweyn dies on February 3. The Danish Navy chooses Canute as king. Instead the English Council decides to elect Æthelred, provided he changes his hard rule. Æthelred sends his son Edvard as a messenger to England and promises to introduce reforms. The English Council and Æthelred, through his delegation, make an agreement that is confirmed by oath. All Danish kings are declared lawless in England forever. Æthelred returns in the spring. Canute makes an agreement with the residents of Lindsey (in Northumbria) to get horses against promise that they will plunder together. Æthelred arrives at Lindsey, which is plundered, but Canute is able to escape by sea. When he reaches Sandwich, he lands the hostage he took after his father. He orders his men to cut off the hands, ears, and noses of the hostages. Canute requests that 21,000 pounds is to be paid to the army located outside Greenwich. On September 28, parts of England are flooded and many people become homeless.[258]

There may have been several reasons for the mutilation of the hostage: (a) as a warning example, (b) as a desperate measure caused by the stressful situation, or (c) as revenge for deceived agreements. Before we get into these possible reasons, some brief comments on the political situation regarding this case will be made. Obviously, Canute was in a precarious situation. Certainly, his own fleet had given him support and chosen him as king. But the English Council had chosen Æthelred. According to the historian Michael K. Lawson, it was likely that this situation would not have occurred if Sweyn had not died.[259] After this event, Canute returned to Denmark where his brother Harald II preceded Sweyn. Harald agreed to help Canute with ships and troops in exchange for Harald to rule Denmark.

In 1014 both sides in this area of confrontations had access to large armies. This meant high self-esteem. During the previous years when Sweyn took hostages, it had a function that did not differ from other forms of hostages. The number of hostages was possibly larger on this occasion than usual, as hostages were given to show a willingness of substitution or 'generosity' rather than something enforced by violence, even if threats of violence were explicit. If one is to apply the gift theory of Mauss to this example, the hostages handed out to Sweyn may be said to have occurred in a situation in which the gifts reached their culmination, including different demands of Danegeld. According to Mauss, the gift meant an obligation to stick to agreements. But what did Canute felt about such commitments?

A ritualistic behaviour?

The mutilations performed at Sandwich can be compared with the execution of Archbishop Ælfeah in 1012. According to the *Anglo-Saxon Chronicle*, the elder Eadric and some councilors came to London and stayed there until the debt of 8,000 pounds was paid.

On Saturday after Easter (April 19), the Danes became annoyed when the archbishop did not want any ransom to be paid for him. Then they took the archbishop and brought him to gathering place, which in the chronicle is called *hustinge* (c.f. ON *húsþing*).[260] They were then drunk on wine. During the Sunday evening after Easter, they killed the archbishop. According to the Chronicle, they threw bones and horns of oxen at him and one of them struck his head with an axe.[261] The Chronicle expresses that Ælfeah's 'holy blood [then] fell on earth' (*his halige blod on ða eorðan feoll*) and his 'holy soul was sent to the kingdom of God' (*his haligan sawle to Godes rice asende*).[262] The body was brought to London in the morning and Bishops Eadnoð and Ælfhun received it with honors, and Ælfeah was buried in St. Paul's Monastery. There he was later declared a martyr.

Ælfeah was not a hostage but a prisoner of war. Nevertheless, the treatment of him is reminiscent of the massacres at Stade and Sandwich; he had to die when the Danes was in a mood of frustration and under the influence of alcohol. The boundary of what can be considered a ritual act and spontaneous violence may have been floating from the perspective of the Scandinavians.

It is quite possible that it was as a part of ritual-based violence that the archbishop was executed; the violence became legitimate because it was a part of a ceremony that the Chronicle merely suggests. From the Christian point of view, the death of Ælfeah was portrayed by miraculous notes of 'holy blood' flowing out and the 'soul' that came to heaven. Obviously, these are later notifications of the chronicler and they are associated with the Christian intention to make Ælfeah a martyr. Nevertheless the actions of the Danes as reported in the Christian-colored context, which are not altogether evident. To conclude: the differences between what can be regarded as 'a ritual act' and what is not is vague. This vagueness can also be observed in the examples with Stade and Sandwich.

In relation to the mutliations of Sandwich, two different legal concepts from the Anglo-Danish area of confrontations can be taken into account: *mundbryce*, 'breach of the mund' and *gripbryce*, 'breach of the peace'. The term *mundr-* meant a personal protection, which, according to Steenstrup, was not used by the Danes.[263] A violation of the *mundr* resulted in a fine in accordance with the person's position. According to Steenstrup, this penalty was therefore part of a hierarchical law system that did not exist in the Scandinavian countries which was based on the rights of the individual, and a part of the King's peace. In the Scandinavian legislation one focused on the character of the deed.[264]

In accordance with the Anglo-Saxon mentality, people in a high social position could have had a position with legal protection that the Danish people was not aware of. The Old English term *gripbryce* encompasses a limited number of crimes, which included crimes against (a) Church peace (*cyric grip*), (b) protection given by the king's hand (*cyniges handgrip* alt. *handseald grip*) and (c) peace in the army.[265] At the same time, Steenstrup indicated that there was a distinction between how in Scandinavian law the name of *grið* was regarded as a peace that originated from an individual – or a place – while the word *grip* in England had a more general meaning and originated from the 'king's peace', which covered the whole society.[266] Canute may not have been unaware of what these breaches meant because they occurred during different peace processes between the Danes and the Anglo-Saxons.

Canute's relationship to the Church of England appears to have been tense at first. Lawson points to the *Sermo Lupi*, by Archbishop Wulfstan, where Canute is, by way of introduction, presented as Antichrist.[267] The marriage with Emma may have helped ease the relationship with the Church because she gave great donations to it. Even though Archbishop Ælfeah was executed by men serving under Sweyn, Canute, according to Lawson, could have attempted to approach the Church by transferring Ælfeah's remnants to Canterbury.[268]

One can nevertheless conclude that Canute still felt so confident that the consequences of worldly lawsuits did not scare him. Even crimes against the canon law – the hostage included many clerks – do not seem to have touched him in this case. Canute thus played a high game with the risk of being excommunicated as Christian.[269] This could be compared to Kosto, who points out that the excomunication was the only tool that was legitimate for the Church to use against combatants.[270] The perception of the *grið* was distinguished between different parties. It is quite conceivable that an authority (a victor) could have had a decisive impact on whether mass violence was practiced. Among other things, this kind of violence did not occur on Canute's way to the throne of England.

At the same time, as Lavelle suggests, questions about authority and responsibility generally appear to have been a gray zone during peace processes in medieval traditions.[271] Nor can it be argued that the Christian, English side was less restrained, which can be seen in the aforementioned St. Brice's Day massacre and Æthelred's plundering of Lindsey in Northumbria in 1014. Naturally this was a reprisal because the residents (or the rulers) made an agreement with Canute. It is likely that Æthelred thought he had the law on his side when the English Council declared each Danish king illegal and the condition for his return to England was that the inhabitants would not act deceitfully against him.[272] Thus, the law, whether canonical or worldly motivated, became means for rulers to use against their enemies.

Concluding remarks

In this part examples are given on how rights, laws, and personal interests were not always compatible when hostages was used. The rights of hostages could be analysed from three perspectives:

(1) the individual's rights;
(2) the laws and agreements; and
(3) the moral perceptions of the different societies.

The legal protection could be viewed through peace agreements, something that is reflected in medieval legislation, both

Continental Germanic and Scandinavian. In these agreements – which often included a bilateral hostage form – interests may have existed for the hostage giver to keep a person with a strong social capital who would be a potential hostage for the hostage taker.

One could note that the hostage had a 'legal capacity' in peace agreements. It could manifest itself in witnessing the agreement and that they were able to swear oaths. Those who delivered the hostage appears to have had a key position when it came to taking responsibility for hostages, because, at least in early medieval societies, they were members of councils and assemblies. A ruler's position of power in Viking-age Scandinavian societies was subjected to pressure from subordinate groups with influence over peace, these groupings were probably also able to influence the choice of hostages.

It can be difficult to discern the practical-political situation that underlies the saga and chronicle material regarding the relationship between a ruler and his subordinates, sometimes loosely organised in groupings with intentions of their own. This relationship is not least evident in the peace agreement between Magnus the Good and Harthacnut, as it is describe in *Ágrip*; the hostages were extradited, while later versions have a softer tone and emphasize the kings' peace efforts. At the same time medieval writers would not mention apparent indulgences towards the opposing side. Although this story is considered to have a low source value, there are different versions of a core story that, fictitious or not, illustrate the difficulties with the saga literature as a source of peace settlements. For medieval writers, it may have been important to report the hostage taking as a triumph of war and peace. The winner's prerogative, to receive hostages, appears in some texts as important. In other cases, hostages ended up in the background, as something unimportant, and in some chronicle traditions they gave way, for example, to stories of victories by divine intervention.

There are other themes in the literature involving persons who acts as hostages: (a) revenge motifs (Vikarr, Walther, Olaf Tryggvason), (b) virtue (William of Malmesbury, Walther) and (c) sacrifice, willingness to volunteer as hostages (William of Malmesbury). In the usual storyline, the hostage situation is depicted as a subordination where it was for the protagonists, who were raised by their hostages, to master the situation by being accepted in the new environment, after which some sort of revenge follows. In some stories, the main character is trusted with important tasks. This could be compared to the gift-giving tradition in which proven loyalty was an important component. These cases can, however, not be explained unambiguously. From the perspective of the hostage taker, they may have been due to a close relationship with the hostages. The hostage could later become a future ally, or the purpose was simply controlling a potential enemy. A hostage may have had an interest in building up a social capital for future relations, but this contrasts with the literary examples of revenge motives.

If a male hostage constituted an important social capital, the same could also have applied to some women, even if this may have varied from culture to culture. There are few cases with female hostages in Roman, Continental German, Old English, and Scandinavian sources. Within the research, it has therefore been assumed that they simply did not become hostages but instead (extradited) wives as a part of a peace process. Although the source material makes it an open question whether female hostages existed (it depends on how one evaluates sources such as *Waltharius*, *Ynglinga saga,* and Malmesbury's English history), they can be attributed to qualities other than just the being the 'good wife'. This applies in particular to women in the 'heathen' societies, where it is difficult to distinguish between categories such as 'religion' and 'politics'.

The social value of the hostage was intimately associated with its legal rights. The rights were contextually conditioned and can be seen in restrictions on the personal freedom described in various sources. There is no evidence that the hostage would have been regarded as 'holy' and thus not inviolable, the value of the hostages can be considered based on their social capital.

When hostages lost their social capital, the protection could also disappear, but the evidence that they, because of bilateral (or unilateral if it were high-ranking persons) agreements, would have been killed or violated is few. Indications of violence against hostages are found in medieval Scandinavian legislation. In some cases, these are private hostages (the *Upplandslagen* and the

Östgötalagen) but in others public hostages (the Upplandslagen). It is quite possible that some of the paragraphs mentioned in this legislation are based on older traditions because there are references to elderly legislations.

From legal texts and sagas it is also apparent that hostages received protection during the peace negotiations and that it could be understood by relating to the Old Norse words for 'peace', *friðr* and *grið*. In the former case, it either concerns the peace that prevails in the hall or an everlasting 'peace' in the society: an ideally condition. Although the etymology behind *grið* is more obscure than *friðr*, it concerned a temporary protection or an asylum. During the peace meetings, envoys, negotiators, and other participants enjoyed this kind of protection. This is evident from formal expressions in medieval Scandinavian legislation such as *mæþ gruþum oc gislum* in the *Äldre västgötalagen* and in *skylde til gilzla oc grutha* in the *Smålandslagen*.

With the unilateral hostage form, hostages could be taken *en masse* for providing a means of pressure towards opposing groupings such as in Norway in the Middle Ages with the underlying threat of a massive execution. At the same time, actual punishment of the hostages seems to have been rare. From two cases, Stade in 994, and Sandwich in 1014, some conclusions can be drawn: Pragmatic reasons determined violent acts, morals, and legal protection. There could have been several reasons: Stressful moments during which people felt crowded made them make the decision more or less in desperation. Alternatively, one party felt that the agreement was breached. Another possible reason was that it could serve as a warning (in an area, a city, etc.). It is not possible to speak of 'morality' in a modern sense. One might be able to talk about some respect for legal rules, but it seems rather to be related to how the law was used and interpreted, naturally from a biased, subjective perspective.

In the meeting between non-Christians and Christians, there may have been different views on such legal rules, which can be explained by the fact that these are different traditions. That some warlords were Christians hardly constituted a guarantee of the security of the hostage. Law, politics, and religion assumed each other in these contexts in a pragmatic way. This can be compared to the hostage phenomenon of the modern times, when it became more associated with retaliation. At the same time, Roscoe Pound claimed that retaliation was an institution 'as old as hostage'. Nevertheless, what was perceived as betrayal and thus the right to reprisals differed. The perception of who was an important person may also have differed. To avoid violence in these contexts, communication and transparency became important for the various parties both during and after the negotiations.

Notes to Part IV

1. von See 1964 103 ff.; Sundqvist 2005: 275.

2. In Sundqvist 2005: 275.

3. Althoff 2004; Kosto 2012: 32 f., 34.

4. Kosto 2012: 31.

5. *Grágás: lagasafn íslenska þjóðveldisins* ([ed.] Gunnar Karlsson et al.): 95 f. (Ch. 23).

6. Kosto 2012: 21, 84.

7. *Annales Alamannici* ([ed.] Pertz): 56 (year 913); Kosto 2012: 84.

8. Tacitus, *Historiarum libri* ([ed.] Fisher): 77 (book 4: 79. 1).

9. Whitney Mathisen 1993: 34; *Passio acaunensium martyrum*.

10. *Beowulf* ([ed.] Klaeber): 472; Brink 2003: 105.

11. *Quellen zur Karolingischen Reichsgeschichte*, Annales Vedastini ([ed.] Rau): 302 f. (year 882).

12. Kershaw 2011: 18.

13. Kosto 2012: 83 f.

14. Kershaw 2011: 18.

15. In Bergman 1990: 199.

16. Jordanes, *Getica* ([ed.] Nordin): 194 f. (Ch. 299); C.f. Kershaw 2011: 21; Olsson 2012: 75.

17. [Plutarchos] *Bíoi Parállēloi* ([ed.] Theander), 209 f. (Ch 29).
18. Plutarchos] *Bíoi Parállēloi* ([ed.] Theander), 209 f. (Ch 29).
19. Weiner 1988; Olsson 2012: 66.
20. Lavelle 2006: 272.
21. von Olberg 1998: 200. I have not been able to confirm this hypothesis in the *Edictus Rothari*.
22. Mathisen 1993: 34.
23. Kosto 2012: 38.
24. Watson1993: 34; Elbern 1990: 97 ff.
25. Watson1993: 34.
26. See Pelteret 2005: 5 ff.
27. Olsson 2012: 68.
28. Cf. Lavelle 2006: 275 f.
29. *Annales Bertiniani* ([ed.] Buchner): 48 ff. (year 839).
30. *Annales Bertiniani* ([ed.] Buchner): 48 ff. (year 839).
31. En þá var Sveinn frá fallinn í Danmǫrku ok svá Knútr faðir hans í Englandi, ok réð þá fyrir Danmǫrku bróðir Sveins, Hǫrða-Knútr at nafni, ok helt her á móti Magnúsi ok fundusk í Brenneyjum. Fóru vitrir menn á meðal ok mæltu til sættar ok gerðu með þeima hætti, at með því at Knúti þótti sem hann ætti rétt tilmæli til Nóregs, þá hafði faðir hans aflat ok bróðir hans at setit–Mǫgnúsi þótti ok illt misheldi þat er faðir hans hafði haft af Knúti, svik ok lands flótta ok lífs aftak– þá slǫru þeir þó máli í þá sætt at sá þeira er lengr lifði skyldi taka við bǫðum landum ok hvárr sínu ríki ráða meðan báðir lifði þeir, ok settu gísla, ok andaðisk Knútr fyrri, en Mǫgnús tók þá við Danmǫrk fyr útan gagnmæli, þvíat synir bǫztu manna vǫru í gíslinginni. *Ágrip af Nóregskonungasǫgum* ([ed.] Driscoll): 48 (text) (Ch. XXXVI).
32. *Ágrip af Nóregskonungasǫgum* ([ed.] Driscoll): 49 (transl.) (Ch. XXXVI).
33. Krag 1995: 169; Bagge 2014: 32.

34. Krag 1995: 169.

35. Fritzner (1883–1896) 1973: 489; *Lexicon poeticum* ([ed.] Finnur Jónsson): 154; Palm 2004: 492.

36. *Fagrskinna* ([ed.] Bjarni Einarsson): 210 (Ch. 47).

37. *Heimskringla* III. *Magnúss saga ins góða* ([ed.] Bjarni Aðalbjarnarson): 12 f. (Ch. 5).

38. Magnus was born about 1024 and Harthacnut about 1018 (P. Sawyer 2001: 65).

39. Ok er þessi ófriðr hafði staðit um hríð milli konunganna þá gørði hvárrtveggi mikinn skaða á annars ríki. Þat leiðisk bœndum ok vildu gøra í millum sín betra vanða. Samnask þá saman bœndr ór hvártveggju ríkinu ok gøra ráð með vizku ok mikilli hamingju fyrir hǫnd fyrir konunganna, er báðir váru œskumenn en auðráð sínum mǫnnum ok hœgir, ok gørðu nú fund í milli sín í Elfi *Morkinskinna* ([ed.] Þórður Ingi Guðjónsson & Ármann Jakobsson): 27 (Ch. 3).

40. *Morkinskinna* ([ed.] Andersson & Gade): 101 (Ch. 2).

41. *Knytlinge saga* ([ed.] Ægidius): 36.

42. Ármann Jakobsson 2005: 397.

43. *Norges kongekrønike* ([ed.] Gunnarssøn): 163 f.

44. *Danmarks middelalderlige annaler* ([ed.] Kroman): 192 f. (stanza 193 f.).

45. Saxo Grammaticus, *Gesta Danorum* = The History of the Danes 1 ([ed.] Friis-Jensen): 775 (Book 10).

46. Allen 2006: 1 ff.

47. Allen 2006: 4.

48. Lavelle 2006: 295.

49. Lavelle 2006: 296.

50. *Commentarii de Bello Gallico* ([ed.] Kraner): 444 f. (Ch. 89, book VII). Dio Cassius ([ed.] Cary): 49 (Ch. 41, book XL).

51. Jón Skaptason 1983: 157.
52. Jón Skaptason 1983: 157.
53. *Annales Bertiniani* ([ed.] Buchner): 50 f. (year 839).
54. Baker 2013: 95.
55. Lynch 1998: 131 f., 215 f.
56. See Rydving 1993: 10 ff.
57. Kosto 2012: 60.
58. Kosto 2012: 60.
59. *Boken om Ansgar* ([ed.] Hallencreutz): 58 (Ch. 30).
60. The number 30 may also be a topos. The missionary Willibrord in the eighth century returned from a visit to the Danish king with 30 boys according to Alcuin (*The Life of Willibrord*, c.796, Ch. 9).
61. Sundqvist (2002: 215 ff.) points out that lottery throwing in favour of Christians is probably a literary topos because it is a recurring theme in other bishop chronicles. It can also be compared to cases where, for example, the devil is said to speak through idols and then is revealed unmasked by missionaries or Christians (see Hultgård 1997: 14 f.).
62. Both silver money and the number 30 are found in the Gospel of Matthew (Matthew 26: 48). Also, Nebuchadnezzar marched againgst Jerusalem in the ninth year of Zedekiah and the ninth day of the fourth month the enemy broke into Jerusalem (2 Kings 25: 1–4).
63. Nerman 1942: 120.
64. Waltharius ([ed.] Ørbæk): 13 f. (stanzas 61–95). *Götreks saga* ([ed.] Malm): 22–27 (Ch. IV).
65. *Ágrip af Nóregskonungasǫgum* ([ed.] Driscoll): 28 (text), 29 (transl.) (Ch. 18). It is the same history in *Heimskringla* I, *Ólafs saga Tryggvasonar* ([ed.] Bjarni Aðalbjarnarson): 230 f. (Ch. 6–7).
66. Jordanes, *Getica* ([ed.] Nordin): 176 f. (text), 179 f. (transl.) (Ch. 270–272).

67. Jordanes, *Getica* ([ed.] Nordin): 184 (text), 185 f. (transl.) (Ch. 282).

68. Tacitus, *Germaniens historie, geografi og befolkning* [*Germania*] ([ed.] Bruun & Lund): 55 f. (Ch. 20); Olsson 2012: 66.

69. Mauss 2002: 16 f.

70. See Allen 2006: 127 ff., 131 ff., 138 ff.

71. Priscus fr. 3; Bury 1958: 241.

72. *Annales regni Francorum* ([ed.] Pertz): 137 (year 812).

73. *The Song of Roland*, the Oxford Version ([ed.] Owen): 101 (stanza 3033).

74. *Nordisk familjebok* (Uggleupplagan): 975 f. Lat.

75. Lavelle 2006: 272, n. 9.

76. *Anglo-Saxon Chronicle* MS F ([ed.] Baker): 105 f. (year 1013).

77. *Anglo-Saxon Chronicle* MS F ([ed.] Baker): 106–111 (years 1014–1017, 1021).

78. *Heimskringla, Ólafs saga helga* ([ed.] Bjarni Aðalbjarnarson): 161–174 (Ch. 97–103). See Beuermann 2011: 110.

79. *Heimskringla* II, *Ólafs saga helga* ([ed.] Bjarni Aðalbjarnarson): 161–168 (Ch. 98–100); *Orkneyinga saga* ([ed.] Finnbogi Guðmundsson): 28–36 (Ch. 13–17).

80. *Heimskringla* II, *Ólafs saga helga* ([ed.] Bjarni Aðalbjarnarson): 168 ff. (Ch. 100, 102); *Orkneyinga saga* ([ed.] Finnbogi Guðmundsson): 36 (Ch. 17).

81. *Heimskringla* II, *Ólafs saga helga* ([ed.] Bjarni Aðalbjarnarson): 168 ff. (Ch. 100); *Orkneyinga saga* ([ed.] Finnbogi Guðmundsson): 35 f. (Ch. 17).

82. *Heimskringla* II, *Ólafs saga helga* ([ed.] Bjarni Aðalbjarnarson): 172 (Ch. 102); *Orkneyinga saga* ([ed.] Finnbogi Guðmundsson): 40 f. (Ch. 19).

83. *Orkneyinga saga* ([ed.] Finnbogi Guðmundsson): 41 (Ch. 19).

84. *Orkneyinga Saga* ([ed.] Hermann Pálsson & P. Edwards): 49 (Ch. 19).

85. *Heimskringla* II ([ed.] Bjarni Aðalbjarnarson): 170 (Ch. 101); *Orkneyinga saga* ([ed.] Finnbogi Guðmundsson): 39 (Ch. 18).

86. *Orkneyinga saga* ([ed.] Finnbogi Guðmundsson): 38 (Ch. 18).

87. *Heimskringla* II ([ed.] Bjarni Aðalbjarnarson): 172 (Ch. 102); *Orkneyinga saga* ([ed.] Finnbogi Guðmundsson): 41 (Ch. 19).

88. In *Heimskringla* II ([ed.] Bjarni Aðalbjarnarson): 172 (Ch. 102); *Orkneyinga saga* ([ed.] Finnbogi Guðmundsson): 41 (Ch. 19).

89. Miller 1990: 123.

90. Miller 1990: 123 ff.

91. Miller 1990: 124.

92. Miller 1990: 124.

93. Miller 1990: 172.

94. *Laxdœla saga* ([ed.] Einar Ól. Sveinsson): 128–132 (Ch. 43); see Olsson 2012: 71 ff.

95. *Sturlunga Saga* I, *Íslendingasaga* ([ed.] Gudbrand Vigfusson [*Guðbrandur Vigfússon*]): 244 (Ch. 43).

96. Miller 1990: 124.

97. Auður Magnúsdóttir 2003: 73.

98. See Auður Magnúsdóttir 2003: 68 f.

99. Jón Viðar Sigurðsson 1999: 210 f., 214, 219 f.; 2011: 101 f.

100. Lavelle 2006: 284.

101. *Anglo-Saxon Chronicle* F ([ed.] Baker): 51 (year 757); Kosto 2012: 64.

102. *Waltharius* ([ed.] Ørbæk): 13 f. (stanzas 61–95).

103. *Gautreks saga* (Ch. 3–4).
The story of Vikar and Herþjofr is largely confirmed by the skaldic poem *Vikarsbalkr* which some believe may originate from the 1000s (see Naumann 2005: 538).

104. Lavelle 2006: 270.

105. Lavelle 2006: 270.

106. Enright 1996: 20 ff., 283 ff. For critical point of views on Enright's hypothesis, see Baker 2013: 183 ff.

107. See Sundqvist 2007: 74, n. 44.

108. *Beowulf* ([ed.] Klaeber et al.): Ch. XVI, 39 (1114–1117).

109. *Waltharius* ([ed.] Ørbæk): 14 (stanzas 113–115), 18 (stanza 260).

110. Kershaw 2011: 21.

111. Sanmark 2014: 94 f.

112. Sanmark 2014: 95 f.; Mundal 1994: 595.

113. Sanmark 2014: 96.

114. *Laxdæla saga* ([ed.] Einar Ól. Sveinsson: 28, 50 f. [Ch. 13, 20]).

115. *Landnámbók*, Sturlubók ([ed.] Finnur Jónsson: 161 [Ch. 112]).

116. Sanmark 2014: 99.

117. Roskrecht (Rosbach: 58 [Ch. 1. 50]).

118. *Germaniens historie, geografi og befolkning* [*Germania*] ([ed.] Bruun & Lund: 44 f. [Ch. 9]).

119. *Statius Silvae* (net edition, *The Latin Library*): 1, 4 (line 90).

120. Näsström 1995: 46 f.; Sundqvist 2007: 70 f.

121. Raudvere 2003: 125 ff.; Sundqvist 2007: 68 f.

122. Raudvere 2003: 125 ff.; Sundqvist 2007: 68 f. A possible counterpart to the presence of 'magicians' has been put forward by Dillmann (2006).

123. Ney 2012: 80, 82, n. 18 f.

124. Cf. Kaliff & Sundqvist 2004: 63 f.

125. Aðalheiður Guðmundsdóttir 2012: 67 ff.

126. *Knytlinge saga* ([ed.] Ægidius) 31. See also *Knútsdrapa*, by Sigvat skald in *Den norsk-islandske skjaldedigtning* A 1 ([ed.] Finnur Jónsson): 248 ff.

127. *Encomium Emmæ Reginae*, Book II, ch. 31.

128. *Encomium Emmæ Reginae*, Book II, ch. 31.

129. Ármann Jakobsson 2005: 398.

130. *Encomium Emmæ Reginae*, Book II, ch. 35.

131. Williams 2003: 53.

132. William of Malmesbury, *Gesta regum Anglorum* (ed. Mynors *et al.*): 300 (text), 301 (transl.) (Ch. 177, 1).

133. William of Malmesbury, *Gesta regum Anglorum* (ed. Mynors *et al.*): 300 (text), 301 (transl.) (Ch. 177, 1). See Fenton 2008: 55.

134. Ney 2006: 71 ff.; Näsström 2009: 172 f.

135. Saxo Grammaticus, *Gesta Danorum = The History of the Danes* 1 ([ed.] Friis-Jensen): 633 ff. (Book 9, 4.1–4.2).

136. Näsström 2009: 172 f.

137. ODCW, 31.

138. Hedenstierna-Jonson et al. 2018: 853 ff.

139. Stylegar blogg http://arkeologi.blogspot.com/2017/10/kvinne-kriger-viking.html.

140. Gardela 2013: 306.

141. Gardela 2013: 306.

142. Den frankiske Rigsannaler, *Vikingerne i Franken* ([ed.] Albrechtsen): 13 ff. (years 804–810).

143. *De Carolo Magno (Gesta Caroli Magni)*, Book II, Chapter 13.

144. Elbern 1990: 110.

145. Walker 2005: kap 1; *Rhōmaikē arkhaiologia*, V: 34: 1–2.

146. Allen 2003: 94.

147. Walker 2005: Ch. 1.

148. Beck 1998: 464. During the Gallic wars, the Suebian ruler Ariovistus fought against Caesar. Caesar wanted to negotiate with Ariovistus and chosed Gaius Valerius Procillus as messenger – a Helvetian who had gained Roman citizenship – and whom Caesar believed the Germans would not misunderstand. He also chose M.

Mettius who had the rights of 'guest friendship' with Ariovistus (*qui hospitio Ariovisti utebatur*) since before. But Ariovistus had them locked up in the belief that they were spies. After the final battle, Caesar found Ariovistus in fetters. Three times had the Suebians cast lots (*sortibus consultum*) to see whether the life of Ariovistus would be spared or not (*C. Iuli Caesaris commentariorum de bello gallico liber primus* [net edition, the Latin Library, Ch. 47]).

149. Widukind, *Sächsiche Geschichten* ([ed.] Hirsch): 10 f. (Book 1, Ch. 6); Althoff 2004: 140.

150. Gylfaginning, *Edda* (a) ([ed.] Faulkes): 26 ff. (Ch. 33–34).

151. Mathiesen 1993: 35.

152. Jordanes, *Getica* ([ed.] Nordin): 129 (text), 130 (transl.) (Ch. 184).

153. *Lex Frisionum*: ch. XX. § 1 (text), (transl.).

154. Kosto 2012: 36 ff.

155. Kosto 2012: 38.

156. Gundersen 1960: 332.

157. *Magnus lagabøters landslov* III ([ed.] Taranger): 31 (Ch. 3, § 4).

158. Orkneyinga þáttr, *Flateyjarbók* II ([ed.] Gudbrandr Vigfusson): 518.

159. E.g. *Orkneyinga saga* ([ed.] Finnbogi Guðmundsson): 170 (Ch. 75).

160. According to the Acts of the Apostles 9: 3–5 Saul (Paulus) is blinded by God. Three days later his sight is restored by Ananias of Damascus (Acts of the Apostles 9: 17).

161. *Heimskringla* II, *Ólafs saga helga* ([ed.] Bjarni Aðalbjarnarson): 105 (Ch. 75).

162. Meyer 1960: 331.

163. Östgötalagen, *Svenska landskapslagar* 1 ([ed.] Holmbäck): 67, n. 8.

164. Östgötalagen, *Svenska landskapslagar* 1 ([ed.] Holmbäck): 54 (Dråpsbalken II, § 2); (Vådamålsbalken XXXIV, § 1); (Rättegångsbalken III, § 2).

165. Amira 1882a: 691; Lutteroth 1922: 25.

166. Manhelgdsbalken, *Upplandslagen* ([ed.] Schlyter): 144 (flock 12, § 8).

167. Manhelgdsbalken, *Upplandslagen* ([ed.] Holmbäck): 95 (flock 12, § 8).

168. Upplandslagen, *Svenska landskapslagar* 1 ([ed.] Holmbäck): 124, n. 83.

169. Upplandslagen, *Svenska landskapslagar* 1 ([ed.] Holmbäck): 94 pp. (Manhelgdsbalken §§ 1–10); *Upplandslagen*, according to Cod. Holm. B 199 and the edition of 1607 ([ed.] Henning): 127 ff. (12, § 1–12).

170. Upplandslagen, *Svenska landskapslagar* 1 ([ed.] Holmbäck): 124, n. 81.

171. Upplandslagen, *Svenska landskapslagar* 1 ([ed.] Holmbäck): 123, n. 72.

172. *Danmarks riges breve* ['The Letters of the Realm of Denmark'] I 1211–1223 ([ed.] Skyum-Nielsen): 190 (diploma nr 217).

173. *Danmarks riges breve* ['The Letters of the Realm of Denmark'] I 1211–1223 ([ed.] Skyum-Nielsen): 192 (diploma nr 217, § 10).

174. indtil hr. ærkebiskoppen av Köln og oftnævnte greve av Schwerin [Henrik] bringer i erfaring, om de kan bevæge Danmarks konger til att erhverve sig hr. kejserens og hr. kongens nåde enten ved betaling eller ved at tilbagegive de lande, som de har berøvet kejser og rige, eller hved hvilke som helst andre midler. *Danmarks riges breve* ['The Letters of the Realm of Denmark'] I 1211–1223 ([ed.] Skyum-Nielsen): 192 (diploma nr 217, § 11).

175. Ulsig 2011: 81 f.

176. Hall & Meritt 2002: 138; *Beowulf* ([ed.] Klaeber et al.): 380.

177. Hall & Meritt 2002: 138 f.

178. Steenstrup (1882) 1972: 248.

179. Kershaw 2011: 30.

180. Erfidrápa Óláfs helga, *Den norsk-islandske skjaldedigtning* A 1 ([ed.] Finnur Jónson): 259 (12, stanza 10). Kuhn 1968: 103.

181. Vellekla, *Den norsk-islandske skjaldedigtning* A 1 ([ed.] Finnur Jónson): 126.

182. *Edda* ([ed.] Neckel & Kuhn): 19 (stanza 16). Hástein Hrómundarson halta (*Hásteinn Hrómundarson halta*), Lausavísur, *Den norsk-islandske skjaldedigtning* A 1 ([ed.] Finnur Jónson): 97 (stanza 4).

183. *Edda* ([ed.] Neckel & Kuhn): 82 (Ch. 29).

184. *Lexicon Poeticum* ([ed.] Finnur Jónsson): 154.

185. Tiefenbach 1995: 595.

186. Elmevik 2013: 42.

187. In Fritzner (1883–96) 1973: 487.

188. See Fritzner (1883–96) 1973: 172.

189. See Peterson 2007: 104.

190. *Eyrbyggja saga* ([ed.] Einar Ól. Sveinsson): 9 (Ch. 4).

191. *Eyrbyggja saga* ([ed.] Einar Ól. Sveinsson): 10 (Ch. 4).

192. *The Annals of Fulda* ([ed.] Reuter): 92 (year 882).

193. *The Annals of Fulda* ([ed.] Reuter): 93 (year 882).

194. Bøe 1960: 463; *Lexicon Poeticum* ([ed.] Finnur Jónson): 203.

195. Erfidrápa um Harald konung harðráða, *Den norsk-islandske skjaldedigtning* A 1 ([ed.] Finnur Jónson): 352 (stanza 15).

196. Af Ragnars saga loðbrókar, *Den norsk-islandske skjaldedigtning* A 2 ([ed.] Finnur Jónson): 232 (II, stanza 3).

197. Atlamál in grœnlenzko, *Edda* ([ed.] Neckel & Kuhn): 252 (Ch. 33); *Den norsk-islandske skjaldedigtning* A 1 ([ed.] Finnur Jónson): 517 (stanza 14 b).

198. *The Concise Oxford Dictionary of English Place Names* ([ed.] Ekwall): 205. In Old English there was likewise a special name for a law that meant a temporary, local peace, *griðlagu* (Borden 1982: 697).

199. *Edda* ([ed.] Neckel & Kuhn): 96. C.f. the historian of religions Tommy Kuusela (2017: 109 f.) who maintains that the use of grið was a part of certain rules of conduct in the halls. Kuusela (2017: 163 ff.) gives examples from various myths on how Odin and Thor (ON *Þórr*) breaks the truces when dealing with the jötnar in halls, the gods which are then mentioned as *griðníðníngr*, 'truce-breaker'.

200. Steenstrup (1882) 1972: 248.

201. *Eyrbyggja saga* ([ed.] Einar Ól. Sveinson): 123 (Ch. 44).

202. Hakonarmál, *Den norsk-islandske skjaldedigtning* A 1 ([ed.] Finnur Jónson): 67 (stanza 16).

203. *Eyrbyggja saga* ([ed.] Einar Ól. Sveinson): 123 (Ch. 44)

204. This formula is comparable to the Old English word *frīðgīsl* (1982: 483).

205. *Grágás, Vígslóði* ([ed.] Gunnar Karlsson et al.): 282 (§ 122).

206. *Heimskringla* II, *Óláfs saga helga* ([ed.] Bjarni Aðalbjarnarson): 115 (Ch. 80).

207. *Upplandslagen*, kungabalken II, ([ed.] Henning): 59.

208. *Grágás: lagasafn íslenska þjóðveldisins* ([ed.] Gunnar Karlsson et al.): 282 (Ch. 122).

209. In Dovring 1947: 258.

210. Smålandslagen, *Svenska landskapslagar* 5 ([ed.] Holmbäck): 423 (1).

211. *Samling af Sveriges gamla lagar* ([ed.] Schlyter): XXI f.

212. Smålandslagen, *Svenska landskapslagar* 5 ([ed.] Holmbäck): 435.

213. See Harrison 2009: 279.

214. Smålandslagen, *Svenska landskapslagar* 5 ([ed.] Holmbäck): 435.

215. Dovring 1947: 259.

216. Dovring 1947: 260.

217. Dovring 1947: 260.

218. Dovring 1947: 260.

219. Hasselberg 1948: 44.

220. In Hasselberg 1948: 45.

221. Hasselberg 1948: 44.

222. Hasselberg 1948: 45.

223. Hasselberg 1948: 45.

224. Hasselberg 1948: 48.

225. Database of the National Archives of Sweden, *Nationell Arkivdatabas* (https://sok.riksarkivet.se) (2015-10-22).

226. Hasselberg 1948: 50.

227. *Edda* ([ed.] Neckel & Kuhn): 103 (stanza 34–35).

228. Alexander Jóhannesson 1956: 306; de Vries 1961: 167; Petersson 2007: 79; see Olsson 2012: 61.

229. Cf. the skaldic poem *Runhenda*: *gisla* and *gjǫldin*.

230. *Anglo-Saxon Chronicle* MS E (ed. Irvine): 82 (year 1048); cf. Steenstrup (1882) 1972: 249, n. 5.

231. Riksarivets databas 2015-03-12; cf. Söderwall 1884–1918: 9.

232. See Söderwall 1884–1918: 399 f.; Hellquist 1922: 281; Ernby 2008: 211.

233. Cf. Lars-Olof Larsson 1975: 16.

234. Haraldssönernas saga, *Nordiska kungasagor* III ([ed]. Johansson): 263 (text), (Ch. 19); *Heimskringla*, History of the Norse Kings: Sigurd, Inge, and Eystein, the sons of Harald Gilli ([ed.] Monsen): 678 (transl.), (Ch. 19).

235. Thietmar, *Chronik* ([ed.] Trillmich): 138 ff. (text), 139 ff. (transl.) (Book 4 Ch. 23).

236. Thietmar, *Chronik* ([ed.] Trillmich): 140 (text), 141 (transl.) (Book 4 Ch. 24).

237. Thietmar, *Chronik* ([ed.] Trillmich): 140 ff. (text), 141 ff. (transl.) (Book 4 Ch. 25).

238. Pound 1959: 186.

239. Pound 1959: 186. According to the legal historian Roscoe Pound, with reference to Lutteroth, a *borgensgeisl* could either be killed or mutilated (Pound 1959: 186).

240. Brink 2012: 191.

241. Brink 2012: 191 ff.

242. See 2012: 193.

243. Brink 2012: 193.

244. Andrén 2014: 98; Halsall 1989; Alcock 2003: 119 ff.

245. Andrén 2014: 99.

246. Andrén 2014: 99.

247. Lavelle 2000: 42.

248. Lavelle 2000: 40.

249. *Anglo-Saxon Chronicle* MS E ([ed.] Irvine): 61 ff. (year 994).

250. *Anglo-Saxon Chronicle* MS E ([ed.] Irvine): 64 ff. (years 1002–1004).

251. *Anglo-Saxon Chronicle* MS E ([ed.] Irvine): 65 (year 1005).

252. *Anglo-Saxon Chronicle* MS E ([ed.] Irvine): 66 (year 1007).

253. *Anglo-Saxon Chronicle* MS E ([ed.] Irvine): 66 ff. (year 1009).

254. *Anglo-Saxon Chronicle* MS E ([ed.] Irvine): 67 ff. (year 1010).

255. *Anglo-Saxon Chronicle* MS E ([ed.] Irvine): 68 ff. (year 1011).

256. *Anglo-Saxon Chronicle* MS E ([ed.] Irvine): 69 (year 1012).

257. *Anglo-Saxon Chronicle* MS E ([ed.] Irvine): 69 ff. (year 1013).

258. *Anglo-Saxon Chronicle* MS E ([ed.] Irvine): 71 (year 1014).

259. Lawson 2004: 27.

260. The *hustinge* was a congregation in 'the prince's' or the warlords own home where he held meetings with the hird (Lexicon Poeticum [(ed.) Finnur Jónson]: 296; Fritzner [1883–96] 1973: 108). In some royal decrees, ancient sagas and medieval laws it is mentioned how the king could convene for the *hustinge* (Fritzner [1883–96] 1973:

108 f.). The king could give custody (*grið*) to a criminal at this place (Fritzner [1883–96] 1973: 108). Obviously, the *hustinge* was multifunctional, where religious, political, and legal elements existed, which can be compared to Stefan Brink's hypothesis about the multifunctionality of the thing (cf. Fritzner [1883–96] 1973: 108).

261. The custom of throwing bones at a person could have a parallel in *Hrólfs saga kraka og Bjarkarímur* ([ed.] Finnur Jónsson): 64 ff.

262. *Anglo-Saxon Chronicle* MS E ([ed.] Irvine): 69 (year 1012).

263. Steenstrup (1882) 1972: 360.

264. Steenstrup (1882) 1972: 360.

265. *Handgrið* was a part of *griðbryce* (Steenstrup [1882] 1972: 363) and is mentioned in the peace treaty (Nov. 921 [– 938?]) between Alfred and Guthrum, *Gesetze der Angelsachsen* 1 ([ed.] Lieberman): 128 [text]).

266. Steenstrup (1882) 1972: 250, 362.

267. Lawson 2004: 119.

268. Lawson 2004: 131 f.

269. Lawson 2004: 120, 131 ff.

270. Kosto 2012: 133.

271. Lavelle 2000: 41.

272. *Anglo-Saxon Chronicle* MS E (ed. Irvine): 71 (year 1014); *Anglo-Saxon Chronicle* MS F (ed. Baker): 106 f. (year 1014).

Part V: Place Names

Place names can provide information about hostages that cannot be obtained from other sources. In his study of sacred place names in the provinces around Lake Mälaren in present Sweden, Vikstrand points out that these names reflect 'a social representativeness' that have grown out of everyday language.[1] As a source, they can therefore represent social groups other than those found in the skaldic poetry which were directed to rulers in the milieu of the hird, and thus primarily give knowledge of performances of the elite.

There are difficulties with analysis of place names, because several aspects of them must be considered. Place names are names of places, but Vikstrand points out that in the term 'place' you can distinguish three components: a geographical locality, a name, and a content that gives meaning to it.[2] The relationship between these components is complicated and it is not always the given geographical location is the right one. For example, local people can ascribe place names an importance that they did not had during the time the researcher investigates.

In this part, the point of departure will be a few place names from mainly eastern Scandinavia and neighboring areas. These are examples of historical provinces in present Sweden, Finland, and Estonia that can provide information about hostages; a comparison is made with an example from Ireland.

In western Scandinavia, corresponding place names with 'hostage' as component do not appear. There are some problems with these place names: they may be mentioned in just one source, the place names are not contemporary, the etymology can be ambiguous,

---

How to cite this book chapter:
Olsson, S. 2019. Place Names. In: Olsson, S. *The Hostages of Northmen: From the Viking Age to the Middle Ages*. Pp. 225–249. Stockholm: Stockholm University Press. DOI: https://doi.org/10.16993/bba.e License: CC-BY.

and the place names can indicate traditions that are not related to hostages. Below, however, a discussion of place names and their relationship with the common denominator 'hostage' is made.

Gummi of Gislamark

In the *Gesta Danorum* ('the Deeds of the Danes') by Saxo Grammaticus there is a place name that can be linked to hostage (Da. *Gislemark*, Sw. *Gislamark*) without ambiguity. The place name is described in Saxo's list of warriors from Svetjud (or Svealand) in the army of King Ring (or Sigurd Hring) at the battle of Bråvalla (OI. *Brávellir*).[3] The battle – which in several texts is mentioned as the largest in Scandinavia in ancient times – has attracted interest from many researchers. From being regarded as a historical battle, it is now viewed as legendary, 'mythical', or merely devised.[4] By 'legendary' I mean a story to which non-historical material was added. By 'mythical' I mean a possible reflection of myths. Saxo's list is attributed, for example, to the mythical, or legendary, character Starkad (ON *Starkaðr*, lat. *Starcatherus*); among other things, the battle has been perceived to be based on the Ragnarök theme or as a part of an Indo-European mythical heritage.[5]

I do not intend to take a position as to whether the battle took place or not, but just to analyse and relate to the list of names with the Swedes. In the Latin text it says:

> At Sueonum fortissimi hi fuere: Ari, Haki, Keclu-Karll, Croc Agrestis, Guthfast, Gummi e Gyslamarchia. Qui quidem Frø dei necessarii erant et fidissimi numinum arbitri.[6]

> The most valiant of the Swedes were: Ari, Haki, Keklu-Karl, Krok the Countryman, Guthfast and Gummi of Gislamark. Indeed, they were kinsmen of the divine Frø and faithful accessories of the gods.[7]
> (Transl. Peter Fisher)

The name Gislamark would refer to a place where hostages would be used in a certain way (see further below). The modifer *Gisla-* would then be derived to the Swedish *gisslan* 'hostage' and the head *-mark* to 'woodland' or 'field'.

In the fragmentary Old Icelandic *Sǫgubrot af fornkonungum* (about 1300) there is a list that partially corresponds to Saxo's:

Þessir váru ofan af Svíaveldi: Nori, Haki, Karl kekkja, Krókarr af Akri, Gunnfastr, Glismakr goði.[8]

These came from above Svetjud: Nori, Haki, Karl kekkja, Krok of Akri, Gunnfastr, Glismakr goði.

(My free translation)

Instead of Gummi and Gislamark, Glismakr goði is mentioned. One can suspect that it is a rewriting by Saxo from 'Glismakr' to 'Gislamark', which has been Latinized to *Gyslamarchia*.[9] But this can be easily explained. The personal name Glismakr, which is not a place name in the text of *Sǫgubrot*, cannot be confirmed by the text material of runestones or other sources. Possibly Glismakr can be a misconception, or rewriting, of the place name Glimåkra, the name of an old church town in the province of Skåne (or Scania), but if so is the case it is a matter of an entirely different region than Svetjud.[10] The philologist Axel Olrik pointed out in an article about the battle of Bråvalla that the author of *Sǫgubrot* in his list must have perceived *goði* as a sobriquet to Glismakr. Glismakr may be about *Guði* (OSw. *Gudhi*), but Olrik thought that it was about an 'unfortunate' corruption in the text of the name Gunni (Gummi) by an Icelandic writer.[11] Even the list of the *Sǫgubrot* can be embroidered with learned elements even if it is less extensive than the version of Saxo.

Gesta Danorum was perhaps completed around 1208, while *Sǫgubrot* was fixed in writing about 1300. However, *Sǫgubrot* can build on the *Skjǫldunga saga* (from about 1180), which is now only found in some fragments and is considered to be based on the even older manuscript by Ari Þorgilsson: *conunga ævi*.[12]

Both productions do not appear to have had the same prerequisites when it comes to the sources. Saxo's list of the warriors of the kings Harold Wartooth (or Harald Hildetand) and Ring is more detailed and could therefore be manipulated and supplemented by learned embroideries, to a greater degree than *Sǫgubrot*'s version. Some of the names that appear can be explained as literary contributions, such as the presence of female warriors (amazons).

Names like the alliterative Skale Scanius (as in the province of Scania) could have been added by Saxo just to include all the parts of the Danish realm of his own time.[13] He may have also manipulated with the time and geographical conditions in the list of warriors. There are names of Jomsvikings who belongs to the 11th century and not the eighth.[14] As a medieval writer, Saxo may have had an interest in allegorically depicting the battle against the Vices: the Swedes is primarily described as idolatry worshipers. On the other hand, Saxo has generally been reassessed by several researchers.[15] Everything is not literary inspiration and learned interpretations.

The historian Inge Skovgaard-Petersen considers the version of *Gesta Danorum* to be closer to the original than the list of *Sǫgubrot*.[16] The historian Nils Blomkvist believes that the list of Saxo – in addition to having more names than *Sǫgubrot* – latinizes the names in order to 'improve them', but when it comes to the names of the Swedes, 'he makes hardly any adjustments at all'.[17]

However, there are no other evidence of Gummi of Gislamark in either Old Eastern Norse or Old Western Norse text sources. The personal name Gunni (or Gunne) is mentioned on 21 rune stones in the province Uppland, while the name form Gummi (or Gumme) occurs on two.[18] Gislamark (or Gislemark) does not exist as a place name in Uppland or in the Mälaren region. Gisslemark and Gilmark, on the other hand, are surnames in Sweden today. But the Swedish Institute for Language and Folklore (Sw. *Institutet för språk och folkminnen*) has no further information about these names in their collections.[19] The theoretical possibility that remains is that the 16th-century editors of the *Gesta Danorum* manipulated the list; however, this is not likely.

Thus, it is not possible to determine whether the personal name of Gummi, with the place name Gislamark, have been inserted in a later stage, or if they stem from a possible older version for certain. But it is possible to relate to hypotheses about the origin of other place name with a similar meaning based on other source material. Through these place names, and the descriptions of them, the function of the hostage can be determined.

Gislamark and gisslalag

Attempts have been made to find the origin of the place name Gislamark in text sources other than *Gesta Danorum*, which is linked to Finland and the Baltic countries. In *A Description of the Northern Peoples* (Sw. *Historia om de nordiska folken*, Lat. *Historien de gentibus septentrionalibus*) from 1555, by the Archbishop (in exile) Olaus Magnus, there is a list of the most important areas in the Nordic region. In this list Olaus Magnus mentions the place name Gislalagen (Lat. *Gislemarchia*).[20]

In the register of the 1976 edition, the ethnologist John Granlund identifies the Gislalagen with the medieval district called *gisslalag* (OSw. *gislalagh*), thus ascribe the area to Finland, which was a part of the Swedish realm between 1249 and 1809.[21] The Gisslalag was a district where the inhabitants were obliged to pay taxes and a hostage was used as security. The inhabitants were also obliged to treat and accommodate the king and his retinue on visit. But the records are few for this territorial division from Finland, and they are found only in medieval texts. The earliest record is found in the *Eric Chronicle* (Sw. *Erikskrönikan*), which mentions how the Swedes abstained from 14 *gisslalag*s to Novgorod (Russia) in the 1290s after the founding of Viborg.[22] The word is also found in the Treaty of Nöteborg from 1323, according to which Novgorod abstained three gisslalags to Sweden (see Figure V.2).[23] However, the place name need not only be ascribed to Finland.

The ethnologist Kustaa Vilkuna asscoiated the gisslalag (Fi. *kihlakunta*) as a place name, with Karelia (c.f. the Karelian place name Kihlakunta) and perceived it as an Eastern Finnish equivalent to the ancient Swedish districts of *hundare* and *härad*. He thus suggested that there should have been a similar former district division in Finland and Karelia.[24] Any permanent country organization did not exist, but according to Vilkuna, Scandinavians could receive a tax from obsolete areas secured by the hostage.[25]

Vilkuna's hypothesis that the hostage may had its roots in an elderly institution in Finland or Karelia has been questioned by modern research. According to the historian Philip Line, there is no sustainable evidence before 1323 that these districts ever existed in Finland and Karelia.[26] But Line ignores the information of the

Figure V.1. Map of Finland including the medieval cities of Viborg and Nöteborg. Source: Sawyer & Sawyer 1993: 68 (By permission from the authors, license CC BY 4.0).

Eric Chronicle, which can confirm that the *gisslalag* functioned as an organisational form in Finland in the 1290s. Nevertheless, none of these text sources can actually tell you how old these traditions are. However, the place name of Kihlakunta may have been much older than the sources where it is recorded.

Vilkuna's statement that a 'king' would take hostages during the journey to the *gisslalag*s with the implied threat that they would be executed – unless the king and his men received the food and drink they expected – must also be noted. This is not in line with the image of the hostage that is given in this book. The hostage was primarily used as a third party to ensure the safety of a person or a group. In this case it seems more probable that it was the king's person who should be secured. Food and other necessities were something that could still be taken through violence. Vilkuna also makes no difference between Finland, Karelia, Ingria, Estonia, and Courland. Different ruling powers had varying degrees of influence over these lands from time to time, which also meant that the use of hostages may have had different purposes.

Despite evidence from the medieval Finland, it is unclear whether an organisational form of *gisslalag* or equivalents ever existed in the 8th–11th centuries, which can be confirmed by the place name Kihlakunta. However, the Estonian word *kihelkond* is of interest because there have been theories that it had a Scandinavian origin. Below, these theories and interpretations of the meaning of the word will be summarized.

The districts of Kihelkond *and* syssel

Vilkuna compared the Old Swedish word *giszlalagh* (alt. *gislalagh*) with the Finnish *kihlakunta*, the Estonian *kihelkond*, the Votic *tshihlago* and the Estonian-Finnish *kunta*. He indicated that the hostage institution in its time (the Middle Ages) stretched from the Livonian area of Courland across the Estonian-Votic area to the Southwestern Karelia. So, it was a matter of large areas. According to Vilkuna, the *gisslalag* was subject to a special 'food tax' or 'guest tax', which was collected in store houses. The food was provieded to the king and his retinue when he made visits.[27] Vilkuna believed that hostages was taken as a security for the payment of the tax and if the tax was not paid, they were killed. Vilkuna also believed that the hostage institution could have existed even before the Middle Ages, something that could be seen through an example from Estonia.[28]

On the island Saaremaa (Sw. *Ösel*) there is a place called Kihelkonna, which can be deduced to the Estonian *kihelkond*, 'parish', a word that indicates a territory where the head -*kond* means 'area' and the modifier *kihla*- is a Nordic loan word (< OWN *gísl*, 'hostage', OE *gisl* 'hostage').[29] Vilkuna could support himself with other researchers who put forward the hypothesis of an ancient district of taxation in Estonia.

The historian Arvi Korhonen argued that smaller tax districts in Estonia already existed in the Viking age before the German

Writer/chronicler	Productions	Composition	Events	Places
Þjóðólfr of Hvinir	Ynglingatal	10th century	The Uppsala ruler Yngvar falls in combat with Estonians	Unknown. Though a fight against *Syslu kind*.
Eyjólfr dáðaskáld	Bandadrápa	ca. 1010	Eiríkr Hákonarson jarl is driven out of Norway. He plunders in Russia in *allar sýslur*.	Various *sýslur* in Russia.
An anonymous monk	Historia Norwegiae	1150s	Death of Yngvar	Eysýsla
Snorri Sturluson	Heimskringla	ca. 1225	Death of Yngvar. The king is buried in a mound	Aðalsýsla
Snorri Sturluson	Saga Ólafs Tryggvarsonar, ch. 90, Heimskringla	ca. 1225	Eiríkr jarl in Russia	Aðalsýsla or Eysýsla
Snorri Sturluson, An anonymous monk	Heimskringla, ch. 8. Ólafs saga helga, ch. 22. Historia Noreuvegiae	ca. 1225 1190? 1150s	Olaf Haraldsson plunders Eysýsla	Eysýsla
	Ágrip, ch 14	ca. 1190		
	Ágrip, ch. 17	ca. 1190	Capture of Olaf Trygvasson	Eysýsla
	Njáls saga, kap. 30	1280–1290?		Eysýsla

Figure V.2. Sources to the presence of Scandinavians in the *sýslur*. Source: Gallén 1972: 650 ff.

conquest in the 13th century. The philologist Paul Johansen made a hypothesis of a territorial division in Estonia organized by Scandinavians. At *Saaremaa* (OI. *Eysýsla*, OGt. *Oysl*, Fi. Saarenmaa), a tax collection system would have been set up by Scandinavians already in the ninth century.[30] A model of the Estonian *maa*-names may also have originated in Scandinavian medieval names of districts. The *syssel*s (ODan. *syssæl*, OSw. *sysel*) were administrative units in the Middle Ages in Scandinavia. In addition, it can be argued that this district organisation in Jutland is considered – at least by an older generation of researchers – to be pre-Christian.[31]

Johansen's interpretations, and Vilkuna's, have been questioned by the philologist Enn Tarvel. The modifier *kihla-* may be a Nordic loan word, but the meaning of the word in Estonian is, according to Tarvel, 'engagement', 'wooing quest', or 'engagement gift'.[32] Only in the Livonian language is there a word that can be translated to 'pledge' or 'hostage' without ambiguity: *kī'l*. Tarvel mentions several reasons that a territorial division with the hostage as security should not have existed during the Viking Age and the early Middle Ages. In particular, he points to the importance of an extensive Scandinavian influence: 'Die Schaffung einer speziellen Besteuerung- und Geiselstellungorganisation würde ja doch eine längere skandinavische Oberherrschaft alls Verbindung notwendig machen'.[33] According to Tarvel, the text sources are not convincing: the *Ynglinga saga* mentions Ivar Vidfamne (ON *Ívarr inn víðfaðmi*), or Erik Emundsson (ON *Eiríkr Eymundsson*) and the Danish Canute the Great as conquerors of Estonia which cannot be confirmed by other sources.[34]

It may not be certain whether the word 'hostage' in the sense that Tarvel claims really contradicts a hostage giving. The *kunda*-areas may have had this function in addition to those described by Tarvel. The philologist Urmas Sutrop believes that the head *-kunta* (alt. *-kunda*) is a loan word from the Germanic *hunta* (*hunda*) and may have occurred as early as in the 100s AD, while the modifier *kihl-* may be (a younger?) loan word.[35] The modifier *kihl-* had several meanings: e.g. the word *kihlused*, 'wedding arrangement', and *kihlvedu*, 'bet', but *kihlkonnad* (alt. *kihelkonnad*) also have had the meaning of hostagegiving.[36] Tarvel claims that an over-rule was required for the establishment of an administrative unit. In my view, a supremacy is not necessarily the prerequisite for an organization around the hostage. In Estonia and Courland, it has not been the question of a Scandinavian over-rule, but rather there have been different spheres of interest. This could be compared to the model for early medieval state formations presented in the introduction. Bagge's model applies primarily to Norway, but can be applied to other Viking communities.[37] In these early pre-state societies, it was the personal ties that were decisive and that the local great men had to rely on. For example, such bonds may have been maintained by and the ambulatory rulership or kingship as described in the Kings' sagas and early medieval Nordic laws.

Regarding the development of a possible tax district organization in Estonia, it may initially, to a limited extent, have emerged without an early Scandinavian influence. According to Line, it could be the reason for the emergence of special fortresses (Est. *Maalinnad*) during the late Iron Age. These fortresses could dominate a territory which eventually became a *kihelkond*.[38] Such fortresses belonged to a local elite. At the same time, these areas may occasionally have been in the sphere of interests of Novgorod and Kiev. The evidence for this to occur earlier than the 1100s is vague,[39] but the presence of the fortresses could indicate that these areas have periodically been subject to taxation – and perhaps hostage takings – from an external power. The establishment of fortresses in Estonia could also have been local defense measures against these charges, and the Kihelkond became an area subject to a local warrior elite. One possibility is that these districts were already organized when Viking raids, and later the crusades, were carried out by Scandinavians or other peopls.

Perhaps the Scandinavians perceived these areas as OSwe. *sȳsla* (pl. *sȳslur*), ON *sýsla*. If the word *sȳsla* ('county', 'district') is older than the Middle Ages, it can be related to the text sources that mention Scandinavian activities in the Baltic areas and on Saaremaa. The historian Jarl Gallén described the sources for where the ON word *sýsla* is used as the designation of Saaremaa, which was the Old Norse *Aðalsýsla*.[40] The head -*sýsla* could be compared to the ancient Scandinavian district.

The presence of Scandinavians in Estonia regarding plundering can be confirmed by several sources independent of each other (Figure V.1). Runic inscriptions also mention Scandinavians in Estonia, Livonia, and Courland.[41] There is archaeological evidence: Two boat graves dated to the eighth century have been found at Saaremaa near the village Salme. In the boat graves (Salme 1–2) the archaeologists found in total 42 skeletons. In the boats there were also remains of grave goods such as pieces for board games, shields, arrowheads, swords, spears, hawks, dogs, and combs.[42] T. D. Douglas Price et al. state that the gravegoods suggest that the boat crews was on a diplomatic mission (perhaps an alliance with local chieftains on Saaremaa). Their analysis seems to confirm that the skeletons are of Scandinavian origins – the tooth enamel is likely to descend from Scandinavia and the weapons are of Scandinavian design.[43] The weapons are decorated with precious metals and garnets; there were also other luxuries as mentioned above, which, according to Price et al., make them suitable as gifts for political alliances.[44] Price et al. also claim that there might have been a Scandinavian settlement on the Sõrve Peninsula of Saaremaa.[45] They also have a hypothesis regarding the death of the warriors:

> The shortest route from Courland to the 'mother country' in the Mälar district ran through the Salme straits. Noblemen from Denmark and the southern coast of the Baltic, along with the Götars [i.e. the Geats], wanted control of that route. It is entirely possible that the dead at Salme were the victims of an armed conflict between these foreign groups that left the Svear seafarers buried near the shoreline. Local Estonians need not have been involved in any way.[46]

Finally, there is an early source that confirms that Scandinavians took tributes and hostages in the Baltic region, that is, the case with Rimbert, whose biography of Ansgar (*Vita Ansgari*) describes how the Swedes received a hostage in 854 from the village of Apuolė in Courland.[47]

The above may suggest that Scandinavians had a knowledge of taxation and hostages that they imposed on the Estonians and Courians. Whether or not the organizational form originated from

Scandinavians or Germans (during the Middle Ages), was based on a domestic organization, or was established under the influence of powers such as Novgorod and Kiev, we can only speculate. Perhaps it was a combination of these forms.

During the peace negotiations between the inhabitants of Saaremaa and the invading armies (or raiding parties) that occurred during the crusades, the terms were dictated by the side that had the upper hand. For example, Valdemar II 'the Victorious' of Denmark tried to build a castle on Saaremaa in 1222.[48] The Saaremaa islanders allied themselves with the Estonians and besieged the castle. After several days, the Danes and some Germans were invited to surrender with a promise of free passage if they left the castle and abandoned Saaremaa. After the Danes gave up, a hostage was taken, including a brother of the bishop of Riga, to consolidate the peace (*obsides ibidem pro pacis confirmatone*).[49] A similar unilateral way of using hostages occurred several times after Christian victories over both islanders, Livonians and Estonians.[50]

The Estonian word *kihelkond* is certainly ambiguous, but it cannot be denied that the activity of the taking and giving of hostages as well as plundering occured. If the use of hostages was the result of a permanent organizational form during the Viking Age in the eastern part of the country, where Swedes carried out plundering, it could give more weight to the argument that the place name Gislamark – as produced by Saxo Grammaticus in the *Gesta Danorum* – can be derived from the Viking Age or earlier.

In addition to the examples from Nordic areas, a comparison can be made with an Irish place name that also occurs in – and may be the result of – various peace agreements: Airgíalla.

Airgíalla in Ireland

In Ireland, hostages have had functions within peace process that are mentioned in several sources. There is a place name that can be linked to the word for 'hostage' in Old Irish traditions called Airgíalla. According to one interpretation the place name might mean 'those who give hostages'.[51] It was a federation of nine different people.

Ireland traditionally had five major areas, 'fifths', or provinces, which were ruled by a provincial king (OIr. *rí ruirech*). The High King (*ard-rí*) had his seat in Tara, but this position was vague and existed only in theory because any permanent supremacy could not be consolidated.[52] Individuals from different family-based groupings, clans, alternately held this position. For such groupings, genealogies were important to legitimise their power positions.[53]

The most powerful clan (or grouping) between the 600s and the 900s in Ireland was called Uí Néill. They claimed their relationship with Niall Noigíallach.[54] Connachta, another grouping, claimed to be descendants of the half-mythical High King Conn Cétchathach ('Conn of the Hundred Battles'). The territories of Connachta are named after them by the collective name *Cúige Chonnact*, 'Connachts Fifth'. According to the *Book of Rights*, Airgíalla would have matched the five major provinces and may have existed already in the fourth century.[55] Perhaps this tribal federation was more likely to have arisen in the seventh century.

A dynasty of kings ruled Airgíalla; sometimes there was no provincial king, but two or three rival kings. It is possible that Airgíalla was dependent on the high kings in Tara. According to the legend, there were three kings, *The Three Collas*: Colla Óss, Colla Fochríth, and Colla Menn. These mythical or legendary figures may have given rise to Airgíalla after defeating a number of Irish tribal federations, including *ulaid*, a people in the historic province of Ulster.[56]

The status of Airgíalla in relation to the five major provinces (*fifths*) is disputed. It is possible that their rulers' genealogies cannot be linked to Connachta or Uí Néill at all. Other individual dynasties within Airgíalla, such as the dynasty Mugdorna, suggest that the federation was founded in the seventh century. It is likely that the dynasty Colla Óss was one of the most important dynasties because it is mentioned in § 8 of *The Airgíalla Charter Poem*.[57]

An etymological explanation of the name *Airgíallne, is that the morpheme -*ne*, was confused with an abstract suffix, -*(ai)ne*, and was supposed to be a diversion of *gíall(n)ae*, 'service' or 'base clientship'. The name Airgíall(n)ae was thus considered to mean 'additional clientship'. Another interpretation suggests that *Airgiallnai, with the head -gíallnae of OI giallae, are comparable to the Latin dicio and deditio.[58] The -gíallnae could also be derived to gíall, 'hostage', 'security'.[59]

The earliest reference to Airgíalla that can be confirmed is found in the Annals of Tigernach (year 677), which also reproduces a ruler – Dúnchad Mac Ultán ('son of Ultán') – who would be 'king' of Airgíalla (Rí Oigirall), but this information is uncertain. The Annals of Ulster of the year 697 describes the ruler Máel Fothartaig Mac Máel Dub ('son of Maeldub') as 'Rex na nAirgialla'.[60] Because Máel Fothartaig and his son Eochu Lemnae are mentioned as guarantors of the Law of Adomnáñan from the 700s, the information about him as a ruler in Airgíalla can be genuine.[61]

In 704 there was a battle between the king of Connacht, Cellach Mac Rogallaig, belonging to a dynasty called Uí Briúin, and Loingsech Mac Óenguso who was rex Hiberniae, 'King of Ireland' and ruler of Tara, who belonged to the Cenél Conaill, a branch of the Uí Neill-dynasty. In the list of people fallen in the battle, Eochu Lemnaes and Fergus Forcraid are found. These belonged to two clans, called Uí Chremthainn and Uí Thuirtri.[62] These groups were allied with Uí Néill. Several alliances between the dynasties of Airgíalla and Uí Néill also occurred before this battle. According to the historian Edel Bhreatnach, Airgíalla was probably a military federation.[63] This is confirmed by a further list of dead from a settlement between two warlords. In 743, Domnall defeated Midi, who belonged to the clan Chlomain Áed Allán of the Cenél federation, who were allied with Airgíalla.[64] Thus, it was alliances and counter alliances over an area of confrontation.

The Airgíalla Charter Poem

The earliest written source which gives information about the foundation Airgíalla is *The Airgíalla Charter Poem*. According to Bhreatnach, there were two main events underlying the creation of the document: (a) the relationship between the dynasties that founded or formed Airgíalla; and (b) the formal definition of the relationship between the dynasties called Arigíalla and Uí Néill.[65]

According to the Celtologist Thomas M. Charles-Edwards, the agreement was thought to be a way of defining the relationship to Uí Néill, and the agreement should have been to Airgíalla's advantage.[66] In *The Airgíalla Charter Poem*, in § 11 there is a reference to Áed Allán, which is interpreted by Bhreathnach: An alliance has existed between the Cenél federation and Airgíalla between 722 and 743.[67] The *Airgíalla Charter Poem* might have been composed at this time.

The poem is divided into four sections with amendments (added articles). These amendments were a result of several different negotiations. The first section, according to Charles-Edwards, is a historical prologue that deals with the land areas and genealogical relationships between Airgíalla and Uí Néill. In the second section, article 14, the case of hostages is mentioned.

14. Ar-dlegat íarara co neuch ar-da-gíalla ar-dlegat fiadnaise it clethe for fíadna.

14. They are entitled to demands together with anyone who gives them hostages.[68]

(Transl. Edel Bhreathnach & Kevin Murray)

Article 14 is about the rights of the *Five Kindreds* (*Na cóic clanda*) of Uí Néill vis-à-vis Airgíalla, the same rights they used, according to Charles-Edwards, against all their subject territories. The hostage that Airgíalla gave the *Five Kindreds* is not specified in this context. The article may also be interpreted so that Airgíalla had certain rights (demands) in the same way as other territories that were subordinated to Uí Néill and were hostage givers.[69]

18. Ar-dlegat a forbanda a suidiu fhlatho acht ma ar-da-gíallatar i rroï chatho.

18. They are entitled to their extra exactions from the seat of a ruler unless hostages are given to them on the field of battle.[70]

(Transl. Edel Bhreathnach & Kevin Murray)

§ 18 belongs to the same section of *The Airgíalla Charter Poem* as § 14.[71] It could be interpreted that Airgíalla was to share the requirements (*exactions*), or privileges, that a ruler (of the *Five Kindreds*) could impose on a defeated enemy unless they could take hostages themselves on the battlefield.

23. Dlegair donaib Airgíallaib córus a ngíallnae slóged trí cóicthiges dïa téora blíadnae.	23. There is due to from the Airgíalla the proper arrangement of their hostageship, a hosting of three fortnights every three years.[72] (Transl. Edel Bhreathnach & Kevin Murray)

The next section of *The Airgíalla Charter Poem* is about the obligations of Airgíalla regarding military service. An obligation called *slógad*, 'hosting', which meant that an army formed through an alliance or agreement could pass through the territory of Airgíalla. § 23 is difficult to interpret, but in the translation of Bhreathnach and the philologist Kevin Murray, there is a word, *ngíallnae*, which they interpret as 'hostageship'.[73] The article is about the obligation to accommodate troops, but what is meant by 'hostageship' is unclear in this case. If Aírgíalla were to make war with other federations, it was necessary with what we today refer to as 'diplomacy'.[74] If an army, in allegiance with Aírgíalla, passed through their territory, they would travel via pre-selected roads and would camp at certain places as specified in § 28.

28. Cumal cacha forbaise fessar co slógib acht manis túissed eolach dia ndúnaib córib.	28. A *cumal* for every camp which spends the night with hosts, unless a knowledge able person should conduct them to their proper encampments.[75] (Transl. Edel Bhreathnach & Kevin Murray)

The following can be interpreted from this: a representative of the visiting army would stay with the hosts overnight at every place they camped, unless a person well-known in Aírgíalla was responsible for their conduct. This person, who represented an area, would probably be valued after his rank.

The last section of the poem leans towards two agreements that should have been made during the sixth century between Aírgíalla and Uí Néill. In this section, mythical elements are included in the text that will guarantee peace. § 40 claims that authorities – which might be percieved as deities – like the 'sea and land with they sky, sun and moon' will guarantee that the peace will be maintained.[76] The next article (41) mentions 'Dew and light, God's apostles from heaven, aged men, prophets, patriarchs and bright angels'.[77] Several researchers argue that these are examples of how Christian and pre-Christian traditions occur side by side.[78]

Another article (46) mentions hostages as a security for the agreement. They are called *aitiri*, 'hostage sureties'.

46. It sruithi a n-aitiri do-chuitchetar már [...].	46. Their hostage sureties are venerable men who have sworn mightily [...]. (Transl. Edel Bhreathnach & Kevin Murray)[79]

According to Charles-Edwards, *aitiri* was used as a guarantee for major public agreements between two or more *túatha*s. The article also shows that the hostage could swear oaths; thus they had a 'legal capacity'. In *The Airgíalla Charter Poem*, much of what is described in previous chapters occurs. Although the proposed etymologies of the place name *Airgíalla* (or *Airgíallnae*) are uncertain, Bhreathnach and Murray believe that the word forms the basis for the federation's relationship to Uí Néill: '*airgíallnae* suggests the tentative translations "additional hostageship" or "additional service"'.[80] Certainly, Airgíalla was subordinated to Uí Néill, but their strength ensured that they could not be totally subjected to other dynasties. Different types of contracts were established because of peace settlements in which hostages served as a security or regulatory factor in the areas of confrontation, but in different ways. The hostage was therefore not only linked to warlike activities but also peace times, something that could be related to my hypothesis about the 'available hostage'. The invocation of mythical elements, both pre-Christian and Christian, as security for peace shows the specific connections to the giving of

The Airgíalla Charter Poem	Examples of cases	Part
(1) A hostage with different purposes that is at disposal.	In 877. The Great Heathen Army gave hostages to Alfred.	III. p. 84 ff.
	In 994. The hostage provided by Æthelred to Olaf Tryggvason.	III. p. 91 ff.
	In the 13th century. The giving of the hostages of the Geats to the king in the province of Västergötland.	VI. p. 251 ff.
(2) Myths and legends about hostages.	The Æsir–Vanir War.	II.
	The legends about Vikar and Walther.	IV. p. 158 ff.
	Semilegendary: The death of Ragnvald Knaphövde in 1130.	
(3) Disputed land areas.	In the 8th to 10th centuries. Negotiations between Danish rulers and the Carolingian royal power. Likewise between Danish and Saxon rulers.	III. p. 95 ff.
	The Orkney Islands in the early 11th century. Clashes between competitive earls.	IV. p. 151 ff.
	The *Gislalag*s in Finland in the 13th century.	V. p. 226 ff.
(4) Oaths. Security.	In 878. The peace processes between Alfred and Guthrum.	I. p. 29 ff.
	Early 10th century. The oath of Earl Brusi Sigurdsson to Olaf Haraldsson.	IV. p. 152.
	Gisla and *grutha* in the medieval Swedish laws.	
(5) Morality and consequences.	Various litterary examples: Vikar and Herthjóf, Walter and Attila.	IV. p. 158 ff.
	The Æsir–Vanir War.	
(6) The social value of hostages.	The value of female hostages.	IV. p. 160 ff.
	Conduct and loyalty.	IV. p. 157 ff.
	The Æsir–Vanir War.	

Figure V.3. Comparsion between different text sources regarding rituals.

hostages. In this settlement legal, religious, and economic aspects presuppose each other.

There are several other points in *The Airgíalla Charter Poem* that can be compared to what has been found in this study, Figure V.3. The Irish examples are interesting from a comparative perspective, although it is not possible to translate the political conditions of the sixth and seventh centuries of Ireland into the Old Norse conditions. In order to emphasize these altering conditions, the hostage giving and taking that is described in the *Elder Westrogothic Law* in the following part will be analysed. The purpose is to describe the power political situation that was specific to this particular area at the time of the law's accession.

Concluding remarks

In this section, some place names are analyzed that may be connected with hostages. Saxo Grammaticus states in *Gesta Danorum* a list of warriors from Sweden (or *Svetjud*) before the mythical or legendary battle of Bråvalla. The list contains name of Gummi from Gislemark (*Gummi e Gyslamarchia*). The place name (*gisl-*, 'hostage') would – although not without some ambiguity – point to a ground where a hostage was used in peace negotiations.

In the Icelandic *Sǫgubrot af fornkonungum*, the name list is reproduced with Swedish warriors before the battle of Bråvalla, but instead of Gummi Glismakr, *goði* is mentioned. This is a personal name and not a place name, which cannot be confirmed by other sources; that it would be a rewriting of the old church village Glimåkra in Scania is far-fetched. Both the authors of *Gesta Danorum* and the *Sǫgubrot* appear to have had access to partly the same source material. Both works show signs of learned work, and when it comes to Saxo's list of Swedish warriors, Nils Blomkvist believes that Saxo hardly makes any changes at all in relation to the source material. There is no other evidence other than Saxo's list that mentions Gummi from Gislemark in Uppland, Mälardalen, or any other parts of the ancient Svetjud. It is, however, not possible to determine with certainty whether the person name Gummi and the place name Gislemark was included in an earlier version of the story about the battle Bråvalla or is a later addition by Saxo.

A hypothesis has been put forward about the possible place name Gislamark. In Olaus Magnus's *A Description of the Northern Peoples* mention is made of the place name *Gyslamarchia*, which Granlund places in Finland, and he believes that it is a rewrite of the medieval districts called *gislalagh*s. These districts are mentioned in sources including *The Eric Chronicle* (Swe. *Erikskrönikan*) and the treaty of Nöteborg (1323). These were districts obliged to pay taxes to the Crown, who used a hostage as a security for the delivery. Kustaa Vilkuna has claimed that an even older district that preceded the *gislalagh*s. These ancient districts would correspond to the Swedish *hundare* ('hundred'). This has been rejected by later research because it is only described in late-medieval text sources. The hypothesis that *Gyslamarchia* in Saxo's list may correspond to the *gislalagh* is therefore uncertain.

Another place name that may be of interest in these contexts is Kihelkonna at Ösel. The Estonian name Kihelkond (or *kihlkonnad*) is a word for a territory where the main path, -con, can mean 'area' and the decision path, Kihle-, can have the possible meaning 'hostage'. However, the philologist Enn Tarvel points out that the word is ambiguous in the Estonian language and can mean both 'hostage' and 'engagement, freedom travel'.

Another place name that may be of interest in these contexts is Kihelkonna at the Island of Saremaa (Swe. *Ösel*). The Estonaian *Kihelkond* is a word for a territory in which the head could mean 'area' and the modifer, Kihel-, can have the possible meaning 'hostage'. The philologist Enn Tarvel points out that the word is ambiguous in the Estonian language and can mean both 'hostage' or 'engagement, wooing quest'.

The tax district organization in Estonia may have arisen in connection with the establishment of special fort (*maalinad*) during the late Iron Age that may have evolved into *kihlekond*. However we can only speculate on, the advent of these districts, but the existence may imply that an organizational form was established that the Scandinavians could utilize even as early as during the Viking Age. The presence of Scandinavians in the Baltic lands is stated in the saga literature, in runic inscriptions, and in the biography of Ansgar, which states how the Swedes received hostages from the city of Apuolė.

One can compare this with the Irish place name Airgíalla, which could have the meaning 'those who give hostage'. It was a tribal federation that corresponded to the great provinces of Ireland. They had a special relationship to the dominant clan (or grouping) called Uí Néill.

The earliest source depicting the foundation of Airgíalla is *The Airgíalla Charter Poem*. The Poem, probably written between 722 and 743, addresses the relationship between the dynasties who founded Airgíalla and their relationship with Uí Néill. In the poem, which is divided into four sections, there are five paragraphs, which mention hostages in different contexts. In a section, heathen deities are also listed alongside God, prophets, patriarchs, and angels as guarantors of peace. A paragraph also shows that the hostage had a legal capacity by being able to bear witness by oath.

Although the etymology of the place name Airgíalla is uncertain, Edel Bhreathnach and Kevin Murray indicate that a possible translation may be 'additional hostageship'. *The Airgíalla Charter Poem* shows that hostages were an important part of the regulation of the relationship between Airgíalla and Uí Néill and that they were thus linked not only to wartime activities but also to peace time, something that can be related to the hypothesis of a hostage that was available. *The Airgíalla Charter Poem* contains many points that can be compared to what has been disccused about place names above.

Notes to Part V

1. Vikstrand 2001: 33.

2. Vikstrand 2001: 19.

3. Saxo Grammaticus, *Gesta Danorum = Danmarkshistorien* I ([ed.] Friis-Jensen): 511–517 (Book 8, Ch. 1, 1–3, 13).

4. See N. Blomkvist 2005: 240 ff.

5. E.g. Skovgaard-Petersen 1987: 179 ff.; Wikander 1960.

6. Saxo Grammaticus, *Gesta Danorum* = *Danmarkshistorien* I ([ed.] Friis-Jensen): 516 (text), (Book 8, Ch. 3, 11).

7. Saxo Grammaticus, *The History of the Danes* ([ed.] Hilda Ellis Davidson): 240 (Book 8).

8. *Sǫgubrot af fornkonungum* (Danakonunuga sǫgur [(ed.) Bjarni Guðnasson]: 64 [Ch. 8]).

9. Müller 1823: 122.

10. According to the *Svenskt ortnamnslexikon* the place name Glimåkra can be traced to the late 14th century. The head, *Glima-, is probably aimed at the river Glimån (*Svenskt ortnamnslexikon* 2016: 98).

11. Olrik 1894: 253.

12. Finnur Jónsson 1920–24: 828; Friis-Jensen 1987: 23; N. Blomkvist 2005: 240 f.

13. Skovgaard-Petersen 1987: 262.

14. N. Blomkvist 2005: 242.

15. See *Saxo og Snorre* (2010).

16. Skovgaard-Petersen 1987: 262.

17. N. Blomkvist 2005: 249.

18. Peterson 2007: 90 ff.

19. E-mail Agneta Sundström, research archivist, Swedish Institute for Language and Folklore.

20. Olaus Magnus, *Historia* [...] (transl. Granlund): 315.

21. Granlund 1976: 543.

22. *Erikskrönikan* ([ed.] Jansson): 73.

23. Gallén & Lind 1991: 314; Tarvel 1998: 193, 198, n. 1; N. Blomkvist 2005: 264.

24. Vilkuna 1964: 9–30.

25. Vilkuna 1960: 9–30, 328.

26. Line 2009: 79.

27. Vilkuna 1960: 328.

28. Vilkuna 1960: 328.

29. de Vries 1977: 168; Tarvel 1998: 193; c.f. Sutrop 2004: 52.

30. Vilkuna 1960: 328.

31. The Philologist Troels Dahlerup (1960: 649) considers that the Danish traditions of the *syssel*s is older than the time for the introduction of Christianity. In Norwegian context, the *syssel* tradition means 'activity', 'work', or 'purpose' and may possibly be earliest recorded in connection with the activities of the king's solicitor in the 900s and 1000s (Andersen 1960: 645). The earliest mention of the *syssel* in Iceland is the law code *Jónsbók* ([ed.] Schulman): 19 (I, 7); 30 (III, 2); 330 (VIII, 26) from about 1270–1280 and the *syssel* could therefore be connected to the traditions of the Icelandic law (Björn Þorsteinsson 1960: 648).

32. Tarvel 1998: 193.

33. Tarvel 1998: 194.

34. Tarvel 1998: 194.

35. Sutrop 2004: 51.

36. Sutrop 2004: 51.

37. See Part I.

38. Line 2009: 79.

39. See Line 2009: 79.

40. Gallén 1972: 650 f.

41. See Peterson 2007: 311, 317, 321, 323 f.

42. Curry 2013: 24 ff.; T. D. Price et al. 2016: 1026 f.

43. T. D. Price et al. 2016: 1030 ff.

44. T. D. Price et al. 2016: 1033.

45. T. D. Price et al. 2016: 1033 f.

46. T. D. Price et al. 2016: 1035.

47. See Part IV.

48. *Livländische Chronik / Chronicon Livoniae* ([ed.] Alb. Bauer): 280 b. (text), 281 b. (Ch. 26, 2)

49. *Livländische Chronik / Chronicon Livoniae* ([ed.] Alb. Bauer): 280 f. (text), 281 f. (transl.) (Ch. 26, 2).

50. See Kala 2009: 169–190.

51. F. J. Byrne 1973: 73; Cróinín 2004: 202.

52. Jaski 2005: 253.

53. See O'Rahilly 1946: 225 ff.; Jaski 2005: 253.

54. P. Byrne 2005: 489 f.

55. Se J. F. Byrne 1973: 47.

56. J. F. Byrne 1973: 47; Bhreathnach 2005: 95..

57. J. F. Byrne 1973: 46; Bhreathnach 2005: 95 f.

58. O'Rahilly 1946: 224; Bhreathnach 2005: 95.

59. Dinneen 1927: 534.

60. See Bhreathnach 2005: 96.

61. Bhreathnach 2005: 96.

62. Bhreathnach 2005: 97 f.

63. Bhreathnach 2005: 98.

64. Bhreathnach 2005: 98.

65. Bhreathnach 2005: 96.

66. Charles-Edwards 2005: 100.

67. Bhreathnach 2005: 98.

68. The Airgialla Charter Poem: Edition, *The Kingship and Landscape of Tara* ([ed.] Bhreathnach & Murray): 130 (text), 131 (transl.).

69. C.f. Charles-Edwards 2005: 101, 117.

70. The Airgialla Charter Poem: Edition, *The Kingship and Landscape of Tara* ([ed.] Bhreathnach & Murray): 132 (text), 133 (transl.).

71. Charles-Edwards 2005: 101.

72. The Airgialla Charter Poem: Edition, *The Kingship and Landscape of Tara* ([ed.] Bhreathnach & Murray): 132 (text), 131 (transl.).

73. The Airgialla Charter Poem: Edition, *The Kingship and Landscape of Tara* ([ed.] Bhreathnach & Murray): 132 (text), 132 (transl.).

74. Charles-Edwards 2005: 100.

75. The Airgialla Charter Poem: Edition, *The Kingship and Landscape of Tara* ([ed.] Bhreathnach & Murray): 134 (text), 135 (transl.).

76. The Airgialla Charter Poem: Edition, *The Kingship and Landscape of Tara* ([ed.] Bhreathnach & Murray): 136 (text), 137 (transl.).

77. The Airgialla Charter Poem: Edition, *The Kingship and Landscape of Tara* ([ed.] Bhreathnach & Murray): 138 (text), 139 (transl.).

78. See Charles-Edwards 2005: 122; Bhreathnach & Murray 2005: 155, n. 40–1.

79. The Airgialla Charter Poem: Edition, *The Kingship and Landscape of Tara* ([ed.] Bhreathnach & Murray): 138 (text), 139 (transl.).

80. Bhreathnach & Murray 2005: 140, n. 1b.

Part VI: Hostages in the Areas of Confrontation Between the Swedes and the Geats

The giving and taking of hostages that is described in the *Westrogothic Law* (Sw. *Västgötalagen*) took place in certain territories in present day Sweden. Because this ritual occurred during the king's so-called *Eriksgata* – the traditional journey of the elected Swedish king – it is necessary to understand the law in the light of the political situation in the provinces of the Swedes (Sw. *svear*) and the Geats (Sw. *götar*) in the 11th to 13th centuries.

Two events that are reported in the *Westrogothic Law* are of particular interest:

(1) The established, law-given practice of hostage giving and taking at the river *Junebäcken* ('the June Brook') at today's city of Jönköping, possibly during the king's *Eriksgata*.[1]

(2) The slaying of King Ragnvald Ingesson Knaphövde at Karleby outside the present day city of Falköping around 1120–1130. Ragnvald was killed because he did not bring the hostage of the Geats to the Thing of all Geats (Sw. *Alla götars ting*), according to the appendix by the priest of Vidhem.

These traditions of hostages can be the result of confrontations between different groupings (or political parties) in different provinces (Sw. *landskap*). To understand these events it is necessary to first scrutinize the sources – the manuscripts of *The Elder Westrogothic Law*. Then a presentation of the sociopolitical and

---

How to cite this book chapter:
Olsson, S. 2019. Hostages in the Areas of Confrontation Between the Swedes and the Geats. In: Olsson, S. *The Hostages of Northmen: From the Viking Age to the Middle Ages.* Pp. 251–320. Stockholm: Stockholm University Press. DOI: https://doi.org/10.16993/bba.f License: CC-BY.

economical situation of the province of Västergötland in the early middle ages will follow.

The manuscripts

The Elder Westrogothic Law (Sw. *Äldre västgötalagen*) is considered to be written in the 1220s. A key person behind its establishment is believed to be the lawman (Sw. *lagman*) Eskil Magnusson (c. 1175–1227).[2] The law is preserved mainly in two manuscripts.[3] Parts of the earliest manuscript, Codex Holmensis B 59, is dated to 1285–1295 (leaves 1–40r), before 1310 (the amendments), and to 1320–1330 (the parts written by the 'D-writer').[4] There is also an older fragment called B 139, which is supposed to stem from an earlier manuscript from the 1240s.[5]

The second main manuscript is dated to 1335 and is called *The Younger Westrogothic Law* (Sw. *Yngre Västgötalagen*) and is more extensive than *The Elder Westrogothic Law*. However, in this chapter it is the accounts of *The Elder Westrogothic Law* that be will be in focus.

The main manuscript, Codex Holmensis B 59, is divided into three parts (a–c). Because the manuscripts B 59a and B 59b mention the episodes that will be analysed in this section, a brief outline of their structure will be given.

The the Book about Lawlessness of *The Elder Westrogothic Law* is a part of the manuscript B 59a and consists of 47 pages.[6] It is written by the so-called 'A-writer'. It can be noted that the 'A-writer' used the 'm'-rune (ᛘ) as was the case in the older fragment B 139.[7] In this part of the manuscript there are also four further amendments by the 'A-writer'.

The information about Ragnvald's death is found in the list of the kings of the Swedes and the Geats (leaves 49r–50r) in B 59a. There are also lists of the bishops and the lawmen of the Geats in the city of Skara (leaves 50v–52r). The philologist Per-Axel Wiktorsson – an interpreter and translator of *The Elder Westrogothic Law* – estimates that the lists were written sometime during the 1240s.[8] Eighty years later, transcriptions were made of the lists by the so-called 'D-writer' also known as Lars Djäkn (*Laurentius Dyakn*) or 'the priest of Vidhem'.[9] Wiktorsson has suggested that the 'A-writer' is actually Lars Djäkn. The 'D-writer' would instead have been the canon and secretary (to the dukes Erik and Valdemar Birgersson) Tyrgils Kristinesson, possibly 1270–1340. In a codicological analysis of the texts in B 59, the classist Monica Hedlund has ascribed these margin notes to Tyrgils Kristinesson.[10]

These analyses of the manuscripts show that the episodes about hostages in *The Elder Westrogothic Law* can be traced to an original from as early as the 1240s. The oldest of these preserved manuscripts was thus written only 15–20 years after the original draft of *The Elder Westrogothic Law*, which is dated to 1220–1225. We shall now turn to the episodes about hostages in the Law.

The texts

The first chapter of the Book about Lawlessness states that the king shall leave hostages after the election at the river of Junabäcken.[11]

> Chapter 1
> To the Svear belongs the right to take a King and to reject him as well. He shall go down with a hostage to Östergötland. Thereafter he shall send his envoys to the assembly of all the Götar. The lawman shall appoint the hostages, two from the southern part of the province, and two from the northern part of the province; thereafter he shall send four other men from the province with them. They shall go to Junabäck to meet him. The hostages of the Östgötar shall follow him there and testify that he has entered their land as their law says. The assembly of all Götar shall be gathered to meet him. When he arrives at the assembly, he shall swear to be faithful to all Götar and not break the law of our province. The lawman first pronounces him to be King and thereafter the others whom he asks to do so.
> §1. The King shall then pardon three men who have not committed a crime of outrage.

> Chapter 2.
> If a bishop is to be chosen, the King shall ask all men of the province whom they want to have. He has to be a householder's son. Thereafter the King shall hand him a staff and a golden ring. Then he is led to the church and placed on the bishop's throne. He has then all the power except consecration.

Chapter 3.
A lawman must be a householder's son. Over this all householders shall decide with God's grace.

(Transl. Thomas Lindkvist)[12]

In B 59 there is a margin note 'about Eriksgata' (*Om Eriks gatu*), an amendment added by Councillor Hogenskild Bielke (1538–1605): The list of Kings of Sweden:[13]

The tenth was
Ragnvald king. Bold and magnanimous [he] went towards Karleby without hostage. And for the disrespect he showed toward all the Western Geats, he had a shamefull death. Then a good lawman ruled
Västergötland and county governor, and then all were
safe in their country.

(My free translation)

In another margin note: 'King Ragnvald Knaphövde' (*k: Rauall knaphöfde*).[14]

Outline of the research

Much of the debate about the hostage episodes in *The Elder Westrogothic Law* have concerned (a) the age of the law, (b) literary impact from Christian and continental ideas, (c) domestic legal traditions that were passed on orally, (d) the relation to other medieval provincial laws, and (e) the *Eriksgata*. The individual perspective has, of course, been based on the discipline of the researcher. We shall return to the debate regarding the *Eriksgata*, but first some perspectives on the age of the law and the question concerning whether there were oral traditions preceding it will be outlined.

During the first half of the 20th century, the oral traditions of the law were emphasized by the researchers. It was supposed that there were layers of an older 'Germanic' legal system embedded in the text. According to the historian Stig Jägerskiöld, *The Elder Westrogothic Law* was an offshoot from 'heathen times'.[15] From the 1970s onwards, more critical voices were raised. The historian Per Nyström maintained that the Medieval Provincial Laws in general emerged as an instrument for the feudal society with continental systems as a role model.[16] An influence of canonical law, an impact of Roman law and a strengthening of the royal power in the 14th century were considered. The legal historian Elsa Sjöholm put forward the hypothesis that the Westrogothic Laws were based on canonical law, which was introduced after a struggle between the royal power and the ecclesiastical power, beginning in the early 1200s. Sjöholm argues that the methods used by previous research originated in were based on Pan-Germanistic ideas and that they had taken too little account of source criticism. For example, researchers believed that there were oral remnants in the provincial laws of a king who acted as 'High Priest' for independent provinces with their 'own legal orders' and 'cult federations'.[17] In Sjöholm's perspective, it is impossible to find a heathen prehistory in the provincial laws. In fact, the laws were not the result of a long tradition but had their foundation in the unification of the Swedish realm and were originally parts of a common legislation; according to Sjöholm, the creation of the law was a strategy used by the royal power when it was weakened in the end of the 13th century.[18] This hypothesis is in contrast to the earlier perception that the older traditions represented a continuity from older societies and were based on oral tradition.[19]

Sjöholm's hypothesis about the origins of the Westrogothic Laws has been questioned by several researchers. According to the historian Dick Harrison, her idea that the provincial laws were only a continental import is based on weak reasoning, because the spiritual and worldly powers would have neither the authority nor the means for such an influence (or ideological direction) and would not have been able to force it on the people.[20] Sundqvist argues on his part that Sjöholm has underestimated the fact that oral tradition could be embedded in the text, for example in formulistic expressions.[21]

Other researchers have, like Sjöholm, stressed the influences of continental legal and church movements in the laws. Recently, the historian Gunilla Tegengren, in her thesis, *Sverige och Nordlanden* ('Sweden and the Sweden and the Northern Provinces'), pointed out that 'theories of reception and influence from continental law' have been restored in relation to 'the historical school's' interpretation of the provincial laws.[22]

In an article in 1999, the legal historian and theologian Göran Inger analysed the influence of the Church Reform Movement (*Libertas ecclesiae*, 'Church Freedom') on the Westrogothic Laws (particularly the Younger). The Reform Movement started in the 11th century and was about the independence of the ecclesiastical power from the secular.[23] At the same time, Inger did not only emphasize the continental influence in the law. In reality the king's role had a strong appearance in the the Book about Lawlessness of *The Elder Westrogothic Law*; for example, he was given a leading role at the Archbishop's inauguration.[24] In fact, there was a resistance to the reform movement through the 'domestic right' as 'built upon decisions by the thing' in every province of Sweden, which was manifested in the provincial laws.[25] The canonical law did not fully win entrance in *The Elder Westrogothic Law* until the end of the 13th century.[26]

Sjöholm did not pay much attention to *The Elder Westrogothic Law* in her study. She noted, however, that there is no acceptable evidence that Eskil Lawman (Sw. *Lagman*) 'wrote' the law.[27] The presumption that he 'wrote' the law can neither be confirmed nor rejected: being 'author' or 'key person' is not the same as being an actual 'writer'. At the same time, as mentioned above, Wiktorsson's analysis shows that parts of the manuscript B 59 can be dated to as early as the 1240s. This does not mean that there was no continental influence, but it must be supported by convincing arguments concerning individual sections (Sw. *balkar*) in the Westrogothic Laws.[28]

The point of departure in this volume, which is supported by the latest research, is that *The Elder Westrogothic Law* has its roots in oral tradition and a legislation of provincial nature. For example, Lindkvist has shown how domestic traditions occur in the Law. There are also references to similar traditions in the introduction the Law of Uppland (Sw. *Upplandslagen*), the provincial law of Uppland.[29] Lindkvist points out the uniqueness of *The Elder Westrogothic Law* in relation to other Swedish legislation. *The Younger Westrogothic Law* shows much more royal influence,

Figure VI.1. The legal districts (Sw. *lagsagor*) of the provincial laws.
Source: Lindkvist & Ågren 1997: 10 (By permission from the authors, license CC BY 4.0).

while the influence of the Church with the canonical law was limited in the province of Västergötland (or Westrogothia) in the late 13th century.[30] There are similarities between the terminology of Norwegian medieval legislation and the *Elder Westrogothic Law*, even though there are no direct 'transmissions' from the Norwegian laws. Consequently, according to Lindkvist, the Law must be understood as a provincial and unique legislation in relation to other provincial laws.[31]

In an article about the role of the lawman, the philologist Inger Larsson has pointed out that the most likely dating of the original lists of lawmen, kings, and bishops in *The Elder Westrogothic Law* is about 1230.[32] The texts about hostages in *The Elder Westrogothic Law* can be understood from the political situation in the 12th and 13th centuries in Västergötland and Svetjud, and in particular from the relationship between the groupings around the kings, the lawmen, and the bishops that are reerred to in the lists and some of the amendments in the law.

The relationship between the kings, the lawmen, and the bishops in Västergötland

The sources that describe the political situation in Sweden during the 12th and 13th centuries are few and sparse in terms of detail. The political situation is therefore difficult to interpret. There has been an idea that Svetjud (a.k.a. *Nordanskog*, 'the Northern forest') and Götaland[33] (a.k.a. *Sunnanskog*, 'the Southern forest') were two individual realms, or rather constellations of several small realms and other types of territories, which grew into a loosely united kingdom of a federal structure after the arrival of Christianity, under a king, perhaps with the starting point in 1008 with the baptism of King Olof Skötkonung (ON *Ólafr skotkonungr*) at the church of Husaby in the province of Västergötland.[34] Since it is the relationship between the provinces (*landskap*) that has been debated, some of the views of modern medieval research will be summarized, without claiming to include all aspects or all research.

In recent years, the theory of social networking communities has been applied to the Scandinavian countries including what would become the unified Swedish realm.[35] The unification of the provinces lay not only in the institutions and written rules, but also in the relationships between families and individuals, that is, in bonds of friendship. In medieval society it was necessary to constantly maintain and renew these bonds.[36] The royal families and groupings around great men (later nobility) who dominated the

Danish, Swedish, and Norwegian realms never managed to control or dominate each other – except in certain areas – because they were separated by sea, mountains, rivers, and other natural obstacles. Between them were also small, more or less independent, territories and large border areas.[37] The rulers focused on these network communities to control their own lands. The most important prerequisites for the network community were that the rulers knew who to turn to, something that is not obvious in a society without communications in modern terms.

Previous research assumed that the names of *Svear*, 'Swedes', and *Götar*, 'Geats', signified ethnic, homogeneous groups with their own languages. According to the social network research, however, the names should instead be interpreted as designations of groupings of different political alliances.[38] In this book these terms are used to distinguish between groupings in the provinces of Västergötland, Östergötland, and Svetjud.[39]

In *Nordanskog*, Old Uppsala (Sw. *Gamla Uppsala*) was a central place where the political, the religious, and the royal powers were gathered. In *Sunnanskog*, however, it is considered that there is no evidence for a similar centre.[40] Place names such as *Götene*, *Göteve* and *Götalunda* suggest that places of regional significance existed during the Viking Age and earlier.[41]

The relationship between the kingdom of the Swedes (Svetjud) and the realms/provinces of Götaland can be presented as follows in a time sequence:[42]

1008. The baptism of Olof Skötkonung in the well at Husaby Church outside the present day municipality of Götene in Västergötland.

1025 (?). Danish influence. The King Anund Jacob was defeated by the Danish Canute the Great who controlled the town of Sigtuna.

1030–1040. The construction of the first stone churches in the village of Varnhem and in the town of Falköping.

1060. Stenkil was recognized as King.

1070. The Swedish King Håkan the Red (Sw. *Håkan Röde*) exerted a limited influence over Västergötland.

1104. The establishment of the archdiocese in the city of Lund.

1120s. No (high) king ruling a unified realm. There were rulers in several provinces.

1120–1130. The slaying of King Ragnvald Knaphövde outside the village of Karleby.

1130. Sverker I recognized as King. He was married to Queen Ulfhild, widow of Inge II. Sverker had close connections to the Cistercian Order. Monasticism was introduced.

1156. The murder of King Sverker I. Erik Jedvardsson, who represented another dynasty, was elected king. Between 1150 and 1200 there were struggles between different groupings, mainly between the descendants of Sverker I and King Erik. But there were also other power constellations.

1160. The murder of King Erik Jedvardsson. Karl Sverkersson was elected king.

1164. The establishment of the archdiocese in the city of Old Uppsala. The king was described as the 'King of the Swedes and the Geats' by the Pope.

1167. King Karl Sverkersson was murdered by Canute, son of Erik Jedvardsson.

1195 (or 1196). Death of Knut Eriksson by natural causes. Sverker II was elected king.

1208. The battle of Lena. Sverker II, supported by Danish troops, was defeated by Erik Knutsson, son of Knut Eriksson.

1210. The battle of Gestilren. Erik Knutsson finally defeated Sverker II.

1216. Death of King Erik Knutsson. Johan Sverkersson, son of Sverker II, was elected king.

1222. Death of King Johan Sverkersson.

1225–1230. The Fixation of *The Elder Westrogothic Law* in writing.

1229–1234. Canute II the Tall (Sw. *Knut Långe*), who belonged to the grouping called Folkung (Sw. *folkungar*), had the power over the realm while Erik Eriksson, son of Erik Knutsson, was in exile in Denmark.

1246. Birger jarl (Birger Magnusson) became de facto ruler of the unified Swedish realm but not elected king.

1250. Valdemar, son of Birger jarl, was elected king.

During these periods, religion played a significant role. Christianity was established earlier in Västergötland and Östergötland than in Svetjud. The earliest Christian realms were found in these provinces and the first monasteries were also established there.[43] Christianity was a crucial part of the unification of the Swedish realm through the introduction of new organizational forms. Recent excavations outside the Varnhem Abbey church have revealed that there was an even older stone church at the hill behind the present church. In the stone church Christian burials were found. The C-14 dating has shown that the oldest of the skeletons were from the first half of the 10th century. The result of this excavation confirms an early establishment of Christianity in Västergötland.

The provinces of Västergötland, Östergötland, and Svetjud (Figure VI.4) became a unified kingdom, partly as a result of the process with the establishment of the archdiocese in Uppsala in 1164,[44] partly when a strong political centre was established in Bjälbo, Östergötland – with the grouping around Birger Jarl – in the early 13th century.

The taxation system was another important reform for the unification of the realm and was introduced mainly in the early 13th century when the tithe was fully established.[45] However, predecessors may have existed as a result of a local ecclesiastical administration.

When the taxes were collected by the Church and by the royal power, it was initially collected through natural products.[46] It wasn't until the second half of the 13th century that Swedish coins began to be used, although local variants of payments witch coins were present earlier.[47]

It is especially important in this context that *The Elder Westrogothic Law* expresses a completely different economy than a coin-based one, which, in contrast, exists in *The Younger Westrogothic Law* and the Ostrogothic Law (Sw. *Östgötalagen*).[48] It thus reinforces the impression of a particular, provincial legislation.

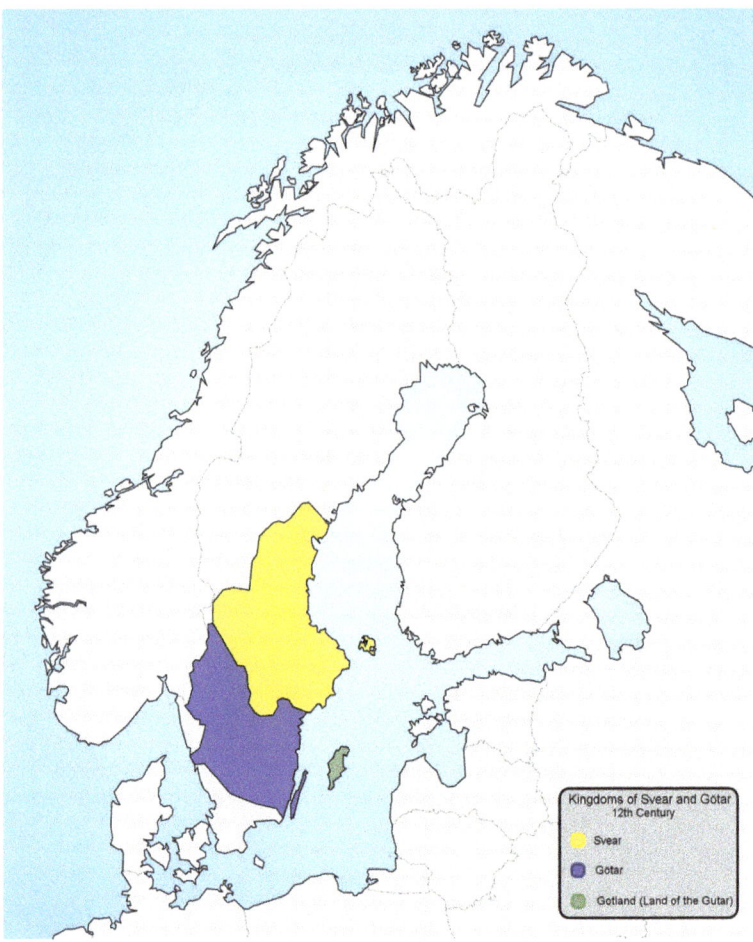

Figure VI.2. Lands of the Geats (blue) and the Swedes (yellow). Source: Wikipedia, Public Domain, File: Scandinavia-12th century. https://en.wikipedia.org/wiki/Swedes_(Germanic_tribe)#/media/File:Scandinavia-12th_century.png (2019-03-23).

There are several references to heathen practices in *The Elder Westrogothic Law,* and it is mentioned that the first lawmen were heathens. This latter information can be interpreted in two different ways: either (a) the lawmen wished to legitimize their position by suggesting genealogical ties to an office which would have existed for a long time, or (b) they were in opposition to other groupings who claimed heredity from ancient times to legitimize their office, such as the bishops or the Christian kings. However, one can only speculate about how Christian the lawmen of the early 10th century really were.

Competitive church movements

During the 10th and 11th centuries, various church movements competed about the missionary work in Scandinavia. In Svetjud, the archdiocese Hamburg-Bremen seems to have had the greatest influence, while Västergötland during the 10th century were influenced by a mission that originated in England. The competition between the German and the English church can be seen in the indignation of Unwan, archbishop of Hamburg-Bremen, who criticized King Canute the Great when he gave bishops from England dioceses in Denmark.[49]

The diocese of Skara formally belonged to the archdiocese of Hamburg-Bremen. The first bishop of the Skara diocese, Thurgot, was sent from the archdiocese of Hamburg-Bremen. However, he is not mentioned in the list of bishops in *The Elder Westrogothic Law*. In the list Sigfrid is mentioned as the first bishop.[50] According to Adam of Bremen, Thurgot and Sigfrid were active at the same time.[51] However, after his death Sigfrid quickly became a saint, explaining what significance he perceived to have for the Skara diocese and Västergötland. According to the list of the kings in *The Elder Westrogothic Law,* Olof Skötkonung was baptized in the well outside the aforementioned church of Husaby.[52]

The competitive missionary initiatives, which were directed toward Västergötland, as mentioned above, primarily from England (Canterbury) and Germany (Hamburg-Bremen), were linked to various political groupings. In Norway, for example, the ruling dynasty had a link to England, while the territories of Svetjud were supported by the archdiocese of Hamburg-Bremen.[53] The conflicts between the missionary dioceses gradually ceased during the 11th century.[54]

It was probably during these conflicts that some of the groupings of great men were linked to the bishoprics. The English influence ended with the missionary period, and domestic bishops were elected as bishops, like the kings and lawmen were elected at the assembly places of the things.[55] In the new eligible dioceses, the aspirant to the bishopric was concerned with obtaining support from different groupings. This relationship can be reflected in the list of bishops in *The Elder Westrogothic Law*.

Competitive bishops in Västergötland

The lists of bishops and lawmen in *The Elder Westrogothic Law* have not been discussed to a large extent in the research.[56] I will here describe how different bishops and lawmen – and competitive groupings around them – were put against one another in the province of Västergötland, as shown by the lists.

The bishops seem to have been dependent on the generosity they showed towards the householders in order to get their support. For example, Bishop Bengt, the twelfth in the order, is mentioned as being immensely rich but generous with contributions to the construction of church buildings, bridges, and roads, and it is noted that he did not demand heavy taxation charges from subordinate householders (or farmers), and in addition, that from his inheritance a share was given to the 'poor men'.[57]

Other bishops, including the sixteenth, Bishop Bengt the Younger (*Biscupær bændikt vngi*), are described as 'warriorlike'. Bengt 'gathered weapons of war, armor and shields, and so administered the stake (crosier) and the chair' (*han samnæðhi hærwapn brynniur oc skyoldæ oc skippæðhi swa stafwi oc stole*).[58] The legacy of Bishop Bengt was that he was 'hard' and 'fierce' towards both laymen and learned and that during his time much property was vandalized.[59]

Obviously, the bishops were contestants of power with other individuals and groupings. They were required to belong to the groupings of great men (see below), but they could not (formally) leave the bishopric to a son. They were, however, a part of an eligible diocese, and the scheme to become popular was through donations to both the Church and the population, which may have been a strategy to secure the bishopric of a successor from the family or a grouping.

Of kings, bishops and lawmen in *The Elder Westrogothic Law*

According to *The Elder Westrogothic Law*, the kings have had some legal privileges that they shared with the bishops which can be seen in the law of the escheat, the so called 'Dane-inheritance' (OSw. *dana arf*), when the inheritance after foreigners, without heirs, would be passed to the king. In the case of a cleric who passed away, the inheritance was taken care of by the bishop.[60]

In the provincial laws of the Swedes – the Law of Uppland (Sw. *Upplandslagen*), the Law of Södermanland (Sw. *Södermannalagen*), and the Country Law of Magnus Eriksson (Sw. *Magnus Erikssons landslag*) – it is stated that the king is entitled to the estates that were the property of the Swedish Crown, the so-called Wealth of Uppsala (Sw. *Uppsala öd*; OSw. *vpsal öþæ*), as well as the fines from the lawsuits of a manslaughter made as a result of revenge (OSw. *duldadrap*).[61]

The king received these privileges after the journey of the *Eriksgata* (see below) when the coronation took place. A prerequisite for the coronation was that the archbishop and his subordinate bishops were present and took part in the ceremony.[62] The bishops had the power to confirm some of the privileges of the king. In the 14th century these prerogatives of the bishops became less authoritative. In *The Country Law of Magnus Eriksson*, from the mid-14th century, it is specified that it would be 'preferable' if the archbishop carried out the coronation of the king for the sake of their mutual 'dignity'.[63] *The Country Law of Magnus Eriksson* further confirms the king's right to the estates of the Wealth of Uppsala (Sw. *Uppsala öd*) and that it was 'his own' right to receive the fines from the lawsuits of the *duldadrap* and the escheat.[64] The bishops still remained influential and continued to be so until the Reformation (see chapter 'Swan song' below).

The opposition to the royal dynasties appears even more clearly in the list of lawmen in the much earlier *Elder Westrogothic Law*, with its provincial character. Certainly, the lawmen swore an oath to the king at the Thing of all Geats (Sw. *Alla götars ting*) and thereby confirmed the loyalty of the province. However, Lindkvist points out that there was a difference between the king's and the lawmen's influence over the interpretation of the law.[65] The king's influence over the jurisdiction in Västergötland was probably weaker than in the rest of the provinces. What the lawmen represented – an elite or whole landscape – is not clear.[66] It is probable that they were associated with the legal districts (OSw. sg. *Lagsagha*, Figure VI.1),[67] and they were probably great landowners.[68] At the things their primary duty was to recite the law.[69] The lawmen were great men with ambitions similar to the ruling dynasties of Svetjud because they are attributed a long history (genealogy) by the list of the lawmen. The groupings around them consisted of wealthy householders. He who aspired to become a lawman or bishop had to be the son of a householder.[70] The dynasties of lawmen used social bonds to relate to groupings that could become contestants or allies in the struggle for power.[71] Through marriages, the groupings around the lawmen made bonds with the royal dynasties and the groupings of great men in Nordanskog (or Svetjtud) and Östergötland. For example, Eskil Lagman ('lawman') was the son of Magnus Minnesköld (or Minnisköld) and half-brother of Birger Magnusson Jarl. He was married to Kristina Nilsdotter who was a descendant of both Erik Jedvardsson and the Norwegian King Håkan Galen Jarl.[72]

The propagandistic legacy of a lawman can be seen in the description of the lawman Karle from Edsvära (OSw. *Karlli af Ezwæri*), number eleven on the list. Karle is attributed with several good qualities, including being 'a father of the native land' (OSw. *faðþir at fostærlandi*), which Lindkvist compares to the honour title of *pater patriæ*, 'father (or protector) of the fatherland',[73] originally used to honour Roman statesmen, generals, and emperors. He is described as 'fair' and as someone who punished those who deserved it but also was merciful. There is also a hint that he did not overuse the hospitality law (the guest right of the rulers).[74] Karle was succeeded by his son, Algot, who did not get the same good obituary testimony in the list.[75]

The last lawman, Folke Lagman (OSw. *Folke laghman*) is mentioned as 'attentive' (*warskær*) and 'lenient' (*milðær*). At the same time there might be a change in *The Elder Westrogothic Law*. It is stated that 'many took the honour of our law' (*toko marghir hedþær af warum laghum*) and the children of mistresses (OSw. sg. *frilla*) were forbidden to inherit.[76] Obviously, here is a breakpoint where there was a dissatisfaction with certain traditions in the legislation such as the institution of mistresses. Who the 'many' refer to is unclear, but since they are opposed to 'our law', they were probably groupings who opposed the lawmen of Västergötland.

In the second half of the 13th century, the province of Västergötland became a political periphery, while Östergötland and Svetjud became administrative centers with a larger population.[77] The role of the lawmen was thus changed vis-à-vis the population of Västergötland: a lawman did not have the same influence over the province he once had.

Powerful women in Västergötland

The Elder Westrogothic Law does not mention anything about women in the groupings around the lawmen and the bishops. From the sources we know that there was a 'queen's institution' at a national level, which – according to Harrison – was surrounded by 'rituals' in the second half of the 13th century.[78] The queens could master different territories, and they could participate in the political game and at least beginning in the 1320s, influenced Swedish national policy.[79] However, it is difficult to know which position women of power had at the beginning of the 13th century in relation to 'national policy' or in relation to the groupings in Västergötland.

Women seem to have had influential positions even earlier in Västergötland. The recent excavation at Varnhem revealed a stone church dated to the 1030s. A burial was also found that contained the remains of a woman with high-status accessories dated to the mid-11th century and a rune stone with the inscription 'Kata'.[80] She was probably the owner of the big farm at Varnhem and the stone church, which stood at the courtyard. It is too early to draw any conclusion about the regional organisation that the church represented, but it was most probably a centre of power and Kata may very well have been one of the key persons in this community.

In the first half of the 12th century, a 'Mrs. (Sw. *Fru*) Sigrid' made a large donation to the monks in Varnhem. She could have belonged to one of the most influential groupings.[81] She was probably a relative to the house of Stenkil as well as to Erik Jedvardsson, according to Harrison and Maria Vretemark.[82] As I have pointed out earlier, the positions of women were dependent on the current situation. If, for example, a master of a household proved incompetent, a more qualified wife could stand out as a leader in the eyes of the nearest relations. This was due to the conditions in a society in which one had to struggle for survival.

Thus, at the political level, the groupings in Västergötland relied on social bonds such as marriages to create alliances over the

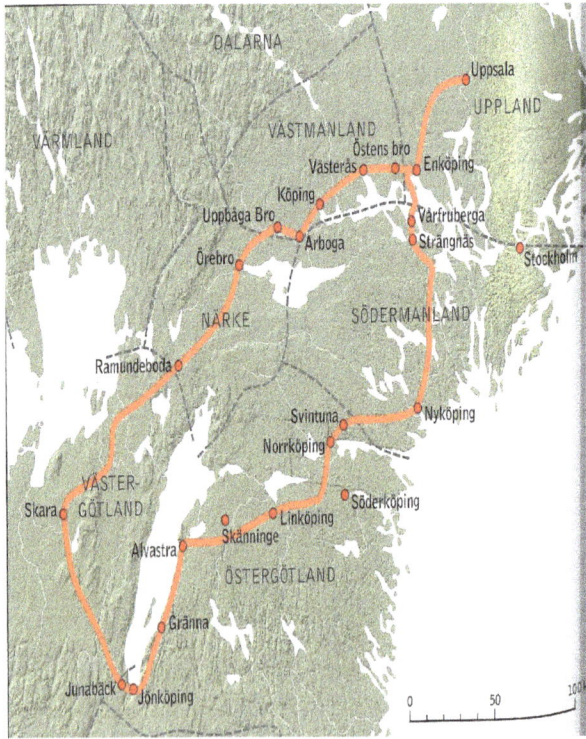

Figure VI.3. 'The hypothetical path of the *Eriksgatan* according to Dick Harrison. Source: *Sveriges historia*. By permission from Dick Harrison (CC BY-NC-ND), Copyright: Norstedts and Dick Harrison.

areas of confrontation between the Geats and the groupings in Svetjud and Östergötland. Other ways to consolidate power – and to avoid or postpone conflicts – were to be more responsive to the demands of the houeseholders rather than to the royal dynasties, perhaps to take stand against increasing taxation charges, but also by preserving indigenous traditions.

The Eriksgata and the election of the king

The ceremonial journey of the Eriksgata[83] appears as a special institution in the Elder and the Younger Westrogothic Law. The journey began after the election at the Stones of Mora (Sw. *Mora stenar*) outside the present city of Uppsala. The king was obliged to visit all the provinces in his realm. When the procession entered Västergötland and came to the Thing of all Geats (Sw. *Alla götars ting*), the Geats would acknowledge the ruler: they were entitled 'to take or reject' (*at taka ok sva vrækæ*) the king; that is, they had the right to acknowledge or deny the throne pretender. It is also stated that it was the duty of the lawman to 'to judge' (OSw. *døma*) the ruler at the thing (see previous chapter) and thereby acknowledge him as king. It is important to note that these ceremonies were performed as two separate ritual actions. The former was linked to the ceremony[84] at the Stones of Mora whereas the

Law	Date	Eriksgata	Election of king
Dalalagen	c. 1250–1350		X
Hälsingelagen	c. 1320		
Magnus Erikssons landslag	(1350s)	X	X
Södermannalagen	1280s	X	X
Upplandslagen	1296	X	X
Västmannalagen	14th c.		
Yngre västgötalagen	1350	X	X
Äldre västgötalagen	1225		X
Östgötalagen	1290	X	

Figure VI.4. Provincial laws with or without stipulations about the election of the king and the Eriksgata.

latter took place at the Thing of all Geats. Whether similar rituals as at the Stones of Mora took place at the

Thing of all Geats is not clear. The Geats, however, still had the formal right to not acknowledge the ruler as king before the coronation, the basis of an elective kingship.

In some of the provincial laws, neither the Eriksgata nor the election of the king (cf. Figure VI.5) is mentioned. When these legal stipulations occur in the laws, details are sparse. In the *Östgötalagen* the Eriksgata is mentioned, but not the election of kings. However, in the *Östgötalagen* it is mentioned that the king had the right to pardon miscreants (Sw. *nidingsmän*) and he had the right to 40 marks[85] from each hundred (Sw. *härad*). These are the same rules as in *The Elder Westrogothic Law* and the Ostrogothic Law.

The Law of Dalecarlia (Sw. *Dalalagen*), the law of the province of Dalarna (or Dalecarlia) – which has been regarded as old-fashioned[86] – only mentions the election of kings, without details, and not the Eriksgata.[87] Neither the Eriksgata nor the election of kings are mentioned in the Law of Helsingia (Sw. *Hälsingelagen*) or the Law of Västmanland (Sw. *Västmannalagen*).[88] But the Law of Sudermania (Sw. *Södermannalagen*) mentions that the king would be elected at the Stones of Mora with some details regarding the taking of oaths and that the king was lifted up on the stones.[89]

In the *Country Law of Magnus Eriksson* there is an important difference in relation to the other provincial laws: the crowning can take place at a more suitable place than Uppsala. This may suggest that Uppsala lost some of its political significance even if it remained as a symbolic important place.

Saxo Grammaticus knew of some of the traditions that were fixed in writing in *The Elder Westrogothic Law* in the 1220s. One of the chapters in book 13 (book 13 in *Gesta Danorum*) may be deduced from the section of *The Elder Westrogothic Law* about 'the right of the Swedes' to elect king. Saxo reports of a Swedish king called Inge who was trampled to death by his horse.[90] This might have been Inge the Younger (Sw. *Inge den yngre*) of the house of Stenkil, who died around 1125. Magnus Nielssøn (alt. Nilsson) from Denmark was then elected king of the Geats. An important point in Saxo's text is that the Geats did that without having the right to elect king. Saxo certainly used Latin terms but referred to an authoritarian past.[91] Thus, the election of kings can be rooted in older traditions, which on the other hand has been a matter of a debate among scholars.

Some opinions about the election of kings and the Eriksgata

During the first half of the 20th century, researchers regarded the Eriksgata and the election of kings as elements based on older traditions. The historian Jerker Rosén argued that the elections were originally performed at the Stones of Mora and that they were rituals with a long history.[92] The lawyer and philosopher Karl Olivecrona believed that the Eriksgata and the election were rituals of a magic character that could be traced back to a (presumed) sacral kingship.[93]

More recent research has focused on other aspects. For example, Sjöholm claims that the Eriksgata was an element that was added later in the provincial laws. She further states that the medieval provincial laws were created as a 14th-century political instrument based on canonical law to legitimize the power of the king; even if Birger Jarl had strong control over different regions, his sons had a weaker position. As a consequence, the king's Eriksgata became an addition to the law as a propaganda tool.[94]

The historian Lars Gahrn examined the main reasons for the unification of the Swedish realm in his thesis *Sveariket i källor och historieskrivning* ('the Swedish realm in sources and historiography' [1988]). According to Gahrn, many researchers had come up with interesting ideas regarding law materials such as *The Elder Westrogothic Law*, but due to the 'poorness' of the laws, these can merely be regarded as 'suggestions'.[95]

Harrison argues that the traditions of the Stones of Mora was probably created during the reign of Magnus Eriksson in the 14th century. But the traditions of the Eriksgata could be much older.[96]

Other interpreters, such as Sundqvist and Hultgård, have pointed out the connection to oral tradition and similarities with continental pre-Christian laws. Sundqvist have these arguments:[97]

(1) Sundqvist believes that there was no rigid distinction between religious and legal ceremonies.

(2) Sjöholm does not take into account that oral traditions can be found in the laws. Other sources outside the law material can be used to confirm older traditions.

(3) The laws cannot be seen as results of Christian ideas alone, but sometimes contradict Canonical law.

(4) When the election of a king is investigated in the legal texts, individual factors must also be taken into consideration and compared with evidence in other sources.

Sundqvist thus shows how religion and jurisprudence presuppose each other in connection with the traditions of the law; for example, the coronation included elements such as the taking of oaths.

Hultgård uses the Eriksgata as an example in his article about 'cultic journeys' (Ger. *kultiske Umfahrt*). Although the term Eriksgata is not mentioned in the Elder Westrogothic Law, there are parallels to the same ritual action in sources such as Tacitus's description of the Nerthus cult, the journey of the Merovingian kings' before their coronation, and there are also other parallels in continental sources. Hultgård, however, does not discuss the relationship between religion and law in this context.[98]

The archaeologists Alexandra Sanmark and Sarah Semple have demonstrated possible archaeological evidence of continuity from earlier times at some places along the king's route.[99] Brink has also observed that the king and his retinue moved between old places in the provinces during the Eriksgata. There are rune stones at several of these places.[100]

One thing to note is how the researchers have methodologically taken the traditions into consideration: religion is either treated as separate from the law or as impossible to distinguish from the law. Researchers of different disciplines tend – quite naturally – to focus on what is perceived as relevant to their own studies.

Below the focus will be on the province of Västergötland in relation to the Eriksgata and the ambulatory kingship. My basic assumption is that *The Elder Westrogothic Law* is based on old traditions. More important, the law also formed after the contemporary political situation in the disorder of the 12th century, when different groupings competed with each other for power and influence. These conflicts continued in the 13th century until Birger Jarl and the groupings around Bjälbo in Östergötland acquired a dominant, nationwide position. By seeing the older traditions as dependent on – and as a result of – the political situaton of that time, one can explain their origin and function without having to distinguish between 'religion' and 'law'. History – whether oral or recorded in text – was important to legitimize the existence of families or groupings.

In order to give a background to the political and economic conditions during the time *The Elder Westrogothic Law* was formulated, in the following a brief description of the ambulatory kingship will be made.

The ambulatory kingship

The Eriksgata was a consequence of the fact that the king did not reside in one location. He constantly moved between staying at the royal estates and staying as a 'guest' of other households. The ritual actions that surrounded the kingship and would define the governmental power of the Swedish society originally had the character of a 'contract' between groupings with different interests.[101]

By traveling between different estates that he owned, the king was able to control large land areas within the kingdom. According to Harrison:

> The Swedish kings of the 1000s and 1100s [...] built their positions on personal networks that were held together by bonds of friendship, marriages, and loyalty. The king's retinue of loyal warriors, the hird and esteemed great men who chosed to reconcile their fate with the king constituted tools of power that could not be underestimated. Without armed men by his side, the king was an easy target of the assassins of the rival throne pretender.[102]

Obviously, the guesting was an insecure moment because the hosting householder was at risk of being ruined.[103] The king risked that the people or the groupings might become dissatisfied with him. The fact that the king had to exploit the guest right in Västergötland was probably due to the fact that there were fewer royal estates there than in the regions of Svetjud.

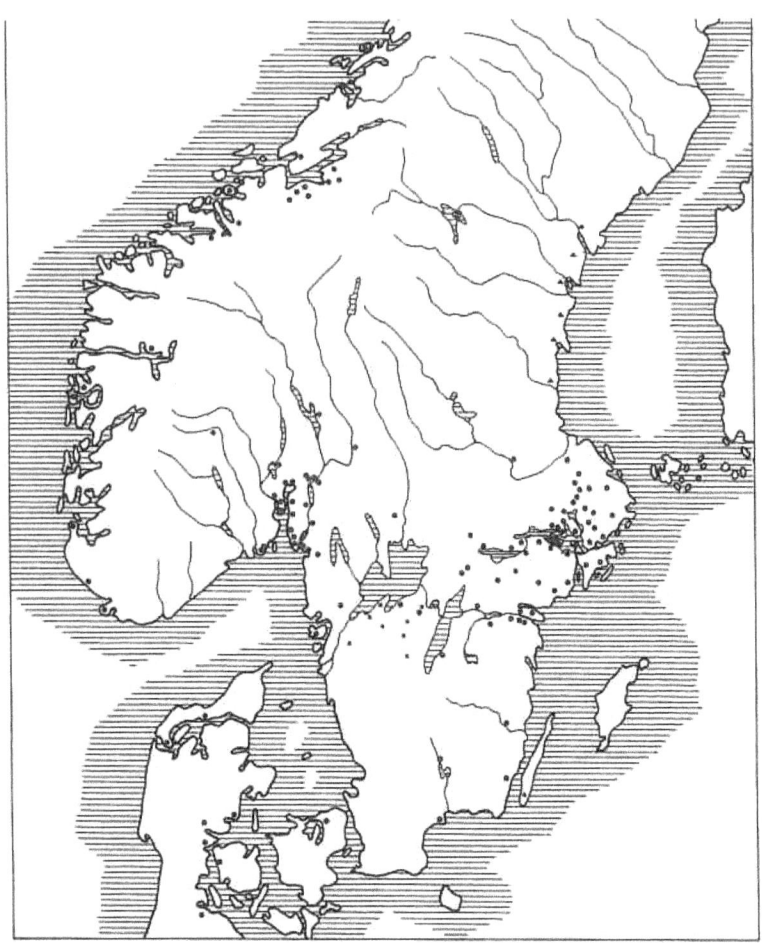

Figure VI.5. The distribution of the *husabyar*, and some of the *Uppsala öd*, in Sweden. Source: Brink 1990: 59. (By permision of the author, license CC BY 4.0).

During the time of Birger Jarl, the guest right was transformed into an added taxation called (OSw.) *gengiærþ*, which the king collected when travelling between his estates. It was paid *in natura* and later in coins.[104]

Some of the royal estates that the king and his retinue ambulated between belonged to the so-called *Uppsala öd* (see above). Other royal estates were called *husabyar* (ON sg. *Húsabýr).[105]

The organization of the *husabyar* has been linked to the administrative division of hundreds (Sw. *hundare*).[106] Brink believes that these villages have been added to the kingship in two different stages: in part, they belonged to the dynasties and were available to the kings as individuals, and in part they endowed the kingship through donations and gifts or through more or less compulsive measures such as confiscation and ransoms. This latter kind of estates in Sweden, mainly the *Uppsala öd*, was called *bona regalia* ('crown lands'), its Danish equivalent in the *kongelev*.[107]

Because the royal estates were made up of large land areas in the Middle Ages,[108] some of them were likely to have been appropriated by violence and thus a significant cause of disputes. At the same time, they had the function of areas of communication (cf. Part I) that could be used for negotiations. The estates could also be used as a base for administration: taxations, legal issues (e.g. fines), and payment to soldiers (sold).

Something that separated Västergötland from other provinces seems to have been the absence of the conscription called *lething* (Sw. *ledung*; OSw. *leþunger*). The royal power had different types of income in different parts of the realm. The lething was an organization for naval operations that consisted of different districts of armaments. These districts were obliged to pay the taxes *in natura*.[109] In Västergötland there was the above-mentioned guest right instead, which later transformed into the taxation of the *gengiærþer*.

Thus, the guest right, the *gengiærþ*, and the leidang formed the body of taxations for different places or individual households in the realm, which can be compared to the hostage district, the Kihlakunta, in the eastern part of the realm (Finland) as mentioned in Part V.

Because the *gengiærþ* and the lething were paid for *in natura*, the goods were stored in the warehouses of the royal estates. From the warehouses, the goods were transported out of the realm via trading networks and sold for money.[110] These funds formed the basis for a modified infrastructure. The coins were used to finance the building of roads and bridges and to hire soldiers.[111] Later the roads became a precondition for the heavy cavalry, and thus a way to control the realm with new form of armed forces.

Taxes and rules for the sale of land can also be seen as regulatory procedures of territories and lands under the king's direct dominion. But the tax collection was not always unconditional and could be imposed under special circumstances concerning the defense of the realm. In the later Country Law of Magnus Eriksson, it is mentioned that if an enemy army, 'Christian' or 'heathen' entered Swedish territory or if anyone within the country made a riot, the king had the right to demand taxes of his subjects.[112] The king also had the right to demand taxes to finance the Eriksgata, when his children were given away in marriages for the building of royal estates. What was once an affair of a prominent family was now a matter for the entire realm. Still, these taxations had to be approved by representatives of the realm: a bishop, lawmen (from each of the *lagsagha*s), members of the privileged class, and the country people.[113] It could be assumed, though, that these taxes, even in this later legislation, were the result of negotiations between the country people, the various groupings and the kingship.

Through the royal estates of the *husabyar* – which in the Middle Ages could include stone churches, warehouses, and castles – there was also another means of controlling power or as a means of communication in order to achieve stability. For example, during times of crises a ruler could distribute grains and corn to the population from the magazines.[114] This kind of distribution was the continuity of the distribution of goods at the ceremonial *blót* feasts during the Viking Age and a part of the gift system,[115] although the religious role of the ruler as a cult leader had been taken over by the clergy. However, the purpose was still the same as in the old gift system: in exchange for the distribution of goods and by sponsoring the feasts, the ruler received loyalty from the people.[116]

Restrictions imposed on the king

According to Brink, the royal estates could be privately owned. The ownership was related to certain legal and ritual regulations.

In the Ostrogothic Law, ceremonial elements are mentioned in case of the transfer of the king's land to a buyer. The king was under the law and subject to the rules as when a householder sold and transferred land. The king's estates should first be offered to his closest kin. At the transfer, the buyer should offer the king three meals, after which the king ceremonially marked the transfer by placing a pinch of soil in the buyer's robe and thus bypassing the purchase. The king had the right of withdrawal from the affair until he had stepped out with his feet over the threshold.[117]

There were also other restrictions concerning the King's right to sell the lands of his estates. In terms of testimonials (Sw. *vitsord*), that is, a statement about the sale and purchase of land, the householder (or farmer) has a special position in *The Elder Westrogothic Law*:

> a vitu firi konunge · ok lændær · Ψ · firi biscupi · ok · bonde firi allum· ·þem · Egho bøndær by · ok annan lændir · mæn skil þem a · þa æghu bønþer uitu ok eigh lændir mæn ·bya þerræ mælli · Boæ bønþær i by mæþ lendum manni ·eig mughu þer uitu mi stæ · þy hældar[118]
>
> A bishop's testimony takes precedence over the king's, and the lenderman's over the bishop's, and the householder's over all of them. If householders own a village and lendermän another village and they disagree, the householders' testimony takes precedence and not that of the lendermän between these villages. If householders live in the same village with a lenderman, they will not lose their testimony.   (transl. Thomas Lindkvist)[119]

So the bishop has the right to appeal and furnish proofs before the king, the great man, and the householder. It must have been about the estates as the king's personal property because the royal estates was not allowed to be sold but should have been handed over to the successor. In a marginal note, the rights between the king and a person who had been given lands are clarified:[120]

Giær · Ψ · i ·	A man gives
gen kononge	[something]
skøtæ · kononger	to the king, since the

hanu*m* jorð	king conveys land to him.
firi · idræs · k*on*onger	If the king regrets
fyr æn han	before he
co*m*bær at hær(að)	comes to the district,
þa ær han ei	then he is not
vald at taka	entitled to withdraw
attær skøtni*n*g	the donation of the land,
æn ha wil ·	if he wishes.
co*m*bær annar	[If] another man
fots sulv · a ·	puts his sole on the
þræskollæ þa	threshold, then
ær skøtnengh	the donation is
me*dh* laghum	legally
fangin	obtained.

(My translation)¹²¹

The word *skøtæ* refers to the fief holders. The ᛦ-rune suggests an old fashioned style and that the text comes from an older original. The ritual act that is described in this text was binding even for the king. Such ritual restrictions were very likely to be of an old order. In the same way that the Roman emperors were formally limited, in some cases, in the city of Rome – as a consul, general, priest or divinity, etc. – had to be approved by the Senate, the Swedish medieval ruler was also restricted by the traditions of the provincial laws. However, this was partially changed with the introduction of the country law and the introduction of the Country and City Laws of Magnus Eriksson. These laws contain the legislation called *edsörelagarna*, which Lindkvist and the historian Kurt Ågren designate as the most important legislation and the first one that was 'valid for the whole realm'.¹²²
The *edsörelagarna* contained stipulations regarding the safety of women, the unlawful entering of a person's residence, peace at the thing, and the sanctity of churches.¹²³ The name of *edsöre* comes from Swedish *ed*, 'oath', and *-söre*, 'swear', and indicates an oath that the king and his great men made to insure that they upheld the laws. This legislation was implemented in the middle of the 13th century.¹²⁴

Trade relations

Archaeologists have shown interest in *The Elder Westrogothic Law* as well as the Eriksgata in connection with excavations of the river Junebäcken in the present city of Jönköping.[125] An archaeological survey of the river Junebäcken has been carried out ahead of a planned expansion of VA pipelines in the streets Junegatan and Friardalen in Jönköping.

One found traces of ironworks workshops from the 13th century 300–400 meters east of the Junebäcken (older: *Junabäcken*).[126] As late as during the 18th century, the present street Västra Storgatan (at that time called *Store Gata*, 'High Street') was part of the Eriksgata. It was the main street from the later part of the 13th century. The investigations have shown that it was coated with pebbles and iron slag from the forging workshops. Another indication that Jönköping was a trade centre already during the 13th century is that the archaeologists have found objects of 'foreign origin'.[127] People thus used the old route of the Eriksgata for commercial purposes.

According to the model I presented in Part I, trade relations are a step in peace processes. Trading locations were areas communication. These places were temporarily established and could be intended for either winter or summer markets and then developed into fixed trading venues, which eventually became cities.[128]

The communications between the trading centers went through maritime links – rivers, lakes and seas – as well as on roads. However, in Götaland and in Svetjud, the infrastructure included the ice-lined rivers and lake systems, with guest resorts.

The trade activity of the Viking Age is considered to have declined as the combination of robbery and trade ceased in the 1100s or even earlier.[129] The trade changed character when trading centers developed into cities and by the expansion of the foreign trade with traders mainly originating in Germany but also from other countries.

Even more extensive than the foreign trade was the local trade, which was often close to the multifunctional thing places.[130]

Aspects	*The Elder Westrogothic Law* c. 1225		→	*The Country Law of Magnus Eriksson* 1350	
	Means		→	Means	
Social & religious factors	Domestic lawmakers and bishops chosen by the Geats. Negotiations between Svetjud and Västergötland. The king will be recognized at the thing. Ambulatory kingship.	Ritual actions must take place in Västergötland: Gifts, marriages between different groupings, oaths.		Elective kingship. Still negotiating relations between the lawmen, the bishops, and the kingship. But in Uppland, advancement of the chivalry and the nobility. Division into castle fiefs (Sw. *slottslän*).	The Eriksgata. There is a continuity of ritual actions, but the place for the coronation can be chosen by the kingship. Gifts in shape of church donations, still marriages and oaths.

Economical factors	Trading centres in competition with cities about trade. There are only limited taxations.	Partial payment *in natura*. Limited coining. Exchange of gifts. The king may not sell the royal estates. Absence of the tax of lething in Västergötland.	→	Cities with full privileges for commerce. Developed taxation. Tithes for the Church.	Payment in hard cash. The kings are not allowed to sell royal estates. The taxation funds the building of castles and payment of professional soldiers.
Judicial factors	There is a law for the province of Västergötland. There is a written law tradition.	There is a limited legislation of the *edsöre*. Individuals are sentenced in their own *lagsaghas*.	→	Nationwide laws. City law. Country law.	Legislation of the *edsöre*.

Figure VI.6. The changing power conditions of the kingship, bishops, lawmen, and country people, according to *The Elder Westrogotic Law* and the Country Law of Magnus Eriksson.

Examples of multifunctional trading centres and thing places were the Disting (OSw. *Disæþing*) at Uppsala, the Lionga Ting at Linköping and the Thing of all Geats outside the town of Skara. Other significant trading places were at the present cities of Kalmar, Visby, and Lödöse.[131]

Finally, it was in the interest of the emerging governmental authorities to control trading places because some of them were illegal (see Figure VI.6). Within the governmental powers there were fiscal interests to control and regulate the trade through customs and other types of taxation. The authorities also restricted the trade to certain days. The new role of the cities as trade metropolises developed into a monopoly for the citizens. There were some counter-movements that challenged the trade monopoly though. Householders had the right to trade for their own consumption and the coastal population had the right to trade on ships by the legislation called (Sw.) *bondeseglationen* (lit. 'householders's navigation'). The rulers and the ecclesiastical powers could, for their part, freely conduct trade.[132]

Regardless of whether the order of the society that is described in *The Elder Westrogothic Law* – in relation to the provincial laws of the Swedes and the Country Law of Magnus Eriksson – can be explained by Bagge's model of the development of medieval societies or not, there is empirical proof for the societal development.[133] To some extent, the development can be described by the three steps of my suggested model:

(1) There was a peaceful order, but it was by no means given. Oral agreements certainly existed before *The Elder Westrogothic Law* as border treaties. Various ceremonies and ritual actions such as gift giving occurred between rival groupings. The actions were important for great men who possessed offices, such as the bishoprics, and for the lawmen, as a way of dealing with the groupings around the kings.

(2) There were several types of cooperation, as, for example, trade relations and road constructions. There was competition between groupings and trading centres, but the collaborations formed a basis for alliances. The establish-

ment of the royal estates can be regarded as examples of both subordination and cooperation.
(3) Legal consolidation. The laws were not nationwide from the beginning but provincial. Peace agreements were concluded between conflicting groupings, which had consequences for the provinces. The laws were later changed and rewritten; past experiences were the basis for the new design. In the 13th century the province of Västergötland had become a political periphery of the realm.

We do not have all information about conflicts and peace relations available. Still, it is through the above-mentioned societal conditions – conflicts between rival groupings, the kingship, and the country people before governmental authorities arises – that the giving of hostages is to be understood in the provincial laws.

The hostages and the kingship

As a single component, the giving and taking of hostages at the river Junebäcken has, in comparison with the Eriksgata and the king's election, attracted surprisingly little interest from researchers who have analysed the above-mentioned episodes of *The Elder Westrogothic Law*. Perhaps this is due in part to the fact that the relationship between the Swedes and the Geats in this section of the law is difficult to interpret. Another factor that contributes to this uncertainty is that Magnus Eriksson (1316–74) was the first king we know for certain who travelled the Eriksgata. The name is mentioned for the first time in the Country Law of Magnus Eriksson. Therefore it may not be possible to determine whether the predecessors of Magnus Eriksson ever rode it, according to some scholars.[134] However, researchers are careful to point out that it does not mean that the Eriksgata would not have taken place earlier.[135]

As for the role of the hostage, there are also some uncertainties. The historian Erik Lönnroth touches upon the king's ride in *The Elder Westrogothic Law* in an essay about the early history of Västergötland. According to Lönnroth, the giving of hostages was a part of the Geats' right to reject the king and his retinue. The king was considered a stranger in Västergötland until he was

Figure VI.7. The Junebäckmonument in Jönköping. Source: Wikipedia. Attribution-ShareAlike 4.0 International, By Bengt Oberger – Own work (License: CC BY-SA 4.0). https://sv.wikipedia.org/wiki/John_Lundqvist#/media/Fil:John_Lundkvist_Juneb%C3%A4cksmonumentet_01.JPG (2018-10-12).

received and celebrated at the Thing of all Geats. The release of the hostage could consequently be a part of and guarantee for the independence of Västergötland.[136] But Lönnroth did not develop this perspective further.

In a monograph about Birger Jarl, Harrison has presented a short survey on the hostage giving at the river Junebäcken. The hostage giving served as a guarantee for the king's office and at the same time a gurantee for the king's saftey.[137] In the later *Sveriges historia: 600–1350* ('The History of Sweden' [2002]) Harrison is more uncertain. Who were the *gisslomän* (see section below), the men who stood as hostage? Whose hostages were they? Did they function as a personal security for the king?[138]

It is obvious that the king's ceremonial duties at the Thing of all Geats emerged as a consequence of negotiations between the Swedes and the Geats even if we do not know to what extent that is the case. Harrison points out that the Geats were not so interested in the rest of the Swedish realm, something that could explain why it was the right of the Swedes to elect king.

In Västergötland there were, as previously mentioned, several groupings of interest that supervised their interests at the things in the province. That was also the case at many other assembly places in Scandinavia during both the Viking Age and the Middle Ages. These interests can be highlighted through an analysis of hostage releases and the ritual actions of the Eriksgata.

The giving and taking of hostages at the Junabäcken as described in the Elder Westrogothic Law is one of the most detailed accounts of the giving and taking of hostages in the Old East Norse and Old West Norse text sources. A division of this section of the text can be made into sequences as follows:

(1) The king travels through the province of Östergötland.
(2) Messengers are sent to the Thing of all Geats.
(3) The lawman of the Geats shall appoint two persons as hostage from the northern part of Västergötland and two from the southern part. An additional four men will travel with them to the river Junebäcken.
(4) The hostages of Östergötland leave the King's retinue at the river Junebäcken. They testify that the king's identity is legally valid, that it is the legitimate king who shall enter into Västergötland.
(5) The king travels to the Thing of all Geats (at Skara) with hostage and his retinue.
(6) The king arrives at the thing. He swears a fidelity to all the Geats. He wows to not break the 'true law'. Then the lawmen and the Geats can acknowledge the king.

(7) When the king is acknowledged, he has the right to perform his ritual and legal obligations: to pardon three men who 'did not perform foul deeds' and to give the elected bishop his staff and ring and to lead the bishop to his chair.

The messengers that were sent to the Thing of all Geats would announce the king's arrival to the thing. This could be a key to understanding the giving of the hostages: the Geats had no knowledge of who the king was, because the election of the king was of elective character – the king was chosen – and the Geats may not have fully understood what dynasty the king belonged to. Thus it was the duty of the messengers to confirm the king's identity and possibly his ancestry. This relationship is also suggested by the hostage giving at the river Junebäcken where the hostage of the Eastern Geats (Sw. *östgötar*) was present. The hostage of the Eastern Geats would testify that the procedure with the king followed their law and thereby confirmed that he was the true king (or pretender to the throne). The fact that the Eastern Geats followed their own law also reinforces the impression of *The Elder Westrogothic Law* as a provincial legislation based on earlier oral traditions.

Who the hostages were,[139] what role they had, and the reason for the selection is partly hidden in the text. Some hypotheses can be presented based on information that can be read between the lines:

(1) The hostage was selected from both the southern and northern parts of Västergötland. The selection could have been pragmatic: one simply wanted representatives from various parts of the province. These people were familiar with the terrain and the villages that the king would pass through.

(2) The hostage would affirm who the king was when they rode through the areas where they were well-known. This procedure was similar to the procedures of the province of Airgíalla where a hostage of the visiting army would stay with the hosts at each campsite unless a person well-known to the inhabitants was in the army.

(3) The selection of hostages may have to do with the changing and different political groupings. For the kingship it would have been beneficial to get a hostage from not just one specific area, but from several areas, far apart. This, however, presupposes that the king had an influence over who became hostage.

(4) The hostage may have served as a status marker for the king, but as discussed in the cases in Part IV, the hostage taking under such circumstances was a result of war actions and a way to symbolize the victory. Nothing like it can be read into this context.

(5) The Geats showed their good intentions by giving hostages, which did not necessarily mean a subordination, but the king was also obliged to show his good intention by accepting the hostage whose identity he probably had little or no knowledge of.

On the selection and purpose of the hostage we can also only make a hypothesis: the lawman who appointed the hostages may have exercised a more decisive influence in this context than has been noted so far. The selection of the hostages might have been decisive – not only for the safety of the king – but also in order to confirm his identity and thereby his future status.

We know very little about the retinue that the king travelled with. The law only mentions the hostages (from Västergötland and Östergötland). We have no information about which persons the king's retinue was composed of. What people rode together with the ruler? Did the king's guard (Sw. *hird*) and chosen parts of his counsel participate? From the perspective of power, an impressive following would certainly have an impact on the people. However, the only text that could give a clue to the size of the retinue is a paragraph in twelfth section of the Country Law of Magnus Eriksson.[140] The retinues of the clergy and noblemen were regulated: the archbishop had four horses in his retinue, the bishop's and the king's officials thirty, the knights and squires (Sw. *svener*) of the king's council twelve, and the knights and squires outside the king's council six horses each. If this information is relevant to the early 1200s, and if some of the council followed the king, the retinue may have included hundreds of people or more.

The retinue went through strategically important junctions, of which Junebäcken was one of the trading centres. This was probably an act that was equally important as showing up on the Thing of all Geats. At the thing, only a limited part of the country people could gather, and the king was bound by the stipulations of the law: the ritual acts. The retinue was also a performative act with a future result: by showing himself to the people – so that those who did not know would him know his appearance – the king made an everlasting impression.[141] Meanwhile during the journey, the hostages were probably within the immediate reach of the king, although this is not clear.

I have mentioned in earlier parts that the person conducting negotiations had a 'sanctioned protection'. There has not been much written about the safe conduct. It is, however, an important issue. For example, it is stated in the provincial laws that there was a safe conduct for the protection of negotiators at the thing.[142] Safe conduct could also be issued for a criminal (for example a killer) so that he could travel to the thing where his case was to be brought up. In the Country Law of Magnus Eriksson it is stated that the king could issue a letter of safe conduct (OSw. *daxbref*).[143] A Norwegian equivalent was the so called *dagsbréf*. The Historian Lars Hamre claimed that the word *grið* could have the same meaning as *dagr-* in *dagsbréf*.[144] Another word corresponding to *dagr-* was *feligr*, a 'protection against assault', which appears in a letter of safe conduct.[145] These terms can be compared to the previous discussion of the formulation *mæþ gruþum oc gislum*, which is also found in *The Elder Westrogothic Law*.[146] At least from the 16th century there are examples of how the safety of the hostage was guaranteed by a letter of safe conduct.[147]

The safe conduct of the king when he entered into Västergötland was intricate. He could hardly issue a letter of safe conduct for himself. In all likelihood, the safe conduct was something that had to be sanctioned by the Geats. It was different from that of the king as a private person in different negotiations about the king's personal purchasing of estates. In both cases, the king was restricted by ritual acts he had to perform. This is an example of what I refer to as a 'contracted role' between groupings of interests.

At the Thing of all Geats, ritual acts were performed similar to those described earlier. The aim was to confirm both the king and the leaders of the Geats, as well as the bishops and lawmen, but also to restrict the king's power. Both worldly and ecclesiastical authorities, as well as the country people, exercised an influence through these ritual acts, symbolically as well as in reality. That is what I refer to as 'regulations' of land areas. These regulations were expressed through the ability to communicate in an area of communication as, for example, the thing. These regulations emerged when different groupings of interest joined forces to achieve a temporary or permanent settlement of a tension or conflict.[148]

At the thing, the king had a limited role, as can be seen from how the oaths were formulated (see above). Since *The Elder Westrogothic Law* focuses on the actual allegiance form, it indicates that the king had to renew his contracted role towards the Geats. Implicitly, one can assume that this contracted role had more the character of an alliance than a true statement of faith. For example, the law does not mention whether the king was perceived as military commander in Västergötland.[149] This military role might have changed with shifting alliances, though. Some rulers relied on the support of groupings in Västergötland against rival groupings in Svetjud.[150] Therefore, the military role of the king during the periodically troubled 12th and 13th centuries would depend on the degree of interaction between the groupings of Västergötland (and Östergötland), the country people, and the kingship. The king's limited influence in Västergötland can also be seen in that he had to adhere to the 'correct law' (of the Geats) when he entered the province.

An interesting aspect is the receiving role of the bishop and the lawman at the thing. The situation is reminiscent of the ceremonial reception other rulers such as, for example, the confirmation of Olaf Tryggvason at Andover in 994. It may be that the interpretation of the long-standing situation between the Danelaw and the Heptarchy was not the same as the one between Västergötland and Svetjud – but as previously stated, Olaf had to give up some of his authority, at least symbolically, in connection with the confirmation ceremony. His primary political interest was directed towards Norway.

Perhaps the Swedish king's interests were in the first place aimed at Svetjud. This might be indicated by the performances of the ritual acts reported in the Elder Westrogothic Law. The purpose with these ceremonies was to get support for the king and to secure his position prior to the final recognition in Uppsala, i.e. the coronation.

What was the purpose of the hostage giving and taking during the king's journey through Västergötland? It has been claimed that the hostage would guarantee the safety of the king's person. But Ragnvald Knaphövde had been killed because he entered Västergötland without having received hostages. Was the king's retinue strong enough to keep him safe? That might have differed between different kings. Maybe the guard was enough, but we do not know if it was present in the retinue. What could the king do if he was assaulted? Perhaps he could fall back to a royal estate, but these were scarce in Västergötland. Waiting for reinforcements from allied groupings was perhaps another option, but how quickly could they come to his aid and what loyalties did they have?

My point with these hypothetical questions is to emphasize that as a power strategy the king had the most to win on an unharmed hostage. The function of the hostage may have had more to do with the king's dignity than being a security against violence. The king could not control which persons were appointed as hostages, something that was extremely important if the true purpose with the hostage was to act as a security.[151]

For the Geats, the hostage was a strategy to show their good intentions, but also a way to control who entered their landscape.

Because Västergötland was a province far from the main territories of the Swedes in the province of Uppland and only sporadically had close contact with the kingship, the hostage was a necessary measure to secure that the person who gave himself out as king really was the king. Perhaps one can see an example when this relationship did not work out in connection with the death of Ragnvald Knaphövde at Karleby in 1130.

The shameful death of Ragnvald

The word Eriksgata is not recorded in the list of kings of *The Elder Westrogothic Law* even if the Eriksgata existed *de facto*.[152] Other types of royal journeys, which may have involved a hostage procedure, could also have occurred. We know, as mentioned above, that the king relied on an ambulatory kingship. I have given other examples in the place name analyses of the legislative districts of *kihlakunta* or *gisslanlag* in the eastern part of the realm and the possible place name Gislemark (or Gislamark) in Svetjud. We can therefore assume that there were other forms of hostages than this case based on the evidence I discussed earlier. At least in the case of the *gisslanlag*, it can be confirmed that it was a disposable hostage,[153] that is, persons who, on request, were given as hostages. As suggested in the analysis of various hypotheses about the Law of Småland, this tradition was not a part of the traditions regarding the Eriksgata. Thus, the purpose of Ragnvald Knaphövde's visit in Västergötland when he was murdered at Karleby (OSw. *karllæpitt*) could have been unclear for the Geats. Ragnvald Knaphövde was elected king of Svetjud after Inge. Saxo does not mention his name but writes that a king was elected after Inge but that he was killed by the Geats; only after that was Magnus accepted as king.[154] However, the important thing for the priest from Vidhem, who wrote the list of kings in *The Elder Westrogothic Law* was the (supposed?) lack of respect Ragnvald showed the Geats when he did not take the hostage from the river Junebäcken to the Thing of all Geats. Therefore, the death of Ragnvald is described as 'shameful'. It implies a violation of a code of conduct. Such codes are brought to the fore when people meet.

The text states that the hostage was a matter of a contractual character between Ragnvald and the Geats (or: different groupings in Västergötland). A clue to understanding the relationship between the Geats and Ragnvald can be seen in the Old Swedish adjective *ogisladher*, 'without (the) hostage', which comes from the verb *gisla*, 'to put someone [in custody] as hostage' in the list of kings.[155]

The Old Swedish verb *gisla* corresponds to the Old English verb *gislian*. According to Lavelle, the Old English *gislian* has evolved from the Old English noun *gisl* and sometimes the OE expression *sealden gislas*, 'giving hostage', appears in texts.[156] The OSw. word *gisla* can therefore be compared to the Old Icelandic *oc seldo at gíslingo goðom* in *Vafþrúðnismál* 39. The hostage was either 'given' or 'put' as an obligation when a treaty was concluded.[157] The word *ogisladher* in the list of kings indicates that there was an agreement about hostage between the Geats and Ragnvald, even if it were no Eriksgata but some other kind of journey.

Ragnvald rode, or 'steered', into Karleby 'bold' (OSw. *baldær* alt. *balder*) and 'magnanimous', or 'presumptuous' (OSw. *huxstor* alt. *hughstor*). According to the Swedish Academy Dictionary, both of these adjectives have a double meaning and express characteristics that may have been perceived as both positive and negative.[158] With this ballad-like description, the writer wants to show how Ragnvald appeared as presumptuous when he violated the rules that were originally agreed upon. It is likely, though, that such characteristics of a person can be related to the hostage as a phenomenon and has to do with the encounter with a foreign collective as discussed earlier in this volume. The ambition to get valuable persons, the right persons, as hostages can be included in the same category. Because no hostage confirmed Ragnvald's identity, he was killed outside or in the village of Karleby.

The events at Karleby can also be seen in the context of the negotiation strategies which could be compared to Anttonen's discussion about the Finnish *pyhä* concept as well as to Bell's discussion about the concept of ritual. Ragnvald's behaviour reinforces the impression that it was a performativity, i.e. a demonstration of his power and authority in competition with the great men of Västergötland (see above). But Ragnvald's performance was not effective, even though that had been the intention.

As stated above, hostages, as described in *The Elder Westrogothic Law*, were more symbolically important than as a true political instrument of power. At the same time, it should be noted that there were different types of hostages. The two cases that are described in *The Elder Westrogothic Law* indicate that there were older traditions that changed over time and that were built on past experiences. The death of Ragnvald was perhaps one of them.

The death of Ragnvald as a story

Just like in the other cases that I discussed earlier, mythical and legendary stories about hostages were created in relation to the areas I refer to as 'areas of confrontation'. It is possible that the manslaughter of Ragnvald Knaphövde was a real event or just a legendary story that was spread among the populace. For whom this kind of story was created, the elite in society or the country people, is, however, not clear.

In the case of Ragnvald, the motive behind the killing was probably to legitimize the grouping around the lawmen of Västergötland in relation to the kingship. There is no other source of this manslaughter accept Saxo's report about the new king elected by the Swedes – after the death of Inge Younger – that was killed by the Geats. In any case, the episode with Ragnvald also illustrates the anticipated conduct in connection with hostages. The story also illustrates what could happen if one did not accepted hostages when the code of conduct demanded such an act.

The impressive hostage

A story from the 16th century exemplifies a model hostage. In Peder Svart's chronicle of the the life of king Gustav Vasa I of Sweden, it is told how a man called the Daljunker ('The Youngster from Dalecarlia') acted as the insurgent and leader of some of the Dalecarlians (Sw. *dalkarlarna*) during the Second Dalecarlian Rebellion (1527–1528) in the province of Dalarna. The Daljunker claimed to be Nils Sture, son of the former ruler Sten Sture the Younger (Sw. *Sten Sture den yngre*).[159] He thereby tried to legitimize his demands on the Swedish throne.

In April 1526 (or 1527?), the levy of the Daljunker encountered the king's army at Börstad (alt. Båtstad) ferry at the Dal River (Sw. *Dalälven*) in the parish (Sw. *socken*) of Stora Tuna. After a number of arrows and crossbow bolts had been fired over the river, the two parties decided to negotiate. Boats were put in the river and hostages – fifteen men from the rebels – were given as security for those people from the royal side who were to negotiate.

The king's side was represented by, among others, the bailiff of mines (Sw. *bergsfogde*) and nobleman Måns Nilsson Svinhufvud. To convince the rebellious Dalecarlians to surrender their weapons, the king's men argued that the Daljunker had lied about his identity and that Nils Sture was actually dead. As a security for this matter, Måns Nilsson offered himself up as a hostage by offering the rebellious Dalecarlians to imprison him and tie him with a rope made of bast until they discovered the truth about the Daljunker.[160] If the Daljunker really turned out to be Nils Sture, they were allowed to chop Måns Nilsson in a hundred pieces. Everyone else in the delegation concurred. This impressed the Dalecarlians.[161]

It is difficult to assess how much truth there is in this story. The chronicle of Peder Svart has been regarded as an exemplary work of fiction but inadequate as a historical source, which can be seen in the portrayal of Gustav Vasa's adventures in Dalarna before the uprising – the so-called Swedish War of Liberation. This text also served as a propaganda tool towards the union-king Christian II. In the case of describing the Dalecarlians who sided with the king, Peder Svart can show them in their most favorable light. It can also be argued that Peder Svart was not present during this negotiation and that he thus could freely construct his text from hearsay (if there were any).

These stories confirm that the use of hostages was formalized in ways that expressed the confidence of the participants during peace meetings. The mentioned stories show that a codified behaviour and certain procedures had to be followed and therefore they constituted a motive that was used in various legendary stories.

Swan song

Even if it is beyond the scope of this survey, which is delimited to the Viking Age and the early Middle Ages, I will in the following section show how the Eriksgata – and thus the giving and taking of hostages – eventually ceased to be a regulatory factor in Sweden. During the period of the Kalmar Union (1397–1523), the Eriksgata gradually became less important for the union kings. This development continued after the introduction of the hereditary monarchy during the reign of Gustav Vasa and his descendants. The last king to ride the Eriksgata was Charles IX (Sw. Karl IX) in 1609.

The Country Law of Magnus Eriksson continued to be valid even during the Kalmar Union. The Country Law of Christopher (1442), which was an update of The Country Law of Magnus Eriksson, contains no changes when it comes to the Eriksgata but was used until the creation of the Civil Code of 1734. The union kings were chosen by a royal election, which was stipulated in the so-called Union Letter of Kalmar from 1397. The kings, however, continued to ride the Eriksgata. Eric of Pomerania, for example, rode his Eriksgata in 1401.[162]

During the Kalmar Union, some restrictions and changes took place regarding the election of kings and the Eriksgata. There were no longer any elections at the Stones of Mora.[163] Nevertheless, in the late 14th century, King Hans made an Eriksgata,[164] and the independence of the provinces was still respected – at least symbolically – which was based on old agreements.

At the beginning of the 16th century, Sweden was at the stage of a new state formation as the Kalmar Union was being dissolved. The conflict lines proposed by the historian Erik Lönnroth in his analysis of the Kalmar Union are certainly probable. According to him, there were conflict lines between the king and the national council, which ended up in the struggle between various groupings of interests, such as the Sture Party (including Sten Sture the Younger) and the Ribbing Party, which were in opposition to the union kings from the mid-1400s.[165] Perhaps one can see an attitude change to the agreements and towards the providences at the end of the union time. It can be seen in the attitude of the union king Christian II to certain peace treaties and contexts where hostages had traditionally been used.

The hostages of the Danes in 1518

There has been almost always a strong bias towards Christian II in Swedish history writing – not least in connection with the

Stockholm Bloodbath – and the descriptions of him in Swedish chronicles are often full of clichés and antipathy. This applies not least to the chronicle of Peder Svart, but also to other sources. Nevertheless, I choose to use Peder's chronicle as a source when I focus on some of the actions of Cristian II in the war of 1518–1521 because they included hostages and descriptions with interesting details.

After the battle of Brännkyrka in September 1518 between the forces of Christian II and Sten Sture the Younger, peace negotiations were initiated in the archipelago of Stockholm. Hostages were given to Christian II as security for his person during the negotiations. Among the hostages were the future king Gustav Eriksson Vasa, the bishop, the military commander, Hemming Gadh, and four noblemen.[166]

However, Cristian II was absent from the agreed meeting, thereby ignoring the armistice. The Danes brought the hostages to Copenhagen, despite being under oaths that included promises that the hostages would not be taken farther than to the town of Kungshamn (in the Norwegian county of Bohuslän). Christian II even guaranteed the security of the hostages in a letter of safe conduct with his seal, according to Svart. Once in Denmark, the hostages were well treated, even though the chronicle describes how they were 'detained'. Later Gustav Eriksson fled to Lübeck, whereas the others were convinced to join the Danish side.[167]

According to the historian Lars-Olof Larsson, the Danes' management of the hostages was 'an obvious breach of all honorable honors and ancient tradition'. Larsson argues that it was about the modern immorality of the supposed benefit of the state of affairs, thus this thinking could be compared with the ideas of Niccolò Machiavelli. Christian's assurance of the safety under oaths was obviouly nothing he had to abide to. Whether this breaking of the oaths says anything about honour or the perception of God is not clear in this context, but it seems obvious that it has to do with a pragmatic behaviour as shown in other examples.[168]

It is not clear whether the hostage perceived their treatment as an offense when they arrived in Denmark. The interpersonal contacts between great men have previously mentioned. The loyalty to countries and nations (and the royal powers) are ideas of later periods. Instead, there was a pragmatic approach to the relations between nobles that was expressed in reward systems. Getting a large estate in a Danish-controlled area was, for example, surely more appealing than getting a smaller one in a Sweden. It is not even certain whether it was perceived as immoral to 'switch sides' among the nobility. It was a behaviour that had existed since at least the early Middle Ages, when professional armies of different feudal lords fought on the continent. The knights and the mercenaries had an influence on the outcome of the battles and could decide when to cease fighting. A defeated army of mercenaries, especially knights, could get a new service (sold) from another feudal lord. It is in the light of this kind of relationship that the betrayal of the 'hostages' of 1518 should be understood.

One could say that Christian II made the choice to 'invest' in the hostages – by treating them kindly and persuading them to switch sides – something which resembles the hostage institution in the Roman Empire, although the conditions for the peace agreements had changed since then. All of Christian's hostages were of significant nobility, and they were also young men, except for Hemming Gadh, Lars and Jörgen Siggesson Sparre, Bengt Nielson, Olof Ryning, and Gustav Eriksson Vasa.[169] As young men from prominent families they had the potential to hold offices as members of councils. Whether Christian actually had a scheme with these hostages from the beginning is unclear. They were, however, hostages that Christian named and requested.[170]

At a later stage, both Christian and Gustav Vasa treated the hostages in a pragmatic way (the way it suited them). Hemmig Gadh, who initially assisted Christian in the conquest of Stockholm in 1520, was sent as an envoy to Finland. But the king had him decapitated at the Raseborg Castle for some unknown reason.[171] Hemming Gadh has since been considered a traitor within Swedish history writing. Lars Siggesson Sparre, on the other hand, joined Gustav Vasa when he returned to Sweden and eventually became a lawman and received knighthood.[172]

The game with hostages and prisoners and illegal actions is an interesting feature of the chronicle of Peder Svart's chronicle: Christian learned that Gustav Vasa was in Lübeck and requested that Gustav should be handed over with reference to his status as prisoner.[173] The chronicle depicts Gustav's answer in a prosaically ornate manner:

> No honest man shall (he said) with any reason whatsoever prove that I am a prisoner, but a hostage. Come forth the one who can justly, and with truth, proof in what skirmish, or in what [other] way, I or the other good Swedish men (that wereso dishonestly abducted with me) took part the time we were captured, or who those were that attacked us. However, since no one with guilty reasons can prove this, we shall not be called prisoners, but assaulted, and betrayed and disappointed, and honest men. By what right can someone be a prisoner, who have never committed [himself] to prison?[174]

In this context the hostage taking by Christian was a breach of written agreements. The writer of the chronicle could relate to violation of the code of conduct by the breach of right and honour and the breaking of an oath. The actual code of conduct with the hostages and relevant documents was a continuity from earlier times and need not be doubted as such. However, in the description of the chronicle, the status of being a hostage or detainee had a decisive impact on Gustav Vasa's (supposed?) answer.

The way of regarding the hostage that the chronicle expresses is a continuation from ancient times; the status was due to how the person in question expected to be treated – with the possibility of being exchanged or released later – and the hostage was the guarantor of peace agreements, as pointed out. In the case of prisoners, who also could be well treated, captivity could lead to a miserable life and eventually death.[175]

In the chronicle it is described how Gustav Vasa should have said that he would never have volunteered for prison. Instead, he could use his status as hostage to protect his person. The violation of the treaty also became a way for Gustav Vasa to designate Christian II as fraudulent and a criminal. Naturally, this pejorative depiction of Christian II in the chronicle was part of the later construction of Gustav Vasa's person, where Christian II and his act in violation of the agreement became an antithesis against which Gustav Vasa was defined. At the same time, it is interesting that the use of hostages still served as a means within an area of confrontation focused on using it properly to influence the outcome of a conflict. In this case it was at the national level.

The Eriksgata of Christian II

The above-mentioned cases concerned members of the higher social strata. There is yet another deed of Christian II that indirectly involved the country people of Sweden. The Stockholm Bloodbath was perhaps directed against nobility, bishops, and the higher bourgeoisie in the first place,[176] but there are indications that the king's violent acts under his Eriksgata also had an impact on the country people. In the long run, these actions had consequences for both the traditional giving of hostages and the status of the provinces.

After the cleansing in Stockholm in December 1520, Christian left the city to ride his Eriksgata. He brought large forces with him. On the way, the king carried out cleansings of those who had joined the Sture Party or other opposing parties. In the cities of Norrköping, Linköping, and Vadstena, executions took place.[177]

At the time of the king's coronation in Stockholm in 1520, an uprising had broken out in the territory called Finnveden, in Småland.[178] The leaders of this uprising and other opposition members from the province of Småland were captured and taken to Jönköping and executed when the king arrived. The king cancelled the rest of the Eriksgata. However, it is the king's exit during the journey that has been most remembered.[179] At Nydala Abbey outside Värnamo he had a number of Cistercian monks executed because of their support for the anti-unionist Ribbing Party. In the yearbook of the Nydala monks, Christian received the nickname that has followed him in Swedish history writing: Tyrant (Sw. *Tyrann*).[180] We will not delve further into the motivation for these cleansings. In such situations, pragmatic considerations may have weighed more heavily than others, ignoring the different interests of groups and individuals who had little to do with the interests of the rulers. Christian II also had Danish opposition to take into account, as well as a financial crisis due to war loans. This may have contributed to his desperation.[181]

Despite these conflicts between the union kings and the anti-unionist parties, the people of the provinces lived their own lives throughout the time of the Kalmar Union. There were movements (or forces) that stood outside politics and formed the basis for peaceful relations. As early as the 14th century, the political boundaries and the boundaries of free trade did not always coincide. In general, trade across the provincial borders was controlled by forces such as demand, supply, and deficits. These were forces that could not always be influenced by political decisions of the royal power or others within the highest strata.[182]

L.-O. Larsson has discussed the border peace of the late Middle Ages. Despite war, peace was possible in the border areas between Denmark and Sweden, for example in the parishes of Möre and Värend at the borders of the provinces Blekinge, Halland, and Småland. This peace meant that the trade and family relations across the national borders continued, as well as a natural desire to keep war and ravages at a distance.[183]

According to the analysis of Österberg, the interaction between the central authority and the local communities was a political culture based on interdependence between the state and the householders that also concerned legal conditions. But internal affairs such as economic transactions (including property disagreements) and civil cases were dealt with on the local level.[184]

For the peasantry and the country people, the executions in Stockholm may have had little to do with their daily life. For more than a hundred years, they had lived under the sovereignty of the union kings and, in turn, the regents (Sw. *riksföreståndare*) of Sweden. But they also had special privileges that were linked to the independence of the provinces and their own lands, not least through their own armaments. However, in two letters from 1521, Christian II announced that all householders should be disarmed.[185] As pointed out by L.-O. Larsson, it meant that the householders' right to defend their own communities disappeared and thus the ability to act against the demands from the alternating authorities (union kings or anti-unionist parties). Additionally, demanding tax burdens might have been required by the bailiff, even if such changes occurred during different periods but such changes had also occured earlier.

The ability of the farmers to influence their dispersed settlements was an important element that the authorities had to relate to, and it was a part of the identity of the provinces. As a symbol, Christian's Eriksgata meant something of an end point for this identity. No sources mention that hostage takings occurred at Christian's Eriksgata, even if the Eriksgata was statutory. Obviously, this action, as well as other ritual actions during the Eriksgata – which were still stipulated in the Country Law of Christopher from 1442[186] – was of secondary significance for the king, if they were carried out at all.

The end of the Eriksgata

During the time of Gustav I and his successors, Sweden became a hereditary monarchy. The uprisings that the kingship had to deal with during the time of Gustav – the Dalecarlian rebellions and the Westrogothian rebellion (Sw. *västgötaherrarnas uppror*) – are considered by the research to be relatively weak, even though the Dacke War (Sw. *Dackefejden*) was a real threat.[187] Even during this period the king could ride into the provinces with a retinue; however, they required increasing strength, which can be seen in the example of Gustav I.

At Candlemas (Feb. 2) 1528, Gustav I mustered a great army at Västerås – according to the chronicle of Gustav Vasa, it was between 12,000 and 14,000 men – 'to mortify a few parts of the country'. But the main goal was to quell the Second Dalecarlian Rebellion. The king went up to Dalarna with his army. Before that, he sent a letter calling for both the people of Western and Eastern Dalarna to meet him at the thing of Tuna (Sw. *Tuna Ting*), the old gathering place, or else he would pay a 'visit' to their homes so that it would 'hurt afterwards'.[188] At Tuna, he surrounded the thing with troops and field artillery, a tactic similar to that of Olaf II of Norway (St. Olaf) 500 years earlier. After that an inquisition (chastisement) was held. The king was able to distinguish those who participated in the council of the Daljunker and had them executed. The other participants of the rebellion were pardoned. The king proceeded to the mines of Kopparberg and then into the province of Helsingia (Sw. Hälsingland), where the people were forced to the thing of Delsbo in the same way as in Dalarna. Finally, the same procedure was executed in the province of Gästrikland before the king returned to Stockholm and dissolved the army. It should be noted, however, that these latter trials were bloodless.[189]

With the actions of Gustav, the respect of the royal power for the boundaries of the provinces had disappeared, as did the order of peace with those who met there. Some restrictions on the king when he was going to ride into the provinces with his retinue (or army) no longer existed. At most, some restrictions survived as a formality; after all, the Eriksgata was conducted as late as in the early 16th century, but it was no longer an act of political significance. Thus, a symbol of the province's ability to ensure its borders disappeared that had lasted for at least 400 years. The above-mentioned event at the river of Dalälven in 1526 was perhaps the last time hostages had a significant role to play in negotiations between the royal power and the provinces, with the exception of the Dacke War (1542–1543). With standing forces[190] – and an infrastructure based on castles and fortresses – it was no longer necessary to fear the householders' uprisings as before, even though the royal power still had to relate to the householders who were responsible for the agricultural production.[191]

The things did not lose their function as an area of communication between the householders and the state. The country people also found out other ways to intervene with the authorities.[192] This could be compared to Österberg, who has demonstrated a 'mutual structural dependence' that characterized the Swedish society, in which householders had the right to make complaints to the crown.[193]

The hostage that was used in connection with the Eriksgata was primarily symbolic. But a symbol, or symbolic (ritual) act, must be provided with a relevant content to make it meaningful.[194] When the relationship – which was characterized by a confrontation – between the provinces and the royal power ceased, the use of the hostage no longer had any meaning. However, during other negotiations and settlements, hostages still had a symbolic significance. Legal historians usually have it that 1748, after the War of the Austrian Succession (1740–48), was an end date for the use of hostages in peace processes.[195]

Concluding remarks

This section discusses the hostage givings that are described in the the Book about Lawlessness (Sw. *Rättslösabalken*) of *The Elder Westrogothic Law* (Sw. *Äldre västgötalagen*) and its list of kings. The first hostage giving is that of the hostages left at the river of Junebäcken at today's city of Jönköping during the king's Eriksgata, the traditional journey of the king before his coronation in Uppsala. The other case is that of the slaying of the king Ragnvald Ingesson Knaphövde outside the village Karleby in Västergötland about 1120–1130 because he did not leave hostages. These traditions of hostages can be the result of confrontations between different groupings in different provinces of the Swedish realm.

The Elder Westrogothic Law is preserved in parts in an old fragment called B 193, while the oldest complete manuscript is called B 59a. It is apparent that episodes in the Law can at least be traced to an original from the 1240s. This early copy was recorded only 15–20 years after the original Elder Westrogothic is supposed to have been fixed in writing.

The scholarly debate over the law has concerned, among other things, its age, Christian influence, whether there is native remnants (including pre-Christian traditions), the relationship with other provincial laws and the traditions of the Eriksgata. During the first half of the 20th century, the connection to older traditions was emphasized. In the 1970s increasingly critical voices emerged, not the least of whom is Elsa Sjöholm, who believes that the purpose of the Law was to mark the influence of the royal and ecclesiastical powers in the 14th century. However, Thomas Lindkvist has shown how native traditions occur in *The Elder Westrogothic Law*. Lindkvist emphasizes the uniqueness of the Law in relation to other medieval Swedish legislation.

Christianity was established earlier in Västergötland and Östergötland than in the rest of the Swedish realm. The earliest Christian kingdoms were founded in the provinces of Västergötland and Östergötland, before a unified realm in 1164. Peace agreements were made that defined the realm. Taxation systems were introduced in the early 13th century.

The three lists of the Elder Westrogothic law, which reports the dynasties of kings, law speakers, and bishops, is found as an appendix of the law. The bishops and the law speakers were representatives of major groupings standing against each other. The bishops were competing for power with other groups. They were required to belong to the families of great men but could not leave their offices to any son.

Lindkvist points out that there was a difference between the king's and the law speakers' influence over the law. The king's jurisdiction was probably weaker than in the rest of the provinces. The kingship had restrictions in Västergötland, which lasted until the 14th century when Magnus Eriksson's national team was fixed in writing. At the same time the dynasties of law speakers and bishops relied on social bounds towards other groupings with possible co-competitors or allies in the struggle for power.

The *eriksgatan* is described in the law as the king's ceremonial rides to the various provinces within the realm after his coronation. The Westrogoths would admit the arrived ruler, something that is expressed by the fact that they had the right 'to take and likewise refuse' (OSw. *at taka ok sva vrækæ*) the king. The king would afterwards be chosen at Mora stones outside Uppsala. In the Law, however, the royal election in Uppsala, or the *eriksgatan*, is not mentioned by name, only in a marginal note from the 16th century. The perception of whether the royal election or the *eriksgatan* are based on older traditions has shifted among researchers. During the first half of the 20th century, *eriksgatan* and the royal election was considered to be a part of an old lineage. Sjöholm, on the other hand, has argued that the *eriksgatan* is a late addition in the provincial laws. Other interpreters, such as Hultgård and Sundqvist, have pointed out the connection to oral traditions and similarities with continental pre-Christian laws. In the study I do not take a position on whether the royal election was an old institution, but I am content with focusing on Västergötland's role in connection with the *eriksgatan* and the ambulatory royal power. However, the premise is that *The Elder Westrogothic Law* is generally based on older traditions. These traditions are partly rooted in 'heathen' time. The law also concerned both the contemporary political situation and its foundations in the unrest of the 12th century, when different groupings competed with each other for power and influence.

The *eriksgatan* was connected to the ambulatory royal power. The ritual acts had at an early stage a 'contractual nature' in the meeting between different groupings with different interests. The ambulatory royal kingdom included forms of taxations. In Västergötland, however, there was the taxation of the *gengiærþer*. The royal power also had some restrictions. The property of the Crown, called *Uppsala Öd*, was not to be sold but would be handed over to the successor. Such partially ritual restrictions were most likely of old order, although such a structure took many different forms.

According to the model (in Part I), trade relations are a step in the peace process. Trading places were areas of communication. These places were initially temporary and could be objects intended for either winter or summer markets, then developed into fixed trading places, which in turn became cities. The trading activities of the Viking Age was considered to have slowed down as the combination of plundering and trade ceased during the 12th century or even earlier. The trade changed as the trading places later developed into cities. The development of society can be described by the three steps of the model:

(1) There was a peaceful order, but it was by no means given.
(2) Several types of collaborations, such as trade relations and road constructions.
(3) Legal consolidation.

We do not have all the information about conflicts and peace conditions available. It is within these societal conditions – conflicts between rival groupings, the royal power, and the country people before a power arises that can subdue all resistance – that hostages must be understood as described in *The Elder Westrogothic Law*.

As far as the role of the hostage is concerned, there are some uncertainties, who the hostages were, what role they had, and the reason for the selection was partly obscured. However, that the king had a role out of an agreement with the Geats can, however, be determined by the behaviour at the Thing of all Geats (Sw.

Alla götars ting) and the ceremonial obligation when appointing the bishop and the law speaker. The legendary story of the death Ragnvald can be an example of the mythification of hostages. The stories carry a message of a codified behaviour that must be followed by certain procedures and therefore constituted a motive for various mythical and legendary stories.

From the time of the kings of the Kalmar Union, the importance of the *eriksgatan* weakened, which culminated in the introduction of the appearance of monarchy during the reign of Gustav Vasa. At the end of the Union, one can see a change of attitude towards the agreements between the provinces and the Crown. It can be seen in the attitude of Christian II towards certain peace treaties and contexts where the hostage was traditionally used.

After the battle at the Battle of Brännkyrka between the forces of Christian II and Sten Sture the Younger in September 1518, peace negotiations were made out in the archipelago. In violation of the agreement, Christian brought the hostages to Denmark. The second incident is after the Stockholm Bloodbath purges in Stockholm in December 1520; Christian left the city to ride his Eriksgata. He brought with him great forces. On the way, the king carried out cleansings of those who took Sten Sture's party. Hostages in connection with the *eriksgatan* were primarily symbolic. But a symbol or symbolic (ritual) action must be provided with a relevant context in order to make it meaningful. When the relationship characterized by a confrontation between the provinces and the royal power ceased, the hostage that had been described in the provincial laws no longer had any meaning.

Notes to part VI

1. The provincial laws are divided into so-called *balkar*, litt. 'wooden beams', but actually 'codes' or 'sections'.
2. I. Larsson 2010: 412 f., 419; Wiktorsson 2011: 11.
3. Wiktorsson 2011: 11 f.
4. Wiktorsson 2011: 29 f.
5. Wiktorsson 2011: 11 f.

6. Wiktorsson 2011: 13.
7. Wiktorsson 2011: 13.
8. Wiktorsson 2011: 15.
9. Wiktorsson 2011: 15.
10. Hedlund 2011: 31 ff.
11. Sveær egho konong at taka ok sva vrækæ · þættæ +
han skal mæþ gislum ovan fara ok **ær retlo**
i · østrægøtaland þa skal han sændi mæn **sæ bolkær** •
hingæt til aldragøta þings · þa skal laghmaþer gislæ
skiptæ tua sunnan af landi · ok tua norþæn af lan
þe · siþan skal aþra fiuræ mæn af landi gæra med
þem · þer skulu til iunæbæk · motæ fara · Østgøta gi
sla skulu þingat fylgiæ ok vittni bæræ at han ær
sva inlændær sum lægh þerræ · sigiæ · þa skal alþragø
tæ · þing i gen hanu*m* gøtom trolæken sværiæ at han
skal eigh ræt lægh a landi varu brytæ · þa skal laghma
þær han fyrst til konungs dømæ ok siþen aþrir · þer · ær
han biþar · K[onongær] skal þa þrim mannum friþ giuæ þem ær eig
hava niþingsværk giort · En biscup skal taka · þa skal ko
nong allandæ at spyriæ huarn þeʀ uiliæ hava han
skal bonþæ sun væræ · þa skal kono*n*gær hanu*m* staf i hand
sæliæ ok gullfingrini siþan han kirkiu leþæ ·
ok i biskups stol sættiæ · þa ær fuldkommen til valdæʀ
uten uixlt Bondæ sun skal lagmaþer væræ · þy skulu
alliʀ bondeʀ ualde mæþ gusz miskun.
Äldre västgötalagen II ([ed.] Wiktorsson): 84 (text), (leaf 21r).

12. *Äldre Västgötalagen*, the Book about Lawlessness ([ed.] Lindkvist): 33 (transl.) ch. 1.

13. Tiundi war
Rangwaldær · konongær · baldær oc huxstor · reð · a · karllæpitt
at vgisllædhu· oc fore þa sæwirðnigh han giorðhe allu*m*
wæstgøtom · þa fek han skiæmðær døðhæ · styrðhi þa goðhær
laghmaðhær · wæstrægøtllandi · oc lanz høffhengiær · oc waru
þa allir tryggir landi sinu·
Äldre västgötalagen II ([ed.] Wiktorsson): 198 (text), (leaf 49v).

14. *Äldre västgötalagen* II ([ed.] Wiktorsson): 198 (text), 199 (transl.) (leaf 49v).

15. Jägerskiöld 1966: 258.

16. Nyström 1974: 77 f.

17. Sjöholm 1988: 47 ff.

18. Sjöholm 1988: 49, 206 ff., 298.

19. Sjöholm 1988: 34, 37 f.

20. Harrison 2009: 293.

21. Sundqvist 2002: 311.

22. Tegengren 2015: 24.

23. Inger 1999: 11. The Reform Movement reached Sweden later (1250) by sending a through a letter to the Archbishop of Uppsala: with the information that the chapter would execute Archbishop without any possibility for the lawmen to influence them (Inger 1999: 11).

24. Inger 1999: 11.

25. Inger 1999: 11 ff., 15.

26. Inger 1999: 15.

27. Sjöholm 1988: 91, 138, 325 f.

28. Cf. Inger 1999. Proof for parallel phenomena in the Norwegian Gulathing Law (No. *Gulatingsloven*) and Frostathing Law (No. *Frostatingsloven*), as well as the Icelandic Gray Goose Laws (Ic. *Grágás*) must also be put forward.

29. Lindkvist 2013: 55.

30. Lindkvist 2013: 58.

31. Lindkvist 2013: 60.

32. I. Larsson 2010: 411.

33. The provinces of Västergötland and Östergötland.

34. See Lindkvist 2008: 669.

35. Harrison 2009: 216 ff.

36. Harrison 2009: 216 ff.

37. Harrison 2009: 218.

38. Se Lindkvist 2008: 669.

39. E.g. Sundqvist (2007: 12) Sundqvist (2007: 12) has, for example, pointed out that the extent of the area is discussed, but it is generally considered that it comprised the current Mälar area, Uppland, Södermanland, and Västmanland (cf. Harrison 2009: 33 ff.).

40. M. G. Larsson 2000; Lindkvist 2008: 669.

41. *Svenskt ortnamnslexikon* 2003: 103 f.

42. Partly after Lindkvist 2008: 670 f.

43. Lindkvist 2008: 671.

44. Sundqvist 2002: 295.

45. Lindkvist 2008: 671.

46. Harrison 2009: 275.

47. Even if coins were minted in the 1150s in the city of Lödöse, the people in the provinces of Västergötland and Värmland did not use money until a hundred years later (Harrison 2009: 276).

48. Harrison 2009: 276.

49. Adam of Bremen ([ed.] Hallencreutz): 100 f. (Book 2, Ch. 54, 55).

50. *Äldre västgötalagen* II ([ed.] Wiktorsson): 202 (text), 203 (transl.) (leaf] 50v).

51. Adam of Bremen ([ed.] Hallencreutz): 231 f. (Book 4, Ch. 34).

52. See Nilsson 1998: 57 f.

53. Even in Svetjud, the influence of the English Church was strong. The German mission may have partially ceased after collapse of Birka, but according to Nilsson (1998: 62), it had a continuation parallel to the English mission. The historian Henrik Janson (1998: 133 ff., 260 ff., 276 f., 295 f., 319 f.) claims that Adam of Bremen's depiction of the 'pagan' Uppsala temple is an allegory of

the conflict lines between the Gregorian reform movement – which opposed the increased influence of the emperors and the kingdoms on church matters – and the archdiocese of Hamburg-Bremen, which would have been close to the German-Roman Emperor Henry IV (1050–1106). According to Janson (1998: 111 ff., 313 f.), the representative of the Gregorian reform movement in Uppsala would have been Bishop Osmund. See Sundqvist (2002: 119 f.), who states that there is no sustainable evidence that Bishop Osmund would ever have been in Uppsala in the middle of the 1000s; see also Nilsson (1998: 38 f., 71), who has put forward the hypothesis that Osmund was possibly linked to Olof Skötkonung's son, Emund, belonged to the Byzantine church tradition, and was 'headless', i.e. a ranging bishop without a concrete mission.

54. The Danish influence of power over the Northern Sea region definitely ceased after the Battle of Hastings in 1066. According to the church historian Bertil Nilsson, '[i]n this way, the sovereignty of Hamburg-Bremen over the Nordic diocese churches was consolidated, and Archbishop Adalbert of Bremen ordained bishops for the Nordic towns. Consequently, influences from the South [the Continent] became dominant' (Nilsson 1998: 62 f.).

55. Nilsson 1998: 61 f.

56. Lindkvist 2013: 59; cf. I. Larsson 2010.

57. *Äldre västgötalagen* II ([ed.] Wiktorsson): 206 (text), 207 (transl.) (leaf 5 1v).

58. *Äldre västgötalagen* II ([ed.] Wiktorsson): 206 (text), 207 (transl.) (leaf 5 1v).

59. *Äldre västgötalagen* II ([ed.] Wiktorsson): 206 (text), 207 (transl.) (leaf 5 1v).

60. *Äldre västgötalagen* II ([ed.] Wiktorsson): 66 (text), 67 (transl.) (flock 14, § 1–2, leaf 16v). Also in the *Manhelgdsbalken* of the *Södermannalagen* ([ed.] Holmbäck och Wessén): 174 (flock 22, § 3).

61. The *duldadrap* meant that a city or township was obliged to pay for a murder when the perpetrator could not be identified.

62. Kungabalken, *Södermannalagen* ([ed.] Holmbäck & Wessén): 43 (flock 3); Kungabalken, *Upplandslagen* ([ed.] Holmbäck & Wessén): 43 f. (flock 3).

63. Kungabalken, *Magnus Erikssons landslag* ([ed.] Holmbäck & Wessén): 8 (flock 8).

64. Ärvdabalken, *Magnus Erikssons landslag* ([ed.] Holmbäck & Wessén): 64 (flock 21).

65. Lindkvist 2013: 61, 673.

66. Lindkvist 2013: 60.

67. The *lagsagha*s were areas with a common law and equivalents to the provinces, which were divided into smaller units such as a *härad* (a hundred) in Västergötland and a *hundare* (a hundred) in Svetjud (Lindkvist & Ågren 1997: 10 f.).

68. Lindkvist 2013: 61.

69. The existence of this duty is confirmed by a letter from the Pope Innocentius III (c. 1160–1216) to the Archbishop in Uppsala 1206 (see I. Larsson 2010: 413).

70. Rättlösabalken, *Äldre västgötalagen* II ([ed.] Wiktorsson): 84 f. (text), 85 f. (transl.) (flock 2–3, leaves 21r–21v).

71. Cf. the model in Part I.

72. Lindkvist 2013: 58 f.

73. Lindkvist 2013: 59; *Äldre västgötalagen* II ([ed.] Wiktorsson): 194 (text), 195 (transl.) (leaf 48v). See *Norstedts latinsk-svenska ordbok* ([ed.] Ahlberg et al.): 631.

74. *Äldre västgötalagen* II ([ed.] Wiktorsson): 192 (text), 193 (transl.) (leaf 48r).

75. *Äldre västgötalagen* II ([ed]. Wiktorsson): 194 (text), 195 (transl.) (leaf 48v).

76. *Äldre västgötalagen* II ([ed]. Wiktorsson): 194 f. (text), 195 f. (transl.) (leaf 48v); cf. Lindkvist 2013: 59.

77. Lindkvist 2013: 62.

78. Harrison 2009: 282.

79. Harrison (2009: 282) gives an example of how the Danish princess Martha of Denmark (1277–1341) married the Swedish King Birger Magnusson (1280–1321) in Stockholm, 1298. Four years later, she was crowned in Söderköping and received, as morning gift, the provinces of *Fjärdunaland* and *Söderköping*. Later she was forced in exile after taking part in the political game. King Magnus Eriksson's mother, Ingeborg, had a leading role in her son's regency council in the 14th century.

80. Vretemark 2014.

81. The manuscript *Sorensis monasterii antiquitatis* is a copy from 1608 by the Danish professor Hans Stephensen (*Johannes Stephanius*) (1561–1625) of an older original from the Cistercian monastery at Sorø in Denmark. The manuscript describes how a woman named 'Mrs Sigrid' made a donation of the big farm Varnhem with its associated land areas, including the old farm church, to the Cistercian Order (excerpt in Edenheim 1982: 50 ff.).

82. Harrison 2009: 175; Vretemark 2014: 132.

83. The Eriksgata is not mentioned by name in the part of the manuscript B59 attributed to the A-writer, that is, the oldest part of the manuscript. The word *eriksgata* is only written in a marginal note. The note was probably made by the Councillor Hogenskild Bielke, or somebody within his circle, in the latter part of the 16th century. For the debate about the origin of the name, see Sundqvist 2002.

84. 'The taking' of a ruler probably meant that the candidate was lifted up on the Stones of Mora (Sw. *Mora stenar*) outside of Uppsala. The expression 'taking a king' (ON *konungstekja*) appears in the Norwegian *Hirdskraa* (5) and meant that the candidate was regarded as a pretender to the throne (ON *konungsefni*) but not as a king before the coronation. There were similar traditions in Denmark (see Sundqvist 2002). According to Sundqvist (2002), the ceremony of 'taking' had parallels in pre-Christian traditions. Ammianus Marcellinus (c. 330–395) reports how the emperor Julian the Apostate (331–363) was raised upon the shield of a legionnaire and hailed by the crowd. According to Magnus Aurelius Cassidorus (c. 485–c. 585) King

Vitiges (d. 540) of the Goths was raised on shields before a battle. The opposite, 'the deeming', meant that the ruler was thrown off the stones and thereby not acknowledged as a throne pretender or ruler. The presence of this ritual is also confirmed by the right 'to dispose' (*vræka*) of a ruler. In *Heimskringla* there is a story about the heathen King Hrollaug of Naumadal, who ritually rolled himself from a high seat down to an earl's seat. Thereby he 'degraded' himself to earl (See Sundqvist 2002).

85. Mark was a medieval measure of weight of noble metals. The value was shifting: The 'Skaramark' has been measured to 213.3 grams and the 'Stockholmmark' to 204.97 (Rasmusson 1966: 423 ff. In total, 40 marks would something like 8198.8–8532g, i.e. 8.2–8.5kg.

86. Dalalagen, *Svenska landskapslagar* 2 ([ed.]. Holmbäck & Wessén): XIX; cf. Sjöholm (1988: 321 f.), who claims that never was any law of the province of the Dalarna; the manuscript B 54 does not have any title (Sjöholm 1988: 327 ff.).

87. *Dalalagen* ([ed.] Holmbäck & Wessén): 21 (flock 1).

88. Hälsingelagen, *Svenska landskapslagar* 3 ([ed.] Holmbäck & Wessén); Västmannalagen, *Svenska landskapslagar* 2 ([ed.] Holmbäck och Wessén).

89. *Södermannalagen* ([ed.] Holmbäck och Wessén): 42 f. (flock 2–3). The *Eric Chronicle* (Sw. *Erikskrönikan*) is the earliest text to mention the election of kings at the Stones of Mora.

90. Saxo Grammaticus, *Gesta Danorum* = *Danmarkshistorien* II ([ed.] Friis-Jensen): 100, 102 (text), 101, 103 (transl.) (Book 13 Ch. 5, 1).

91. The expression *penes Sueones arbitrium erat* in *Gesta Danorum* is comparable to the Old Swedish *sveær egho konong at taka ok sva vrækæ*. Saxo, however, does not use the verb, *ēligō*, which more specifically means 'choose', but the noun *arbitrium* which may also mean 'judgement', 'decision', and 'opinion' (*Norstedts latinsk-svenska ordbok* (red. Ahlberg et al.): 72 f.; Sundqvist 2002: 313).

92. Rosén 1939: 383 ff.

93. Olivecrona 1942. A central concept in Olivecrona's hypothesis, the verb *døma*; see Sundqvist 2002 about the debate regarding the sacral kingship.

94. Sjöholm 1988: 50, 206 ff., 298.

95. Gahrn 1988: 32, 99, 134.

96. Harrison 2009: 277 f., 280.

97. Sundqvist 2002: 311.

98. Hultgård 2001.

99. Sanmark & Semple 2008: 249 ff.

100. Brink 2000b: 52 f.

101. Harrison 2002: 284.

102. Harrison 2009: 273, 284.

103. C.f. the *gislalagh*s in Part V.

104. *Svenska landskapslagar* 3 ([ed.] Holmbäck & Wessén): 57, n. 16; Dovring 1951: 43; Lindkvist 1988: 23.

105. Brink 2000a: 66.

106. See, for example, Hyenstrand 1974.

107. Brink 2000a: 70 f.

108. Sundqvist 2002: 87.

109. Harrison 2009: 283.

110. Rosén 1966: 305.

111. Rosén 1966: 305.

112. *Magnus Erikssons landslag* ([ed.] Holmbäck & Wessén): 5 (flock V, § 6).

113. *Magnus Erikssons landslag* ([ed.] Holmbäck & Wessén): 5 (flock V, § 6).

114. See C. Andersson (2013: 220 ff.) for the research history.

115. The historian Catharina Andersson (2013: 219 ff.) has shown that the gift exchange continued in the 13th and 14th centuries as

'religious gifts'. A nobleman or a noblewoman could choose to donate to a monastery. The donation could also include giving away their daughters, primarily as nuns, to the monastery. Sons too could be donated to monasteries. There were several benefits with this gift strategy. Not only did it strengthen the religious capital of the donor but also the social. It could be rewarding to support the ecclesiastical power, for example in the appointment of a ministry (C. Andersson 2013: 226 ff., 232 ff.). The giving of children as gifts to the monasteries was a continuation of the practice of giving children as foster children (OI *fóstri*) to subordinate families (C. Andersson 2013: 244 f.).

116. See Sundqvist 2002: 344 f. for a discussion.

117. *Östgötalagen* ([ed.] Holmbäck & Wessén): 141 f. (flock 4).

118. Jordabalken, *Äldre västgötalagen* II ([ed.] Wiktorsson): 104 (text), 105 (transl.) (flock 5, leaf 26[r]).

119. Jordabalken, *The older version of the Västgöta Law* (Äldre Västgötalagen) ([ed.] Lindkvist): 41 (Ch. 5).

120. Rosén 1966: 253; Harrison 2009: 284.

121. *Äldre västgötalagen* II ([ed.] Wiktorsson): 104 (text), 105 (transl.) (leaf 26[r]).

122. Lindkvist & Ågren 1997: 14.

123. Lindkvist & Ågren 1997: 14.

124. Lindkvist & Ågren 1997: 14.

125. See Kallerskog & Franzén 2012.

126. Kallerskog & Franzén 2012: 9.

127. Kallerskog & Franzén 2012: 9.

128. Lindkvist & Ågren 1997: 53 f.

129. Rosén 1966: 301.

130. Lindkvist & Ågren 1997: 53 f.

131. Rosén 1966: 300; Lindkvist & Ågren 1997: 54.

132. Lindkvist & Ågren 1997: 54.

133. See Part I, p. 39 f.

134. See for example Rosén 1966: 252; Harrison 2009: 279; Kallerskog & Franzén 2012: 9.

135. Rosén 1966: 252; Harrison 2009: 279.

136. Lönnroth 1985: 21.

137. Harrison 2002: 122.

138. Harrison 2009: 280.

139. It is likely that the hostage was made up of only men in these cases because only men had access to the thing.

140. Kungabalken, *Magnus Erikssons landslag* ([ed.] Holmbäck & Wessén): (section 12).

141. Cf. Bell 1997: 81 f.

142. Liedgren 1965: 469.

143. The letter of safe conduct could be a guarantee of security in addition to the time the criminal had to travel from the thing to the king and back (Liedgren 1965: 469). The letter could also contain some other stipulations (Liedgren 1965: 469). In the database of the National Archives (https://sok.riksarkivet.se; 2015-11-01) there are many examples of letters of safe conduct from the time-period 1298–1697.

144. Hamre 1965: 468.

145. Hamre 1965: 468. In the database of the National Archives (https://sok.riksarkivet.se; 2015-11-01) there is a letter of conduct (SHDK-No: 41772) dated 29 July 1378. It was issued by Håkan Magnusson, 'King of Sweden and Norway', and safe conduct is given for the great man Aslak Neridsson. The term 'letter of *grið*' is used in this case.

146. See Part IV.

147. Liedgren 1965: 469.

148. Cf. Österberg 1989.

149. It can for example be compared to *Sveriges historia* ('The History of Sweden') by the historian Ingvar Andersson (1969: 60),

which states that the king had a role as 'warlord' and 'representation figure' before 1250 in the Swedish realm.

150. See the list on conflicts.

151. See Part IV.

152. It is possible that the Eriksgata took place as early as during the Viking age, but in such cases it was probably a more limited journey that might only have covered the people of Uppland (Sundqvist 2002: 318; Hultgård 2001: 439 f.; Sanmark & Semple 2008: 250).

153. The hostage of the Geats could also have been a disposable hostage, which is indicated by the fact that it was statutory and applied during peacekeeping conditions.

154. Saxo Grammaticus, *Gesta Danorum* = *Danmarkshistorien* II ([ed.] Friis-Jensen): 100, 102 (text), 101, 103 (transl.) (Book 13 Ch. 5, 1).

155. Söderwall 1884–1918: 402; 1900–1918: 151.

156. Lavelle 2006: 273.

157. See Fritzner (1883–96) 1973: 600; Söderwall 1900–1918: 151.

158. *SAOB* http://g3.spraakdata.gu.se/saob/ (2015-10-23).

159. *Gustav Vasas krönika* ([ed.] Mosesson): 109 (anno 1526). L.-O. Larsson (2003b: 149–163) has argued that the Daljunkern was actually identical with Nils Sture. Sten Sture died of his wounds after the battle of Bogesund in February 1520.

160. According to Pound (1959: 187) it was customary to leave the hostage tied.

161. *Gustav Vasas krönika* ([ed.] Mosesson): 108 f. (ann. 1526).

162. Lönnroth 1969: 45 ff.; L.-O. Larsson 2003a: 83 ff.

163. The king's election had changed in a way that the lawmen did not have to come as representatives of their *lagasagha*s to confirm the king's election. Instead, the election was carried out at different places by great men; it was something that had already begun with the Country Law of Magnus Eriksson. Only after the general

elections could the election and tribute ceremonies be performed at the Stones of Mora (Yrwing 1964: 365 f.).

164. Skyum-Nielsen 1964: 158 ff.

165. Lönnroth 1969.

166. *Gustav Vasas krönika* ([ed.] Mosesson): 11 ff. (ann. 1490).

167. *Gustav Vasas krönika* ([ed.] Mosesson): 15 (ann. 1490).

168. L.-O. Larsson 2003a: 432. During the negotiations with Sten Sture, Christian II asked him to come to the archipelago personally (Lauring 1963: 103). Sten Sture was willing if a hostage could be given as security for his person (Lauring 1963: 103). According to the chronicle of Peder Svart ([ed.] Mosesson): 11 (ann. 1490), the offered hostage was not valuable enough to function as a real security: they could be sacrificed on the 'slaughtering-block'. The hostage was sent back, and according to Lauring (1963: 103), it was perceived as an offence by Christian. Christian would then have declared that he was willing to come ashore and negotiate if a hostage would be granted as security for his person (Lauring 1963: 103). Christian later tried to justify his behaviour in some letters to German cities. He had no plans whatsoever to come ashore for the meeting but took it as an insult when Sten Sture sent his hostage back (Lauring 1963: 104). The battle and its aftermaths is are depicted in a ballad in the *Stora rimkrönikan (Sturekrönikan), Svenska medeltids dikter och rim* ([ed.] Klemming): 471 ff. (ch. 22).

L.-O. Larsson (2003a: 432) argues that this way of breaking the safe conduct began with the murder of the Norwegian nobleman Knut Alvsson Tre Rosor during a peace treaty in 1502. Knut was in one way or another in league with a Swedish insurgency against the union king Hans Knut, who was one of most powerful men of Norway and had most of his support in Western Norway. His leading rival, the Danish Henrik Krummedige, a member of the Danish Council of the Realm (Da. *Rigsraadet*), was commander at the Bohus (No. *Båhus*) Fortress in the Norwegian province of Bohuslän (No. *Båhuslen*) (Lauring 1962: 196; Larsson 2003a: 392 f.). Knut made a campaign against southern Norway and reached the Bohus Fortress, which was besieged. The siege was broken and Danish reinforcements were sent to Bohuslän. On August 18, 1502, Henrik Krummedige and Knut met on the former's ship in the port of Oslo for negotiations. Although Knut had been given safe conduct, he was murdered on the ship (Lauring 1962: 198; Hamre 1965: 469; L.-O. Larsson 2003a: 396). This violence was subsequently sanctioned by King Hans, according to L.-O. Larsson (2003a: 396).

169. *Gustav Vasas krönika* ([ed.] Mosesson): 12 (ann. 1490).

170. *Gustav Vasas krönika* ([ed.] Mosesson): 12 (ann. 1490).

171. The database of Riksarkivet, https://sok.riksarkivet.se (2015-11-01); L-O. Larsson 2003a: 447.

172. *Svenskt biografiskt lexikon* 1906: 487 f.

173. *Gustav Vasas krönika* ([ed.] Mosesson): 15 (anno 1490).

174. Det skall ingen ärlig man (sade han) med någen skäl bevisa att jag är en fånge, utan en gisslare. Komme den fram som rättvisligen och med sanning bevisa kan uti vad skärmytsel eller på vad rum jag eller de andra gode Svenske män (med mig så sveklige bortförde bleve) stadde vore den tid vi vorde fångade, eller vem de vore som oss angripe. Men all den stund det ingen med skäl bevisa kan, bör oss icke vara kallade fångar, utan överfallne förraskne och besvikne, och ärlige män. Heller med vad rätt kan den vara en fånge, vilken aldrig fängelse klappat haver?
Gustav Vasas krönika ([ed.] Mosesson): 15 (ann. 1490).

175. See Part I.

176. L.-O. Larsson 2003a: 444 f. During the Bloodbath, 7–9 November 1520, about 100 persons were executed after a brief trial. Before the trial, the widow of Sten Sture the Younger, Christina Nilsdotter Gyllenstierna, who led the defense of Sweden, received a letter from Christian II that assured her and the members of anti-unionist parties amnesty if they surrendered. However, after the surrender Christian broke his promise.

177. L.-O. Larsson 2003a: 448.

178. Finnveden was one of the lands that constituted the province of Småland.

179. L.-O. Larsson 2003a: 448.

180. L.-O. Larsson 2003a: 448; 2003b: 57; *Gustav Vasas krönika* ([ed.] Mosesson): 16 f. (ann. 1490). In reality, this nickname was never used for Christian II during his lifetime.

181. Christian's uncle, Frederik I of Denmark, led an insurgency at Jutland in the early 1520s.

182. L.-O. Larsson 2003a: 78.

183. L.-O. Larsson 2003a: 413.

184. Österberg 1989: 74 ff.

185. L.-O. Larsson 2003a: 450.

186. *Kristofers landslag*. Corpus iuris sueo-gotorum antiqui (Samling af Sweriges gamla lagar, på kongl. maj:ts nådigste befallning utgifven af d. C. J. Schlyter 12).

187. Österberg 1989: 88; L.-O. Larsson 2003b: 195 ff.

188. *Gustav Vasas krönika* ([ed.] Mosesson): 116 (ann. 1527).

189. *Gustav Vasas krönika* ([ed.] Mosesson): 117 f. (ann. 1527).

190. Cf. L.-O. Larsson 2003b: 171.

191. Österberg 1989: 83.

192. Cf. Österberg 1989: 81.

193. Österberg 1989: 89 f.

194. Cf. Anttonen 2000.

195. See Pound 1959: 185. Following the War of the Austrian Succession 1740–48, a negotiation peace was conducted. Different constellations stood against each other, Great Britain, fighting on the side of the Habsburg monarchy and France on the side of the other constellation (including Sweden). The Cape Breton Island off the Canadian East Coast was received by Great Britain through the Aix-la-Chapelle (Aachen) Treaty in 1748. As security for the island, two English nobles as hostages were sent to France (Pound 1959: 185). This was a breaking point: After this event the hostages were considered to have occurred mostly as a part of reprisals (Pound 1959: 186).

Part VII: Summary and Conclusions

The aim of this study is to investigate the taking and giving of hostages in peace processes during the Viking Age and early Middle Ages in Scandinavia and adjacent areas. The giving and taking of hostages is understood as a ritual act in peace negotiations and as an opportunity for both parties – winners and losers – to influence their negotiating position and also as a way to exert influence on relations within as well as between societies.

In Part I previous research on hostage-taking and hostage in the Viking and Early Medieval traditions in Scandinavia is presented. A summary of Roman, Continental Germanic, and Old English hostage traditions is put forward. In this part, the problems of a methodology is discussed. In order to adopt a new approach to hostages in relation to war and peace treaties, I present a theoretical model of peace processes and, in addition, various perspectives on 'ritual acts' are given.

Part II deals with the myth of the Æsir–Vanir War in various text sources, with special focus on how hostages were presented, and a discussion of earlier research on this myth. The peace processes and ritual acts as described in the myth of the war between the Æsir and the Vanir are analysed.

In Part III the theoretical approaches outlined in the first part to examples of hostage exchanges in Viking Age societies is applied to societies such as the Danelaw in England and the encounters between Scandinavians and Franks during the Merovingian rule. This part concludes with a synthesis that gives an overview of various ritual acts within peace processes.

How to cite this book chapter:
Olsson, S. 2019. Summary and Conclusions. In: Olsson, S. *The Hostages of Northmen: From the Viking Age to the Middle Ages.* Pp. 321–330. Stockholm: Stockholm University Press. DOI: https://doi.org/10.16993/bba.g License: CC-BY.

Part IV addresses two themes: who became a hostage and his or her rights. The relationship between law and tradition is discussed using examples from various parts of Scandinavia and from areas with a Scandinavian population outside Scandinavia. Because the examples are retrieved from different texts it is relevant to try to understand the intentions of the writers. This raises the question of who was made subordinate, something that was not always evident. Further, the possibility of female hostages is discussed. The information is scarce, but some sources indicate that women could be leaders – at least in various ritual contexts – which might have made them politically valuable and therefore possible hostages. The question of violence against and violation of the hostages is also discussed. Medieval Scandinavian contexts governing violence against hostages are analysed. Finally, two major case studies with examples of mutilation of hostages and their ethical and moral implications are considered in relation to areas of confrontation.

In Part V, the idea of what I refer to as 'available hostages' is further developed. This phenomenon can be found in place names that suggest organizational forms around the hostages. In this part the Swedish place name *Gyslamarchia*, mentioned in the *Gesta Danorum*, is discussed. This place name is then put in relation to place names with a similar meaning in Finland and Estonia.

In Part VI all the threads in the thesis are tied together in an analysis of *The Elder Westrogothic Law* (Sw. *Äldre västgötalagen*). The focus is on two cases of hostage taking during the so-called Eriksgata, the ritual royal tour before the coronation. The study closes with an analysis of Christian II's royal Eriksgata in the early 16th century and the possible end of hostage taking as a mean to control the *landskap*, the provinces, in Sweden.

In the introduction, five research questions were formulated as a starting point for the investigation. These are answered as follows.

1. *How and why can the giving and taking of hostage be understood as a ritual act in peace processes during the Viking era until the late Middle Ages (16th century) in Scandinavia? How did the hostages function as objectives of negotiations?*

In order for an action to qualify as a ritual act it must be filled with content. When it comes to hostages – bilateral as well as unilateral – the 'content' can be related to many contexts. In this study, I have particularly stressed the social, religious, economic, and legal factors. Ritual acts often took place at specific locations. Research on Old Scandinavian religion has therefore often emphasized the connection between ritual acts and fixed places (in the landscape), such as *vi*-places. At these places, both judicial and religious acts were associated with 'ritual taboos' and 'ritual restrictions'. I have related taboos and restrictions to what I refer to as 'sanctioned protection'. This type of protection could be applied at places that were temporarily established – or fixed in the landscape – during a conflict (they could later be fixed in the landscape). These mobile (cult) sites included temporarily established *vi*-places around which *vi*-bonds were tied. As described in the book, areas of communication were established temporarily as meeting places, for example at the mouth of the River Göta in the border areas between the Danes and the Norwegians. At these places hostages were used, who probably had some kind of protection, even if we do not know exactly how this protection was designed.

Even if we cannot know exactly how the 'sanctioned' protection of the hostages was expressed in the areas of communication during the Viking Age, it may be related to terms like *grið* and *friðr*, found in the source material from both the Viking Age (skaldic poetry and Edda poetry) and the early Middle Ages (laws), through the Old Swedish formula *mæþ gruþum oc gislum*, 'with peace and hostages'. Hostages and peace are then closely connected, and the legal texts seem to indicate that the two concepts presupposed each other and denoted protection to a third part. Some medieval laws specify it as an offense to harm hostages (Old Swedish *gislingabrut*), even though the offense may have concerned private hostages. Legal and religious aspects are in this case mutually dependent. Although protection may have been prescribed for hostages, this does not mean that they were inviolable in the sense of enjoying 'sacred protection'; the sanctioned protection only existed within certain boundaries.

The above-mentioned examples can be compared with Anttonen's discussion about the boundaries of the sacred, with the help of the

Finnish term *pyhä*, 'sacred', as an analytical category. In order for something to be perceived as sacred, it must be filled with a content that usually appears when people interact during meetings. The interaction rather than the theological position determines the ritual content of the ritual act. *Pyhä* can be defined as something that is not questioned by the performers of the ritual acts. Similar arrangements can be found at things and other types of areas of communication, where existing agreements on hostages were not allowed to be broken.

The giving, taking, or exchange of hostages as a ritual act can also be related to the performative ritual models that point to active rather than passive roles for the participants. A performative model was proposed by Catherine Bell and applied to the study of Old Scandinavian religion by Olof Sundqvist. The latter points out that a 'ritual' has the capacity to change society: the ritual action has a 'power' or 'effect' on the group (the community).

Formally, hostages were used as security within an area of confrontation, with negotiations taking place at an area of communication. The purpose of the hostages during negotiations was as a form of security for a person. But hostages were, of course – as Ryan Lavelle states – also important as a symbolic factor indicating the ruler's dignity, or they could be used to facilitate relations between different groups, as in Anglo-Saxon England. To 'give' and 'take' hostages were ritual acts; hostages therefore became important as a means to acknowledge people's identity, something that is generally important in ritual contexts. These ritual acts, among other things, determined the superiority or inferiority of the participants, but were also a means to relate to one another. Thus hostage taking, along with other ritual acts, was important to rulers and the identities of different groupings. In Part IV, several examples of these issues from different areas of confrontation, Anglo-Danish/Norwegian as well as Anglo-French, and with different ritual acts such as gift giving, oaths/pledges, the performance of skaldic poems and other praises, baptisms, the casting of lots, and other kinds of events, including feasts and hunts, are given.

All these ritual acts were thus designed both to confirm a ruler's person and the status of a grouping, although the intent of the ritual acts could vary. Various rulers (and groupings) could have different intentions. Olaf Haraldsson's confirmation exemplifies different perceptions of what confirmation meant as a symbol. In cases like this, the superiority or inferiority of the different participants was not always evident from the symbolic display. This can also be seen in the early medieval traditions described in *The Elder Westrogothic Law* (Sw. *Äldre västgötalagen*). According to this law, the purpose of the hostage was to confirm the identity of the king-to-be during the Eriksgata, his ritual journey before his election. When the king arrived at the Thing of all Geats (Sw. *Alla götars ting*), he had to be recognized by the lawmen, bishops, and other members of the community (Sw. *tingsmenigheten*). Even more important was that the king could use the Eriksgata as a form of propaganda, with the hostages – who were known to the Geats – confirming him as king in the eyes of the country folk. In this case, the hostage constituted more of a symbolic component than a real means of exerting pressure or a 'life insurance policy'. For the society (province; Sw. *landskap*), the hostage handover was important because it meant that one could relate to the new royal power, which in turn thereby had its formal supremacy confirmed. In this way, both parties made their views known, and a change – or confirmation – of society had taken place.

2. *Were there similarities and differences between hostage traditions in different parts of Scandinavia and continuities from the Iron Age into medieval Scandinavian societies?*

It is uncertain how far back in time the hostage phenomenon can be traced in Scandinavia. The age of Eddic poetry is debated, and the skaldic poetry that mentions hostages is from the early 11th century at the earliest. In medieval law codes, alliterative and formulaic expressions that contain a word for 'hostage' could indicate old traditions. Therefore alternative sources (besides the text sources), such as inscriptions and place names, source categories previously ignored by the research on hostages, have been referred to.

The place-name evidence that is referred to is not so ambiguous when it comes to words for 'hostage'. However, it is uncertain how old these names are. Although the place name *Gyslamarchia* is referred to by Saxo, it is unclear what sources he had access to. The *gisslalag* in Finland – earliest attested in the *Erikskrönikan* – was fixed in writing in the 1320s. The Estonian *maa*names, however, confirm that the *gisslalag* was an old organization. In addition, place names may be much older than the sources where they are first mentioned. These place names – from the Viking Age or older – indicate an ancient organization that can confirm that hostage taking and hostage giving was fairly routine. The evidence also leads us to assume that hostages were probably used in a similar manner in eastern Scandinavia as they were in Danish and Norwegian confrontation areas (in England and France) during the Viking Age. Myths and legends often build on oral traditions, and if they do so here, then it is reasonable to infer that hostage taking was an established practice long before these stories were fixed in writing. For example, the *Ynglinga saga*, compiled by Snorri, could be based on older models when it comes to the hostage tradition in the story of the Æsir-Vanir war. Other stories about hostages – primarily in continental chronicles – highlight the assumption that hostages were an important theme in the narrative traditions; the continental and Old English chronicles confirm early forms of hostage practices. Thus it is quite possible that many traditions about hostages were first fixed in writing in these chronicles, where, however, the perspective of the adversary is sometimes neglected or missing. The relationship can be compared with my model of peace processes, which characterizes the areas of confrontation: the experiences drawn from previous conflicts influenced the way peace agreements were designed. The peace processes were long, drawn-out processes in which both parties could have various degrees of influence.

The above-mentioned sources are independent of each other and, therefore, independently suggest that these are older traditions – dating back at least to the early Viking Age – although we do not know exactly how old they are. The sources indicate that hostages were used in both Western and Eastern Nordic countries, but only sporadically in Iceland. In other words, hostages were used primarily by the Norwegian monarchy.

The traditions that survived into the Middle Ages include the issuing of safe conduct letters, which, at least according to a late medieval source, meant protection for the hostages. The purpose of the hostages during this time was as security in the interaction between individuals (i.e. kings and nobles), but also between different provinces, which were more or less loosely organized. In the 16th century, however, the latter type of hostage lost its importance as a factor in regulating the Swedish provinces.

3. What kind of relationships or social bonds occured between hostages and hostage takers? How were the power hierarchies and influences expressed? Were these relations violent or non-violent?

The investigation has shown that there could be close bonds between hostages and hostage takers, but these were not unconditional, because the hostages were integrated into a new collective.

There was a close connection between the *fóstri* institution and growing up as a hostage in a foreign collective (with the hostage-taker). Some literary examples, both Continental Germanic and Old Scandinavian, mention that it would be a question of subordination in which the moral may be that the main character – given as hostage as a young person – could turn against the hostage taker. But some cases – such as *Getica*'s story of Theodoric (the Great) and *Heimskringla*'s depiction of Rögnvald, Earl Brusi's son – give examples to the contrary. This reflects, therefore, that construction of superiority and subordination is not always evident in peace processes.

Kosto has pointed out that the status of the hostages was determined by how they were expected to be treated. But even the actual hostage giving might have been crucial for the hostage's welfare. It was important to get the right person as hostage, and consequently, knowledge about possible hostages was important for both sides. It was probably the lack of information (the hostages did not identify the ruler) that was the reason for the killing of the king-to-be Ragnvald Knaphövde outside Karleby in the province of Västergötland in the early 12th century. The desire to retain valuable people can be explained by Annette Weiner's paradox 'keeping while giving'.

Hostages seem generally to have been treated well, and the conclusion must be that violence directed towards hostages was extremely rare. The exceptions consisted of unilateral hostages, which in the first place were taken *en masse*, and some examples of individual hostages, as in the case with Archbishop Ælfeah, who was taken hostage in order to stand as security for a tribute. One cannot point to any general reason for violence, however. Possible mechanisms could be stressful situations resulting from a crisis, the desire for revenge or to enact a warning, or even a misconception about the value of the people given (their social capital). The aspect of power was crucial, and thus how 'safe' the hostage taker felt in relation to the other party, something that did not necessarily have to do with military power, but could also be due to the degree of trust in the other party. The more distant one was from the counter-party, the more inclined one was to use violence, as is illustrated by, for example, the mass mutilations at Stade and Sandwich. In both cases people were dehumanized.

4. What methodological concerns does one encounter in studying hostage practices? How can hostages be understood theoretically in the light of peace agreements between communities where Scandinavians acted?

In the material that deals with hostages and concerns Scandinavia, text sources are few, and many of them are written from a Christian perspective and influenced by continental literary text traditions. This bias may be seen in the continental Bishop Chronicles, such as Rimbert's description of the siege of Apulia.

As Adam J. Kosto points out, the fact that women are not mentioned as often as hostages does not mean that they did not function as hostages. The reason for this is that the use of hostages was likely to appear in chronicles and annals without being mentioned as such, and also that women did not constitute central themes in the stories by and about men. To give women away was humiliating for men and would therefore be avoided as a literary theme. Women, however, were politically and socially important and active in various ways in different times and spaces, something which might have made them attractive as targets for hostage taking. An example of a source category – outside the text traditions – that depicts women in such active roles is the Gotland picture stones.

Obviously, the fact that all the entries in the chronicles, annals, and other literary works are so brief can be explained in a number of ways. Even a single word like *ginslingu* may indicate that hostages were 'positioned' (during the giving or taking of hostages), and it may imply a more tedious process than the text material describes.

Peace agreements in the Viking Ages and in particular the Middle Ages were not linear processes. In the context of peace negotiations, hostages were used as a resource by both parties to the conflict, but sometimes in different ways. This could be compared to Lavelle's remark that hostages had 'multi-layered meanings'. By analyzing societies affected by conflicts that were interrupted by lengthy periods of peace, the giving or taking of hostages can thus be understood as an advocacy opportunity, together with several other ritual acts. It is when analysing such complex situations that my model is useful, because it values the religious, social, economic, and legal aspects related to the development of society. 'The societies' could be lands and properties on the micro level or kingdoms on the macro level, as was described in the initial case descriptions based on material from *Landnámabók* and *Íslendingabók* and the settlement between Guthrum and Alfred. The fact that several aspects were involved implies that the perspectives of different groups can be analysed even if they do not usually feature in the sources, especially the peasantry, which was the basis of production. Hostages are thus put into context and not only determined by the actions of the elite. These are aspects that emerge in the discussions about the Eriksgata in the *Äldre västgötalagen*, of Snorri's story about Dala-Gudbrand, and some other cases.

5. What are the similarities and differences between Christian and non-Christian traditions and values of peace agreements and negotiation processes that involved hostages? What were attitudes towards the agreements that became established?

This question cannot be fully answered but some observations are possible: It can be noted that both Christian and heathen rulers who concluded a contract had a pragmatic approach to the peace treaties. Regarding the perception of superiority and subordination, this might have been something that had different symbolic implications in relation to the ritual acts that were important (or central) to the respective culture. For example, in the Christian context it was important to illustrate father-and-son type relationships during baptism and confirmation, a symbolism that might have been lost on the 'heathens', as they appear to have had a more pragmatic approach to ritual acts.

There may, for example, have been a symbol that was difficult to interpret behind the assassination of Ælfeah, because he was executed under circumstances that were possibly ritualistic, something that appears to have gone unnoticed, however, by the Christian chronicler. As acts, the mass mutilations at Stade and Sandwich might have been about the boundary between categories like 'ritual', 'legal', and 'criminal', as the status of the hostages was unclear (were they prisoners or hostages?) and as the hostages were not actually murdered. The event at Sandwich shows that it is not possible to conclude that the mutilation was something that was 'pagan', because it was the Christian King Canute who was responsible. The identity of hostages – including their status and relationship to the hostage taker – was probably crucial for their protection. This seems to have been the case in both Viking Age and early medieval contexts. The hostage was also important as an 'investment opportunity' for a possible future alliance. It was likewise important to have the right person as security when it came to protecting borders during a restless period.

Abbreviations

Arab. = Arabic
Da. = Danish
Est. = Estonian
Fi. = Finnish
Fr. = French
Ger. = German
Ice. = Icelandic
n. = neuter
Lat. = Latin
No. = Norwegian
ODan. = Old Danish
OE. = Old English
OGt. = Old Gutnish
OI. = Old Icelandic
OIr. = Old Irish
ON = Old Norse
OSw. = Old Swedish
OWN = Old West Norse
Sw. = Swedish

References

Sources

Ágrip af Nóregskonungasǫgum: A Twelfth-century Synoptic History of the Kings of Norway (Text series / Viking Society for Northern Research). Ed. Matthew Driscoll. London 1995: Viking Society for Northern Research.

The Airgialla Charter Poem: Edition *The Kingship and Landscape of Tara*, pp. 124–158. Eds. Edel Bhreathnach & Kevin Murray. Dublin 2005: Four Courts Press.

[The Anglo-Saxon Chronicle]. *The Anglo-Saxon Chronicle: A Collaborative Edition* 3, MS A [891 to mid-11th century.]. Ed. Janet M. Bately, Simon Keynes & David N. Dumville. Cambridge 1986: Brewer.

——— *The Anglo-Saxon Chronicle: A Semi-Diplomatic Edition with Introduction and Indices* 7, MS E Eds. Susan Irvine, Simon Keynes & David N. Dumville. Cambridge 2004: Brewer.

——— *The Anglo-Saxon Chronicle: A Semi-Diplomatic Edition with Introduction and Indices* 8, MS F Eds. Peter S. Baker, Simon Keynes & David N. Dumville. Cambridge 2000: Brewer.

Annales Alamannici [8th–11th century.]. Annales Laureshamenses, Alamannici, Guelferbytani et nazariani. *Monumenta Germaniae historica*. Ed. Georgius Heinricus Pertz. Hannover 1826: Hahn.

Annales Bertiniani [9th century.]. *Quellen zur karolingischen Reichsgeschichte* (Ausgewählte Quellen zur deutschen Geschichte des Mittelalters), pp. 11–287. Ed. Ruldolf Buchner, Transl. Reinhold Rau. Darmstadt 1955 (1966): Wissenschaftliche Buchgesellschaft.

Annales regni Francorum inde ab a. 742 usque ad a. 829 qui dicuntur (Scriptores rerum Germanicarum in usum scholarum ex monumentis Germaniae historicis separatim editi) [8th–9th century].

Annales Laurissenses maiores et Einhardi. Eds. Georgius Heinricus Pertz & Fridericus Kurze. Hannoverae 1895: Impensis bibliopolii Hahniani.

The Annals of Fulda (Ninth-Century Histories 2) [9th century]. Ed. & transl. Timothy Reuter. Manchester 1992: Manchester University Press.

[Ari Þorgilsson den lärde (*Ari Þorgilsson hinn fróði*)] Íslendingabók. *Íslendingabók, Landnámabók* (Íslenzk fornrit 1). [Ed.] Jakob Benediktsson. Reykjavík 1968: Hið íslenzka fornritafélag.

—— Íslendingabók. *Íslendingabók, Kristni Saga / The Book of the Icelanders, The Story of the Conversion* (Text series / Viking Society for Northern Research 18), pp. 3–34. Eds. Faulkes & Finlay, transl. Siân Grønlie. London 2006: Viking Society for Northern Research.

[Asser, John d. ca 908/909]. *The Medieval Life of King Alfred the Great: A Translation and Commentary on the Text Attributed to Asser.* Ed. Alfred P. Smyth. Basingstoke 2002: Palgrave.

Die beiden Verträgen mit den Dänen in Ostanglien [late 11th century]. *Die Gesetze der Angelsachsen* 1. Ed. & transl. Felix Liebermann. Aalen (1903) 1960: Scientia.

[Beowulf]. *Klaeber's Beowulf and the Fight at Finnsburg* (Toronto Old English Series 21), pp. 1–109. Eds. D. Fulk & Robert E. Bjork & John D. Niles. Toronto 2008: University of Toronto Press (4 uppl.).

[Chanson de Roland] *The Song of Roland (Chanson de Roland): The Oxford Text* [1129–1165]. Ed. D.D.R. (Roy) Owen. London 1972: Allen and Unwin.

Corpus iuris sueo-gotorum antiqui. *Samling af Sweriges gamla lagar, på kongl. maj:ts nådigste befallning utgifven af d. C.J. Schlyter* (vol. 6). *Codex iuris Helsingici = Helsinge-lagen ; Codicis iuris Smalandici pars de re ecclesiastica = Kristnu-balken af Smålands-lagen; et, Juris urbici codex antiquior = och, Bjärköa-rätten.* Eds. Carl Johan Schlyter & Hans Samuel Collin. Lund 1844: Berlingska boktryckeriet.

[Caesar = Gaius Julius Caesar, d. 44 f.Kr.]. *Commentarii de Bello Gallico*. Eds. Friedrich Kraner & Wilhelm Dittenberger. Berlin 1960: Weidmannsche Verlagshandlung.

Dalalagen. *Svenska landskapslagar: tolkade och förklarade för nutidens svenskar*. 2, Dalalagen och Västmannalagen. Eds. Åke Holmbäck & Elias Wessén. Stockholm 1979: AWE/Geber.

Danakonunga sǫgur. *Danakonunga sǫgur, Skjǫldunga saga, Knýtlinga saga, Ágrip af sǫgu danakonunga* (Íslenzk fornrit 35). Ed. Bjarni Guðnason. Reykjavík 1982: Hið íslenzka fornritafélag.

Danmarks middelalderlige annaler. Ed. Erik Kroman på grundlag af M. Cl. Gertz, Marcus Lorenzens og Ellen Jørgensens udgaver. København 1980: Selskabet for udgivelse af kilder til dansk historie.

Danmarks riges breve I, 1211–1223. Ed. Niels Skyum-Nielsen. København 1957: Danske Sprog- og Litteraturselskab & Ejnar Munksgards Forlag.

[Dio Cassius d. ca 235]. *Dio's Roman History* III [Ῥωμαϊκὴ Ἱστορία, *Historia Romana*]. Ed. Earnest Cary, transl. Herbert Foster. Cambridge, Mass 1914–1927: Harvard University Press.

[Dudo av Saint-Quentin d. ca. 1042–1043]. *Normandiets historie under de første Hertuger*. Transl. Erling Albrectsen. Odense 1979: Odense Universitetsforlag.

[The Poetic Edda] *Edda: die Lieder des Codex Regius nebst verwandten Denkmälern*. 1, Text. Eds. Gustav Neckel & Hans Kuhn. Heidelberg (1914) 1962: Carl Winter Universitätsverlag.

——*The Poetic Edda* ([ed. and transl.] Lee M. Hollander): Austin, Tex.: Univ. of Texas Press, 1962

Edictus Rothari [mid-8th century]. *Monumenta Germaniae historica* (Legum Tomus 4). Ed. Georgius Henricus Pertz. Hannoverae 1868: Impensis Bibliopolii Hahniani.

Egils saga Skalla-Grímssonar [first half of the 13th century] (Íslenzk fornrit 2). Ed. Sigurður Nordal. Reykjavík 1933: Hið íslenzka fornritafélag.

———Egils saga. Islänningasagorna: samtliga släktsagor och fyrtionio tåtar. 1, pp. 1–152. Eds. Kristinn Jóhannesson, Gunnar D. Hansson & Karl G. Johansson. Reykjavík 2014: Saga.

[Ermoldus Nigellus d. 838?]. In Honor of Louis, *Charlemagne and Louis the Pious*. Ed. Thomas F. X. Noble. Pennsylvania 2009: Pennsylvania State University Press, cop.

Encomium Emmae Reginae [ca 1041]. Edited for the Royal Historical Society. Ed. Alistair Campbell. London 1949: Offices of the Royal Historicla Society.

Erikskrönikan. Ed. Sven-Bertil Jansson. Stockholm 1985: Tiden.

[Eyrbyggja saga, 13th century]. *The Story of the Ere-dwellers (Eyrbyggja Saga): With the Story of the Heath-slayings (Heiðarvíga Saga) as Appendix*. Ed. Bernard Quaritch, transl. Eiríkr Magnússon & William Morris. London 1892: Bernard Quaritch.

———*Eyrbyggja saga*. Eyrbyggja saga, Brands þáttr örva, Eiríks saga rauða, Grœnlendiga saga, Grœnlendiga þáttr (Íslenzk fornrit 4), pp. 1–186. [Eds.] Einar Ól. Sveinsson & Matthias Þórðarson. Reykjavík (1935) 1985: Hið íslenzka fornritafélag.

[Flateyjarbók, completed in 1394]. *Flateyjarbok: en samling af norske konge-sagaer med indskudte mindre fortællinger om begivenheder i og udenfor Norge samt annaler* (1). Eds. Gudbrand Vigfusson (Guðbrandur Vigfússon) & Carl Rikard Unger. Christiania 1860: P. T. Mallings forlagsboghandel.

Grágás [1117]. *Grágás: lagasafn íslenska þjóðveldisins*. Eds. Gunnar Karlsson, Kristján Sveinsson & Mörður Árnason. Reykjavík 1992: Mál og menning.

Hálfs saga ok Hálfsrekka (Altnordische Saga-Bibliothek 14). Ed. Albert Le Roy Andrews. Halle 1909: Niemeyer.

[Henry of Livonia d. 1259] *Livländische Chronik* [*Chronicon Livoniae*] (Ausgewählte Quellen zur deutschen Geschichte des Mittelalters 24). Ed. and transl. Albert Bauer. Darmstadt 1959: Wissenschaftliche Buchgesellschaft.

Hirdloven til Norges konge og hans håndgangne menn: etter AM 322 fol [*Hirðskrá*, completed in the 1270s]. [Ed.] and transl. Steinar Imsen. Oslo 2000: Riksarkivet.

Hrólfs saga kraka og Bjarkarímur (Samfund til Udgivelse af gammel nordisk litteratur 32). Ed. Finnur Jónsson. København 1904: Møllers Bogtr.

Helsinge-lagen. Hälsingelagen. *Svenska landskapslagar: tolkade och förklarade för nutidens svenskar*, 3. Södermannalagen och Hälsingelagen. Eds. Åke Holmbäck & Elias Wessén. Stockholm 1979: AWE/Geber.

Jónsbók: The Laws of Later Iceland: The Icelandic Text According to MS AM 351 fol. Skálholtsbók eldri (Bibliotheca germanica, Series nova 4). Ed. and transl. Jana K. Schulman. Saarbrücken 2010: AQ-Verlag.

[Jordanes, 6th century] *Getica: om goternas ursprung och bedrifter = de origine actibusque Getarum* (Atlantis väljer ur världslitteraturen). Transl. Andreas Nordin. Stockholm 1997: Atlantis.

Keltiske myter (Verdens hellige skrifter). Transl. Jenny Graver, Mads Haga & Jan Erik Rekdal. Oslo 2006: De norske bokklubbene.

Knytlinge saga [*Knýtlinga saga*]. Knytlinge saga: Knud den Store, Knud den Hellige og deres mænd, deres slægt. [Eds.] Jens Peter Ægidius, Hans Bekker-Nielsen & Ole Widding. København 1977: Gad.

Kristofers landslag. Corpus iuris sueo-gotorum antiqui (Samling af Sweriges gamla lagar, på kongl. maj:ts nådigste befallning utgifven af d. C. J. Schlyter 12). Eds. Carl Johan Schlyter & Hans Samuel Collin. Lund 1869: Berlingska boktryckeriet.

Kristnisaga. Kristnisaga; Þáttr Þorvalds ens víðfǫrla; Þáttr Ísleifs biskups Gizurarsonar; Hungrvaka (Altnordische Saga-Bibliothek). Ed. Bernhard Kahle. Halle 1905: Niemeyer.

Landnámabók I–III: Hauksbók, Sturlubók, Melabók m.m. Ed. Finnur Jónsson (udgiven af det Kgl. nordiske oldskrift-selskab). København 1900: Thiele bogtrykkeri.

Laxdœla saga [first half of the 13th century]. *Laxdœla saga*: Halldórs þættir Snorrasonar. Stúfs þáttr (Íslenzk fornrit 5). [Ed.] Einar Ól. Sveinsson. Reykjavik 1934: Hið íslenzka fornritafélag.

Lex Frisionum [8th century]. Latin text, English transl. http://www.keesn.nl/lex/ 2016-04-08.

Lexicon poeticum antiquae linguae septentrionalis. Eds. Finnur Jónsson & Sveinbjörn Egilsson (forøget og påny udgivet for det Kongelige nordiske oldskriftselskab). København 1966: Atlas bogtryk.

[Alcuin, 8th century]. *The Life of Willibrord, c.796.* Fondham University. https://sourcebooks.fordham.edu/basis/alcuin-willbrord.asp 2018-05-07.

Magnus Erikssons landslag [mid-14th century]. (Skrifter utgivna av Institutet för rättshistorisk forskning, grundat av Gustav och Carin Olin. Serien 1, Rättshistoriskt bibliotek 6). [Eds. and transl.] Åke Holmbäck & Elias Wessén. Stockholm 1962: Nordiska Bokhandeln.

Magnus lagabøters landslov (Scandinavian university books). Ed. and transl. Absalon Taranger. Oslo 1962: Universitetsforlaget.

Morkinskinna (Íslenzk fornrit 23–24). Eds. Þórður Ingi Guðjónsson & Ármann Jakobsson. Reykjavík 2011: Hið íslenzka fornritafélag.

——— *Morkinskinna: The Earliest Icelandic Chronicle of the Norwegian Kings (1030–1157)* (Islandica 51). Eds. Theodore M. Andersson and Kari E. Gade. Ithaca, NY, 2000: Cornell University Press.

Norges kongekrønike [*Chronicon Regum Norvegiæ*] (Oslohumanistene. Skrifter i utvalg). Eds. Halvard Gunnarssøn & Inger Ekrem. Oslo 1992: Universitetsforlaget.

Den norsk-islandske skjaldedigtning. A, Tekst efter håndskrifterne, Bd 1, 800–1200. Ed. Finnur Jónsson. København 1967: Rosenkilde & Bagger.

——— *Den norsk-islandske skjaldedigtning.* A, Tekst efter håndskrifterne, Bd 2, 1200–1400. Ed. Finnur Jónsson. København 1967: Rosenkilde & Bagger.

[Olaus Magnus] *Historia om de nordiska folken = Historia de gentibus septentrionalibus.* Ed. John Granlund. Stockholm 1976: Gidlund i samarbete med Inst. för folklivsforskning vid Nordiska museet och Stockholms universitet.

Orkneyinga saga [13th century]. Orkneyinga saga, Legenda de sancto Magno, Magnúss saga skemmri, Magnúss saga lengri, Helga þattr ok Úlfs (Íslenzk fornrit 34). Ed. Finnbogi Guðmundsson. Reykjavík 1965: Hið íslenzka fornritafélag.

[Peder Svart (alt. Peder Swart) d. 1562]. *Gustav Vasas krönika.* Göteborg 2014: Mimer.

[Plutarchos d. ca 120 AD] *Levnadsteckningar över berömda greker och romare* [*Vitae parallelae*]. Eds. Carl Theander, Ivar Harrie & Hugo Bergstedt Theander. Stockholm 1947: Bokførlaget Natur och Kultur.

Riksarkivets databas, Nationell Arkivdatabas https://sok.riksarkivet. se (2015-10-22).

[Rimbert d. 888]. *Boken om Ansgar* (Skrifter utgivna av Samfundet Pro fide et christianismo). Eds. Carl Fredrik Hallencreutz & Tore Hållander, [transl.] Eva Odelman. Stockholm 1986: Proprius.

[Saxo Grammaticus d. ca. 1204]. Saxo Grammaticus, *The History of the Danes: Books I–IX.* Ed. Hilda Ellis Davidson, transl. Peter Fisher. Cambridge 1979–1980: Brewer.

——— *Gesta Danorum = Danmarkshistorien* 1–2. Ed. Karsten Friis-Jensen, transl. Peter Zeeberg. København 2005: Det Danske Sprog- og Litteraturselskab & Gads Forlag.

Skaldic database. https://www.abdn.ac.uk/skaldic/m.php?p=skaldic (2015-12-07).

Smålandslagen [alt. Tiohäradslagen]. Corpus iuris sueo-gotorum antiqui. (Samling af Sweriges gamla lagar, på kongl. maj:ts nådigste befallning utgifven af d. C.J. Schlyter 6). Eds. Carl Johan Schlyter & Hans Samuel Collin. Lund 1844: Berlingska boktryckeriet.

——— *Smålandslagen* [alt. Tiohäradslagen]. *Svenska landskapslagar: tolkade och förklarade för nutidens svenskar.* 5, Äldre västgötalagen,

Yngre västgötalagen, Smålandslagens kyrkobalk och Bjärköarätten. Eds. Åke Holmbäck & Elias Wessén. Stockholm 1979: AWE/Geber.

[Snorri Sturluson d. 1241]. *Edda: Prologue and Gylfaginning* (a). Ed. Anthony Faulkes. London 1988: Viking Society for Northern Research.

———*Edda: Skáldskaparmál* (b). 1, Introduction, Text and Notes. Ed. Anthony Faulkes. London 1998: Viking Society for Northern Research.

———*Edda: Háttatál* (c). Ed. Anthony Faulkes. Oxford 1991: Clarendon Press.

———*Edda*. Ed. & transl. London and Vermont 1995: J. M. Dent & Charles E. Tuttle.

[Snorri Sturluson] *Heimskringla* 1–3 (Íslenzk fornrit 26–28). Ed. Bjarni Aðalbjarnarson. Reykjavík (1941, 1945, 1951) 1979: Hið íslenzka fornritafélag.

———The History of St. Olav, *Heimskringla, Or the Lives of The Norse Kings*. Ed. and transl. Erling Monsen & Albert Hugh Smith). New York (1932) 1990: Dover.

———Nordiska kungasagor. *1, Från Ynglingasagan till Olav Tryggvasons saga*. Ed. and transl. Karl G. Johansson. Stockholm 1991: Fabel.

———Nordiska kungasagor. *2, Olav den heliges saga*. Ed. and transl. Karl G. Johansson. Stockholm 1992: Fabel.

———Nordiska kungasagor. *3, Magnus den gode till Magnus Erlingsson*. Ed. and transl. Karl G. Johansson. Stockholm 1993: Fabel.

[Snorri Sturluson & Magnús Ólafsson d. 1636] *Laufás Edda*. Two versions of Snorra Edda from the 17th century, vol. 1, Edda Magnúsar Ólafssonar: (Laufás) (Rit stofnun Árna Magnússonar á Íslandi 13). Ed. Anthony Faulkes. Reykjavík 1979: Stofnun Árna Magnússonar.

Sǫgubrot af fornkonungum. Danakonunuga sǫgur: Skjǫldunga saga, Knýtlinga saga, Ágrip af Sǫgu danakonunga (Íslenzk fornrit 35), pp. 46–71. Ed. Bjarni Guðnasson. Reykjavík 1982: Hið íslenzka fornritafélag.

[Statius Publius Papinius d. ca 96 e.Kr.] *Statius Silvae* (Netedition, the Latin Library): http://www.thelatinlibrary.com/statius.html. 2014-09-01

[Sturla Þórðarson] *Sturlunga Saga, Including the Íslendinga Saga of Lawman Sturla Thordsson and Other Works*, 1–2. Ed. Gudbrand Vigfusson (alt. Guðbrandur Vigfússon). Oxford 1878: Clarendon Press.

Svenska medeltidsdikter och rim (Svenska fornskrift-sällskapet) [Stora rimkrönikan]. Ed. Gustaf Edvard Klemming. Stockholm 1881–1882: Norstedt.

Södermannalagen. Svenska landskapslagar: tolkade och förklarade för nutidens svenskar. 3, Södermannalagen och Hälsingelagen. Eds. Åke Holmbäck & Elias Wessén. Stockholm 1979: AWE/Geber.

[Tacitus = Publius Cornelius Tacitus d. ca 120 AD] *Cornelii Taciti Historiarum libri*. Recognovit brevique adnotatione critica instruxit Charles Dennis Fisher. Scriptorum classicorum bibliotheca Oxoniensis. Oxonii 1911: E Typographeo Clarendoniano.

——*Germaniens historie, geografi og befolkning = De origine et situ Germanorum*. Eds. Niels W. Bruun & Allan A. Lund. Århus 1974: Wormianum.

[Thietmar av Merseburg d. 1018] *Chronik* (Ausgewählte Quellen zur deutschen Geschichte des Mittelalters 9). Ed Werner Trillmich. Darmstadt 1966: Wissenschaftliche Buchgesellschaft.

Um Þorgeirsbola. Netútgáfan. http://www.snerpa.is/net/thjod/thorgeir.htm (2014-12-09)

[Vilhelm av Jumièges d. in the 1070s]. *To normanniske krøniker*. Ed. and transl. Erling Albrectsen. Odense 1980: Odense universitetsforlag.

Upplandslagen. Corpus iuris sueo-gotorum antiqui. Samling af Sweriges gamla lagar, på kongl. maj:ts nådigste befallning utgifven d. C.J. Schlyter. Vol. 3, Codex iuris Uplandici = Uplands-lagen.

Eds. Carl Johan Schlyter & Hans Samuel Collin. Stockholm, 1834: P. A. Norstedt & Söner.

——— Upplandslagen. *Svenska landskapslagar: tolkade och förklarade för nutidens svenskar* 1, Östgötalagen och Upplandslagen. Eds. and transl. Åke Holmbäck & Elias Wessén. Stockholm 1979: AWE/Geber.

Uppsala Edda. Handritið DG 11 4to. Ed. Heimir Pálsson. Reykjavík 2013: Bókaútgafan Opna.

Vikingerne i Franken: skriftlige kilder fra det 9. århundrede. Ed. and transl. Erling Albrectsen. Odense 1976: Odense Universitetsforlag.

Västmannalagen. *Svenska landskapslagar: tolkade och förklarade för nutidens svenskar*. 2, Dalalagen och Västmannalagen. Eds. and transl. Åke Holmbäck & Elias Wessén. Stockholm 1979: AWE/Geber.

Vǫlundarkviða > Edda.

Waltharius: et latinsk heltedigt fra middelalderen. Ed. and transl. Hans Ørbæk. København 2008: Museum Tusculanums forlag.

[Widukind av Corvey d. ca 973]. Sächsiche Geschichten [*Res gestae saxonicae*]. Ed. Paul Hirsch, [transl.] Reinhold Schottin. New York (1931) 1965: Johnson.

[William av Malmesbury d. 1143] *Gesta regum Anglorum: The History of the English Kings*, 1–2 (Oxford Medieval Texts). Ed. and transl. Roger A. B. Mynors; completed by Rodney M. Thomson & Michael Winterbottom. Oxford 1998–99: Clarendon Press.

[Äldre västgötalagen ca 1225] Äldre västgötalagen. *Svenska landskapslagar: tolkade och förklarade för nutidens svenskar*. 5, Äldre västgötalagen, Yngre västgötalagen, Smålandslagens kyrkobalk och Bjärköarätten. Eds. Åke Holmbäck & Elias Wessén. Stockholm 1979: AWE/Geber.

——— *Äldre västgötalagen och dess bilagor: i Cod. Holm. B 59*, del I–II (Skara stiftshistoriska sällskaps skriftserie 60), pp. 11–38. Ed. P. A. Wiktorsson. [Skara] 2011: Föreningen för Västgötalitteratur.

——— *The older version of the Västgöta Law* (Äldre Västgötalagen). Ed. and transl. Thomas Lindkvist. Unpublished manuscript.

Östergötlands runinskrifter (Sveriges runinskrifter 2). Ed. Erik Brate. Stockholm 1911–18: Kungl. Vitterhets historie och antikvitets akademien.

Östgötalagen. *Svenska landskapslagar: tolkade och förklarade för nutidens svenskar.* 1, Östgötalagen och Upplandslagen. Eds. Åke Holmbäck & Elias Wessén. Stockholm 1979: AWE/Geber.

Secondary Literature

Abram, Christopher. 2011. *Myths of the Pagan North: The Gods of the Norsemen*. London: Continuum.

Aðalheiður Guðmundsdóttir. 2012. Sagomotiv på de gotländska bildstenarna: fallet Hild Högnadotter. *Gotlands bildstenar: järnålderns gåtfulla budbärare*, pp. 59–71. Ed. Maria Herlin Karnell. Transl. Bertil Sjöblom. Visby: Gotlands museum.

Alcock, Leslie. 2003. *Kings and Warriors, Craftsmen and Priests in Northern Britain AD 550–850*. Edinburgh: Society of Antiquarities of Scotland.

Alexander Jóhannesson. 1956. *Isländisches etymologisches Wörterbuch*. Bern: Francke Verlag.

Allen, Joel. 2006. *Hostages and Hostage-Taking in the Roman Empire*. Cambridge: Cambridge University Press.

Althoff, Gerd. 2004. *Family, Friends and Followers: Political and Social Bonds in Medieval Europe*. Transl. Christopher Carroll. New York: Cambridge University Press.

von Amira, Karl. 1882. *Nordgermanisches Obligationenrecht*. 1, Altschwedisches Obligationenrecht. Leipzig: Verlag von Veit.

——— 1895. *Nordgermanisches Obligationenrecht*. 2, Westnordisches Obligationenrecht. Leipzig: Verlag von Veit.

Andersen, Per Sveaas. 1960. Gisslelag. Norge. *Kulturhistorisk leksikon for nordisk middelalder* 5, pp. 645–648. Ed. Finn Hødnebø et al. Oslo: Gyldendal.

Anderson, Carl Edlund. 1999. *Formation and Resolution of Ideological Contrast in the Early History of Scandinavia* (PhD

Dissertation). University of Cambridge: Department of Anglo-Saxon, Norse & Celtic (Faculty of English).

Andersson, Catharina. 2013. Gifts and society in fourteenth-century Sweden. *Disputing Strategies in Medieval Scandinavia* (Medieval Law and its Practice 16), pp. 218–245. Ed. Kim Esmark *et al.* Leiden: Brill.

Andersson, Ingvar. (1943) 1969. *Sveriges historia: 600–1350*. Stockholm: Natur och kultur.

Andersson, Theodore M. 1988. Lore and literature in a Scandinavian conversion episode. *Idee, Gestalt, Geschichte: Festschrift Klaus von See*, pp. 261–284. Ed. Gerd Wolfgang Weber. Odense: Odense University Press.

Andersson, Thorsten. 1992a. Orts- und Personennamen als Aussagequelle für die altgermanische Religion. *Germanische Religionsgeschichte: Quellen und Quellenprobleme*, pp. 508–540. Ed. Heinrich Beck et al. Berlin: de Gruyter.

———1992b. Kultplatsbeteckningar i nordiska ortnamn. *Sakrale navne* (NORNA-rapporter 48), pp. 77–105. Eds. Gillian Fellows-Jensen & Bente Holmberg. Uppsala: NORNA-förlaget.

———1992c. Haupttypen sakraler Ortsnamen Ostskandinaviens. *Der historische Horizont der Götterbild-Amulette aus der Übergangsepoche von der Spätantike zum Frühmittelalter* (Abhandlungen der Akademie der Wissenschaften in Göttingen. Philologisch-historische Klasse F. 3, 200), pp. 241–256. Ed. Karl Hauck. Göttingen: Vamdenhoek und Ruprecht.

———1993. Sakrala personnamn – eller profana: klassifikations- och gränsdragningsproblem i det gamla nordiska personnamnsförrådet. *Personnamn i nordiska och andra germanska fornspråk* (NORNA-rapporter 51), pp. 39–60. Ed. Lena Peterson. Uppsala: NORNA-förlaget.

Andrén, Anders. 2014. *Tracing Old Norse Cosmology: The World Tree, Middle Earth, and the Sun from Archaeological Perspectives* (Vägar till Midgård 16). Lund: Nordic Academic Press.

Anttonen, Veikko. 2000. The sacred. *Guide to the Study of Religion*, pp. 271–282. Eds. Willi Braun & Russell T. McCutcheon. London: Cassell.

Ármann Jakobsson. 2005. Royal Biography. *Old Norse-Icelandic Literature and Culture*, pp. 388–402. Ed. Rory McTurk. Oxford: Blackwell Publishing.

Auður Magnúsdóttir. 2003. Älska, giftas, stötta, slåss. *Nätverk som social resurs: historiska exempel*, pp. 61–81. Eds. Einar Hreinsson & Tomas Nilson. Lund: Studentlitteratur.

Aymard, André. 1961. Les otages barbares au debut de l'empire. *The Journal of Roman Studies* 51, pp. 136–142. London: Society for the Promotion of Roman Studies.

Bagge, Sverre. 1986. Borgerkrig og statsutvikling i Norge i middelaldern. [Norsk] *Historisk tidsskrift* 65, pp. 145–197. Oslo: Universitetsforlaget.

———2014. *Cross & Scepter: The Rise of the Scandinavian Kingdoms from the Vikings to the Reformation*. Princeton: Princeton University Press.

Baker, Peter S. (2003) 2007. *Introduction to Old English*. Malden, MA: Blackwell.

———2013. *Honour, Exchange and Violence in Beowulf* (Anglo-Saxon Studies 20). Woodbridge: D.S. Brewer.

Beck, Heinrich. 1998. Gast und Gastfreundschaft. *Reallexikon der germanischen Altertumskunde* 10, pp. 462–466. Ed. Heinrich Beck *et al*. Berlin: de Gruyter.

Bell, Catherine. 1997. *Ritual: Perspectives and Dimensions*. New York: Oxford University Press.

Bergman, Gösta. (1977) 1990. *Ord med historia*. Stockholm: Prisma.

Berresford, Peter. 1999. *The Chronicles of the Celts: New Tellings of Their Myths and Legends*. London: Robinson.

Beuermann, Ian. 2011. *Jarla Sǫgur Orkneyja*: Status and power of the Earls of Orkney according to their Sagas. *Ideology and Power in the Viking and Middle Ages: Scandinavia, Iceland, Ireland, Orkney and the Faeroes* (The Northern World: North Europe and the Baltic c. 400–1700 A.D. Peoples, Economics and Cultures 52), pp. 109–162. Ed. Gro Steinsland *et al.* Leiden: Brill.

Beyerle, Franz. 1927. Der Ursprung der Bürgschaft: ein Deutungsversuch vom germanischen Rechte her. *Zeitschrift der Savigny-Stiftung für Rechtsgeschichte*: Germanische Abteilung 47, pp. 567–645. Weimar: Böhlau.

Bhreathnach, Edel. 2005. The Airgialla Charter poem: The political context. *The Kingship and Landscape of Tara*, pp. 95–99. Ed. Edel Breatnach. Dublin: Four Courts Press.

Bhreathnach, Edel & Murray, Kevin. 2005. Notes [to *The Airgialla Charter Poem: Edition*]. *The Kingship and Landscape of Tara*, pp. 140–158. Ed. Edel Breatnach. Dublin: Four Courts Press.

Björn Þorsteinsson. 1960. Gisslelag. Island. *Kulturhistorisk leksikon for nordisk middelalder* 5, pp. 648–649. Ed. Finn Hødnebø *et al.* Oslo: Gyldendal.

Blomkvist, Nils. 2005. *The Discovery of the Baltic: The Reception of a Catholic World-System in the European North (AD 1075–1225)* (The Northern World 15). Leiden: Brill.

Blomkvist, Torsten. 2002. *Från ritualiserad tradition till institutionaliserad religion: strategier för maktlegitimering på Gotland under järnålder och medeltid*. Uppsala: Teologiska institutionen, Uppsala universitet.

Blomkvist, Torsten & Sundqvist, Olof. 2006. Religionsbegreppets tillämpning i handböcker om fornskandinavisk religion. *Nya mål?: religionsdidaktik i en tid av förändring*, pp. 20–37. Eds. Birgit Lindgren Odén & Peder Thalén. Uppsala: Swedish Science Press.

Borden, Arthur. 1982. *A Comprehensive Old-English Dictionary*. Lanham: University Press of America.

Brink, Stefan. 1990. *Sockenbildning och sockennamn: Studier i äldre territoriell indelning i Norden*. Acta Academiae Regiae Gustavi Adolphi 57, Studier till en svensk ortnamnsatlas. Uppsala: Stockholm.

―― 1997. Political and social structures in Early Scandinavia: 2, aspects of space and territoriality – the settlement district. *Tor: meddelanden från Uppsala universitets museum för nordiska fornsaker* 28, pp. 389–437. Uppsala: Uppsala universitets museum för nordiska fornsaker.

―― 1999. Social order in the early Scandinavian landscape. *Settlement and Landscape: Proceedings of a Conference in Århus, Denmark, May 4–7 1998* (Jysk Arkæologisk Selskabs skrifter), pp. 423–439. Eds. Charlotte Fabech & Jytte Ringtved. Højbjerg: Jutland Archaeological Society.

―― 2000a. Nordens husabyar – unga eller gamla? *Et hus med mange rom: venne -bok til Bjørn Myhre på 60-årsdagen*, pp. 283–291. Ed. Ingrid Fuglestvedt. Stavanger: Arkeologisk museum i Stavanger.

―― 2000b. Forntida vägar. *Vägar och vägmiljöer* (Bebyggelsehistorisk tidskrift 39), pp. 23–64. Ed. Jan-Olof Montelius. Uppsala: Swedish Science Press.

―― 2003. Ambátt, seta, deigja – Þræll, Þjónn, bryti: termer för trälar belyser träldomens äldre historia. *Trälar: ofria i agrarsamhället från vikingatid till medeltid* (Skrifter om skogs- och lantbrukshistoria 17), pp. 103–117. Eds. Thomas Lindkvist & Janken Myrdal. Stockholm: Nordiska museet.

―― 2012. *Vikingarnas slavar: den nordiska träldomen under yngre järnålder och äldsta medeltid*. Stockholm: Atlantis.

Budge, Wallis. (1911) 1973. *Osiris and the Egyptian Resurrection*. New York: Dover Publications.

Bugge, 1910. See *Södermanlands runinskrifter*.

Bull, Edvard. 1917. Det hedenske kultcentrum i Søndre Gudbrandsdalen. *Maal og minne: norske studier*, pp. 156–162. Ed. Magnus Olsen. Kristiania: Bymaals-lagets forlag.

Bury, John Bagnell. (1923) 1958. *A History of the Later Roman Empire: From the Death of Theodosius to the Death of Justinian* 1. New York: Dover Publications.

Byrne, Francis John. 1973. *Irish Kings and High-Kings*. London: Batsford.

Byrne, Paul. 2005. Uí Néill. *Medieval Ireland: An Encyclopedia*, pp. 489–490. Ed. Seán Duffy et al. New York: Routledge.

Bøe, Arne. 1960. Grið. Norge. *Kulturhistorisk leksikon for nordisk middelalder* 5, pp. 463–464. Ed. Finn Hødnebo et al. Gyldendal: Oslo.

CD = *The Chambers Dictionary*. Ed. Allied Chambers. Edinburgh 1998: Chambers.

Chapman Stacey, Robin. 2007. *Dark Speech: The Performance of Law in Early Ireland* (The Middle Ages Series). Philadelphia: University of Pennsylvania Press.

Charles-Edwards, Thomas M. 2005. The Airgíalla Charter poem: the legal content. *The Kingship and Landscape of Tara*, pp. 100–123. Ed. Edel Breatnach. Dublin: Four Courts Press.

Clunies Ross, Margaret. 1998. *Hedniska ekon: myt och samhälle i fornnordisk litteratur*. Transl. Suzanne Almqvist. Gråbo: Anthropos.

——— 2010. *The Cambridge Introduction to the Old Norse-Icelandic Saga* (Cambridge Introductions to Literature). Cambridge: Cambridge University Press.

The Concise Oxford Dictionary of English Place-names. Ed. Eilert Ekwall. London 1960: Clarendon Press.

Cróinín, Dáibhí Ó. 2004. Ireland, 400–800. *A New History of Ireland*. 1, Prehistoric and Early Ireland, pp. 182–234. Ed. Dáibhí Ó Cróinín. Oxford: Oxford University Press.

Curry, Andrew. 2013. The first Vikings. *Archaeology: A Publication of the Archaeological Institute of America* 66, pp. 24–29. New York: Archaeological Institute of America.

Dahlerup, Troels. 1960. Gisslelag (Danmark). *Kulturhistorisk leksikon for nordisk middelalder* 5, p. 649–650. Ed. Finn Hødnebø et al. Gyldendal: Oslo.

Dillmann, François-Xavier. 2001. Mimir. *Reallexikon der germanischen Altertumskunde* 16, pp. 38–43. Ed. Heinrich Beck et al. Berlin: de Gruyter.

―――― 2006. *Les magiciens dans l'Islande ancienne: études sur la représentation de la magie islandaise et de ses agents dans les sources littéraires norroises* (Acta Academiae Regiae Gustavi Adolphi 92). Uppsala: Kungl. Gustav Adolfs akademien för svensk folkkultur.

Dinneen, Patrick. 1927. ...[Celt.] *An Irish-English Dictionary, Being a Thesaurus of the Words, Phrases and Idioms of the Modern Irish Language*. Dublin.

Dols, Michael W. 1992. *Majnūn: The Madman in Medieval Islamic Society*. Ed. Diana E. Immisch. Oxford: Clarendon Press.

Dovring, Folke. 1947. "Gilzla oc grutha" i Smålandslagen. *Arkiv för nordisk filologi*, pp. 258–260. Lund: C. W. K. Gleerups förlag.

―――― 1951. *De stående skatterna på jord 1400–1600* (Acta Regiae Societatis humaniorum litterarum Lundensis). Lund: Gleerup.

Drieskens, Barbara. 2008. *Living with Djinns: Understanding and Dealing with the Invisible in Cairo*. London: Saqi.

Drobin, Ulf. 1991. "Mjödet och offersymboliken i fornnordisk religion". *Studier i religionshistoria tillägnade Åke Hultkrantz*, pp. 97–141. Ed. Per-Arne Berglie et al. Löberöd: Bokförlaget Plus Ultra.

DuBois, Thomas A. 1999. *Nordic Religions in the Viking Age* (The Middle Ages). Philadelphia: University of Pennsylvania Press.

Dumézil, Georges. (1962) 1966. *De nordiska gudarna: en undersökning av den skandinaviska religionen* (Aldus-böckerna 50). Stockholm: Aldus/Bonnier.

Edenheim, Ralph. 1982. Medeltidens byggnadshistoria. *Varnhems klosterkyrka, Valle härad, Västergötland*, pp. 50–67. Eds. Ralph Edenheim & Ingrid Rosell. Stockholm: Almqvist & Wiksell.

Elbern, Stephan. 1990. Geiseln in Rom. *Athenaeum* 78, pp. 97–140. Pavia: Amministrazione di Athenæum, Università.

Elmevik, Lennart. 1999. Sockennamnet Villberga och Lindholmsamulettens sawilagaR. *Saga och sed*, pp. 137–146. Uppsala: Kungl. Gustav Adolfs akademien.

——— 2003. En svensk ortnamnsgrupp och hednisk prästtitel. *Ortnamnssällskapets i Uppsala årsskrift*, pp. 68–78. Uppsala: Ortnamnssällskapet i Uppsala.

——— 2013. Ortnamn jag stött och blött. *Ortnamnssällskapets i Uppsala årsskrift* 2013, pp. 41–53. Uppsala: Ortnamnssällskapet i Uppsala.

Engen, Arnfinn. 2010. Hovudtrekk i Gudbrandsdalens historie. *Gudbrandsdalen, en kulturhistorisk veiviser: historie, landskap, byggeskikk, folketradisjoner*, pp. 28–59. Ed. Arnfinn Engen. Oslo: ARFO.

Enright, Michael. 1996. *Lady With a Mead Cup: Ritual, Prophecy, and Lordship in the European Warband from La Tène to the Viking Age*. Dublin: Four Courts Press.

Ernby, Birgitta. 2008. *Norstedts etymologiska ordbok*. Stockholm: Norstedts akademiska förlag.

Etimološki slovar slovenskega jezika. France Bezlaj. Ljubljana 1982: Slovenska akademija znanosti in umetnosti.

Fenton, Kirsten A. 2008. *Gender, Nation and Conquest in the Works of William of Malmesbury* (Gender in the Middle Ages 4). Woodbridge: Boydell Press.

Finnur Jónsson. (1894–1902) 1920–1924. *Den oldnorske og oldislandske litteraturs historie* 2: 2. København: Gad.

Friis-Jensen, Karsten. 1987. *Saxo Grammaticus as Latin Poet: Studies in the Verse Passages of the* Gesta Danorum (Analecta Romana Instituti Danici. Supplementum 14). Roma: Bretschneider.

Fritzner, Johan. (1883–1896) 1973. *Ordbog over det gamle norske sprog* 1–3. Oslo: Universitetsforlaget.

Gahrn, Lars. 1988. *Sveariket i källor och historieskrivning* (Meddelanden från Historiska institutionen i Göteborg 36). Göteborg: Historiska institutionen, Göteborgs universitet.

Gallén, Jarl. 1972. Gisslelag (Estland). *Kulturhistorisk leksikon for nordisk middelalder* 5, p. 650–651. Ed. Finn Hødnebø et al. Gyldendal: Oslo.

Gallén, Jarl & Lind, John. 1991. *Nöteborgsfreden och Finlands medeltida östgräns* 2. Helsingfors: Svenska litteratursällskapet.

van Gennep, Arnold. (1960) 1977. *The Rites of Passage*. London: Routledge & Kegan Paul.

Gardeła, Leszek. 2013. 'Warrior-women' in Viking Age Scandinavia? A preliminary archaeological study. *Analecta Archaeologica Ressoviensia* (vol. 8), pp. 273–339. Instytut Archeologii Uniwersytetu Rzeszowskiego: University of Rzeszów.

Ginzburg, Carlo. 1989. *Clues, Myths, and the Historical Method*. Baltimore: Johns Hopkins University Press.

Gísli Sigurðsson. 2007. Völuspá. *Reallexikon der Germanischen Altertumskunde* 35, pp. 524–533. Ed. Heinrich Beck *et al*. Berlin: de Gruyter.

Granlund, John. (1951) 1976. Kommentar. *Historia om de nordiska folken*. 4. [By] Olaus Magnus. Stockholm: Gidlund i samarbete med Institutionen för folklivsforskning vid Nordiska museet och Stockholms universitet.

Gustavson, Helmer. 2003. *Gamla och nya runor: artiklar 1982–2001* (Runica et mediævalia. Opuscula 9). Stockholm: Sällskapet Runica et mediævalia.

Hadley, Dawn M. 2000. 'Hamlet and the princess of Denmark': Lordship of the Danelaw, c. 860–954. *Cultures in Contact: Scandinavian Settlement in England in the Ninth and Tenth Centuries* (Studies in the Early Middle Ages), pp. 107–132. Eds. Dawn M. Hadley & Julian D. Richards. Turnhout: Brepols.

Hall, John Clark & Meritt, Herbert. (1960) 2002. *A Concise Anglo-Saxon Dictionary*. Cambridge: Cambridge University Press.

Halsall, Guy. 1989. Anthropology and the study of pre-conquest warfare and society: The ritual war in Anglo-Saxon England. *Weapons and Warfare in Anglo-Saxon England* (Oxford University, Committee for Archaeology. Monograph 21), pp. 157–177. Ed. Sonia Chadwick Hawkes. Oxford: Oxford University Committee for Archaeology.

Hamre, Lars. 1965. Lejde. Noreg. *Kulturhistorisk leksikon for nordisk middelalder* 10, pp. 468–469. [Ed.] Finn Hødnebø et al. Oslo: Gyldendal.

Harrison, Dick. 2002. *Jarlens sekel: en berättelse om 1200-talets Sverige.* Stockholm: Ordfront.

——— 2009. *Sveriges historia: 600–1350.* Stockholm: Norstedts.

Hasselberg, Gösta. 1948. Om Smålandslagens inledningsord. *Saga och sed* 1948, pp. 44–52. [Ed.] Jöran Sahlgren. Uppsala: Kungl. Gustav Adolfs akademien för svensk folkkultur.

Haugen, Einar Ingvald. 1967. The mythical structure of the Ancient Scandinavians. *To Honor Roman Jakobson: Essays on the Occasion of his Seventieth Birthday, 11 October 1966* 2 (Janua linguarum. Series major 32), pp. 885–868. The Hague: Mouton.

Hayeur Smith, Michèle. 2004. *Draupnir's Sweat and Mardöll's Tears: An Archaeology of Jewellery, Gender and Identity in Viking Age Iceland* (British Archaeological Reports. International Series 1276). Oxford: Hedges.

Hedlund, Monica. 2011. De "osynliga texterna" i B 59. *Biblis: tidskrift för bokhistoria, bibliografi, bokhantverk, samlande* 54, pp. 31–36. Stockholm: Föreningen Biblis.

Hellberg, Lars. 1984. Hedendomens spår i Uppländska ortnamn. *Ortnamnssällskapets i Uppsala årsskrift* 1984, pp. 40–71. Uppsala: Ortnamnssällskapet i Uppsala.

Hellquist, Elof. 1922. *Svensk etymologisk ordbok* 1–2. Lund: Gleerup.

Helmbrecht, Michaela. 2012. "En mansvärld": berättande bilder på stenarna i grupp C och D. *Gotlands bildstenar: järnålderns gåtfulla budbärare*, pp. 83–90. Ed. Maria Herlin Karnell. Visby: Gotlands museum.

Hemmingsen, Lars. 1989. *Behind Beowulf: A New Theory of the Historical Background of the Poem* (Unifol). København: Reitzel.

Hermanson, Lars. 2000. *Släkt, vänner och makt: en studie av elitens politiska kultur i 1100-talets Danmark* (Avhandlingar från Historiska institutionen i Göteborg 2), Göteborg: Historiska institutionen.

―――― 2009. *Bärande band: vänskap, kärlek och brödraskap i det medeltida Europa ca 1000–1200*. Lund: Nordic Academic Press.

Hill, David. 2001. Mercians: the dwellers on the boundary. *Mercia: An Anglo-Saxon Kingdom in Europe* (Studies in the Early History of Europe), pp. 173–182. Eds. Michelle P. Brown & Carol Ann Farr. London: Leicester University Press.

―――― 1970. *Norrøn mytologi: tro og myter i vikingtiden*. Oslo: Det norske samlaget.

Honko, Lauri. 1975. Zur Klassifikationen der Riten. *Temenos: Studies in Comparative Religion Presented by Scholars in Denmark, Finland, Norway and Sweden* 11, pp. 61–77. Helsinki: Suomen uskontotieteellinen seura.

Hultgård, Anders. 1993. Altskandinavische Opferrituale und das Problem der Quellen. *The Problem of Ritual: Based on Papers Read at the Symposium on Religious Rites held at Åbo, Finland, on the 13th–16th of August 1991* (Scripta Instituti Donneriani Aboensis 15), pp. 221–259. Ed. Tore Ahlbäck. Åbo: Donnerska institutet för religionshistorisk och kulturhistorisk forskning.

―――― 1996. Fornskandinavisk kult – finns det skriftliga källor? *Religion från stenålder till medeltid: artiklar baserade på Religionsarkeologiska nätverksgruppens konferens på Lövstadbruk den 1–3 december 1995* (Riksantikvarieämbetet. Arkeologiska undersökningar 19), pp. 25–57. Eds. Kerstin Engdahl & Anders Kaliff. Linköping: Riksantikvarieämbetet.

―――― 1997. Från ögonvittnesskildring till retorik: Adam av Bremens notiser om Uppsalakulten i religionshistorisk belysning. *Uppsalakulten och Adam av Bremen* (Religionshistoriska forskningsrapporter från Uppsala 11), pp. 9–50. Ed. Anders Hultgård. Nora: Nya Doxa.

―――― 2001. Kultische Umfahrt. *Reallexikon der germanischen Altertumskunde* 17, pp. 437–442. Ed. Heinrich Beck et al. Berlin: de Gruyter.

―――― 2011. Óðinn, Valhǫll and the Einherjar: eschatological myth and ideology in the late Viking period. *Ideology and Power in the*

Viking and Middle Ages: Scandinavia, Iceland, Ireland, Orkney, and the Faeroes (The Northern World 52), pp. 297–328. Ed. Gro Steinsland et al. Leiden: Brill.

——2016. Den sista striden och den framtida freden. *Krig och fred i vendel- och vikingatida traditioner* (Stockholm Studies in Comparative Religion 37). Eds. Håkan Rydving & Stefan Olsson. Stockholm: Stockholm University Press.

Humphrey, Caroline & Laidlaw, James. 1994. *The Archetypal Actions of Ritual: A Theory of Ritual Illustrated by the Jain Rite of Worship* (Oxford Studies in Social and Cultural Anthropology). Oxford: Clarendon Press.

Hyenstrand, Åke. 1974. *Centralbygd - randbygd: strukturella, ekonomiska och administrativa huvudlinjer i mellansvensk yngre järnålder* (Studies in North-European archaeology 5). Stockholm.

Höckert, Robert. 1926. *Vǫluspá och vanakulten*. 1. Uppsala: Almqvist & Wiksell.

Inger, Göran. 1999. Kanonisk och inhemsk rätt under biskop Brynolf Algotssons tid. *Kyrkohistorisk årsskrift* 99, pp. 9–16. Uppsala: Svenska kyrkohistoriska föreningen.

Íslensk orðabók. Ed. Árni Böðvarsson. Reykjavík (1962) 1992: Mál og menning.

Jakob Benediktsson. 1969. *Landnámabók: Some Remarks on its Value as a Historical Source. Saga-Book* 18, pp. 275–292. London: Viking Club.

Janson, Henrik. 1998. *Templum nobilissimum: Adam av Bremen, Uppsalatemplet och konfliktlinjerna i Europa kring år 1075* (Avhandlingar från Historiska institutionen i Göteborg). Göteborg: Historiska institutionen, Göteborgs universitet.

Johansen, Paul. 1950. Der altnordische Name Ösels als verfassungsgeschichtliches Problem. *Festschrift Karl Haff zum siebzigsten Geburtstag dargebracht*, pp. 95–110. Eds. Karl Haff, Kurt Bussmann & Nikolaus Grass. Innsbruck: Wagner.

Jón Skaptason. 1983. Material for an Edition and Translation of the Poems of Sigvat Thortharson, Skald (Ph.D. dissertation, State

University of New York at Stony Brook). Ann Arbor, MI: University Microfilms.

Jón Viðar Sigurðsson. 1999. *Chieftains and Power in the Icelandic Commonwealth* (The Viking Collection 12). Transl. Jean Lundskær-Nielsen. Odense: Odense University Press.

———2008. *Det norrøne samfunnet: vikingen, kongen, erkebiskopen og bonden.* Oslo: Pax.

———2010. *Den vennlige vikingen: vennskapets makt i Norge og på Island ca. 900–1300.* Oslo: Pax forlag.

———2011. Skattlandet Island: fra høvdingmakt til kongemakt. *Nordens plass i middelalderens nye Europa: samfunnsomdanning, sentralmakt og periferier: rapporter til det 27. nordiske historikermøte, Tromsø 11.–14. august 2011* (Speculum Boreale 16), pp. 89–104. Ed. Lars Ivar Hansen et al. Stamsund: Orkana akademisk.

Jägerskiöld, Stig. 1966. Landskapslagarna. *Den svenska historien.* 1, Forntid, vikingatid och tidig medeltid till 1319, pp. 256–260. Ed. Jan Cornell et al. Stockholm: Bonnier.

Jørgensen, Bent. 1994. *Stednavneordbog* (Gyldendals små røde ordbøger). København: Gyldendal.

Kala, Tiina. 2009. Rural society and religious innovation: acceptance and rejection of Catholicism among the native inhabitants of medieval Livonia. *The Clash of Cultures on the Medieval Baltic Frontier*, pp. 169–190. Ed. Alan V. Murray. Farnham: Ashgate.

Kaliff, Anders & Olof Sundqvist. 2004. *Oden och Mithraskulten: religiös akulturation under romersk järnålder och folkvandringstid* (Occasional Papers in Archaeology 35). Uppsala: Institutionen för arkeologi och antik historia.

Kallerskog, Linnéa & Franzén, Ådel V. 2012. *Junebäcken – ett vattendrag med skiftande öden.* Arkeologisk utredning etapp 1 inför planerad utbyggnad av VA-ledningar i Junegatan och Friaredalen, Jönköpingsstad, Jönköpings län (Arkeologisk rapport 2012: 37). Jönköping: Jönköpings läns museum.

Kershaw, Paul. 2000. The Alfred-Guthrum treaty: Scripting accommodation and interaction in Viking-Age England. *Cultures in*

Contact: Scandinavian Settlement in England in the Ninth and Tenth Centuries (Studies in the Early Middle Ages 2), pp. 43–64. Eds. Dawn M. Hadley & Richards, Julian D. Turnhout: Brepols.

——— 2011. *Peaceful Kings: Peace, Power, and the Early Medieval Political Imagination.* Oxford: Oxford University Press.

Kiernan, Kevin S. 1981. *Beowulf and the Beowulf Manuscript.* New Brunswick: Rutgers University Press.

af Klintberg, Bengt. 1988 (1965). *Svenska trollformler.* Stockholm: Wahlström & Widstrand.

Kommentar zu den Liedern der Edda, Bd 2, Götterlieder (Skírnismál, Hárbarðslióð, Hymiskviða, Lokasenna, Þrymskviða). Ed. Klaus von See. Heidelberg 1997: Winter.

Korhonen, Arvi. 1923. *Vakkalaitos: yhteiskuntahistoriallinen tutkimus* (Historiallisia tutkimuksia 6). Helsinki: Suomen historiallinen seura.

Kosto, Adam J. 2012. *Hostages in the Middle Ages.* Oxford: Oxford University Press.

Krag, Claus. 1995. *Aschehougs norgeshistorie.* 2, Vikingtid og rikssamling: 800–1130. Ed. Knut Helle et al. Oslo: Aschehoug.

Kuhn, Hans. (1927) 1968. *Edda: die Lieder des Codex regius nebst verwandten Denkmälern.* 2, Kurzes Wörterbuch. Ed. Gustav Neckel. Heidelberg 1968: Carl Winter Universitätsverlag.

Kuusela, Tommy. 2017. *"Hallen var lyst i helig frid": Krig och fred mellan gudar och jättar i en fornnordisk hallmiljö.* Stockholms universitet: Institutionen för etnologi, religionshistoria och genusvetenskap.

Larsson, Inger. 2010. The role of the Swedish lawman in the spread of lay literacy. *Along the Oral-Written Continuum: Types of Texts, Relations and their Implications* (Utrecht Studies in Medieval Literacy 20), pp. 411–427. Eds. Slavica Rankovic, Leidulf Melve & Else Mundal. Turnhout: Brepols.

Larsson, Lars-Olof. (1974) 1975. *Historia om Småland.* Växjö: Diploma.

—— (1997) 2003a. *Kalmarunionens tid: från drottning Margareta till Kristian II.* Stockholm: Prisma.

—— 2003b. *Gustav Vasa: landsfader eller tyrann?* Stockholm: Prisma.

Larsson, Mats G. 1987. 2000. *Götarnas riken: upptäcktsfärder till Sveriges enande.* Stockholm: Atlantis.

—— 2008. *Tre gälder i England: i vikingarnas kölvatten över Nordsjön.* Stockholm: Atlantis.

Lassen, Annette. 2010. Saxo og Snorri som mytografer: hedenskaben i Gesta Danorum og Heimskringla. *Saxo og Snorre,* pp. 209–230. Ed. Jon Gunnar Jørgensen et al. København: Museum Tusculanums Forlag.

Lauring, Palle. 1962. *Unionskrigene* (Författarens Danmarkshistorie 5). København: Det Schønbergske forlag.

—— 1963. *Fejder og reformation: (1513–1536).* København: Schønberg.

Lavelle, Ryan. 2000. Peacemaking in Anglo-Saxon England. *Peace and Negotiation: Strategies for Coexistence in the Middle Ages and Renaissance* (Arizona Studies in the Middle Ages and the Renaissance 4), pp. 39–55. Ed. Diane Wolfthal. Turnhout: Brepols.

—— 2006. The use and abuse of hostages in later Anglo-Saxon England. *Early Medieval Europe* 14, pp. 269–296. Oxford: Blackwell.

—— 2007. *Royal Estates in Anglo-Saxon Wessex: Land, Politics and Family Strategies* (BAR British Series 439). Oxford: Archaeopress.

Lawson, Michael K. 2004. *Cnut: England's Viking King.* Stroud: Tempus.

Lexicon poeticum antiquae linguae septentrionalis. Eds. Finnur Jónsson & Sveinbjörn Egilsson. København 1966: Atlas Bogtryk.

Liedgren, Jan. 1965. Lejde. Sverige. *Kulturhistorisk leksikon for nordisk middelalder,* p. 469. Ed. Finn Hødnebo et al. Oslo: Gyldendal.

Liestøl, Aslak. 1964. Runer frå Bryggen. *Viking: tidsskrift for norrøn arkeologi* 27, pp. 5–53. Oslo: Norsk arkeologisk selskap.

Lindkvist, Thomas. 1988. *Plundring, skatter och den feodala statens framväxt: organisatoriska tendenser i Sverige under övergången från vikingatid till tidig medeltid* (Opuscula historica Upsaliensia 1). Uppsala: Uppsala universitet.

——— 2008. The emergence of Sweden. *The Viking World* (The Routledge Worlds), pp. 668–674. Eds. Stefan Brink & Neil Price. Abingdon: Routledge.

——— 2013. Chapter 3: Västergötland as a Community and the making of a Provinical Law. *Legislation and State Formation: Norway and its Neighbours in the Middle Ages* ("Norgesveldet", occasional papers 4), pp. 55–65. Ed. Steinar Imsen. Oslo: Akademika.

Lindkvist, Thomas & Ågren, Kurt. (1985) 1997. *Sveriges medeltid*. Solna: Almqvist & Wiksell.

Lindqvist, Sune. 1936. *Uppsala högar och Ottarshögen* (Kungl. Vitterhets-, historie- och antikvitetsakademien). Stockholm: Wahlström & Widstrand.

Line, Philip. 2009. Sweden's conquest of Finland: A clash of cultures? *The Clash of Cultures on the Medieval Baltic Frontier*, pp. 73–99. Ed. Alan V. Murray. Farnham: Ashgate.

Lundgreen, Michael. 1995. Friedensschluss. *Reallexikon der germanischen Altertumskunde* 9, pp. 603–610. Ed. Heinrich Beck *et al.* Berlin: de Gruyter.

Lutteroth, Ascan. 1922. *Der Geisel im Rechtsleben: ein Beitrag zur allgemeinen Rechtsgeschichte und dem geltenden Völkerrecht* (Abhandlungen aus dem Staats- und Verwaltungsrecht mit Einschluß des Kolonialrechts und des Völkerrechts 36). Breslau: M. & H. Marcus.

Lynch, Joseph H. 1986. *Godparents and Kinship in Early Medieval Europe*. Princeton: Princeton University Press.

——— 1998. *Christianizing Kinship: Ritual Sponsorship in Anglo-Saxon England*. Ithaca, NY: Cornell University Press.

Lönnroth, Erik. (1934) 1969. *Sverige och Kalmarunionen 1397–1457* (Studia historica Gothoburgensia 10). Göteborg: Akademiförlaget.

———1985. Västergötlands tidiga historia. *Västergötlands äldre historia: fakta och hypoteser: 12 inlägg i en aktuell debatt*, pp. 13–24. Eds. Göran Behre & Erik Wegraeus. Vänersborg: Stiftelsen Älvsborgs länsmuseum.

MacKillop, James. 1998. *Dictionary of Celtic Mythology*. Oxford: Oxford University Press.

Marold, Edith. 2012. Þjóðólfr ór Hvini. *Poetry from the King's Sagas* (Skaldic Poetry of the Scandinavian Middle Ages 1) 1: 1, pp. 3–66. Ed. Diana Whaley. Turnhout: Brepols.

Mathiesen, Ralph Whitney. 1993. *Roman Aristocrats in Barbarian Gaul: Strategies for Survival in an Age of Transition*. Austin, TX: University of Texas Press.

Matthews, John. 1989. Hostages, philosophers, pilgrims, and the diffusion of ideas in the late Roman Mediterranean and Near East. *Tradition and Innovation in Late Antiquity* (Wisconsin Studies in Classics), pp. 29–49. Eds. Frank M. Clover & Stephen R. Humphreys. Madison, WI: University of Wisconsin Press.

Mauss, Marcel. (1950) 2002. *The Gift: The Form and Reason for Exchange in Archaic Societies*. London: Routledge.

McCorduck, Pamela. (1979) 2004. *Machines Who Think: A Personal Inquiry Into the History and Prospects of Artificial Intelligence*. Natick, MA: AK Peters.

McKinnell, John. 2008. Völuspá and the feast of Easter. *Alvíssmál: Forschungen zur mittelalterlichen Kultur Skandinaviens* 12, pp. 3–28. Berlin: Verlag für Wissenschaft und Bildung.

Medieval Ireland: An Encyclopedia. Ed. Seán Duffy et al. New York 2005: Routledge.

Meulengracht Sørensen, Preben. 1991. Om eddadigtenes alder. *Nordisk Hedendom: et symposium*, pp. 217–228. Ed. Gro Steinsland. Odense: Odense Universitetsforlag.

———1992. Fra mundtlig digtning til litteratur. *Från vikingar till korsfarare: Norden och Europa 800–1200*, pp. 166–171. Ed. Else Roesdahl. Stockholm: Föreningen Norden.

——— 1993. *Fortælling og ære: studier i islændingesagaerne*. Århus: Aarhus Universitetsforlag

Meyer, Poul. 1960. Gisslan. Danmark. *Kulturhistorisk leksikon for nordisk middelalder* 5, p. 331. Ed. Finn Hødnebø et al. Oslo: Gyldendal.

Miller, William Ian. 1990. *Bloodtaking and Peacemaking: Feud, Law, and Society in Saga Iceland*. Chicago: University of Chicago Press.

Mortensen, Lars Boje. 2010. Litterær teknik og sprogets repræsentative effekt. *Saxo og Snorre*, pp. 113–129. Eds. Jon Gunnar Jørgensen, Karsten Friis-Jensen & Else Mundal.

Müller, Peter Erasmus. 1823. *Critisk undersögelse af Danmarks og Norges sagnhistorie eller om trowærdigheden af Saxos og Snorros kilder*. Kiöbenhavn: Den gyldendalske boghandel.

Mundal, Else. 1994. Kvinner som vitne i norske og islandske lover i mellomalderen. *Sagnaþing helgað Jónasi Kristjánssyni sjötugum 10. apríl 1994*, pp. 593–602. Ed. Jónas Kristjánsson et al. Reykjavík: Hið íslenska bókmenntafélag.

——— 2013. Edda og skaldedikting. *Handbok i norrøn filologi* (Skriftserie, Landslaget for norskundervising 157), pp. 356–416. Ed. O. E. Haugen. Bergen: Fagbokforlaget.

Naumann, Hans-Peter. 2005. Starkaðr. *Reallexikon der germanischen Altertumskunde* 29, pp. 538–541. Ed. Heinrich Beck et al. Berlin: de Gruyter.

Nerman, Birger. 1942. *Sveriges första storhetstid*. Stockholm: Skoglunds bokförlag.

Ney, Agneta. 2005. *Drottningar och sköldmör: Gränsöverskridande kvinnor i medeltida myt och verklighet ca 400–1400*. Hedemora: Gidlund.

——— 2012. Välkomstmotivet på gotländska bildstenar i jämförelse med litterära källor från vikingatid och medeltid. *Gotlands bildstenar: järnålderns gåtfulla budbärare*, pp. 73–82. Ed. Maria Herlin Karnell. Visby: Gotlands museum.

Nielsen, Niels Åge. 1976. Myten om krigen og fredsslutningen mellem aserne og vanerne. *Festskrift tillägnad Gösta Holm på 60-årsdagen den 8 juli 1976*, pp. 310–315. Ed. Lars Svensson. Lund: Studentlitteratur.

Nilsson, Bertil. 1998. *Sveriges kyrkohistoria*. 1, Missionstid och tidig medeltid. Ed. Lennart Tegborg et al. Stockholm: Verbum i samarbete med Svenska kyrkans forskningsråd

Nordberg, Andreas. 2003. *Krigarna i Odins sal: dödsföreställningar och krigarkult i fornnordisk religion*. Stockholm: Stockholms universitet.

Nordisk familjebok [Electronic resource]: *konversationslexikon och realencyklopedi* 1909. Uggleupplagan. Stockholm: Nordisk familjeboks förlag.

Nyström, Per. 1974. *Historieskrivningens dilemma och andra studier* (En PAN-bok). Ed. Tomas Forser. Stockholm: PAN/Norstedt.

Näsström, Britt-Mari. 1995. *Freyja: The Great Goddess of the North* (Lund Studies in History of Religions 5). Stockholm: Almqvist & Wiksell International.

——— 2001. *Blot: tro og offer i det førkristne Norden*. Oslo: Pax.

——— 2009. *De nordiska gudinnorna: nytolkningar av den förkristna mytologin*. Falun: Scandbook.

The Oxford Dictionary of the Classical World. Ed. John Roberts. Oxford 2005: Oxford University Press.

The Oxford English Dictionary 1–20. Eds. J. A. Simpson & E. S. C. Weiner. Oxford 1989: Clarendon Press.

Oehrl, Sigmund. 2017. Documenting and Interpreting the Picture Stones of Gotland. *Current Swedish Archaeology* (vol. 25), pp. 87–122. Eds. Fredrik Fahlander & Anders Högberg. Lund: Nordic Academic Press.

von Olberg, Gabriele. 1998. Geisel. *Reallexikon der germanischen Altertumskunde* 10, pp. 573–576. Ed. Heinrich Beck et al. Berlin: de Gruyter.

Olivecrona, Karl. 1942. *Döma till konung: en rättshistorisk undersökning* (Skrifter utgivna av Juridiska fakulteten i Lund 1). Lund: Gleerup.

Olrik, Axel. 1894. Bråvallakvadets kæmperække. *Arkiv for nordisk filologi* 10, pp. 223–287. Lund: C.W.K. Gleerups förlag.

——— 1902. Om Ragnarok. *Årbøger for nordisk oldkyndighed og historie* 1902, pp. 157–291. København: Det Kongelige Nordiske Oldskriftselskab.

Olsson, Stefan. 2012. Gisslan i vikingatida och tidigmedeltida traditioner. *Chaos: skandinavisk tidsskrift for religionshistoriske studier* 58, pp. 59–82. København: Museum Tusculanum.

——— 2016. Fredsöverenskommelser genom riter i konfrontationsområden: exempel från vikingatidens England och Island. *Krig och fred i vendel- och vikingatida traditioner* (Stockholm Studies in Comparative Religion 37), pp. 266–275. Eds. Håkan Rydving & Stefan Olsson. Stockholm: Stockholm University Press.

——— 2018. Religion and law. *Religion, Law and Justice*, pp. 159–170. Eds. Håkan Rydving and Stefan Olsson. Novus forlag.

O'Rahilly, Thomas F. 1946. *Early Irish History and Mythology*. Dublin: Dublin Institute for Advanced Studies.

Orri Vésteinsson, 1998–2001. Pattern of settlement in Iceland: A study in prehistory. *Saga-Book* 25, pp. 1–29. London: Viking Club.

Oxford Advanced Learner's Dictionary of Current English. A.S. Hornby; Ed. Joanna Turnbull *et al*. Oxford 2010: Oxford University Press.

Palm, Rune. 2004. *Vikingarnas språk: 750–1100*. Stockholm: Norstedt.

Pelteret, David A. E. 2005. *The Ealdorman of Alfred's reign*. (Revised version of a paper presented at the First Session of the International Medieval Congress, University of Leeds, on 12 July 2004) Prospography of Anglo-Saxon England.

Peterson, Lena. 2007. *Nordiskt runnamnslexikon*. Uppsala: Institutet för språk och folkminnen.

Phillipson, Coleman. 1911. *The International Law and Custom of Ancient Greece and Rome*. London: Macmillan.

Pound, Roscoe. 1959. *Jurisprudence*. Vol. 3, Part 4, The Scope and Subject of Law. Part 5, Sources, Forms, Modes of Growth. St. Paul, MN: West Publishing Co.

Rasmusson, Nils L. 1966. Mark. Medeltida. *Kulturhistoriskt lexikon för nordisk medeltid*, pp. 423–425. Ed. Johan Granlund *et al.* Malmö: Allhems förlag.

Raudvere, Catharina. 2003. *Kunskap och insikt i norrön tradition: mytologi, ritualer och trolldomsanklagelser* (Vägar till Midgård 3). Lund: Nordic Academic Press.

Reitzenstein, Richard. 1924. Weltuntergangsvorstellungen: eine Studie zur vergleichenden Religionsgeschichte. *Kyrkohistorisk årsskrift* 24, pp. 129–212. Uppsala: Svenska kyrkohistoriska föreningen.

Reallexikon der germanischen Altertumskunde 1–35 [2nd ed.]. Ed. Heinrich Beck et al. Berlin 1968/1973–2007: Walter de Gruyter.

Ritual, Performatives, and Political Order in Northern Europe, c. 650–1350 (Ritus et Artes 7). Ed. Wojtek Jezierski *et al.* Turnhout 2015: Brepols.

Rosén, Jerker. 1939. *Striden mellan Birger Magnusson och hans bröder. Studier i nordisk politisk historia 1302–1319*. Lund: Gleerup.

—— 1966. Handelsförbindelser och näringsliv. *Den svenska historien*. 1, Forntid, vikingatid och tidig medeltid till 1319, pp. 300–307. Ed. Jan Cornell *et al.* Stockholm: Bonnier.

Rydving, Håkan. 1990. Ortnamn som religionshistoriskt källmaterial. *Saga och sed*, pp. 167–177. Uppsala: Kungl. Gustav Adolfs akademien.

—— 1993. *The End of Drum-Time: Religious Change among the Lule Saami, 1670s–1740s* (Acta Universitatis Upsalensis. Historia religionum 12). Stockholm: Almqvist & Wiksell International.

Røthe, Gunnhild. 2010. *I Odins tid: norrøn religion i fornaldersagaene*. Hafrsfjord: Saga bok.

Sahlgren, Jöran. 1924. *Eddica et scaldica* 2: 1. Lund: Gleerup.

Salin, Bernhard. 1903. Heimskringlas tradition om asarnes invandring. *Studier tillägnade Oscar Montelius 19 9/9 03*, pp. 133–141. Eds. Bernhard Salin, Oscar Almgren & Sune Ambrosiani. Stockholm: Norstedt.

Sanmark, Alexandra. 2014. Women at the Thing. *Kvinner i vikingtid*, pp. 89–106. Eds. Nancy L. Coleman & Nanna Løkka. Oslo: Scandinavian Academic Press.

Sanmark, Alexandra & Sarah Semple. 2008. Places of assembly: New discoveries in Sweden and England. *Fornvännen* 103, pp. 245–259. Stockholm: Kungl. Vitterhets historie och antikvitetsakademien.

Svenska akademiens ordbok (Swedish Academy Dictionary). Göteborg: OSA-projektet. http://g3.spraakdata.gu.se/saob/ (2014-03-03).

Sawyer, Birgit and Sawyer, Peter. 1993. *Medieval Scandinavia: From Conversion to Reformation circa 800–1500* (The Nordic Series 17). Minneapolis, MN: University of Minnesota Press.

Saxo og Snorre. Eds. Jon Gunnar Jørgensen, Karsten Friis-Jensen & Else Mundal. København 2010: Museum Tusculanum Forlag.

Schier, Kurt. 1981. Zur Mythologie der Snorra Edda: einige Quellenprobleme. *Speculum Norroenum: Norse Studies in Memory of Gabriel Turville-Petre*, pp. 405–420. Ed. Ursula Dronke. Odense: Odense University Press.

Schjødt, Jens Peter. 1991. Relationen mellem aser og vaner og dens ideologiske implikationer. *Nordisk hedendom: et symposium*, pp. 303–319. Ed. Gro Steinsland et al. Odense: Odense universitetsforlag.

——— 1999. *Det førkristne Norden: religion og mytologi*. København: Spektrum.

——— 2008. *Initiation Between Two Worlds: Structure and Symbolism in Pre-Christian Scandinavian Religion* (The Viking Collection 17). Odense: University Press of Southern Denmark.

Schweinfurth, Georg August. 1874. *The Heart of Africa: Three Years' Travels and Adventures in the Unexplored Regions of Central Africa from 1868 to 1871* 1. London: Sampson Low.

von See, Klaus. 1964. *Altnordische Rechtswörter: philologische Studien zur Rechtsauffassung und Rechtsgesinnung der Germanen* (Hermaea N.F. 16). Tübingen: Niemeyer.

Simek, Rudolf. (1984) 1993. *Dictionary of Northern Mythology*. Cambridge: Brewer.

―――2010. The Vanir: An Obituary. *The Retrospective Methods Network Newsletter*, pp. 10–19. Ed. Frog et al. Helsinki: University of Helsiniki.

Sjöholm, Elsa. 1988. *Sveriges medeltidslagar: europeisk rättstradition i politisk omvandling* (Skrifter utgivna av Institutet för rättshistorisk forskning 41). Stockholm: Institutet för rättshistorisk forskning.

Skovgaard-Petersen, Inge. 1987. *Da tidernes Herre var nær: studier i Saxos historiesyn*. København: Den danske historiske forening.

Skyum-Nielsen, Niels. 1964. *Blodbadet i Stockholm og dets juridiske maskering* (Scandinavian University Books). København: Munksgaard.

Die Slawen in Deutschland: ein Handbuch. Ed. Joachim Herrmann. Berlin 1985: Akademie-Verlag.

Spiro, Melford. 1982. *Buddhism and Society: A Great Tradition and its Burmese Vicissitudes*. Berkeley: University of California Press.

Steenstrup, Johannes. (1882) 1972. *Normannerne* (Reprografisk genutgivet og forlagt af Selskapet for udgivelse af kilder til dansk historie). København: Rudolph Klein.

Steinsland, Gro. 1999. Voluspå og volven. *Voluspå*, pp. 31–38. Eds. Red. Gro Steinsland & Preben Meulengracht Sørensen. Oslo: Pax.

―――2000. *Den hellige kongen: om religion og herskermakt fra vikingtid til middelalder*. Oslo: Pax.

―――2005. *Norrøn religion: myter, riter, samfunn*. Oslo: Pax.

Steinsland, Gro & Meulengracht Sørensen, Preben. 1994. *Menneske og makter i vikingenes verden*. Oslo: Universitetsforlaget.

Ström, Folke. (1961) 1997. *Nordisk hedendom: tro och sed i förkristen tid*. Göteborg: Akad.-förl./Gumpert.

Stübe, Rudolf. 1924. Kvasir und der magische Gebrauch des Speichels. *Festschrift Eugen Mogk zum 70. Geburtstag 19. Juli 1924*, pp. 500–509. Ed. Eugen Mogk. Halle an der Saale: Niemeyer.

[Stylegar, Frans-Arne H.] Frans-Arne H. *Stylegars sider om arkeologi og historie*. http://arkeologi.blogspot.no (2015-10-12).

Sundqvist, Olof. 2002. *Freyr's Offspring: Rulers and Religion in Ancient Svea Society* (Acta Universitatis Upsaliensis. Historia religionum 21). Uppsala: Uppsala University Library.

———2005. Siðr. *Reallexikon der germanischen Altertumskunde 28*, pp. 249–260. Ed. Heinrich Beck et al. Berlin: de Gruyter.

———2007. *Kultledare i fornskandinavisk religion* (Occasional Papers in Archaeology 41). Uppsala: Institutionen för arkeologi och antik historia, Uppsala universitet.

———2012. Var sejdhjällen (fvn. *seidhjallr, hjallr*) en permanent konstruktion vid kultplatser och i kultbyggnader? *Fornvännen* 107, pp. 280–285. Stockholm: Kungl. Vitterhets historie och antikvitetsakademien.

———2015. Custodian of the sanctuary: protecting sacred space as a ritual strategy for gaining legitimacy and power in pre-Christian Scandinavia. *Ritual, Performatives, and Political Order in Northern Europe, c. 650–1350* (Ritus et Artes 7), pp. 113–135. Ed. Wojtek Jezierski et al. Turnhout: Brepols.

———2016. Vapen, våld och *vi*-platser: skändande av helgedomar som maktstrategi i det vikingatida Skandinavien. *Krig och fred i vendel- och vikingatida traditioner* (Stockholm Studies in Comparative Religion 37), pp. 167–195. Eds. Håkan Rydving & Stefan Olsson. Stockholm: Stockholm University Press. DOI: https://doi.org/10.16993/bay.

Sutrop, Urmas. 2004. Taarapita: the great god of the Oeselians. *Folklore* [Electronic resource] (Eesti Keele Instituut) 26, pp. 25–64. Tartu: Institute of the Estonian Language.

Sveinbjörn Rafnsson. 2001. *Sögugerð Landnámabókar: um íslenska sagnaritun á 12. og 13. öld* (Ritsafn Sagnfræðistofnunar 35). Reykjavik: Sagnfræðistofnun Háskóla Íslands.

Svenskt biografiskt lexikon. 1906. http://runeberg.org/sbh/b0488.html (2015-11-06).

Svenskt ortnamnslexikon. 2016. Utarbetat inom Språk- och folkminnesinstitutet och Institutionen för nordiska språk vid Uppsala universitet. Ed. Mats Wahlberg. Uppsala: Språk- och folkminnesinstitutet.

Söderwall, Knut Fredrik. 1884–1918. *Ordbok öfver svenska medeltidsspråket*. 1–3 (Samlingar utgivna av Svenska fornskriftsällskapet. 1, Svenska skrifter). Lund: Berlingska boktryckeri.

Tarvel, Enn. 1998. Die Gauinstitution in Estland am Anfang des 13. Jahrhunderts. *Culture Clash or Compromise?: The Europeanisation of the Baltic Sea Area 1100–1400 AD* (Acta Visbyensia 11), pp. 192–199. [Ed.] Nils Blomkvist. Visby: Centrum för Östersjöstudier, Högskolan på Gotland.

Tegengren, Gunilla. 2015. *Sverige och Nordlanden: förvaltning och nordlig expansion 1250–1550* (Kungl. Skytteanska samfundets handlingar 72). Göteborg: Göteborgs universitet.

Tiefenbach, Heinrich. 1995. Friede. *Reallexikon der germanischen Altertumskunde* 9, pp. 594–596. Ed. Heinrich Beck et al. Berlin: de Gruyter.

Turner, Victor W. 1969. *The Ritual Process: Structure and Anti-Structure*. London: Routledge & Kegan Paul.

Turville-Petre, E. O. Gabriel. 1964. *Myth and Religion of the North: The Religion of Ancient Scandinavia* (History of Religion). London: Weidenfeld and Nicolson.

Ulsig, Erik. 2011. *Danmark 900–1300: kongemakt og samfund*. Århus: Aarhus universitetsforlag.

Vikstrand, Per. 2001. *Gudarnas platser: förkristna sakrala ortnamn i Mälarlandskapen* (Acta Academiae Regiae Gustavi Adolphi 77. Studier till en svensk ortnamnsatlas 17). Uppsala: Kungl. Gustav Adolfs akademien för svensk folkkultur.

Vilkuna, Kuusta. 1960. Gisslalag. Finland. *Kulturhistorisk leksikon for nordisk middelalder* 5, pp. 327–329. Ed. Finn Hødnebø et al. Oslo: Gyldendal.

——— 1964. *Kihlakuntaja häävuode: tutkielmia suomalaisen yhteiskunnan järjestymisen vaiheilta*. Helsinki: Otava.

Vretemark, Maria. 2014. Fru Sigrids gård i Varnhem. *Medeltida storgårdar: 15 uppsatser om ett tvärvetenskapligt forskningsproblem* (Acta Academiae Regiae Gustavi Adolphi), pp. 131–143. Eds. Olof Karsvall & Kristofer Jupiter. Uppsala: Kungl. Gustav Adolfs akademien för svensk folkkultur.

de Vries, Jan. 1961. *Altnordisches etymologisches Wörterbuch*. Leiden: Brill.

———(1956–57) 1970. *Altgermanische Religionsgeschichte*. 1–2 (Grundriss der germanischen Philologie 12: 1–2). Berlin: de Gruyter.

———(1961) 1977. *Altnordisches etymologisches Wörterbuch*. Leiden: Brill.

Walker Cheryl L. 2005. *Hostages in Republican Rome*. Washington, DC: Center for Hellenic Studies. http://chs.harvard.edu/CHS/article/displays/5571 (2012-05-16).

Watson, Alan. 1993. *International Law in Archaic Rome: War and Religion*. Baltimore, MD: Johns Hopkins University Press.

Weiner, Anette. 1988. *The Trobrianders of Papua New Guinea*. New York: Holt, Rinehart and Winston.

Wikander, Stig. 1960. Från Bråvalla till Kurukshetra. *Arkiv för nordisk filologi* 75, pp. 183–193. Lund: C.W.K. Gleerups förlag.

Wiktorsson, Per-Axel. 2011. Inledning. *Äldre västgötalagen och dess bilagor: i Cod. Holm. B 59*, del I (Skara stiftshistoriska sällskaps skriftserie 60), pp. 11–38. Ed. Per-Axel Wiktorsson. [Skara]: Föreningen för Västgötalitteratur.

Williams, Ann. 2003. *Æthelred the Unready: The Ill-Counselled King*. London: Hambledon and London.

Yrwing, Hugo. 1964. Konungavalet i Strängnäs 1523. *Scandia: tidskrift för historisk forskning* 2, pp. 357–383. Stockholm: Bokförlaget Natur och kultur.

Österberg, Eva. 1989. Bönder och centralmakt i det tidigmoderna Sverige: konflikt – kompromiss – politisk kultur. *Scandia: tidskrift för historisk forskning* 55, pp. 73–96. Stockholm: Natur och kultur.

Östvold, Torbjörg. 1969. The war of the Æsir and the Vanir: a myth of the fall in Nordic religion. *Temenos: Studies in Comparative Religion Presented by Scholars in Denmark, Finland, Norway and Sweden* 5, pp. 169–202. Helsinki: Suomen uskontotieteellinen seura.

Index

A
Abram, Christopher, 13
Aðalheiður Gudmundsdóttir, 166
Adam of Bremen, 19, 78, 169, 263, 309
A Description of the Northern Peoples, 229, 244
Áed Allán, 238–239
Afgärþabyagilzli, 194
Agreement, 2–3, 6, 10–11, 25, 28, 31–33, 40, 46, 53, 55, 57, 60, 67, 70, 82–84, 86–87, 89, 104, 111–112, 115, 125–127, 131–133, 135–140, 143, 152–153, 170, 172, 174–176, 179–180, 196–197, 200, 203–204, 206–209, 236, 239–241, 282–283, 292, 295, 297–298, 303, 305–306, 324, 326, 328–329
Airgíalla, 236–245, 286
Airgíalla Charter Poem, 132, 237–243, 245
Alfred the Great, 29, 46, 83
Althoff, Gerd, 114
Anglo-Saxons, 29–31, 86–91, 101, 126, 158, 168, 181, 202, 205
Anglo-Saxon Chronicle, 19, 21, 82, 84, 88–92, 94, 111, 116
Annales Bertianni, 134

Ágrip, 135–137, 141, 148, 207, 232
Allen, Joel, 141–142, 172
Amali, 149
Amalaberga, 130
Andersson, Theodore, 108, 110, 138
Andersson, Thorsten, 17
Annales Vedastini, 129
The Annals of Fulda, 184
'Annals of Ryd', 139
Anttonen, Veikko, 37–38, 47, 292, 323
Apuolė, 131, 146, 148, 235, 245
Areas of communication, 97, 160, 172, 179, 182, 275, 305, 323–324
Areas of confrontation, 24–25, 27–29, 33–35, 46, 81, 95, 97–99, 101, 110, 112, 114, 131, 153, 162, 181–182, 241, 251, 269, 293, 322, 324, 326
Ármann Jakobsson, 167
Ariovistus, 163
Askøy, 158
Asplin, Anne, 108
Asser, 29, 31, 82, 84, 89, 91, 111, 117
Athelney, 84

Attila, 158, 161, 242
Aud the Deep-Minded, 160
Auður Magnusdóttir, 155–156

B

Bagge, Sverre, 27, 234, 282
Baker, Peter S., 145
Banquet, 28, 92, 99, 100, 160, 184
Batavi, 128, 164
Bell, Catherine, 30, 41–42, 44, 47
Beowulf, 19, 20, 78, 129, 161, 164
Bíoi Parállēloi, 130
Biography of Alfred, 84, 111
Blomkvist, Nils, 27, 228, 243
Blomkvist, Torsten, 26
Brenneyjar, 135–137, 139
Brevis Historia Regum Dacie, 32
Borgensgeisel, 1, 6, 176, 197
Bohuslän, 196, 296, 318
Bres, 71
Bructeri, 164
Brusi Sigurdsson, 152–153, 242, 237
Bull, Edvard, 107
Byrhtnoth, 158
Byzantine Empire, 150

C

Caesar, 26, 143–144, 163
Caithness, 175
Canute the Great, 93, 135, 151, 167, 197, 201–206, 233, 259–260, 263, 330
Canterbury, 201–202, 205, 263
Capratine, 131
Carolingian Empire, 1, 4, 6, 8, 20–22, 45, 81, 95–97, 145, 150–151
von Celse, Magnus, 193
Cimusclus, 144
Charlemagne, 20, 95–96, 111, 119, 150–151, 170
Charles-Edwards, Thomas, 239, 241
Charles the Fat, 129, 200–201
Charles the Simple, 113
Childebert, 173
Christian II of Denmark, 4, 10, 294–300, 306, 318–319, 322
Christianity, 8, 18–19, 22, 29, 71, 92, 100–108, 110, 144–145, 168, 258, 261, 303
Chronicon Regum Norvegiæ, 139
Chronicon Roskildense, 16
Clovis I, 173
Clunies Ross, Margaret, 64
Codex holmensis, 252–253
Conduct, 2, 4, 8, 43, 46, 91–92, 101, 113, 148, 157, 159, 162, 172, 183, 185–194, 221, 240, 242, 282, 288, 291, 293, 296, 298, 302, 318, 326
Conflicts, 1, 4, 12, 14, 15, 19–20, 25–26, 28–29, 33–34, 42, 46, 82, 89, 95, 125, 137, 154–155, 160, 164, 185, 199–200, 252, 263, 269, 273, 283, 300, 305, 326, 329
Country Law of Christopher, 295, 301

Cyneheard, 158
Cynewulf, 158

D

Dale-Gudbrand, 105, 107–109, 110, 116
Dalarna, 270, 293–294, 301–302, 313
Danes, 16, 19, 21, 29–31, 78, 82–83, 86–91, 93, 95–98, 101–102, 115, 147, 149–151, 168, 173, 180–181, 197, 201–202, 204–205, 226, 236, 295, 323
De Bello Gallica, 20, 143
Denmark, 10, 15–16, 20, 78, 81, 91, 97, 99–100, 105, 114–115, 135, 137, 139–140, 151, 179–180, 201, 203, 235–236, 260, 263, 270, 296, 300, 306, 312
Dillmann, François-Xavier, 60
Dovring, Folke, 192–195
Drobin, Ulf, 61
Duels, 34
Dumézil, Georges, 22, 60, 64, 65, 70, 73

E

East Anglia, 29, 31, 82–83, 86, 151, 202
Edel Bhretnach, 238–241, 245
Eddic Poems, 13–14, 55, 58, 66–67, 69, 72, 78, 182–183, 187–188, 194
Edictus Rothari, 132
Einar Helgason, 182
Elbern, Stephan, 15, 47, 172, 178

Elder Westrogothic law, 18, 23, 87, 133, 243, 251–258, 260–267, 270–273, 277, 279–293, 303–305, 322, 325
Elmevik, Lennart, 17, 183
Emma of Normandy, 167, 205
Encomium Emmæ Reginae, 167
England, 4, 29, 82, 85, 91, 93–94, 100, 114, 135, 199, 140, 143, 146, 151, 167–168, 199–203, 205–206, 263, 321, 324, 326
Enright, Michael, 160
Eric Chronicle, 229–230, 244
Erik the Red, 34
Erfidrápa Óláfs Helga, 144
Envoys, 12, 29, 95, 102, 111, 39
Eriksgata, 18, 20, 134, 177–178, 190–191, 193, 251, 254, 265, 268–273, 276, 279–280, 283, 285, 291–292, 294–295, 299, 301–306, 312, 322, 325, 329
Ermold the Black, 98
Eskil Lagman, 252, 256, 266
Eucherius, 129

F

Female hostages, 4, 128–129, 159, 208, 242, 322
Fenrir, 173
Fetiales, 133
Finland, 4, 225, 229–231, 242, 244, 275, 297, 322, 326
Five Kindred, 239–240
Fjalar and Galar, 59, 61
Flokkr, 101, 111, 186
foedus aequum, 133

foedus deditio, 133
foedus iniquum, 133
Folke lagman, 266
fornaldarsögur, 149
Fostering, 7, 35, 127–128, 151, 154–155
Foster children, 18, 23, 150, 154–155
fóstrlaun, 127
Frankish Royal annals, 20
Franks, 4, 6, 96–97, 99, 113, 115, 174, 185, 321
Freyja, 56, 61–65, 67–68, 112
Freyr (Frø), 55, 62–63, 65–66, 69, 72, 76, 169
friðr, 136, 138, 180–184, 189, 189, 209, 323
Friesland, 96, 99, 129, 134, 170, 184
Fróða friðbygg, 182
Frog, 67
Frostatings law, 18
friðbann, 182
friðland, 182
friðgerð, 183
friðstaðr, 184
frið glepsk, 183

G

Gabinius (Suebian ruler), 173
Gaiseric, 173–174
Gallic War, 20, 23, 143, 163
Gardeła, Leszek, 169
Geats, 18–19, 134, 235, 242, 251–252, 254, 259–260, 262, 265, 269–270, 280, 282–293, 305, 317, 325

Germania, 20
Germans, 5, 113, 149, 236
gengiærþ, 274–275, 305
van Gennep, Arnold, 102
Gesta Hammaburgensis, 19, 169
Gesta Danorum, 16, 20, 140, 169, 226–229, 236, 243, 270, 322
Getica, 149, 173, 327
gilzla, 188, 190–193, 195, 209
Ginzburg, Carlo, 22
gisslalag, 229–231, 326
Grágás, 18–19, 127, 162, 189–190
Great Heathen Army, 82–88, 90, 199, 242
Great men, 27, 43, 86, 96, 103, 113, 134–135, 137–140, 143, 156, 158, 164, 200, 234, 258, 263–264, 266, 273, 278, 282, 292, 206, 304
grið, 74, 109, 121, 136, 180–182, 185–190, 194, 202, 205–206, 209
griðbítr, 187, 189
griðamark, 62
griðastaðr, 188
griðkona, 185, 187
griðmaðr, 185
grutha, 188, 190–193, 209, 242
Godafrid, 184–185
godfather, 30, 92
Godfred, 95–97, 170–171
godparent, 92
Gotland, 20, 23, 27, 87, 164–166, 176, 329

Gribthorpe, 188
grip, 188, 194, 205
Gudrøðr (ruler), 176
Gulaþing law, 18
Gullveig, 56–57, 69
Gummi, 226–228, 243
Gundersen, Dag, 175
Gunnhild, 167–168
Gunnlöð, 59
Gustav Vasa, 10, 293–298, 301, 306
Guthrum, 29–32, 46, 84–85, 87–89, 93, 112, 126, 145, 242, 329
Göta Älv (river), 101–102, 115, 134, 137, 139, 140
Götreks saga, 148

H

Hálfs saga ok Hálfsrekka, 61
Halli stirði, 101, 104, 115
Hamburg-Bremen (archdiocese), 263
Harald Hardrada, 101–102, 115, 134, 185
Harald Wartooth, 227
Harrison, Dick, 255, 267–268, 271, 273, 284–285
Harzburg, 179
Hasselberg, Gösta, 193–195
Háttatal, 182
Hauksbók, 13, 40, 56
heilagr, 37–40, 46–47
Heimskringla, 15, 55, 62–64, 76, 101–102, 105, 107–109, 111–112, 116, 138, 151, 153, 189, 232, 313, 327

Hellberg, Lars, 17
Hemming Gadh, 296–297
Henry of Schwerin, 180
Hermanfrid, 130
Heptarchy, 82, 87, 104, 289
Hermanson, Lars, 7
Herthjóf, 158, 242
Hild, 166
Hiltgund, 158, 161
Hirdskraa, 26, 40, 92, 312
Histories, 128
Hogenskild, Bielke, 254, 312
Holmbäck, Åke, 178, 191, 195
Honko, Lauri, 35–36, 46
Horic, 134
Hostages, 1–12, 14–32, 35–36, 44–47, 55, 57, 62, 65–73, 81–98, 100–101, 104–106, 109–111, 113–116, 125–137, 139, 141–164, 166–181, 184–198, 200–204, 206–210, 225–226, 228–231, 233–245, 251, 253–254, 258, 275, 283–288, 290–299, 301–303, 305–306, 321–330
Householder, 25, 102, 104–106, 110, 115, 122, 138–139, 156, 171, 175, 253–254, 264, 266, 273, 277, 282, 300, 302
Hultgård, Anders, 14, 271–272, 304
Hunde, 153, 171
Hundtorp (farm), 105, 107
husabyar, 274–276
Håkon IV Håkonsson, 155

I

Icelandic sagas, 9, 15, 39, 79
Íslendingabók, 14–15, 29,
    32–34, 46, 112, 126, 155, 329

J

Jón Viðar Sigurðsson, 7, 156
Junebäcken, 192, 251, 279,
    283–286, 288, 291, 303
Jönköping, 192, 251, 279,
    284, 303

K

Kalmar Union, 294–295,
    300, 306
Karleby, 251, 254, 260,
    290–292, 303, 327
Kent, 82, 86, 91, 201–202
Kershaw, Paul, 9, 129, 161, 182
Kjartan Olafsson, 155
Knytlinge saga, 167
konungasǫgur, 15
Kosto, Adam J., 6, 8–11, 45,
    87, 125, 127–130, 132, 143,
    146, 158–159, 174, 180,
    195, 201, 206, 327–328
Krag, Claus, 135
Kvasir, 55, 58–62, 65, 68

L

Lagertha, 169
Laidlaw, James, 42, 44, 47
Lake Mälaren, 17, 148, 169,
    225, 228
Landnámabók, 14, 26, 29,
    32–34, 39, 46, 112
Lars Djäkn, 23, 252–253
Larsson, Inger, 258
Larsson, Lars-Olof, 296, 300
Lassen, Annette, 68
Latins, 130–131
Lavelle, Ryan, 6, 45, 88–90,
    93–94, 131, 142–143, 151,
    158–159, 199–200, 206,
    292, 317, 324
Laxdœla saga, 155, 160, 163
Legendary sagas, 15–16, 149
Lex Frisionum, 174, 197
Lex Salica, 197
Lindkvist, Thomas, 27, 254,
    256–257, 266, 277–278,
    303–304, 307
Lindsey, 82–83, 203, 206
Liutward, 183–185
Livius Postumius, 130
Ljufvina, 163
London, 83, 91–92, 167,
    201–202, 204
Lothar, 99, 129
Louis the Pious, 114–115, 134
Lucius Tarquinius Superbus, 172
Lutteroth, Ascan, 6–7
Loyalty, 7, 140, 145, 156–159,
    171, 175, 209, 242, 266,
    273, 276, 296
Lynch, Joseph H., 93, 99, 144

M

Mada, 60
Mag Tured, 71
Magnus Erikssons landslag, 18,
    191, 265, 269
Magnus the Good, 135, 207
Magnus lagabøters landslov,
    174–175, 179, 195

Marcel Mauss, 88, 113, 131, 149, 203
Marcian (Emperor), 149
Marriage, 2, 35–36, 66, 113, 128–130, 135, 160, 162, 167, 173–174, 205, 266, 268, 273, 276, 280
McKinnell, John, 56
Mead of Poetry, 58, 72
Melkorka, 162
Mercia, 82–84, 86–87, 115, 201–202
Messengers, 64, 96, 134, 170, 172–173, 285–286
Meulengracht Sørensen, Preben, 13, 23–24,
Miller, Ian, 7, 154–155
Morkinskinna, 138–139
Motz, Lotte, 67
Mundal, Else, 162
Meyer, Poul, 176
Måns Nilsson Svinhufvud, 294
Mälardalen, 243

N

Nasatyas, 60
Negotiations, 3, 10, 12, 38, 40, 43, 45–46, 60, 81, 86, 88, 90–91, 94–95, 97, 101, 103–105, 110–111, 115–116, 126–128, 132–133, 135–136, 145–147, 152–153, 162, 167, 170, 172–173, 175–176, 178–185, 188–189, 209–210, 236, 239, 242–243, 275–276, 280, 285, 288, 296, 302, 306, 318–319, 321–322, 324, 329

Niall, Noígíallach, 71, 144, 237
Njǫrðr, 55, 62–63, 65–69, 72, 76, 79
Nonae Caprotinae, 130
Northumberland, 82
Norway, 18, 27, 33, 39, 56, 81, 91, 105, 108, 112, 115, 135, 139–140, 153, 158, 162, 169, 171, 176, 179, 189, 209, 232, 234, 263, 290, 301, 318
Novgorod, 135, 148, 229, 234, 236
Nydala monastery, 299
Nyström, Per, 255
Näsström, Britt-Mari, 168–169

O

Oath, 9, 23, 28–32, 35, 39–40, 46, 82–84, 86, 88–90, 93, 100–102, 104–105, 111, 113, 115, 118, 132, 139–140, 143–145, 152, 167, 170, 203, 207, 241–242, 245
Odin, 7, 21, 57, 59, 61, 64–65, 68, 70–72, 78–79, 158, 166
Ogier the Dane, 150–151
Olaf Haraldsson (St Olaf), 105, 108–109, 112, 116, 152, 159, 176, 182, 189, 232, 242, 325
Olaf Tryggvason, 7, 91, 99, 115, 146, 148, 155, 171, 201, 207, 242, 289
Óláfr Þórðarson hvítaskald, 139
Olaus Magnus, 229, 244
von Olberg, Gabrielle, 6, 132
Old Uppsala, 259–260

Olof Skötkonung, 112, 189, 263, 258–259, 310
Orkney islands, 43, 148, 152–153, 171, 175, 242
Orkneyinga þáttr, 175
Orkneyinga saga, 43, 47, 151–153, 171, 175
Óttar the Black, 153

P
Paulinius of Pela, 129, 132
Peace processes, 2–4, 6, 8–9, 12, 16, 25, 28–31, 36, 39, 46–47, 61–62, 81–82, 95, 110, 113, 115, 125–126, 130–131
Peder Svart, 293–294, 296–297
Peterson, Lena, 17
Philip V, 141
Plutarch, 130–131
The Poetic Edda, 13, 55–56, 58
Pound, Roscoe, 210
pyhä, 37–38, 47, 292, 324

R
Ragnar Lodbrok, 169, 185–186, 226
Ragnarök, 56–57, 67, 226
Ragnvald Knaphövde, 23, 87, 242, 251–252, 254, 260, 290–293, 303, 306, 327
Raudvere, Catharina, 164
Repton, 82–83
Reric, 95, 114
Rex Justus, 110, 116
Ribbing Party, 295, 299
Rimbert, 19, 100, 146–147, 235
Rituals, 7–8, 24, 26, 28–32, 35–36, 40–42, 44, 46, 60, 100, 115–116, 125, 143, 163–164, 242, 267, 270–271
Roman Empire, 5, 22, 45, 71, 133, 141, 149–150, 172, 178, 297
Roman legal system, 173
Ronaldsay, 43
Roper, Jonathan, 67
Royal Frankish Annals, 21, 95, 98, 111, 150, 170
Russel, James C., 108
Rögnvald Kali Kolsson, 43
Rüstringen, 99–100

S
Sanmark, Alexandra, 27, 161–163, 272
Saga of Magnus góði, 138
Saga of St. Olof, 105, 107, 189, 232
Saga of Harald Hardrada, 101–102
Saxons, 6, 21–22, 95–98, 144–145
Semple, Sara, 272
St Brice's Day massakre, 168
Schier, Kurt, 56
Schjødt, Jens Peter, 13, 63, 70, 73
Schlyter, Carl Johan, 190–193
Schweinfurth, Georg August, 61
von See, Klaus, 126
Settlement, 12, 14, 33, 36, 44, 61, 70, 87, 99, 126, 133, 136, 139, 146, 150–151,

170, 183, 207, 235, 238, 241, 243, 289, 301–302, 329
Shetland Islands, 152, 154
siðr, 108, 126
Sigrid, 268
Sigvatr skald, 144
Simek, Rudolf, 67, 78
Sjöholm, Elsa, 255–256, 271–272, 303–304
Skáldskaparmál, 59–63, 74
Skjǫldunga saga, 227
Skovgaard-Petersen, Inge, 228
Smålandslagen, 190–192, 195, 209
Snorra Edda, 13, 55, 57–59, 62, 67–69, 72
Song of Roland, 151
Sigurd Hlodvirsson, 171
Sorbs, 144–145
Spiro, Melford, 35–36, 46, 145
Starkad, 148, 158, 226
Steinsland, Gro, 107–108, 110
Sten Sture the Younger, 10, 293, 295–296, 306
Stockholm Bloodbath, 296, 299, 306
Ström, Folke, 56, 58, 60
Stockholm, 296–297, 299, 300, 302
Stones of Mora, 269–271, 295
Sture Party, 295, 299
Sturlunga saga, 15
Stylegar, Frans-Arne, 169
Stübe, Rudolf, 60
Suebi, 163–163, 173

Sundqvist, Olof, 26, 37, 42–43, 126, 164, 255, 271–272, 304, 310, 324
Sussex, 91
Suttungr, 59, 74
Svein Knutsson, 135
Swedes, 19–19, 131, 146–148, 189, 226, 228–229, 235–236, 245, 251–252, 259–260, 262, 265, 270, 282–283, 285, 290, 293
Sweden (Svetjud), 23, 25, 96, 101, 112, 132, 146–148, 191, 225, 228–229, 243, 251, 254–256, 258, 274–275, 284, 293–295, 297, 299–301
Sweyn Asleifson, 43–44
Sweyn II Estridsson, 101, 134
Sweyn Forkbeard, 91, 115, 151, 168, 201
sætt, 44, 76, 103, 136, 138, 188, 195
Sǫgubrot af fornkonungum, 243, 277

T

Tacitus, 20, 128, 149, 164, 272
Tanakvisl, 64
Tegengren, Gunilla, 255
Thing (*ting*), 20, 25–26, 28, 32, 34–35, 109, 152, 161–163, 193, 264, 266, 285, 302, 324
Theoderic the Great, 149–150, 173
Theoretical model, 3, 4, 46, 149–150, 173, 321

Thietmar of Merseburg,
  196–197, 199
Thuringians, 173
Thorfinn Sigurdsson, 152–153,
  175
Thorkel the Tall, 151, 201–202
Thrasco, 95, 98
Titus Quinctius Flaminius, 141
Treaty of Alfred and Guthrum,
  31–32
Treaty of Nöteborg, 229, 244
Treaty of Wedmore, 32
Truce shield, 43, 184–185
Trøndelag, 12, 18, 33, 169
Tuatha Dé Danann, 71
Turner, Victor, 102
Turville-Petre, Gabriel, 63, 70
Tutula, 131
Tyrgils Kristinesson, 253
Týr, 173

U

Uí Néill, 237–239, 241, 245
Unwan, 263
Upplandslagen, 176–177, 191,
  208–209, 256, 265, 269
Upplönd (Opplönd), 144
Uppsala, 40, 62–63, 74, 169,
  189, 232, 259–261, 265,
  269–270, 274–275, 282,
  290, 303–305, 310

V

Vafþrúðnismál, 66, 68, 194, 292
Valamir, 149
Valdemar II of Denmark,
  179–180, 194

Valdemar, prince of Denmark,
  179–180
Vanaheimr, 62, 64, 67
Vandals, 173
*veb*ǫ*nd*, 26, 39–40, 183
Veleti, 95, 98
Vestfold, 12, 56
vilvé, 38–47
Vikar, 16, 148, 207, 242
Vilkuna, Kustaa, 229–231, 233,
  244
Vikstrand, Per, 17, 79, 225
Vita Ansgarii, 19, 100
Vita Karoli Magni, 20
vitrir men, 136
Vretemark, Maria, 268
de Vries, Jan, 59
Västergötland, 23, 87, 134, 183,
  189, 242, 252, 254, 257–
  261, 263–264, 266–269,
  272–273, 275, 280–293,
  303–304, 305, 327
*v*ǫ*lur*, 164
*V*ǫ*luspá*, 14, 55–57, 66–70, 72

W

War of the Austrian Succession,
  302
Wales, 22, 87
Walker, Cheryl, 172
Weolþeow, 160–161
Wessén, Elias, 191, 195
Wessex, 29, 31, 82–88, 90–91,
  115, 158, 201
Widukind, 95
Wiktorsson, Per-Axel, 252,
  256

Index 381

William of Jumièges, 78, 114
William of Malmesbury, 78, 168, 207
Worldpeace, 137
Women as cultleaders, 163–168
Women as warriors, 168–170

Y
Ynglinga saga, 62–65, 68–69, 72, 76, 208, 233, 326
Yorkshire, 188
The Younger Westrogothic law, 252

Þ
Þiðreks saga, 129
Þjóðolfr of Hvinir, 63, 232
Þórvaldr Koðránsson, 43

Å
Ågren, Kurt, 257

Æ
Ælfeah, 202, 204–205, 328, 330
The Æsir–Vanir War, 4, 55, 57, 59–62, 64, 67, 70–71, 242
Æthelred, 83, 91–94, 99, 126, 146, 151, 168, 201–203, 206, 242

Ö
Österberg, Eva, 25, 300, 302
Östgötalagen, 176, 209, 261, 269– 270
Östvold, Torbjörg, 70

www.ingramcontent.com/pod-product-compliance
Lightning Source LLC
Chambersburg PA
CBHW061245230426
43662CB00021B/2435